# dot.con

# dot.con

## the greatest story ever sold

## john cassidy

ALLEN LANE

THE PENGUIN PRESS

ALLEN LANE
THE PENGUIN PRESS

Published by the Penguin Group
Penguin Books Ltd, 80 Strand, London, WC2R 0RL, England
Penguin Putnam Inc., 375 Hudson Street, New York, New York 10014, USA
Penguin Books Australia Ltd, 250 Camberwell Road, Camberwell, Victoria 3124, Australia
Penguin Books Canada Ltd, 10 Alcorn Avenue, Toronto, Ontario, Canada M4V 3B2
Penguin Books India (P) Ltd, 11, Community Centre, Panchsheel Park, New Delhi – 110 017, India
Penguin Books (NZ) Ltd, Cnr Rosedale and Airborne Roads, Albany, Auckland, New Zealand
Penguin Books (South Africa) (Pty) Ltd, 24 Sturdee Avenue, Rosebank 2196, South Africa

Penguin Books Ltd, Registered Offices: 80 Strand, London, WC2R 0RL, England

www.penguin.com

First published in the USA by HarperCollins 2002
First published in Great Britain by Allen Lane The Penguin Press 2002
Reprinted with minor corrections 2002
4

Copyright © John Cassidy, 2002

The moral right of the author has been asserted

Printed and bound in Great Britain by Clays Ltd, St Ives plc

A CIP catalogue record for this book is available from the British Library

ISBN 0–713–99598–X

# contents

# preface to the british edition

**A few years ago, a British journalist who has lived and worked in the** United States for longer than he cares to remember received a phone call from an old British friend whom he met at university. The old friend had a question: Would the journalist be interested in helping to set up a British Internet company, a financial Web site modelled on TheStreet.com, an American start-up that was attracting a lot of publicity? The journalist said several things: he didn't want to leave New York; he didn't have much faith in Internet commerce, certainly not enough to invest his savings in it; and he had heard that TheStreet.com was losing a small fortune. The old friend, who had worked for a major British company and an international consulting firm before striking out as an Internet entrepreneur, dismissed these objections. There would be no need to move to London, he said. All the journalist had to do was lend his name to the new firm and act as an adviser. The key to success was building credibility in the financial community. As a former Business Editor of the *Sunday Times*, the journalist would be a useful asset. As for putting up some of his own money: that was out of the question. Outside investors would supply the cash in the hopes of making a handsome return when the company eventually issued stock. The lucky hack would receive equity for nothing.

The journalist had often heard this sort of reasoning from eager young American MBAs, but it sounded strange on the lips of his old friend, a caustic British businessman who was the wrong side of thirty-five. Apparently, Internet fever had spread to the United Kingdom. What about potential competitors, the journalist asked. The old friend admitted that competition was important, but only as an argument for moving fast. If they got in quickly, they would be able to raise plenty of money, he said. The journalist, after sounding a few more doubtful notes, agreed to have lunch with his old friend's partner, another former management consultant, who would be passing through New York a few weeks later on his way back from Silicon Valley.

When this would-be Internet mogul arrived he reminded the journalist of Jeff Bezos, the founder of Amazon.com. He was smart, polite, earnest and totally single-minded in his infatuation with online commerce. Individual share ownership was exploding in Germany and France, and it was also rising steadily in Italy, Spain and many other European countries, he pointed out. The new Web site would be based in Britain, but joint ventures with financial and media companies in other countries would allow it to provide 'content' in several languages. Plans were already advanced. After stopping off in London, the former consultant was going on to Paris, Frankfurt and several other cities to meet some potential partners.

For a moment, the journalist had visions of himself as the Rupert Murdoch of the online era, presiding over a far-flung media empire. Then he asked a few questions. How many reporters would the Web site employ? What sort of stories would they write? How much would the readers have to pay? It was immediately obvious that the former consultant, while immensely knowledgeable about the Internet, knew relatively little about journalism. The business would follow a 'subscription model', but its charges were yet to be determined, he said. Ten or twenty reporters would be enough to go along with – young, thrusting types, who would work cheaply and produce 'interesting' stories that 'moved markets'. The journalist pointed out that the *Financial Times* employs several hundred reporters and editors, and the *Wall Street Journal*'s European edition employs almost as many. Moreover, most American news sites were having great difficulty attracting paying subscribers. The would-be Bezos was not to be put off. This was an Internet company, he pointed out, and it couldn't be compared to old media companies. Pricing was an issue, but it would be sorted out down the road.

The journalist wished his visitor luck. Privately, he didn't think the new venture would come to anything, but he couldn't be sure. Crazier Internet schemes had made it all the way to the Nasdaq, conferring immense paper wealth on their founders. Soon after, TheStreet.com and the *Financial Times* both announced plans for ambitious Web sites based in the UK. Clearly, there was no chance of raising money for a third financial site. A few months later, the old friend got back in touch with the journalist. Things had moved on, he said. Consumer sites like TheStreet.com and FT.com were yesterday's news. The wave of the future was 'business-to-business' commerce, and that was where he and his partner were now directing their efforts. The journalist suppressed a smile. It was hard to open an American newspaper without seeing yet another article about the latest 'B2B' company that was heading for the Nasdaq at an outrageous valuation.

Sadly, the journalist never became a New Media mogul. Instead, he wrote this book, which tells how a liberating and remarkable technology was seized upon and transformed into an enormous and unprecedented speculative bubble. It starts with an account of the historic development of the Internet, from 1945 onwards, and it ends with an assessment of what remains of the Internet economy. Although primarily an attempt to understand events in the United States, the narrative contains much that is germane to what happened in Britain, where there was a parallel bubble, albeit of much smaller radius.

In general, the British Internet boom mirrored what had happened on the other side of the Atlantic a year or two earlier. In March 2000, for example, Lastminute.com, the most widely hyped of all British Internet companies, issued stock on the London Stock Exchange and achieved a valuation, albeit fleetingly, of more than £800 million. From an American perspective, this was a replay of events twelve months previously, when Priceline.com issued stock on the Nasdaq and ended its first day as a public company worth almost $10 billion. Priceline.com allowed airlines and hotels to unload their spare capacity cheaply online; it made heavy losses; and Morgan Stanley, a leading Wall Street investment bank, marketed its shares to the public. Lastminute.com shared all of these attributes.

The principal difference between the British bubble and the

American bubble was one of scale. In Britain, the Internet start-up phenomenon was largely restricted to a small group of young, highly educated professionals, who lived and worked in London, or so it appeared from afar. Three of the best-known Internet companies – Lastminute.com, Oxygen.com and Clickmango.com – were headed by an old Etonian (Brent Hoberman), a well-connected public relations executive (Matthew Freud) and a media baron's son (Toby Rowland), respectively. In the United States, by contrast, while most Internet entrepreneurs were also young and highly educated, the geographic and social spread was much wider.

It began in August 1995, when Netscape, the company that invented the Netscape Navigator Web browser, went public, and it ended, for all intents and purposes, in April 2000, when the Nasdaq crashed. Between those dates, more than three hundred Internet companies went public, and young men like Bezos, Marc Andreesen (the founder of Netscape) and Jerry Yang (the cofounder of Yahoo!) turned into American icons, their cherubic faces staring out from a thousand magazine covers. At the same time, millions of ordinary Americans bought Internet stocks, and a good number of them gave up their regular jobs to invest full-time. Even the US government got caught up in the hysteria, claiming that the Internet and other forms of information technology had created a 'New Economy'.

This book contains the histories of Amazon.com, Netscape, Yahoo! and many other Internet companies, but it is not an exhaustive business history. Rather, it is an attempt to explain how a sophisticated modern society like the United States could become embroiled in a speculative mania. Such manias have occurred periodically ever since the rise of organized capitalism, but they seem to be getting more frequent. In the past couple of decades alone, there have been damaging speculative bubbles in Britain (the property boom of the 1980s), Scandinavia, Japan, Russia and much of South-East Asia, as well as the United States.

In all speculative bubbles, two sorts of causal factors are involved. The first are universal human failings, such as greed, credulity and a susceptibility to herd behaviour. The second are historical factors unique to each situation. In the case of the Internet bubble, the historical factors included the ending of the Cold War, the development of a populist stock market culture, the rise of technological utopianism, the accommodating policies of Alan Greenspan, the head of the US central bank, and the development of the Internet itself, which made it a lot easier for ordinary people to buy and sell stocks. Together, these factors had a seriously detrimental impact on the judgement of the American people. By the eve of the millennium, many of them had come to believe that the US economy was destined for eternal prosperity and that the stock market only moved in one direction. In the weeks and months after April 2000, this dual faith was badly shaken. On 11 September 2001, it received yet another blow. The ultimate consequences of the terrorist attacks on the World Trade Center and the Pentagon are impossible to predict, but in economic terms they made a bad situation worse. America was facing, simultaneously, the consequences of a speculative bust and a war on terrorism.

No doubt, the country will survive this challenge, as it has survived many before. For all its faults, it remains an admirably open and vibrant society, and one that attracts immigrants from all over the globe. But the myth of American economic invulnerability, like the myth of American military invulnerability, has been shattered.

New York
November 2001

# acknowledgments

I would like to thank everybody who helped me to write *dot.con*. At HarperCollins: David Hirshey, Jeff Kellogg, Cathy Hemming, Adrian Zackheim, Cindy Achar. At the *New Yorker:* David Remnick, Dorothy Wickenden, Pam McCarthy, Henry Finder, John Bennet, and, especially, Cressida Leyshon. At the Wylie Agency: Andrew Wylie and Jeffrey Posternak. Thanks also to: Katherine Zoepf, for checking facts and compiling the footnotes; Greg Kyle, at Pegasus Research, for compiling the figures in the appendix; Alice Rose, for inspiring the title. The material in this book is drawn from a combination of firsthand reporting, government economic statistics, SEC filings, corporate press releases, contemporary newspaper and magazine stories, research reports, academic periodicals, and books. Whenever practical, I have tried to indicate the relevant sources. All the opinions expressed are my own.

This book is dedicated to my parents, John and Julie Cassidy.

"Ever get the feeling you've been cheated?"

**—Johnny Rotten**

# dot.con

# prologue

**One of the strange things about history is how certain periods from** long ago can seem recent, while some events that just happened, relatively speaking, can appear ancient. As these words are being written, President George W. Bush has declared war on terrorism, and American warplanes are heading for Central Asia. Suddenly the Cold War, with its attendant undercurrent of fear, feels a lot closer, while the carefree 1990s seem like a distant age. It is too early to judge the ultimate historic significance of the terrorist attacks that were carried out on the World Trade Center and the Pentagon on September 11, 2001, but one thing is clear: they changed America's view of itself. The belief in U.S. military and economic invulnerability, which grew stronger by the year during the 1990s, until it was taken for granted by many, has been violently undermined. In the wake of the attacks, America's attention has shifted from the secondary human concerns that dominated during the 1990s boom (saving for old age, getting rich) to the primary matters of human survival (staying safe, providing a livelihood for one's family).

Already, it is hard to fathom that just a couple of years ago many intelligent Americans believed that the marriage of computers and communications networks had ushered in a new era of permanent peace and prosperity. Depending on which Wall Street or Silicon Valley guru you listened to, the Internet was the most revolutionary development since the electric dynamo, the printing press, or the wheel. The most striking manifestation of this thinking was the extraordinary prices that people were willing to pay to invest in Internet companies. In nearly every sector of the economy, entrepreneurs, many barely out of college, were rushing to establish online firms and issue stock on the Nasdaq, which was heading upward at a vertiginous rate. Names like Marc Andreessen, Jerry Yang, and Jeff Bezos were being uttered with awe.

In March 1999, Priceline.com, an Internet company that operated a site on the World Wide Web where people could name their price for airline tickets, was preparing to do an initial public offering (IPO). In order to introduce Priceline.com's executives to Wall Street analysts and fund managers, Morgan Stanley, the investment bank that was managing the IPO, hired a ballroom at the Metropolitan Club, at 1 East Sixtieth Street, a fitting location. The Metropolitan, which John Pierpont Morgan founded and Stanford White designed, is a lavish remnant of a previous gilded age. Four stories high, its white marble exterior is fronted by six Roman columns and an ornate cornice. After the guests had picked at their lunch, Richard S. Braddock, Priceline.com's chairman and chief executive, told them that his firm had the potential to revolutionize not just the travel business, but automobile sales and financial services, too. This was a grand claim from a start-up that had been in business for less than a year and employed fewer than two hundred people, but nobody in the room queried Braddock's presentation.

By the standards of the time, Priceline.com had impressive credentials. Jay S. Walker, the company's founder, was a Connecticut entrepreneur who had already made one fortune by peddling magazine subscriptions in credit card bills. Braddock was a former president of Citicorp, and Priceline.com's board of directors included Paul Allaire, a former chairman of Xerox Corporation, N.J. Nicholas Jr., a former president of Time Inc., and Marshall Loeb, a former managing editor of *Fortune* magazine. William Shatner, the actor who played Captain Kirk in *Star Trek,* had appeared in a series of popular radio ads for the firm. Morgan Stanley's star analyst, Mary Meeker, recently dubbed "Queen of the 'Net" by *Barron's,* the weekly investment newspaper, had helped coach the Priceline.com team for their presentation, and she was sitting in the back of the room as they spoke.[1]

The word on Wall Street was that Priceline.com would follow the path of America Online, Yahoo!, and eBay to become an "Internet blue chip." The only question people in the investment community were asking was how much stock they would be able to lay their hands on. Underwriters reserved Internet IPOs for their most favored clients. Other investors had to wait until trading started on the open market before they could buy any stock. On the morning of March 30, 10 million shares of Priceline.com opened on the Nasdaq National Market under the symbol PCLN. They were issued at $16 each, but the price immediately jumped to $85. At the close of trading, the stock stood at $68; it had risen 425 percent on the day. Priceline.com was valued at almost $10 billion—more than United Airlines, Continental Airlines and Northwest Airlines combined. Walker's stake in the company was worth $4.3 billion.

Airlines like United and Continental own valuable terminals, landing slots, and well-known brand names—not to mention their planes. Priceline.com owned some software, a couple of powerful computers, and an untested brand name. Despite this disparity, few on Wall Street were surprised by Priceline.com's IPO. Such events had become an everyday occurrence. *The New York Times* didn't think the story merited a mention on the front page of the next day's edition and instead relegated it to the business section. "It doesn't matter what these companies do or how they are priced," David Simons, an analyst at Digital Video Investments, told the paper. "Each new Internet IPO is nothing more than red meat to the mad dogs." Penny Keo, a stock analyst at Renaissance Capital, saw things differently. "We like Priceline's business model," she said.[2]

This was an interesting statement. Priceline.com started operating on April 6, 1998. By the end of the year it had sold slightly more than $35 million worth of airline tickets, which cost it $36.5 million. That sentence bears rereading. Here was a firm looking for investors that was selling goods for less than it had paid for them—and as a result had made a trading loss of more than a million dollars. This loss did not include any of the money Priceline.com had spent developing its Web site and marketing itself to consumers. When these expenditures were accounted for, it had lost more than $54 million. Even that figure wasn't what accountants consider the bottom line. In order to persuade the airlines to supply it with tickets, Priceline.com had given them stock options worth almost $60 million. Putting all these costs together, the company had lost more than $114 million in 1998.

How could a start-up retailer that was losing three dollars for every dollar it earned come to be valued, on its first day as a public company, at more than United Airlines, Continental Airlines, and Northwest Airlines put together? To answer that question we must investigate what the nineteenth-century British historian Charles Mackay called "the madness of crowds."[3] Few investors, acting in isolation, would buy stock in a company like Priceline.com. To be willing to take such a risk, people needed to see others doing the same thing—and see them making money doing it. This is exactly what happened. Investors who bought stock in early Internet companies like Netscape, Yahoo!, and Amazon.com made a lot of money—at least for a while. None of these firms could boast much in the way of revenues when they went public, let alone profits, but that didn't seem to matter. Seeing what was happening, other people started to buy Internet stocks, and other types of stocks too, not because the underlying companies were good businesses with solid earnings prospects, but simply because stock prices were going up. As history has repeatedly demonstrated, this is the point when a rising market turns into a speculative bubble.

Speculation, according to the *McGraw-Hill Dictionary of Modern Economics,* is "the act of knowingly assuming above-average risks with the hope of gaining above-average returns on a business or financial transaction."[4] There is no settled definition of a speculative bubble. Like pornography, it is easier to spot one than to define it. Broadly speaking, if the price of an asset—a stock, a house, a gold ring, or any other item of value—rises beyond anything that can be justified on economic grounds, and then keeps on rising for an extended period, it is a speculative bubble.

All speculative bubbles go through four stages, each with its own internal logic. The first stage, which is sometimes referred to as the "displacement," starts when something changes people's expectations about the future—a shift in government policy, a discovery, a fabulous new invention. A few well-informed souls try to cash in on the displacement by investing in the new vehicle of speculation, but most investors stay on the sidelines. The early investors make extremely high returns, and this attracts the attention of others. Next comes the boom stage, when prices are rising sharply and skepticism gives way to greed. The sight of easy money being made lures people into the market, which keeps prices rising, which, in turn, attracts more investors. Eventually, those upstanding citizens who haven't joined in the festivities feel left out. Not just left out. They feel like fools. If their daughter's boyfriend, who does nothing all day but sit around and play with his computer, can make fifty thousand dollars on his America Online stock, why can't they? Boom passes into euphoria. Established rules of investing, and often mere common sense, are dispensed with. Prices lose all connection with reality. Investors know this situation can't last forever, and they vie to cash in before the bubble bursts. As Charles Kindleberger, an MIT economic historian, wrote in his book *Manias, Panics, and Crashes: A History of Financial Crises,* "Speculation tends to detach itself from really valuable objects and turns to delusive ones. A larger and larger group of people seeks to become rich without a real understanding of the processes involved. Not surprisingly, swindlers and catchpenny schemes flourish."[5] Finally, inevitably, comes the bust. Sometimes there is clear reason for the break; sometimes, the market implodes of its own accord. Either way, prices plummet, speculators and companies go bankrupt, and the economy heads into recession. A few months later, everybody looks back in amazement, asking: "How did that happen?"

The Greater Fool Theory of investing provides part of the answer. Few investors really believed that Priceline.com was worth $10 billion. On page three of Priceline.com's prospectus—the legal document that all companies have to file with the Securities and Exchange Commission before they issue stock to the public—the following headline appeared in bold type: "We Are Not Profitable and Expect to Continue to Incur Losses." Other headlines in the first twenty pages included: "Our Business Model is Novel and Unproven"; "Our Brand May Not Achieve the Broad Recognition Necessary to Succeed"; and "We May Be Unable to Meet Our Future Capital Requirements."[6] Short of printing a warning from the Surgeon General, it is hard to see what else could have been done to alert the public to the dangers of investing in Priceline.com. Investors ignored these warnings because they had persuaded themselves that there would always be somebody else, a greater fool, ready to buy their Priceline.com stock at a higher price. For a while they were proved right.

The Greater Fool Theory explains how the bubble sustained itself but not why it started or what it signified. Those questions can only be addressed by placing what happened in its proper historical context. The stock market boom, which extended well beyond Internet stocks, was about more than day traders trying to get rich on the Nasdaq and twenty-four-year-old computer science graduates trying to become the next Bill Gates. It was about both of those things, of course, but it was also about a lone superpower that believed it had discovered the secret of eternal prosperity. It was about a group of pundits promoting the next "big thing." It was about Wall Street bankers eager to cash in on an unprecedented source of revenues. It was about newspapers, magazines, and television programs that pumped enough hot air into the Internet bubble to float a blimp. It was about economists and other "experts" who refused to learn the lessons of history. It was about a chairman of the Federal Reserve who had convinced himself that miraculous things were happening to the American economy. Above all, it was about ordinary Americans, enticed by the prospect of instant wealth, parting with their hard-earned money for worthless pieces of paper. In short, the Internet boom and bust was about America—how it works and what it thought of itself in that short interregnum between the end of the Cold War and September 2001. America, therefore, is the underlying subject of this book.

Gold rushes are an established feature of American history. In 1849, the year after the United States seized California from Mexico, gold was discovered in the Sierra Nevada Mountains. "At once a host of fortune hunters poured forth, some by sea and some by overland trail, to the canyons and gulches where nuggets could be washed out in pots and pans," Allan Nevins and Henry Steele Commager recounted in their classic history of the United States. "The mountains filled with roaring camps; San Francisco sprang overnight into a lusty little metropolis, full of vice, luxury, and energy; and California was converted in a twinkling from a sleepy, romantic community of Spanish-American ranchers into a hustling and populous commonwealth of Anglo-Saxons." The discovery of gold on the Internet can be dated, with some precision, to August 1995, when Netscape, the maker of the Netscape Navigator Web browser, held its IPO. Like the strike in the Sierra Nevada, the Netscape IPO attracted a host of prospectors, but they bore little resemblance to the forty-niners. Instead of illiterate farmers, they were mostly highly educated professionals, and they came armed, not with picks and shovels, but with Harvard MBAs and subscriptions to *The Wall Street Journal*. As for vices, any that they had were hidden behind a bland façade of chinos and caffe latte. And unlike the Californian gold rush, the Internet mania was not geographically confined. It started out in Silicon Valley but spread to all corners of the country, all age groups, and all social groups with enough money to invest in the stock market.

This book tracks the development of the Internet bubble, and the broader stock market boom of the late 1990s, from the period immediately after the Second World War, when scientists had the first inklings of a decentralized communications network that would be beyond the control of any single authority. The Internet is often portrayed as a triumph of American private enterprise, but that is a myth. The U.S. government designed and built the Internet, and a European academic invented the application that turned it into a mass medium. Even in the mid-1980s, when the Internet had been up and running for almost two decades, most companies dismissed it as an obscure research tool. Not until the early 1990s, when millions of people around the world were already using the network to communicate with each other, did the private sector show much of an interest.

When Wall Street and corporate America did discover the Internet, they adopted it with the zeal of converts, and the bubble started to inflate. Once that happened, the process was self-reinforcing, with everybody involved trapped in the peculiar competitive logic of a speculative boom. In elementary economics textbooks, competition forces people to act rationally, and it also leads to an efficient allocation of resources. But in the real world, where people are judged relative to their peers, competition can have perverse effects. The venture capitalists that invested in Pets.com and Webvan didn't necessarily believe the Internet was the best way to sell pet food and groceries, but they knew that if they didn't finance these firms their competitors would. If the Nasdaq kept going up, and few doubted that it would, their rivals would be able to cash in their investments at a profit after the planned IPO. In such circumstances, the "sensible" thing to do was to keep pouring money into the Internet sector. Consequently, virtually any company with the suffix ".com" after its name could raise money. Investment bankers and mutual fund managers faced similar incentives. If they refused to have anything to do with Internet companies, as some of them did, at least in the early stages, their performance suffered compared to that of competitors who were managing Internet IPOs and buying Internet stocks.

Journalists weren't immune to the logic of the bubble. In the early stages of a speculative boom it is easy for a financial columnist to be a skeptic, but after a year or two of rising prices, most readers get tired of pieces predicting a crash. The news is that investors are getting rich. Other people want to know how to mimic them; editors want to satisfy this demand. Tip-sheet journalism replaces probing reporting—a process that becomes more advanced the longer the bubble persists. By the euphoria stage, most observers have a vested interest in avoiding stating the obvious—that delusion has replaced reality. Journalists and media companies that are supposed to be objective are themselves benefiting from the bubble. Ditto economic policy makers. Nothing improves the reputation of a Fed chairman or a Treasury secretary like a soaring stock market and a booming economy.

With nobody left to prick them, speculative bubbles tend to go to extremes. A few weeks after Priceline.com's IPO, its stock reached $150, at which point the tiny company was worth more than the entire U.S. airline industry. Two years later, the stock was trading at less than $2, and the entire market capitalization of Priceline.com would not have covered the cost of two Boeing 747s.

But that is getting ahead of our tale.

# chapter 1 from memex to world wide web

I

**The Internet story begins with a familiar figure in American history:** the Yankee inventor. Vannevar Bush (no relation to the political family of the same name) was born into a middle-class family in Chelsea, Massachusetts, in March 1890. Adept with numbers and fascinated by gadgets, he studied engineering at Tufts University, where, in 1913, he invented a device to measure distances over uneven ground. Made from a bicycle wheel, a rotating drum, some gears and a pen, this contraption, which was called a Prolific Tracer, earned Bush a master's degree and his first patent. Two years later, Harvard and Massachusetts Institute of Technology jointly awarded him a Ph.D. for his research into how electrical currents behave in power lines. Bush then moved into the private sector. He returned to academic life in 1919, joining the electrical engineering faculty at MIT, where he was to remain until the Second World War.

During the interwar years, a series of revolutionary inventions transformed daily life. For the first time, ordinary Americans gained access to electricity, motor cars, refrigerators, and radios, Economists spoke of a "New Era" of technology-based prosperity. The stock market crash of October 1929 and the subsequent Great Depression put paid to such language, but scientific progress continued unabated, especially in Bush's field of electrical engineering, where useful applications seemed to emerge from the laboratory every week. MIT has always had close links to industry, and Bush lent his expertise to numerous manufacturing ventures, including firms that later became part of Texas Instruments and the Raytheon Corporation.

In 1931, Bush and his students invented an unwieldy contraption consisting of levers, gears, shafts, wheels, and discs, all mounted on a large metal frame, which they called a "differential analyzer." The first digital computer, the ENIAC, wasn't invented for another decade and a half, but Bush's invention was a mechanical computer designed to mechanize the solution to differential equations, a mathematical problem that had tormented students for decades. It cemented his reputation as an ingenious engineer. During the Second World War, the U.S. Navy used an updated version of the differential analyzer, one weighing a hundred tons, to help it calculate missile flight trajectories.

In 1938, Bush was appointed president of the Carnegie Institution, a prestigious research institute based in Washington. After moving to the capital, he became friendly with Harry Hopkins, a senior aide to President Roosevelt. Hopkins and Roosevelt were keen to mobilize the nation's scientists and engineers behind the war effort, and they picked Bush as the man for the job. In 1941, Roosevelt named Bush as director of the newly formed Office of Scientific Research and Development, which operated independently of the Pentagon and the civilian agencies. Bush quickly justified his selection. Riding roughshod over bureaucrats, military and civilian alike, he granted military research contracts to Harvard, MIT, Cal Tech, and other leading universities. At the war's peak, he had more than six thousand scientists working for him. The research carried out by these scientists facilitated the development of the proximity fuse, radar, and the hydrogen bomb.

In 1944, Roosevelt asked Bush to explore how scientists and the government could work together when the war was over. The following year, Bush published *Science, the Endless Frontier,* in which he proposed federal financing of basic scientific research, especially in the fields of health and national security. This report led directly to the creation of the National Science Foundation, which became the main government agency for supporting scientific research. Bush also dusted off an essay about the future that he had written before the war, when he had been doing some research into information retrieval systems. He did a bit of rewriting and published the essay in the July 1945 edition of *Atlantic Monthly* under the title "As We May Think."

According to Bush, the biggest problem facing scientists after the war would be information overload. "The investigator is staggered by the findings of thousands and thousands of other workers—conclusions which he cannot find time to grasp, much less to remember, as they appear. Yet specialization becomes increasingly necessary for progress, and the effort to bridge between disciplines is correspondingly superficial."[1] Fortunately, Bush went on, the very phenomenon that had caused the problem—the explosion of scientific research—also provided two potential solutions to it: microphotography and the cathode ray tube. The former could reduce the *Encyclopaedia Britannica* to the volume of a matchbox. The latter could be used to display text and pictures on glass screens. Put them together, Bush wrote, and you could construct a device "in which an individual stores all his books, records, and communications, and which is mechanized, so that it may be consulted with exceeding speed and flexibility."[2]

Bush called his proposed machine a "memex." He said it would feature "translucent screens, on which material can be projected for convenient reading. There is a keyboard, and sets of buttons and levers. Otherwise it looks like an ordinary desk."[3] All entries in the memex would be indexed by title and by subject, just as in a regular library, but users could also move between items of interest more directly, via what Bush called "trails." Each time a researcher created a new file, he would be able, by tapping in a code, to link it to a second file of his choosing, which, in turn, could be linked to a third, and so on. Thereafter, anybody looking at the first file could call up the other files by pressing a couple of buttons. The great attraction of this filing system, Bush argued, was that it would mimic the human mind and work by "association." Vast amounts of related information would be grouped together in an easily accessible format. "The lawyer has at his touch the associated opinions and decisions of his whole experience, and of the experience of friends and authorities," Bush explained. "The patent attorney has on call the millions of issued patents, with familiar trails to every point of his client's interest. The physician, puzzled by a patient's reactions, strikes the trail established in studying an earlier similar case, and runs rapidly through analogous case histories, with side references to the classics for the pertinent anatomy and histology."[4]

Bush's memex was never built, but his information "trails" were the intellectual forerunner of the World Wide Web, although the road between them was long and circuitous. In the early 1960s, Ted Nelson, an iconoclastic New Yorker who decided as a schoolchild that "most people are stupid, most authority is malignant, God does not exist and everything is wrong," realized that digital computers, with their enormous storage capacity, provided the technical means to make Bush's ideas a reality.[5] Nelson envisioned all the knowledge in the world being collected on an enormous database, where it would be available to anybody who could use a computer. The information would be presented in what Nelson called "hypertext"—the first use of the word—and computer users would be able to jump from one hypertext file to another, just as in Bush's memex. Nelson called his ambitious project Xanadu. It was never implemented, but the idea of hypertext caught on. In 1968, Doug Engelbart, a Stanford researcher who had come across "As We May Think" while stationed in the Philippines, demonstrated the first working hypertext program, the "oNLine System." Engelbart, who dedicated his life to creating software designed to augment human intelligence, was years ahead of his time. His oNLine software allowed users to browse through multiple windows of text using a small block of wood mounted on a ball to direct the cursor—a prototype mouse.

The early hypertext systems inspired a devoted band of enthusiasts, but it would be another twenty-five years before the invention of the World Wide Web. The reasons for the delay were technological and sociological. In the late 1960s, computers were big, expensive, difficult to program, and largely incompatible. They didn't communicate easily, and neither did many of their users, who tended to be young men with long greasy hair, thick glasses, and an obsessive interest in science fiction. The computer "geeks" tended to congregate in university science departments, where, for reasons of economy and camaraderie, they often worked through the night. Many of them held the outside world in contempt, and the feeling was generally reciprocated.

It took the emergence of the personal computer to bring down the barriers between the computer literate and the rest of society. In 1971, Ted Hoff, an engineer at Intel, a technology firm based in Northern California, invented the microprocessor—a computer on a silicon chip the size of a thumbnail. By today's standards, Hoff's microchip was primitive—it contained 2,300 transistors, had a memory of 1,024 bits, and ran at 0.5 megahertz; Intel's 1995 Pentium chip contained more than 3 million transistors, had a memory of 256 megabytes, and ran at 150 megahertz—but it was a truly historic invention. Once Hoff had demonstrated that a computer didn't have to be the size of a room, the profit motive did the rest. In 1975, Ed Roberts, the founder of MITS, a calculator company based in Albuquerque, New Mexico, put a microchip in a box with a screen and called his invention the Altair, after a character from *Star Wars*. The following year, Steve Jobs and Steve Wozniak, two high school dropouts in Menlo Park, California, used the Altair as the basis for the Apple I, the first commercially successful microcomputer. In 1977, a pair of Harvard dropouts, Bill Gates and Paul Allen, wrote some software for the Altair and set up a company to market it, which they called Microsoft. Four years later, Gates and Allen licensed a version of their software to IBM, the mainframe computer giant, which used it in a new product line: the IBM Personal Computer.

For all the wealth and praise subsequently heaped on Gates and Jobs, their technical achievements were modest. Much more important were the scientists at the Xerox Palo Alto Research Center who developed both the graphical user interface that Apple used and a commercial version of Engelbart's mouse. These two inventions replaced the blinking cursor with point-and-click computing. The other essential component of the PC age is Moore's law, named after Gordon Moore, the founder of Intel, which decrees that the processing capacity of microchips doubles every eighteen months or so. There is no irrevocable physical principle determining that Moore's law must hold, but it has worked for almost forty years. As a result, computing gets cheaper all the time. In 1960, the cost of carrying out a million operations on a computer was about seventy-five dollars; by 1990, the cost had fallen to less than a thousandth of a cent. But despite the technical leaps of the 1970s and 1980s, the PC remained a limited tool—useful for processing words and crunching numbers, but little else besides. When all was said and done, it was still an isolated, lifeless box.

## II

**It was the Pentagon that brought the PC to life. For decades, strate-**gists had been thinking about how to enable the U.S. military's communications system to survive a nuclear first strike, which would, in all likelihood, knock out large parts of the network. In the early 1960s, Paul Baran, a Polish-born engineer at the Rand Corporation, a Pentagon-financed research institute in Santa Monica, California, came up with a potential solution. Baran proposed to allow individual units on the ground to communicate with each other without going through a centralized command and control structure. The key to this idea was something called "packet switching." In the old days (pre-Baran), most communications networks, such as the Bell phone system, were based on analog circuits. When somebody dialed a number, a switch at a local telephone exchange assigned a wire to the call. When the caller talked into his receiver, his voice was converted into an electronic imprint (analog), which traveled along the wire to another local exchange and then onto the recipient's handset, where it was reconverted into voice waves. Throughout the call, a single connection was maintained. (These days, the principle is the same but the practice is more complicated. Hundreds of calls can be sent, or "multiplexed," down the same wire at one time.) Circuit technology worked well most of the time, but if the circuit was broken at any point, as might well happen during a nuclear attack, the call would be lost. To get around this problem, Baran was forced to forgo the analog world and think in terms of digital technology.

Digitization was one of the great inventions of the twentieth century. It involves converting any form of information—text, voice, pictures, music, video—to numbers (hence the term "digital"). In digitizing a black-and-white photograph, for example, the number 0 may be ascribed to white and 1,000 to black, with each shade of gray somewhere between the two. If a fine grid is superimposed on the photograph, each square in the grid can be given a number, and the resultant string of numbers represents the digital version of the photograph. If these numbers are sent down a phone line, then reconverted to colors at the other end, the result is an almost perfect impression of the original. For technical reasons, the numbers used are not the decimal ones we see every day, which work in multiples of ten, but binary numbers, which work in multiples of two. In the binary number system, any number consists of just two digits: 0 and 1. For example, the binary expression of the decimal number 4 is 100. With only two digits, binary numbers can be transmitted as electrical impulses. "Off" means 0; "on" means 1. Each 1 or 0 is usually referred to as a "bit." A string of eight bits is called a "byte." A million bytes is called a "megabyte."

Baran combined digitization with a new way of sending information called "packet switching." Once a stream of voice or data had been converted into digital form, it would be split into a number of small pieces, called "packets." Each packet would include a "header," or address, to tell the routing switches on the network which direction to send it in. The packets would be dispatched across the network individually, and they wouldn't necessarily travel by the same route. If one route was blocked, perhaps because it had been destroyed, the switches would choose another route. They would keep sending each packet until it had been received. At the final address, a piece of software would gather all the packets together and reassemble them in the original order.

Baran's fellow scientists hailed his design, which was published in 1964, but it took the U.S. government several years to realize its implications. In 1968, the Advanced Research Projects Agency (ARPA), a generously funded Pentagon body that was set up in the wake of the *Sputnik* launch, decided to build a computer network linking several university departments that carried out research for the Department of Defense. ARPA's motives in commissioning the network were not purely military. Since the early 1960s, when J. C. R. Licklider, an MIT computer scientist who had started out as an experimental psychologist, headed it up, ARPA's computing division had financed interesting research wherever it arose. One of Licklider's successors, Bob Taylor, was particularly interested in getting computers to work together more effectively. The obvious answer, circuit switching (direct lines between each computer), was problematic because on a big network there are so many possible connections. Eventually, somebody remembered Baran's idea for a packet-switched network. Bolt, Beranek, and Newman, a technology firm with close links to MIT, landed the contract to build the new network. Honeywell Corporation supplied the computer hardware. AT&T provided the telephone cables. On October 1, 1969, the ARPANET went online. A researcher at the University of California at Los Angeles tried to send a message to the Stanford Research Institute. In one of history's little ironies, the network crashed, but the Pentagon persisted. Within months, the ARPANET was delivering messages between UCLA, Stanford, the University of California at Santa Barbara, and the University of Utah. Eventually, the network was expanded to other universities across the country.

The ARPANET was an important step forward, but it still wasn't easy for computers to communicate, especially if they were on different networks. They used many languages, and they didn't even follow the same rules of conversation. For example, they sometimes tried to talk at the same time. In 1973, Vinton Cerf, of Stanford, and Robert Kahn, of ARPA, addressed these problems by writing a new rule book for how computers should communicate on the ARPANET and elsewhere. Cerf and Kahn had two guiding principles: their rules would allow different networks to be linked together in an internetwork, or "internet"; and all types of communications would be treated equally. An order from the Pentagon to a battalion commander would be passed across the network in the same way as a digitized picture of Niagara Falls being sent to National Geographic. Cerf and Kahn encapsulated these ideas in two new standards: the Transmission Control Protocol (TCP), which detailed how information should be split into packets and reassembled at the destination; and the Internet Protocol (IP), which specified how the packets should be sent across the network. Different networks would be tied together via "gateways," special computers that would redirect the packets from one network to another, translating them as necessary. The Cerf and Kahn design, which was later modified by other computer scientists, proved flexible enough to incorporate vastly different networks and robust enough to withstand rapid growth. It allowed the ARPANET, a single network, to develop into the Internet—an internetwork of hundreds of thousands of networks.

This transformation didn't take place overnight, but the ARPANET proved popular with scientists, who used it to exchange informal messages as well as research. Ray Tomlinson, an MIT-trained computer scientist, designed the first e-mail program for ARPANET users, using the symbol "@" to separate the name of the sender from his or her network address. E-mail facilitated the development of online communities that had nothing to do with scientific research. One of the most popular mailing lists among early ARPANET users was devoted to science fiction. By the start of 1982, there were more than a dozen networks connected to the ARPANET. A year later, the ARPANET was split in two. One half of it (the MILNET) was reserved for military users. The other half (the ARPANET) was given over to scientific researchers. Rival networks were also growing up. In 1982, the National Science Foundation launched the CSFNET, which was open to any research institution willing to pay the dues and ban commercial use. It didn't make much sense for the federal government to be financing two different networks. In the late 1980s, Congress approved the construction of the NSFNET, a new high-speed national network that would replace the ARPANET, which was becoming technically obsolete, as the Internet's backbone. A number of regional networks were also built and linked to the NSFNET, such as BARRNet in Northern California and NYSER-Net in the Northeast. On February 28, 1990, the Pentagon closed down the ARPANET, leaving the Internet in the hands of the National Science Foundation. To mark the occasion, Vinton Cerf penned a poem that ended with the line "Lay down thy packet, now O friend, and sleep."[6]

Computer networking was no longer esoteric. Many big companies had their own internal networks, which were called Local Area Networks (LANs). When these LANs were connected to the Internet, the network expanded dramatically. There were also a number of networks that had been built by independent "hackers," a term that didn't have the negative connotations it does now. In 1978, two Chicago students, Randy Seuss and Ward Christensen, invented the modem, which allowed computer users to exchange files without going through a host system. A year later, Tom Truscott and Steve Bellovin, two students at Duke University, modified the popular Unix operating system so that people could exchange files over regular telephone wires. This led to the growth of the USENET, a community of online bulletin boards that was sometimes referred to as "a poor man's ARPANET." In 1983, Tom Jennings, a California software developer, demonstrated how to post bulletin boards on PCs and helped set up FIDONET, the first big PC network. By 1991, FIDONET had tens of thousands of users around the world, many of them in countries where freedom of communication was previously unknown.

At the end of the 1980s, according to some estimates, several million computers were connected to networks. On the Internet alone, there were more than 800 networks and more than 150,000 registered addresses. However, for all but the expert, logging onto the Internet remained a fraught exercise. In order to retrieve a file from a computer on the network, a person might have to use one program to access the other computer, another program to locate the file he wanted, and a third program to translate it into something his own computer could understand, if that was even possible. Not surprisingly, online communication remained largely the preserve of computer geeks who liked the technical challenge. Things would have stayed this way for longer if it hadn't been for a reserved Englishman living in Switzerland.

## III

**Tim Berners-Lee was brought up in London. His mother and father** were computer scientists. After high school, he studied physics at Oxford University, where he built his own personal computer with an old television, a microprocessor, and a soldering iron. Berners-Lee left Oxford in 1976 and spent a few years as a software engineer. In 1980, he landed a temporary post at CERN, the European particle physics laboratory that nestles beneath Mont Blanc just outside Geneva. The scientists at CERN came from all over Europe, and they brought their own computers and software with them, which made it difficult to record their activities. Berners-Lee wrote some software to keep track of what the scientists were up to and which computer programs they were using. He called his own program Enquire, short for *Enquire Within About Everything*, a Victorian book he had read as a child that offered advice on everything from cleaning clothes to investing. Enquire was simple, little more than an address book, really, but it reflected a bigger ambition on Berners-Lee's part, as he later recalled: "Suppose all the information stored on computers everywhere were linked, I thought. Suppose I could program my computer to create a space in which every computer at CERN, and on the planet, would be available to me and to anyone else. There would be a single, global information space."[7]

In 1984, Berners-Lee returned to CERN, this time as a full-time researcher. A colleague directed him to the Internet, which was then little known in Europe. Berners-Lee was impressed by the decentralized nature of the American network, and the fact that it could be accessed by various operating systems, but he found it cumbersome to use. How much simpler things would be if each file on the Internet had its own label and if users could jump between related files using hypertext, just as Vannevar Bush and Ted Nelson had envisaged. Berners-Lee believed such a system was now technically feasible, and he set out to write some software to prove it. By 1990, he had made enough progress to try and name his project. His first thought was "The Information Mesh," but that sounded too messy. "The Information Mine" was too egocentric. (Its acronym was TIM.) In the end, Berners-Lee settled on "The World Wide Web."

Berners-Lee's design was deceptively simple. (That was its great strength.) The World Wide Web would sit on top of the Internet, utilizing its communications protocols and packet-switching technology, as well as existing computers and phone lines. It would consist of just three elements: (1) A computer language for formatting hypertext files, which Berners-Lee called Hypertext Markup Language (HTML); (2) A method of jumping between files, which Berners-Lee called the Hypertext Transfer Protocol (HTTP); (3) A unique address code attached to each file that could be used to call up any file on the Web instantly. Berners-Lee called his address code a

Universal Resource Identifier (URI). The word "identifier" was later replaced with "locator," leading to the acronym that is used today, "URL."

Once Berners-Lee had drawn up the basic architecture of the World Wide Web, he needed some content to show how it would work. Using his own computer as the host, he created the first Web site, www.info.cern.ch, which contained a description of HTML, HTTP, and URI, together with some notes. With the help of a French colleague, Robert Cialliau, and a visiting English graduate student, Nicola Pellow, Berners-Lee also designed a primitive Web browser that allowed users to read and edit files. By the end of 1990, the World Wide Web was running on several computers at CERN. The following spring, Berners-Lee demonstrated his creation to a seminar of computer scientists. A few months later, in August 1991, he posted details of the World Wide Web at several locations on the Internet, including alt.hypertext, a bulletin board favored by hypertext enthusiasts. The posting directed users to the CERN Web site, where they could download software to set up their own site. Four months later, Paul Kunz, a Stanford computer scientist who had visited CERN, launched the first American Web site.

To begin with, less than a hundred people a day visited Berners-Lee's site, but the number gradually increased. Every three months or so, it doubled. In the summer of 1992, when Berners-Lee plotted the "hits" on a graph, he ended up with a curved line that got steeper as it moved from left to right. This pattern, which mathematicians call an exponential curve, was to become a basic feature of the online world. For a long time it would seem that any statistic to do with the World Wide Web—the number of Web sites, the number of networks attached to the Web, the number of Web users—followed the same uplifting pattern. Eventually, the exponential curve would achieve talismanic status, especially on Wall Street. It would get to the stage where no presentation about the Internet was complete without a graph showing the magic pattern; and entire business plans would be based on creating one and riding it out.

Despite its growing popularity, Berners-Lee's invention initially confused many people. The World Wide Web was not a place or a thing. It didn't have a single piece of hardware at the center of it or an organization overseeing it. Essentially, it was just a set of conventions for exchanging information over the Internet. "I told people that the Web was like a market economy," Berners-Lee would later write. "In a market economy, anybody can trade with anybody, and they don't have to go to a market square to do it. What they do need, however, are a few practices everyone has to agree to, such as the currency used for trade, and the rules of fair-trading. The equivalent of rules for fair-trading, on the Web, are the rules about what a URI means as an address, and the language the computers use—HTTP—whose rules define things like which one speaks first, and how they speak in turn."[8]

The comparison of the World Wide Web to a market economy was prophetic. But before Berners-Lee's invention could be developed commercially it would have to become easier and more pleasant to use. In the early days, the World Wide Web was a sea of gray text, which Berners-Lee's browser displayed one line at a time. A number of scientists developed more powerful Web browsers, but none of them really took off. The most popular browser at the time was an Internet browser called Gopher, which Mark McCahill, a computer scientist at the University of Minnesota, designed. Gopher located files via a system of menus and grouped them together in related topics. By early 1993 it had become so popular that the University of Minnesota decided to charge an annual license fee to nonacademic users. "This was an act of treason in the academic community and the Internet community," Berners-Lee noted. "Even if the university never charged anyone a dime, the fact that the school had announced it was reserving the right to charge people for the use of Gopher protocols meant it had crossed the line."[9] Internet enthusiasts were used to using the network free of charge. Professional software developers feared being sued if they worked on what had become proprietary technology. Usage of Gopher fell dramatically and never recovered.

The same thing could easily have happened to the World Wide Web. CERN owned the intellectual property rights to Berners-Lee's programs, and it was unclear what it would do with them. Berners-Lee pressed his bosses to release the rights and, after some hesitation, they agreed. On April 30, 1993, CERN announced that from now on anybody anywhere in the world could use the World Wide Web protocols without paying a royalty or observing any legal constraints. This farsighted move created a global electronic commons where people could come together, talk, play, and, before too long, buy refreshments.

## IV

**At the start of 1993, the Internet had more than a million computers** attached to it, but Internet commerce was still an oxymoron. In order to prevent companies from profiting from taxpayer subsidies, the U.S. government had proscribed using the Internet for commercial activities. Anybody who wanted access to the NSFNET, the Internet's backbone, had to abide by an "Acceptable Use Policy," which restricted it to "research and education." A few specialist bookstores had skirted this ban by posting discreet advertisements on online bulletin boards, but by and large the Internet remained commerce-free— often militantly so. Whenever somebody tried to use the Internet to make money the online community reacted by deluging the offender with aggressive e-mails, a practice known as "flaming."

In a few years, all this changed and the Internet was transformed from an idealistic community of technology enthusiasts to a global bazaar. The key figure behind this transformation was a little-known public official, Stephen S. Wolff, the program director for computer networking at the National Science Foundation, which, following the shutdown of the ARPANET, was responsible for running the Internet's backbone. In 1990 and 1991, Wolff initiated a series of discussions with other government departments and representatives from the private sector about what to do next with the Internet. Back in 1987 the NSF had awarded a five-year contract to the Michigan Educational Research Information Triad (MERIT), a nonprofit computer network based in Michigan, to build and operate the NSFNET. This contract was coming up for renewal, and a number of commercial network providers were pressing the NSF to let them enter the Internet market. Some of these companies, such as Performance Systems International (later known as PSI NET) and Advanced Network Services (ANS), were new ventures that had grown out of regional not-for-profit networks. Others were established telecommunications carriers, such as MCI, AT&T, and Sprint, which were building their own high-speed networks.

Wolff, who would later become a senior executive at Cisco Systems, the biggest manufacturer of networking gear for the Internet, had no interest in running the Internet indefinitely as a public utility, although this is what some Internet activists were calling for. Wolff believed the government's role was to foster important technologies, then let the private sector take over. The "NSF recognizes limitations and only has so much money," he argued. "If you don't stop doing old things, then you can't start any new things. And when something gets to the point that it becomes a commodity product there is no reason for the NSF to be supporting it."[10] As far back as the mid-1970s, Pentagon officials had thought about allowing a private operator to take over the ARPANET, but they couldn't find any companies interested. Now the private sector was keen to exploit what it saw as a big potential market. Wolff decided the best thing would be to allow several companies to build and operate backbone networks. This would prevent any single company from dominating the Internet, while allowing the NSF to bow out.

In November 1991, the NSF issued a proposal reflecting Wolff's thinking, which proposed to shut down the NSFNET over the ensuing few years and replace it with competing commercial networks. These systems would be linked by a series of electronic gateways, so it would appear to the individual Internet user that he or she was using a single network. The government would create a separate "very-high-speed Backbone Network Service" restricted to scientific researchers and supported by taxpayers' money. All other Internet users would have to sign up with a commercial Internet Service Provider (ISP). Since each company would own and operate its own network, the Acceptable Use Policy would become redundant, and the Internet would turn into a capitalist free-for-all. There was remarkably little public discussion about this plan, which revolutionized the Internet. A few hearings were held on Capitol Hill, but they were attended mainly by lobbyists from the telecommunications industry who supported privatization. The NSF asked companies to submit bids to operate the new system, and it awarded contracts to a number of them, including MCI, Sprint, and Bellcore. On April 30, 1995, the NSFNET was closed down. The Internet was now a private-sector enterprise.

# chapter 2 popular capitalism

**I**

**Speculative bubbles have occurred as far apart as Holland in the sev-**enteenth century, Florida in the 1920s, and Japan in the 1980s. No one explanation fits all of them, but some common antecedents have been identified. Many bubbles, such as the 1840s railway mania in England and the Wall Street boom of the 1920s, are associated with exciting new inventions that create exaggerated hopes of profits. (In the 1920s, there were radio, talking pictures, and passenger aircraft.) War, particularly the end of a war, is another frequent precursor. The South Sea Bubble of 1720 followed the peace agreement that finally ended the hundred-year war between Britain and France. Here in America, it was after the Civil War that rascals like Jay Gould and Jay Cook organized their speculative pools, which helped send stock prices (temporarily) into the stratosphere. And bubbles are usually associated with periods of prosperity, when the future seems bright, investors are cocky, and there is easy access to money and credit. The Japanese bubble of the late 1980s followed twenty years of unprece-dented economic success.

The Internet bubble fit the broad historic pattern, but it had its own idiosyncrasies. Technology provided the focus for the specula-tive mania, but it can't fully explain what happened. Revolutionary inventions are nothing new, after all. Television and the jet aircraft arguably changed people's lives more than the World Wide Web, but neither led to a speculative binge. Evidently, there was something about American society in the middle of the 1990s that made it susceptible to an outbreak of stock market hysteria.

The end of the Cold War surely played a role. In the wake of Nagasaki and Hiroshima, technological progress was associated in many people's minds with nuclear destruction. It was difficult to be bullish about a trend that seemed likely to result in the destruction of humanity. From Thomas Pynchon's *Gravity's Rainbow* to Stanley Kubrick's *Dr. Strangelove,* the books, plays, and movies of the Cold War era were filled with apocalyptic imagery. When the Warsaw Pact collapsed, popular attitudes toward technology changed. For the first time in decades, people felt safe. Science and technology began to appear as benign forces that had created the color television, the PC, and numerous lifesaving medicines. As the 1990s progressed, Theodore Kaczynski (a.k.a. the Unabomber) and a few others apart, it became difficult to find anybody who remained opposed to technical progress.

Socialism's demise had other important consequences. Capitalism—American capitalism specifically—was almost universally accepted as the only viable model for economic development. People the world over looked to the United States not just for military leadership, but also for lessons in economics. The key to American success was widely believed to be a combination of free markets and technical progress. Janos Kornai, a Hungarian economist who now teaches at Harvard, encapsulated this thinking in an essay in the *Journal of Economic Perspectives* on the eve of the millennium. The twentieth century yielded two lessons, Kornai argued: capitalism is a necessary condition for democracy; and socialism cannot survive because it doesn't foster enough technological innovation.[1] When the Internet arrived, it was seen as the latest triumph of American enterprise. The fact that Pentagon-funded academics created the network and a European invented its most important application didn't seem to matter. In Britain, for example, Tony Blair's New Labor government was consumed with trying to replicate the freewheeling culture of Silicon Valley.

The Internet's appeal was partly ideological. In the summer of 1989, Francis Fukuyama, a senior official at the State Department, argued that history, viewed as the ongoing clash of rival ideologies, had ended. Writing in *The National Interest,* Fukuyama argued that liberal democracy of the type pioneered by the United States may constitute "the final form of human government."[2] The significance of Fukuyama's piece was widely debated (partly because it was written in the mystifying argot of G. W. F. Hegel, an obscurantist German philosopher), but it captured a moment when the future seemed blurred. If the ancient debate about how society ought to be organized was over, what was to be the new organizing principle for history? Where was mankind to go next? The Internet enthusiasts had a ready answer: into cyberspace. Here was a medium that transcended the old divisions of class, geography, and nation-state. The Internet was global and anonymous, but also personal. From Lima to Lagos to Laos, anybody with a phone line and a computer could communicate with people on the other side of the Earth. And once a person was online, no government could tell him or her what to do. A student in Shanghai could log on to the White House Web site (www.whitehouse.gov), which was launched in 1993, and read what the president's spokesman had said about U.S.-China relations in his press briefing that morning. A researcher in Stockholm could swap notes with a colleague in Rome. A teacher in Sydney could have online sex with an accountant in Chicago.

To borrow an ugly phrase from the social sciences, the Internet represented a new paradigm for human development. Paradigms are stories (not necessarily true stories) that help people to organize their thoughts. Most of us use paradigms, even though we sometimes don't realize it. The straight line is a paradigm. Nobody has ever seen a perfectly straight line, but it's hard to imagine the world without the concept. The Internet paradigm was one that liberal utopians like Bertrand Russell and Robert Owen had dreamed about: a worldwide community in which distance had been conquered, national hatreds had disappeared, and borders meant nothing. "Computing is not about computers anymore. It is about living," Nicholas Negroponte, head of the Media Lab at MIT, wrote in his 1995 book *Being Digital*.[3] "As we interconnect ourselves, many of the values of a nation-state will give way to those of both larger and smaller electronic communities. We will socialize in digital neighborhoods in which physical space will be irrelevant and time will play a different role. Twenty-five years from now, when you look out a window, what you see may be five thousand miles and six time zones away. When you watch an hour of television, it may have been delivered to your home in less than a second. Reading about Patagonia can include the sensory experience of going there. A book by William Buckley can be a conversation with him."

## II

**Thursday, August 12, 1982, didn't seem like a momentous day in** American history. Events in the Middle East dominated the news. The Israeli military, which had been invading Lebanon for two months, launched its biggest air raid yet on Beirut, killing more than a hundred people, many of them civilians. President Reagan expressed "outrage" at the Israeli attack, but the Israeli prime minister, Menachem Begin, appeared to take little notice. In Beverly Hills, Henry Fonda died at seventy-seven following a long illness. In sports, the White Sox handed the Yankees their third straight loss. On Wall Street, it was a quiet day. With the economy stuck in a slump, there was little interest in buying stocks. The Dow Jones Industrial Average fell by 0.29 points, closing at 776.92. The fledgling Nasdaq National Market fell by 0.93 points, to 159.84. Nobody realized it at the time, but when the closing bell rang at the New York Stock Exchange the last bear market of the twentieth century had ended. The following morning, the Federal Reserve, led by Paul Volcker, cut short-term interest rates by half a percent in an effort to revive the economy. It was the third rate reduction in six weeks, and it worked. From then on, the stock market and the economy recovered in tandem. By the end of 1982, the Dow was trading above 1,000. The greatest bull market ever—one that would see the Dow rise more than tenfold and the Nasdaq rise almost thirtyfold—was under way.

An entire generation of newborns would get their driver's licenses before the stock market would see another lengthy downturn. High school students would go to college, get married, have children, and approach middle age to the accompaniment of a rising stock chart. Given the longevity of the bull market, it is hardly surprising that so many Americans came to regard buying stocks as an easy way to get rich. The Internet stock mania during the late 1990s was like the frenzy on the dance floor at the end of a wedding party. The disc jockey may have prompted the excitement by playing a popular tune, but the real reason that people were singing at the tops of their lungs and waving their hands above their heads was that the free bar had been open all day.

The stock market's sustained ascent was the central and dominating fact of American history in the 1980s and 1990s. It was based on a restructuring of American capitalism. At the end of the 1970s, the conventional wisdom among economists was that overseas firms, especially Japanese firms, had become a lot more efficient than their American rivals. Starting in the recession of 1982–1983, firms like General Electric and General Motors slashed their payrolls, invested in laborsaving equipment, and shifted production to cheaper locations abroad. American workers suffered, at least in the short term, but corporate profits picked up sharply. Since a stock certificate is simply a claim on a firm's future earnings, stock prices rose to reflect the brighter outlook for profits. By the summer of 1987, the Dow was trading above 2000.

At the same time as firms were restructuring, popular attitudes toward saving and investing were changing. Traditionally, many Americans viewed Wall Street with suspicion. Putting money into the stock market was seen as a rich man's game. In 1983, the wealthiest 1 percent of households in America owned 90 percent of all stocks. The vast majority of households—about three out of four—owned no stocks at all. Most of these families, if they had any surplus income, kept it in the bank. Fifteen years later, in 1998, things had changed substantially. Almost half of American households owned stocks, either through individual shareholdings or through mutual funds, and the proportion of stocks owned by the top 1 percent had fallen to about 80 percent—still a very unequal share, but less so than it used to be.

The emergence of popular capitalism was largely an accident. During the 1970s, many economists were concerned that Americans were saving too little for retirement, thereby putting the Social Security system under strain and depriving businesses of the funds needed for investment. To encourage thrift, Congress introduced a series of tax incentives for saving. In 1974, the first individual retirement accounts (IRAs) were introduced, but the standards for qualifying were strict, and they didn't really catch on. In the Tax Reform Act of 1978, legislators loosened things up a bit by allowing workers to contribute their cash bonuses to retirement savings accounts on a tax-deferred basis. The wording of this clause, number 401(k), was vague, and it attracted the attention of R. Theodore Benna, an employee benefits consultant in Langhorne, Pennsylvania.

One Saturday afternoon in 1980, Benna, who was then thirty-nine years old, was helping one of his clients, a local bank, to redesign its employee pension plan when he had a thought. If cash bonuses could be sheltered from tax under clause 401(k), then why couldn't regular income be sheltered in the same way? There didn't appear to be anything in the statute that specifically ruled it out. "My approach was that if the code doesn't say, 'Thou shalt not,' then thou should be able to," Benna, a devout Baptist, later recalled.[4] Acting on this flash of inspiration, Benna designed a retirement plan that would allow employees to contribute a portion of their paychecks on a pretax basis to a savings account. A few months later, Benna's own firm, the Johnson Companies, launched the first 401(k) plan. In November 1981, the Internal Revenue Service gave Benna's creation its official blessing. With legal approval, the new saving plans spread rapidly, and by 1985 more than 10 million employees had one. This was only the beginning. At the end of 2000, more than 40 million Americans had 401(k) plans, and the accounts contained about $1.7 trillion in assets—enough to put every public student in the country through Ivy League schools.

Through their 401(k) plans, tens of millions of middle-class families were introduced to the stock market. In most cases, the initiation was via mutual funds—investment companies that pool their shareholders' money and invest it in a range of financial assets. Mutual funds have been around for decades, but it wasn't until the arrival of the 401(k) plan that they became a part of everyday life. The first mutual fund, it is generally agreed, was the Massachusetts Investors Trust, which opened its doors in 1924 with a promise to invest its shareholders' money soundly and publish its holdings. At the time, such openness was a novelty. Many investment funds—or "investment trusts," as they were then called—were run by swindlers and rogues, who spent their shareholders' money as they saw fit. In the stock market crash of October 1929, many investment trusts, including some operated by eminent Wall Street firms, went broke. After that experience, most Americans with money chose to invest it on their own behalf, and this remained the case despite the Investment Company Act of 1940, which regulated investment pools. At the beginning of 1980, the total amount invested in stock and bond mutual funds was just $49 billion.

The growth of 401(k) plans and IRAs transformed the mutual fund industry. Between 1981 and 1985 the number of mutual funds increased from 665 to 1,527. Initially, much of the new money went into money market funds, but this soon changed. In 1985, for the first time, the total amount in stock and bond funds surpassed the amount in money market funds. It is no accident that the bull market and the development of the mutual fund industry coincided. Rising stock prices drew money into mutual funds, and mutual funds poured money into the stock market. During 1995, Americans invested more than $100 billion in stock funds, and the figure went up from there. Between 1996 and 1999, almost $170 billion a year flowed into stock funds.

By the middle of the 1990s, there were about 130 million mutual fund accounts, and names like Fidelity and T. Rowe Price were as familiar to Americans as Citicorp and Chase Manhattan. At the end of 2000, mutual funds contained more money than the banking system—about $7 trillion, of which more than $4 trillion was in stock funds. New funds were being created every day, and the mutual fund listings were taking up almost as much space as the stock tables. At the start of 2001, the point of absurdity was reached. The number of mutual funds topped eight thousand, which meant there were more mutual funds than there were stocks listed on the New York Stock Exchange and the Nasdaq combined.

## III

**It is a curious fact of history that mass movements often invent their** own vocabularies. The Jacobins did during the French Revolution;

the antiwar protesters did during the 1960s; and stock market investors did during the 1980s and 1990s. Much of the jargon they adopted dates from the 1950s and 1960s, when economists like Harry Markowitz, of the University of Chicago, William Sharpe, of Stanford, and Paul Samuelson, of MIT, invented the field of financial economics. (All three were later awarded Nobel Prizes for their work.) Before the 1950s, economists regarded the stock market as an emotional and unpredictable beast, which was better studied with the tools of psychology. John Maynard Keynes compared stock picking to a newspaper beauty contest in which readers are asked to pick the six prettiest girls from a hundred photographs, the winner being the person whose choices correspond most closely to the selections of the entrants as a whole. "It is not a case of choosing those which, to the best of one's judgement, are really the prettiest, nor even those which average opinion genuinely thinks the prettiest," Keynes wrote in *The General Theory of Employment, Interest and Money*. "We have reached the third degree where we devote our intelligences to anticipating what average opinion expects average opinion to be. And there are some, I believe, who practice the fourth, fifth and higher degrees."[5]

Some people (including this author) would argue that Keynes's metaphor remains an apt way of describing the way investors behave, especially during a speculative mania, but the economists of the post-war era looked at things differently. To them, stock market investing represented a straightforward scientific problem: How could prospective returns be maximized for a given level of risk? Or, equivalently, how could risk be minimized for a given level of desired returns? The solution that Markowitz *et al.* came up with, after many pages of complicated mathematics, was surprisingly simple: invest in a diverse portfolio of stocks and bonds, then hold on to it for as long as possible. Some of the investments will fall and others will rise, but over the long term the investor will do a lot better than he would by leaving his money in the bank or by studying the newspaper and buying individual stocks.

To mutual fund managers, who made their living providing investors with diversification, this conclusion was greatly welcome. The mutual fund industry spent heavily to inform the public about the purported benefits of "risk management," "portfolio diversification," and "long-term investing." (Not surprisingly, the way to achieve these goals was to buy more mutual funds.) Academics and financial journalists also helped spread the message that investing had been reduced to a formula, as did magazines like *Money, Smart Money,* and *Fortune.* Publishing investment guidebooks became a lucrative industry, although much of what these books said could be encapsulated in a short sentence: "Invest for the long term and spread your risk." By the mid-1980s millions of Americans regarded the two mantras of scientific investing—"diversify" and "buy and hold"—as gospel. Then, on October 19, 1987, the Dow fell by 508 points, or 22.8 percent, its biggest-ever drop. Black Monday, as it came to be known, presented a challenge to the new investment doctrines. Diversification didn't help investors much during the market's collapse, because virtually every stock on the New York Stock Exchange plummeted, as did the vast majority on the Nasdaq and the American Stock Exchange. "Buy and hold" also took a severe knock. For several months before the crash, numerous analysts had been saying that the market was due for a fall. Investors who acted on this advice saved a lot of money.

The crash shook the public's faith in the stock market, but didn't break it. During 1988, American households took more money out of stock mutual funds than they put into them. Then, as stock prices recovered, confidence returned. In August 1988, the Dow passed its September 1987 peak. Ultimately, the message that many Americans took from October 1987 was that the market always comes back, so selling in a downturn is a big mistake. "Investors learned firsthand in the 1980s that it's usually smart to stick," Jane Bryant Quinn, *Newsweek's* personal finance maven, wrote in September 1993, when some analysts were fretting that the Dow, then perched at about 3,650, was heading for a fall. "If you'd held every stock in the Standard & Poors 50 Stock Index over every five-year period since 1926, and reinvested the dividends, you'd have made money 89 percent of the time, reports Ibbotson Associates in Chicago. So quit worrying about your mutual-fund investments and worry about Bosnia instead."[6]

Jeremy Siegel, a professor of finance at the Wharton business school, was the most influential proponent of the "buy and hold" philosophy. In 1994, Siegel published a book called *Stocks for the Long Run,* in which he argued that "stocks have been chronically undervalued throughout history."[7] Siegel was nothing if not thorough. He calculated that stocks had outperformed bonds in every single ten-year period since 1802. On the basis of this evidence, Siegel claimed it was always a good idea to buy stocks, regardless of how far prices had risen in previous months and years. Similarly, he argued, "there is no compelling reason for long-term investors to significantly reduce their stockholdings, no matter how high the market seems."[8] Even people who bought stocks on the eve of October 1929 achieved decent returns if they held on to them for long enough, Siegel demonstrated. Not surprisingly, this message proved popular on Wall Street. Siegel became something of a celebrity, appearing on television regularly and speaking at investment conferences all over the country. At one point, he was even summoned to make a presentation to Alan Greenspan and his fellow governors at the Fed.

## IV

**Between 1946 and 1964, 76 million Americans were born, a** demographic bulge that has been variously ascribed to postwar euphoria, increasing prosperity, and the lack of diverting pursuits during the Truman and Eisenhower years. Whatever its origin, the surge in births inspired a popular theory that explains much of recent American history in terms of the aging of the baby boomers. "From V-J Day forward, whatever age bracket Boomers have occupied has been the cultural and spiritual focal point for American society as a whole," William Sterling and Stephen Waite wrote in their 1998 book, *Boomernomics.* In the halcyon 1950s, according to this simple narrative, the boomers grew up; in the 1960s, they discovered drugs and rock and roll; in the 1970s, Richard Nixon and Jimmy Carter disillusioned them; in the 1980s and 1990s, they had kids, started saving for retirement and discovered the stock market. Harry S. Dent Jr., a former management consultant, was the first person to trace the stock market's rise to the boomers' encounter with middle age. In *The Great Boom Ahead*, which was published in 1992, Dent compared historic data on birthrates to the subsequent path of stock prices. "Plot the two, and it looks like the same chart with a forty-five-year lag," he claimed.[9] Dent's work yielded a simple prediction: the more people that were turning forty-five, the more saving there would be, and the higher the stock market would go. Since the number of boomers in their forties was increasing rapidly, Dent concluded that the Dow could "streak to around 8500 between 2006 and 2010." In 1992 this seemed like an outlandish prediction.

The boomer theory of stock market behavior remains popular with journalists and Wall Street stock strategists, but it has major weaknesses. For one thing, there is no evidence that the postwar generation is saving more than its predecessors did. To the contrary, personal savings rates in the United States have dropped to levels rarely seen before in the developed world. Back in the 1970s, when economists started to worry about a lack of thrift, Americans saved about ten cents out of each dollar they earned. In the mid-1990s, they saved about five cents on the dollar, but the amount was still falling. In 1999, the personal savings rate turned negative, at least according to some measurements, which meant that, on average, people were borrowing money to finance their spending. Far from saving more for retirement, Americans were on an unprecedented binge—buying 7,500-square-foot McMansions, light trucks disguised as "utility vehicles," and $5,000 outdoor grills.

True, more of the saving that did take place during the 1990s found its way into the stock market, but this had as much to do with economics as demographics. Following the recession of the early 1980s, inflation and interest rates on bank deposits fell in tandem, which made stocks look relatively attractive. But they looked attractive to Americans of all ages, not just to boomers. As always older people, who have more money, were the biggest buyers of stocks. If the aging of the boomers had any affect on stock prices, it was indirect. By taking part in the biggest spending spree in American history, they provided a fast-growing market for many businesses, which, in turn, led to rising profits and higher stock prices. In the auto industry, for example, annual sales of cars and light trucks rose from about 12 million in the early 1990s to 17 million in 2000. There may also have been something to the argument that the "me generation," with its openness to individual experimentation, came to view investing in stocks as another form of self-expression. When Joey Ramone, the late punk rock icon, was writing a stock market newsletter, something significant had happened to American culture.

Since popular attitudes are so difficult to measure, such cultural generalizations must remain the currency of pop sociologists and media directors. The fact is that the stock market culture was based on the growth of 401(k) plans and IRAs. Between 1983 and 1998, the share of American households with some type of retirement savings account rose from 11 percent to 23 percent. During the same period, hourly wages hardly grew at all for production workers, especially unskilled workers, and middle-class families struggled to maintain the standard of living that they had come to expect. For many American households that were investing in the stock market for the first time, their 401(k) plans and IRAs offered the only prospect of a decent increase in spending power. This wasn't the upbeat message that the financial industry wanted to portray, but it was a fact. Rising interest in the stock market also coincided with a big run-up in consumer debt—another sign that many were struggling to achieve their financial goals.

Some Americans invested in the stock market simply because they liked to gamble. According to a study done for Congress, during 1998 more than 125 million Americans wagered money in one way or another, and more than 7 million were problem gamblers. In lotteries and in the casinos, the odds are stacked heavily against the gamblers. On Wall Street, at least for a time, the chances of making money seemed more favorable.

# chapter 3 information superhighway

I

**In March 2000, CNN anchorman Wolf Blitzer asked Al Gore what**
set him apart from Bill Bradley, his main rival for the Democratic
nomination for the presidency. As part of his answer, Gore said:
"During my service in the United States Congress, I took the initiative in creating the Internet."[1] The statement dogged Gore for the
rest of the campaign, which was hardly surprising, as the Internet had
been created years before he arrived in Washington. But Gore *has*
always been something of a geek. In the late 1970s, he called for the
construction of a high-speed data network to link the nation's major
libraries, although nobody took much notice of the freshman Congressman from Tennessee. In 1985, when Gore entered the Senate, he
persuaded Congress to finance a study into the feasibility of building a
national network of supercomputers (high-performance machines
that can perform billions of calculations a second). The Reagan
administration resisted Gore's plans, but in 1989 President George
Bush signed into law the National High-Performance Computer
Technology Act, a five-year program that allocated $1.7 billion for
research into high-performance computer networks. Gore was the
bill's primary sponsor in the Senate. None of this amounts to taking
"the initiative in creating the Internet," but it wasn't totally insignifi-
cant. And Gore also made another contribution: he introduced the

phrase "information superhighway" to the political lexicon. In July 1990, in a lengthy piece in the Outlook section of *The Washington Post*, Gore wrote:

> Just as the Interstate highway system made sense for a post-war America with lots of automobiles clogging the crooked two-lane roads, a nationwide network of information superhighways now is needed to move the vast quantities of data that are creating a kind of information gridlock.[2]

And he added:

> If we had the information superhighway we need, a school child could plug into the Library of Congress every afternoon and explore a universe of knowledge, jumping from one subject to another, according to the curiosity of the moment. A doctor in Carthage, Tennessee, could consult with doctors at the Mayo Clinic in Minnesota on a patient's CAT scan in the middle of an emergency. Teams of scientists and engineers working on the same problem in different locations could work together in a 'co-laboratory' if their supercomputers were linked.

As the column inches devoted to the information superhighway multiplied, this sort of passage would become commonplace, with only the details varying. The vignettes made the reader say "Wow," but they didn't prompt much further thought. More than a moment's consideration might have led to some uncomfortable questions for the technology boosters, such as: Why would an eighth-grader need to "plug into" the Library of Congress every afternoon? Wouldn't she be better off studying her algebra and English grammar? And how would the information superhighway differ from the Internet, which had been in existence for twenty years?

During the 1992 presidential campaign, Gore and Bill Clinton promised to wire up every classroom in the country if they were victorious, and they must have repeated the term "information superhighway" thousands of times. Even when they entered the White House, there was no relief. In February 1993, the president and vice president visited Silicon Valley to launch what was billed as a $17 billion high-technology program. (The fine print revealed that less than $500 million would go toward construction of the information superhighway.) Later in 1993, the White House published an Agenda for Action aimed at ensuring universal access to the information superhighway. In 1994, the White House created an interagency National Information Infrastructure Task Force, which included officials from the Commerce Department, the Treasury, the Pentagon, the Office of Management and Budget, and the Internal Revenue Service. None of this activity meant much, but it kept journalists busy. According to a search of Nexis, the online database, in 1994 the phrase "information superhighway" cropped up almost nine thousand times in major newspapers and magazines. Thereafter, as media interest switched to the Internet, and the Clinton administration became consumed by other subjects, the number of stories mentioning the information superhighway fell sharply. By 2000, it merited just fifteen hundred mentions in major newspaper and magazines, many of them in stories about Gore's past.

In many ways, the hubbub over the information superhighway helped to create the soggy environment in which the Internet tulips sprouted and took root. In both cases a promising new technology was hyped out of all proportion, prompting a flurry of media coverage and a blaze of Wall Street deal making that ended in heavy losses. Far less money was lost in the information superhighway mania than in the Internet boom, but the cast of characters was similar: self-promoting technology "gurus," credulous journalists, wily investment bankers, ambitious entrepreneurs, and gullible investors. And what exactly was the information superhighway? Despite all the ink spilled on the subject, it is still impossible to say for sure. Some, such as Gore, saw the information superhighway as a research tool. Others saw it as a high-bandwidth entertainment medium that would replace the clunky, text-based Internet. Yet others saw it as a new way of life. Vagueness was the key to the project's appeal. As long as the information superhighway couldn't be pinned down to a specific design, it couldn't be evaluated objectively and its promise remained limitless. As a senior AT&T executive pointed out in 1994: "The information superhighway is a convenient metaphor, but it's largely a mythical thing. In a strict sense, it doesn't exist and will never exist. And in another sense, it's here already."[3]

## II

**Al Gore wasn't the only person smitten with digital technology.** During the late 1980s and the early 1990s, an unlikely alliance of liberal and conservative thinkers promoted computer networks as the key to human salvation. "We are seeing a revitalization of society," Michael Hauben, the coauthor of *Netizens: On the History and Impact of Usenet and the Internet,* wrote. "The frameworks are being redesigned from the bottom up. A new more democratic world is becoming possible."[4] Hauben teaches communications at Columbia Teachers College. He and other liberal intellectuals were particularly taken by the fact that neither governments nor corporations could control the Internet. "People now have the ability to broadcast [their] observations or questions around the world and [have] other people respond," Hauben wrote. "The computer networks form a new grassroots connection that allows the excluded sections of society to have a voice."[5] This optimistic view of technology seemed to be confirmed in 1991 when Russian liberals used the Internet to help foil an attempted Communist coup.

Closer to home, online bulletin boards, such as the Well, based in San Francisco, provided a virtual meeting place for activists and dreamers of all descriptions. The intelligentsia's infatuation with computers dates back to the 1984 publication of William Gibson's *Neuromancer*, though this science fiction novel was hardly a manifesto for technology-based liberation.[6] In Gibson's nightmarish vision of the future, the world was being run by anonymous corporations, the environment had been stricken by catastrophe, and many people were living in a criminal underworld, renting out parts of their brains as storage devices. *Neuromancer* was highly influential. At a time when the old frames of reference seemed to be worn out, the concept of "cyberspace" that Gibson introduced proved attractive to many artists and writers. In the "cyberpunk" movement, which emerged soon after, they used computers to interpret the world around them in new ways, with, it must be said, varying degrees of success.

The feminist Donna Haraway seized upon technology as a means of superceding gender differences. In her 1991 book *Cyborgs, Simians and Women: The Reinvention of Nature*, Haraway argued that, because in cyberspace a person's sex didn't make any difference, there was the possibility to create an entirely new relationship between men and women.[7] The novelist Susie Bright, in her book *Susie Bright's Book of Virtual Sex*, and the editors of *Mondo 2000*, a glossy magazine aimed at the computer fetishist, saw the sexual potential of cyberspace in more graphic terms. The theme of personal liberation even attracted some icons of the 1960s counterculture, notably Timothy Leary, the former Harvard professor who had famously advised his students to "Tune in, turn on, drop out," before taking his own advice and repairing to an ashram in upstate New York. In the late 1980s, Leary reemerged in Southern California as an apostle of cyberpunk. Leary still advocated stimulation of the senses, but this time he encouraged people to get high by booting up rather than by taking LSD.

The conservative technology lovers were equally guilty of hyperbole. But largely because they had more money behind them than the liberals did, they were more effective at spreading their message. George Gilder, a political-speechwriter-turned-journalist, was the high priest of the conservative technology cult, although, in many ways, he was an unlikely futurist. The scion of an old New England family, Gilder was brought up partly on a Massachusetts farm and partly in a Manhattan rooming house that his mother kept after his father was killed in World War II. His father's roommate at Harvard, David Rockefeller, paid for Gilder to be educated at Exeter, an exclusive private school, where he finished last in his class, and at Harvard, where he had an equally undistinguished academic career. After college, Gilder wrote speeches for a number of moderate Republicans, including Jacob Javits and Nelson Rockefeller, then moved sharply to the right. During the 1970s he wrote three political books, the last of which, *Visible Man*, sold 578 copies.

Gilder seemed destined for a life as a little-known ideologue when, in 1981, at the age of forty-one, he published *Wealth and*

*Poverty*, a defense of supply-side economics that lambasted Adam Smith and William Buckley for being insufficiently supportive of capitalism. The timing couldn't have been better. Ronald Reagan had just entered the White House promising big tax cuts for the rich. Gilder provided the new administration with a moral, as well as an economic, argument for trickle-down economics, namely that it provided the greatest wealth and liberty for the greatest number of people. David Stockman, Reagan's budget director, lauded Gilder's "Promethean" vision, and William J. Casey, the director of the Central Intelligence Agency, said *Wealth and Poverty* would "serve as an inspiration and guide for the new Administration." Even the president himself, while not going so far as to read Gilder's book—that would have been asking a lot—gave copies to his friends. All the attention turned *Wealth and Poverty* into a bestseller and Gilder into a public figure.

While Gilder was writing *Wealth and Poverty*, Peter Sprague, the chairman of National Semiconductor, introduced him to the microprocessor and to Moore's law. The idea of thousands of minute electrical circuits being arranged on a piece of silicon the size of a pinhead struck Gilder like a revelation. "It just seemed to me to be the most important thing that was going on," he later recounted. "I didn't think our literature was especially impressive, or our poetry, art, or films. They were not as representative of what this era was accomplishing as the microchip. The microchip is the Gothic Cathedral of our time."[8] In 1989, Gilder published *Microcosm*, in which he exalted the microchip. The following year, in *Life After Television*, he tried to demonstrate how "the microchip will reshape not only the television and computer industries but also the telecommunications industry and all other information services. It will transform business, education and art. It can renew our entire culture."[9]

Gilder's embrace of the computer had almost as much to do with religion as with technology. A devout Christian, who also believes in ESP, he has long viewed America as a fallen society, corrupted by the "depraved" medium of broadcast television, which appealed to the prurience of tens of millions of viewers. But television's hegemony was based on the scarcity of the electromagnetic spectrum, which could support only a few channels. In the coming digital age, there would be thousands of channels to choose from. "The position of the broadcasters parallels the stance of mass magazines before the rise of television and the proliferation of a thousand specialized magazines," Gilder exulted. "The TV networks are the *Look* and *Life*, the *Collier's* and *Saturday Evening Post*, of the current cultural scene."[10] In the near future, the "dumb terminal" in the corner of the living room would be replaced by a "telecomputer, a personal computer adapted for video processing and connected by fiber-optic threads to other tele-computers all around the world."

Gilder continued:

> Tired of watching TV? With artful programming of telecomputers, you could spend a day interacting with Henry Kissinger, Kim Basinger, or Billy Graham. Celebrities could produce and sell their own software or make themselves available for two-way personal video communica-tion. You could take a fully interactive course in physics or computer science with the world's most exciting professors, who respond to your questions and let you move at your own learning speed. You could have a fully interactive workday without commuting to the office or run a global corporation without ever getting on a plane.
>
> You could watch your child play baseball at a high school across the county, view the Super Bowl from any point in the stadium that you choose, or soar above the basket with Michael Jordan. You could fly an aeroplane over the Alps or climb Mount Everest—all on a powerful high-resolution display.[11]

The fact that this passage reads like Gore's *Washington Post* article is no coincidence. The allure of the information superhighway went beyond party politics. The concept appealed to the adventurous little boy or little girl inside every grown-up. Having heard all the things that this fabulous invention could do, who could resist it?

## III

**With so many exciting things apparently about to happen, the digital** revolution was crying out for a chronicler. He arrived in the form of Louis Rossetto, a forty-something magazine editor who had spent most of the 1980s working on computer industry publications like *Electric Word* and *Language Technology*. Rossetto sported a ponytail, smoked pot, and had written two books: *Takeover*, a political thriller that he published under his own name; and *Ultimate Porno*, which was inspired by the film *Caligula*, and came out under a pseudonym. In the early 1990s, Rossetto and his girlfriend, Jane Metcalfe, moved to San Francisco and created *Wired*, a glossy magazine aimed at the "Vanguard of the Digital Revolution." The first issue, which appeared in January 1993, was financed by a number of investors, including Nicholas Negroponte, the head of the Media Lab at MIT, and Charlie Jackson, a Silicon Valley entrepreneur. *Wired* was meant to be a lifestyle magazine as well as a technology guide. Sections like "Fetish" and "Street Cred" told readers which new gadgets to buy, while "Idees Forte" and "Jargon Watch" told them what to think and say. The most striking thing about Wired was its garish design. Rossetto had no time for the "old media" idea of readability. His new magazine sometimes featured yellow text on purple background, with indecipherable graphics as a bonus.

Rossetto hoped the first few issues of *Wired* would attract a few thousand upscale readers, but he underestimated his potential market. After only a year, *Wired* had attracted 30,000 subscribers and a substantial investment from S. I. Newhouse, the chairman of Conde Nast Publications, which owns *Vogue* and *Vanity Fair*. After two years, *Wired* had a monthly circulation of about 200,000 and a National Magazine Award to its credit. Like all successful magazines, *Wired* helped to create the culture that it reported on. It made no pretense at objectivity or historical perspective. In his first editor's note, Rossetto said the digital revolution was creating "social changes so profound that their only parallel is probably the discovery of fire."[12] He told a reporter from *The New York Times Magazine* that "within ten or twenty years the world will be completely transformed. Everything we know will be different. Not just a change from L.B.J. to Nixon, but whether there will be a President at all. I think Alvin Toffler's basically right: we're in a phase change of civilizations."[13]

Toffler, the author of *Future Shock* and *The Third Wave*, became part of a right-wing intellectual coterie that surrounded *Wired*, and so did Gilder. Both of them granted long interviews to the magazine. "It's very hard to think outside the boxes—cultural box, institutional box, political box, religious box—that we are all, every one of us, imprisoned in," Toffler lamented.[14] *Wired* liked to see itself as above politics, but in reality it was the editorial voice of the rich, highly educated capitalists who created Silicon Valley. Such men had little time for history and even less for government. One of them was Mitchell Kapor, founder of Lotus Development Corporation, helped set up the Electronic Frontier Foundation to lobby against any form of government interference in the new digital media. The fact that the federal government had built the Internet and operated it for more than twenty years didn't dampen Kapor's libertarian ardor. In *Wired*'s third issue he wrote a long article under the headline: "Where Is the Digital Highway Really Heading?"[15] The piece called on the government to step aside and let the private sector build and operate the new network.

Rossetto also employed some fiction writers. Michael Crichton contributed an article predicting the demise of newspapers. Douglas Coupland wrote a thinly disguised story about the internal culture of Microsoft, which he subsequently turned into a best-selling book, *Microserfs*. Negroponte, who wrote a regular back-page column, was one of the magazine's most popular contributors. The dapper son of a Greek shipping family, educated at an exclusive Swiss school, Negroponte was the perfect spokesman for the rootless culture of technology-driven global capitalism that *Wired* was promoting. He went to MIT in 1961 to study architecture, and a few years later he joined the faculty as a professor specializing in computers and design. In 1983, Negroponte persuaded MIT's then president, Jerome Wiesner, to set up the Media Lab, an interdisciplinary research department whose initial staff included a filmmaker, a graphic designer, and a composer, as well as a famous physicist and two mathematicians. With the explosive growth of the PC industry, Negroponte had little difficulty attracting corporate sponsors for his creation. Apple Computer, Time Warner, and NEC all gave money.

The Media Lab supported a number of interesting projects, but its best-known product was Negroponte himself. He did a lot of flying around the world, giving speeches and rubbing shoulders with CEOs and politicians. In futurology, modesty and intellectual caution are false virtues. Negroponte wasn't overburdened with either, as he made clear in *Being Digital*, a book that he published in 1995 based on his columns in *Wired*. "When I met with the Japanese Prime Minister Kiichi Miyazawa in 1992, he was startled to learn that Hi-vision"—high-definition television—"was obsolete," Negroponte wrote. "Margaret Thatcher, however, did listen to me."[16]

*Being Digital* was translated into thirty languages, and it established Negroponte as the world's leading technology guru, a role he reveled in. The book wasn't all dubious. Its early chapters, which explained the meaning of "bits," "bandwidth," and other technical terms, were clear and lucid. But when Negroponte went on to describe what life would be like in the not-too-distant future, he sounded as if he had just emerged from Timothy Leary's ashram. The following extracts were fairly typical:

> The idea that twenty years from now you will be talking to a group of eight-inch-high holographic assistants walking across your desk is not farfetched.[17]

> My VCR of the future will say to me when I come home, "Nicholas, I looked at five thousand hours of television and recorded six segments for you, which total forty minutes. Your old high-school classmate was on the 'Today' show, there was a documentary on the Dodecomese Island, etc."[18]

> Future rooms will know that you just sat down to eat, that you have gone to sleep, just stepped into the shower, took the dog for a walk. A phone would never ring. If you are not there, it won't ring because you are not there. If you are there and the digital butler decides to connect you, the nearest doorknob may say, "Excuse me, Madam," and make the connection.[19]

Negroponte appeared to be deadly serious. He predicted that within a few years *The New York Times* and *The Boston Globe* would be usurped by *The Daily Me*, an online newspaper that would scour the Internet for stories of interest to the individual reader. Video stores like Blockbuster "will go out of business in less than ten years,"

Negroponte asserted. Michael Crichton will "make more money selling his books direct" to readers online. And the information superhighway, while it "may be mostly hype today," will prove to be "an
understatement about tomorrow. It will exist beyond people's wildest
predictions."

Hyperbole aside, the most striking thing in retrospect about the
*Wired* crowd is how they missed the significance of the Internet.
Caught up in elusive visions of telecomputers and information super-
highways, they looked down on the anarchic text-based network. In
Gilder's *Life After Television* the Internet didn't appear at all. The first
few issues of *Wired* hardly mentioned it either. The index to *Being
Digital* included five entries for "interactive television" and five for
"information superhighway" but none at all for "Tim Berners-Lee"
or "World Wide Web." After Berners-Lee's creation took off, Rossetto and his colleagues scrambled to catch up, and the myth was created that they had been in the vanguard of the Internet revolution. In
fact, they were just as surprised by the World Wide Web's remarkable
growth as everybody else was.


## IV


**If Al Gore ever really intended that the federal government should**
build the information superhighway in the same way it built the interstate highways during the 1950s, he had changed his mind by the time
he entered the White House. The cost of constructing a nationwide
high-speed network was estimated at anywhere between $500 billion
and $1 trillion. For an administration intent on reducing government
deficits, spending such a sum was out of the question. In March 1993
Gore moved to lower expectations, telling *The National Journal*, "The
idea of the federal government constructing, owning and operating a
nationwide fiber network to the home is a straw man. No one—at
least nobody associated with me—has made such a proposal."[20] This
was inaccurate—in his 1990 article in *The Washington Post* Gore had
said the new network would be "supported by the federal government"—but at least it cleared things up. The Clinton administration
would act as a cheerleader for the information superhighway, but that

would be all. The task of getting the new network up and running would fall to private industry, just as Mitch Kapor and others wanted.

This meant that the telephone companies and cable television companies would have to do the job. Both of these industries already had wires going into tens of millions of homes, but they each faced big challenges. The long-distance telephone companies, such as AT&T and MCI, had built their own high-capacity fiber-optic networks, but they depended on the regional Baby Bells, which had been created when AT&T was broken up, to reach their customers. The Baby Bells, such as Bell Atlantic and BellSouth, still largely relied on old-fashioned copper wires. If the telephone network was to be transformed into the information superhighway, these wires would have to be upgraded, which would cost a fortune.

The cable companies, for their part, could transport video and sound into homes, but they lacked the switching technology and powerful computer servers necessary for interactive television of the type Gilder had envisaged. The set-top boxes of the early 1990s were primitive devices that worked by blocking certain channels, depending on which service package the customer had purchased. They couldn't transmit signals from the viewer to the cable provider. If the cable industry were to deliver interactivity, it would have to invest heavily in computer technology. But most cable companies were already heavily indebted from the cost of laying their cables.

The strongest cable company was Time Warner. Early in 1993, Gerald Levin, Time Warner's chairman, decided to build a pilot version of the information superhighway in Orlando, Florida, offering video-on-demand, games, and online shopping. Scientific Atlanta and Toshiba agreed to build the interactive set-top boxes, Silicon Graphics agreed to provide powerful network servers, and Hewlett-Packard promised to deliver specially modified color printers, which would allow viewers to print out on-screen advertisements. The Orlando system, which Levin christened "the Full Service Network," would initially be restricted to 4,000 upscale households, but Time Warner told advertisers that within five years it could be expanded to 14 million homes. "Our new electronic superhighway will change the way people use television," Levin said. "By having the consumer access unlimited services, the Full Service Network will render irrelevant the notion of sequential channels on a TV set."[21] Time Warner's announcement prompted a mad scramble to enter a market that John Sculley, the chairman of Apple Computer, claimed could be as large as $3.5 trillion early in the twenty-first century. (This estimate, which amounted to about half the Gross Domestic Product, was ludicrous.) AT&T teamed up with Viacom, the owner of MTV and Nickelodeon, to build a rival interactive television system in Castro Valley, California. Microsoft joined TCI Inc., the nation's biggest cable company, to set up a pilot system in Seattle. And US West, a Baby Bell based in Denver, combined with computer manufacturer Digital Equipment Corporation to launch a similar project in Omaha, Nebraska.

This spurt of activity delighted the investment bankers on Wall Street, who helped to broker many of the deals. Whenever a new industry emerges, or an old one goes into decline, investment bankers rub their hands. There are always lucrative fees to be earned in bringing companies together and breaking them up. Wall Street research analysts helped to promote deals by publicly debating which old media companies would end up as "roadkill" on the information superhighway. The early conventional wisdom was "content is king," and this adage helped to fuel a bidding war for Paramount Pictures, one of Hollywood's oldest film studios. The week after Labor Day of 1993, Viacom agreed to pay $8.2 billion for Paramount. Two weeks later, QVC, a home-shopping network based in Pennsylvania, upped Viacom's bid by more than a billion dollars. QVC's main asset was its chairman, Barry Diller, a Hollywood executive with a well-earned reputation as a wheeler-dealer. The siege of Paramount lasted for six months and ensnared more than half a dozen other big companies. On Viacom's side, they included Nynex and BellSouth, two Baby Bells, and Blockbuster. In QVC's camp were Comcast and Cox, two cable providers. After the last lawsuit had been filed, and the final investment banker had received down payment on his summerhouse, the Viacom-led alliance emerged victorious.

While the battle for Paramount was going on, Bell Atlantic, another Baby Bell, agreed to merge with TCI. The deal, if it had gone through, would have been worth about $26 billion, making it the biggest corporate merger yet. "This is a perfect information-age marriage," Ray Smith, the chairman of Bell Atlantic, declared. "Together we will help make the information superhighway a reality."[22] These words proved to be empty. The prospect of a big telephone monopoly merging with a big cable monopoly raised objections in Washington. Telephone and cable companies were supposed to be competing to build the information superhighway, not joining together. Bell Atlantic, when it inspected Tele-Communication Inc.'s books, also had second thoughts. TCI wasn't the high-technology colossus that its mercurial boss, John Malone, claimed it was. In reality, it was a sprawling assembly of aging cable systems, most of which needed heavy investment if they were to provide interactive television service. In early 1994, Bell Atlantic called off the merger. It wouldn't be building the information superhighway after all.

Meanwhile, down in Florida, the launch of Full Service Network was being repeatedly delayed. The set-top boxes and the network server didn't work properly together, and the launch date was postponed from the beginning until the end of 1994. When the experiment did finally get up and running, only a handful of viewers were online. In the middle of 1995, there were still fewer than fifty homes on the network, and many of the promised services, such as news on demand, online banking, and home delivery of fast food, remained unavailable. Finally, at the start of 1996, four thousand homes were connected, and viewers were given the option to order pizza. Even then, things didn't go as planned. Video-on-demand proved popular, but other services languished, and technical problems continued. Time Warner started to distance itself from the Full Service Network, describing it as just one of several options for interactive television that the firm was pursuing. In May 1997, when the Orlando network had been fully operational for little more than a year, Time Warner announced its closure. The media giant wouldn't say how much it had spent, but some estimates put the total cost at more than $150 million. One by one, the other interactive television trials were also shut down. By then, though, hardly anybody noticed. Wall Street and Silicon Valley had finally realized that the information superhighway already existed and it was called the Internet. Even George Gilder had caught on.

# chapter 4  netscape

I

**On Saturday, January 23, 1993, at seven twenty-one in the morning,**
the following message appeared on several Internet bulletin boards:

> By the power vested in me by nobody in particular, alpha/beta
> version of 0.5 of NCSA's Motif-based information systems and
> World Wide Web browser, X Mosaic, is hereby released,
> Cheers,
> Marc[1]

Marc was Marc Andreessen, a twenty-one-year-old computer science major at the University of Illinois in Urbana-Champaign. NCSA
was the National Center for Supercomputing Applications, where
Andreessen had been working part-time as a software programmer.
Mosaic (the X was later dropped) was the first Web browser that was
easy to use, easy to install, and able to work on a variety of operating
systems, including Microsoft Windows and Apple Macintosh. Ten
minutes after Andreessen posted a copy of Mosaic on the supercomputing center's Internet site somebody downloaded it. After half an
hour, a hundred copies had been downloaded. Thereafter Mosaic
"spread like a virus," to use Andreessen's own words. Nobody kept
exact count, but by the summer of 1993 hundreds of thousands of
people were using Mosaic to surf the World Wide Web—and the
numbers were getting bigger all the time.

Before Mosaic, navigating the Internet was a trial. Many casual users connected to the network via online communities, such as the Well in Northern California and Echo in New York. For ten or twenty dollars a month, these services allowed people to sign up with their newsgroups and chat rooms. Once online, the intrepid surfer could also strike out on his or her own, but to do this he or she had to be familiar with the Unix operating system and the TCP/IP communications protocols. There was no central directory of Internet addresses, and many sites were difficult to access. Getting onto the World Wide Web was even harder. The browser that Berners-Lee released with his www protocols displayed text a line at a time, like a teletype machine, and it ran only on NeXT workstations. Most computer professionals used Unix-based machines, and most ordinary people used Microsoft Windows or Apple Macintosh. During 1992, three different sets of scientists (at Helsinki University of Technology, Berkeley, and Stanford) developed Web browsers for Unix, called, respectively, "Erwise," "Viola," and "Midas." Each one of these browsers was an improvement over Berners-Lee's version, but they all had shortcomings. Viola, for example, was notoriously difficult to install.

When Mosaic appeared, less than 1 percent of Internet traffic was on the World Wide Web. Two years later, the Web was the most popular thing on the Internet, accounting for about a quarter of all traffic. Mosaic was responsible for the transformation. The new browser displayed Web pages inside a window, which made users of Microsoft Windows and Apple Macintosh feel at home. There were familiar scroll bars, buttons, and pull-down menus. On each Web page some of the text was highlighted. Clicking on this text caused another page to appear. "Back" and "Forward" buttons made it easy to move to and fro. Mosaic also allowed users to create their own Web pages. And, most important of all, it allowed graphic images to be displayed alongside words. What hitherto had been a dry, text-based medium was suddenly transformed into a bright, colorful place.

It was Andreessen who came up with the idea of building a user-friendly Web browser. A native of New Lisbon, Wisconsin (population 1,491), he was tall (six four), thin, antsy, and he sported a shock of blond hair. Andreessen hailed from a modest background: his father was a seed salesman, his mother a shipping clerk. Growing up, he hated sports, preferring to spend his time learning the BASIC programming language from a library book. At high school, he favored math and computing, but he also had wider interests. "Say we were talking about God or something," a classmate told *Fortune* magazine. "He would talk about it in a more complete way, with more than one view. And we'd sit back on our heels and say, 'Wow, oh yeah.' "[2] After high school, Andreessen chose the University of Illinois at Urbana-Champaign, which was only a four-hour drive from New Lisbon and boasted a world-class computer science department, as well as the NCSA. He thought about majoring in electrical engineering, but eventually he settled on computer science.

Like many computer buffs, Andreessen was fascinated by the World Wide Web but frustrated with how difficult it was to use. None of the prototype Web browsers had the point-and-click capability that had been popularized by Apple. Andreessen suspected that many of the scientists using the Web were happy to keep things as they were. "There was a definite element of not wanting to make it easier, of actually wanting to keep the riffraff out," he said in 1995.[3] The supercomputing center, where Andreessen wrote three-dimensional graphics programs after class for $6.85 an hour, also left him cold. "It had a very large established budget—many millions of dollars a year—and a fairly large staff and, frankly, not enough to do," he would later recall.[4] Andreessen had a point. Supercomputing had had its day. The PC workstations that firms like Sun Microsystems and Silicon Graphics were building could do many of the same things that a supercomputer could do.

Andreessen thought it would be fun to create a graphics-based browser for the Web, and he tried to interest Eric Bina, a full-time programmer at the supercomputing center, in his idea. Bina said he was too busy, but Andreessen persisted. Eventually, Bina caved in, and his boss, Joseph Hardin, approved the project. Starting in late 1992, Andreessen and Bina worked around the clock for two months. They made a good team. Andreessen, brash and voluble, was the ideas man. Bina, a reserved and punctilious programmer, wrote most of the 9,000 lines of code using a Unix-based tool kit called Motifs. As the work progressed, Andreessen and Bina recruited others to write versions of the new Web browser for Microsoft and Apple. Jon Mittelhauser, a graduate student, took on the Microsoft job, with the help of a friend, Chris Wilson. Aleks Totic, a Yugoslav known as "Mac Daddy," agreed to write the Apple code along with another student, Mike McCool.

Andreessen argued that Mosaic should have the capacity to incorporate images alongside text. Bina was initially against the idea. Graphics files are a lot bigger than text files, and he feared that people would abuse them, choking up the Internet with frivolous images. Andreessen, who spent a lot of time in Internet chat rooms, was insistent. Users would love the pictures, he argued. Even if the network did get overloaded for a while, then its transmission capacity could easily be increased. The other members of the programming team sided with Andreessen. The idea of adding a color photograph to a Web page just for the sake of it made eminent sense to them because, as Mittelhauser explained, "Face it, they made pages look cool."[5] Looking back a couple of years later, Bina could see both sides of the argument: "I was right," he said. "People abused it horribly. . . . But Marc was also right. As a result of the glitz and glitter, thousands of people wasted time to put pretty pictures and valuable information on the Web, and millions of people use it."[6]

Mosaic wasn't perfect—it had a tendency to crash—but even unsophisticated users could learn how to operate it in an hour or two. As Bina noted, many people used it to create personal "home pages," featuring pictures of themselves and their families. Pornographic images also proliferated. Berners-Lee, who saw his creation primarily as a research tool, disliked these developments. In the summer of 1993 he met Andreessen at a conference and "Tim bawled me out . . . for adding visual images to the thing," Andreessen later recalled.[7] But Berners-Lee was no longer in control of the Web, and he couldn't prevent it from being transformed into a popular medium. Nobody could. As more and more material was posted on the Web, more and more people were attracted to the network, which, in turn, encouraged the development of new sites. Berners-Lee's creation was benefiting from a positive feedback mechanism that arises on all networks, from the Bell telephone system to the airline routing system. Put simply, a network's usefulness increases with size. With only two airports in the country, an airline is of limited value. With dozens of airports, air travel is indispensable. The same applies to the phone system. If just one person has a phone it is useless, but when two people have one the network comes alive. As the number of people connected increases, the number of ways to communicate grows exponentially. With three people, there are 6 possibilities. (A talks to B; B talks to A; A talks to C; C talks to A; B talks to C; C talks to B.) With four people on the network, there are 12 possible connections; with twenty people there are 380. And so on.

As Web usage increased, firms from all over the country called up the NCSA with inquiries about Mosaic. Some of them wanted to install the new Web browser on their internal computer systems. Others wanted to buy the distribution rights and sell Mosaic to the public. The computer code was the property of the supercomputing center. There was nothing to prevent Andreessen and his colleagues from quitting the university, incorporating themselves, and licensing Mosaic from their former employer, but such an idea seemed outlandish. This was rural Illinois, not Silicon Valley. "There's no infrastructure at all in Illinois for a start-up company," Andreessen told Robert Reid, the author *Architects of the Web*. "It's not there. No one does it."[8]

Having created Mosaic, Andreessen and his colleagues were forced into the background while the officials who ran the NCSA decided what to do with it. Tensions grew between the two sides, especially when, in December 1993, John Markoff, the computer correspondent of *The New York Times*, published an article on Mosaic in which he said it was "so different and so obviously useful" that it could possibly "create a new industry from scratch."[9] The person Markoff quoted most was Larry Smarr, the NCSA's director. Andreessen and his fellow programmers weren't even mentioned.

Andreessen was understandably embittered. The same month that the *Times* piece appeared he graduated and moved to Silicon Valley, where he tried to forget about Mosaic and took a job at a small software company, Enterprise Integration Technologies. He had been in California for a couple of months when he received an e-mail:

Marc. You may not know me, but I'm the founder and former chairman of Silicon Graphics. As you may have read in the press lately, I'm leaving SGI. I plan to form a new company. I would like to discuss the possibility of your joining me. Jim Clark.[10]

## II

**Jim Clark was born into a poor family in Plainview, Texas, in 1942.** After dropping out of high school he joined the navy, where he discovered that he had a gift for mathematics and electronics. After four years in the service, he went back to high school, then on to the University of New Orleans, where he picked up a master's in physics, and to the University of Utah, where he did his Ph.D. in computer science. In 1981, when Clark was working at Stanford as an associate professor of electrical engineering, he borrowed $25,000 and created Silicon Graphics. The firm's personal computer workstations, which could perform many tasks that had previously demanded a mainframe, proved popular with engineers, financial firms, and film producers. (Universal Pictures used them to create *Jurassic Park*.) Clark got rich, but he didn't get lazy. He was far too driven for that. As well as being an engineer and an entrepreneur, he was a pilot, a sailor, a biker, a driver of fast cars, and an all-round piece of work. "Along with its brother, impatience, irritability was the sensation Clark felt most keenly," the journalist Michael Lewis wrote in *The New New Thing*, his entertaining book about Clark and Silicon Valley that was published in 1999. "He was rarely irritated by machines, but he was often irritated by people, especially when they stood between him and what he was after. His face would redden, and his mouth would twist up into a mouth-of-the-volcano pucker as if it were trying to suppress the inevitable lava."[11]

Eventually, even Silicon Graphics annoyed Clark. Ed McCracken, the firm's chief executive, drove him to distraction. ("Fucking Ed McCracken," he called him.) In January 1994, Clark resigned as chairman of Silicon Graphics and announced that he was going to create a new firm, where he would be free of McCracken. For a while, it wasn't clear, least of all to Clark, what the new firm would be. His first thought was to build some sort of online network. Speaking at a conference in 1992, Clark had said that within four or five years "high-speed computer systems" would be able to deliver "audio and movies on demand, virtual reality games, digital forms of daily newspapers, weekly and monthly magazines, libraries, encyclopedias and interactive books." It was he who got Silicon Graphics involved in Time Warner's abortive Full Service Network in Orlando, Florida, and despite the problems that project faced he was still fascinated by the idea of an information superhighway.

In early February, while Clark was deciding what to do next, Bill Foss, an associate of his, gave him a copy of the Mosaic browser to play with. Serious businessmen like Clark and Foss still tended to look on the Internet as a curiosity, but when Foss had first used Mosaic he had been mightily impressed. "This *is* an information superhighway," he said to himself.[12] Clark was equally fascinated by the new gizmo, and he decided to get in touch with Andreessen. Even if nothing else happened, he needed some bright engineers. Andreessen replied to Clark's e-mail almost immediately, and the pair agreed to meet the next day. They had breakfast at Caffe Verona, a restaurant in Palo Alto, and talked about Clark's plans. Andreessen was still seething about his experience in Illinois. "I'm finished with all that Mosaic shit," he told Clark.[13]

Clark didn't press matters, but he invited Andreessen to join an informal group of advisers that he had put together. Over the next few weeks, Andreessen and Clark worked on an abortive plan to create an online Nintendo network. Then, one night after dinner, Andreessen said to Clark: "Well, we could always build a Mosaic killer."[14] Clark's interest perked up. During the previous few weeks, he had been thinking a lot about the Internet. Like many in Silicon Valley, he originally viewed it as a chaotic place, where it was impossible to make money because everything was free. But the startling growth of the World Wide Web prompted Clark to reassess his views. During 1993 traffic on the Web had increased by 341,631 percent. "How could anybody make money on the Internet?" he later recalled. "I didn't have a specific answer to that yet, but I figured that with the Web-and-Mosaic-enabled Internet already growing exponentially, you couldn't help but make money. It was just the law of large numbers at work—even a small amount of money per user would yield a big business."[15] After a short discussion, Clark made Andreessen an offer: "If you can hire the entire Mosaic team to do this I'll invest in it. Screw the business plan and the conventional investors."[16]

A few days later, Andreessen sent an e-mail to his former colleagues in Urbana-Champaign saying that he and Clark would be coming to town. When they got there, Clark told the programmers that he could make them rich if they built a commercial browser to replace Mosaic. Seven members of the group that had created Mosaic including Bina, Mittelhauser, and Totic agreed to join the new firm. Clark took out his laptop and wrote their employment contracts, which included generous ownership stakes. Then everybody went out and celebrated in a local bar. Clark committed about $3 million to the venture, about a fifth of his net worth. On April 4, 1994, Mosaic Communications was officially incorporated. When it opened for business in Mountain View, a nondescript town south of Palo Alto, there was already a potential competitor on the horizon. After Andreessen left Illinois, the NCSA had licensed the Mosaic code to a new company called Spyglass. Clark wasn't too worried. He had faith in his engineers.

Throughout the spring and summer, Andreessen and the others, along with some Silicon Graphics veterans recruited by Clark, rebuilt Mosaic from scratch. For legal reasons, they couldn't use any of the original code. The programmers worked in three teams: one for Unix, one for Macintosh, and one for Microsoft. For the Mosaic team it was like old times, with people working through the night fortified by pizza and soda. Somebody created a big paper lizard, called it Mozilla, and hung it on the wall. The reptile served as the company's mascot and provided a nickname for the new browser. Andreessen started out in a hands-on role but quickly shifted aside to become the firm's strategist, cheerleader, and spokesman. One of Clark's first moves was to hire a press person, Rosanne Siino. "We had this twenty-two-year-old kid who was pretty damn interesting, and I thought, 'There's a story right there,'" Siino later recalled. "And we had this crew of kids who had come out from Illinois and I thought, 'There's a story there too.'"[17] Andreessen was somewhat shy, but he realized the value of publicity. "If you get more visibility, it would count as advertising," he said. "And it doesn't cost anything." The press coverage of Mosaic Communications provided an early indication of how the media would promote the Internet boom. Most journalists that visited Mountain View were happy to puff the firm despite the fact that it didn't yet have a product or a business plan, let alone any profits. "He's Young, He's Hot, and He's Here," one newspaper claimed of Andreessen. In July, *Fortune* picked Mosaic Communications as one of its "25 Cool Companies."

## III

**For the first few months, Mosaic Communications subsisted on** Clark's $3 million. Clark was reluctant to bring in outside investors. "When you ask people for millions of dollars, you have to at least rationalize what the hell you're doing, and at that point I wasn't really rational," he explained. "My only rationale was a cold, gut feeling."[18] By the early summer of 1994, Clark had a better idea of what he was doing, and he also needed money to hire more workers. Fortunately, he could tap into the unique ecosystem that existed in Silicon Valley to support new enterprises. It was an ecosystem that had turned the thirty-mile stretch of land between San Francisco International Airport and San Jose into a major industrial center, the headquarters of firms like Intel, Hewlett-Packard, 3Com, and Clark's own Silicon Graphics.

Capitalism is, in large part, a process of experimentation and discovery. At any one time, there are thousands, perhaps millions, of business ideas out there that might, or might not, make money. The traditional way for these ideas to be developed is for established firms to invest in them and then try out the resulting products on the public. With Sony's PlayStation and Pfizer's Viagra the tryouts proved wildly successful; with Classic Coke and high-definition television the results were disastrous. But some ideas are just too risky or revolutionary for existing corporations to finance, because they threaten to cannibalize the firms' other products. It wouldn't make much commercial sense, for example, for General Motors to develop a family sedan that did 500,000 miles before breaking down, because if it did, families wouldn't need a new car every three years. Products like these—"disruptive technologies" in the phrase of Clayton Christiansen, a professor at Harvard Business School—have to be developed outside the system, and that is where Silicon Valley comes in. In the past forty years or so, an alternative economic system has developed there that is based on starting up companies to challenge existing ways of doing things.

The scientific research institutes attached to and surrounding Stanford University act as the fulcrum for this system, but the fuel that keeps the levers turning is provided by venture capitalists—investment firms that give money to hopeful entrepreneurs in return for stakes in their companies. Arthur Rock, a transplanted New York investment banker, is usually credited with setting up the first Silicon Valley venture capital firm in the 1960s. Rock helped to finance Fairchild Semiconductor and Intel, two firms that helped to create Silicon Valley. By 1974, the region was home to more than 150 venture capitalists, or "VCs," many of whom were technology entrepreneurs in their own right, such as Eugene Kleiner, a founding partner of Fairchild Semiconductor, and Tom Perkins, a former Hewlett-Packard executive. In 1972, Kleiner and Perkins set up Kleiner Perkins Caulfield & Byers, which went on to become the leading venture capital firm in the country.

By the middle of the 1990s, there were dozens of venture capital firms in Silicon Valley, many of them headquartered on Sand Hill Road in Menlo Park. Buttoned-down MBAs had largely replaced the old-style entrepreneur VCs, but the legal structure of the industry remained the same as it had been in the 1970s. Most of the firms were partnerships, with the general partners—the VCs—charging the limited partners—the investors—an annual management fee of 2 or 3 percent, as well as taking 25 or 30 percent of the profits. The investors included wealthy individuals, pension funds, and other institutional investors, such as the Harvard and Stanford endowments. Some venture capital funds were as large as $250 million, and the management fees on this money ensured generous salaries for the VCs even before they made any investments. Despite the punitive fees involved, investing in venture capital funds was often extremely profitable, with average annual returns topping 20 percent. As a result, tens of billions of dollars poured into the industry.

The presence of such a large pool of risk capital was a key reason for Silicon Valley's growth. In her 1996 book *Regional Advantage*, Annalee Saxenian, a professor of geography at Berkeley, compared the Silicon Valley VCs to their more conservative brethren in Massachusetts, which is also a world-class center of science and technology. "When I started Convergent I got commitments for $2.5 million in twenty minutes from three people over lunch who saw me write the business plan on the back of a napkin," a Silicon Valley engineer told Saxenian. "They believed in me. In Boston, you can't do that. It's much more formal. People in New England would rather invest in a tennis court than high technology."[19] According to Saxenian, the stultified nature of the Massachusetts venture capital community hastened the demise of the high-technology industry that surrounded Route 128. In Silicon Valley, by contrast, the venture capital firms were the "financial engine" of the entrepreneurial process, providing business start-ups with expert advice and operating experience, as well as hard cash.[20]

In deciding whether to invest in a project the Silicon Valley VCs tended to look at three things: the size of the potential market, the originality of the idea, and the smartness of the people proposing to carry it out. Mosaic Communications satisfied all of these conditions, but that didn't mean a deal was automatic. The problem was Clark, who took a much dimmer view of VCs than Saxenian did. To him, they were "velociraptors," financial predators that bought entrepreneurs' ideas on the cheap and kept most of the rewards. Clark based this view on his own experience. When he set up Silicon Graphics, he had been forced to give away most of his company to the VCs who financed him—at least that is how he saw it. With Mosaic Communications, he vowed, things would be different. He would eventually allow the VCs to invest in Mosaic Communications—he had little choice—but only on two conditions: that he would retain 25 percent of the company: and that the buyer would have to pay three times as much for its shares as he had paid for his.

These terms caused consternation on Sand Hill Road. The VCs were accustomed to dictating to entrepreneurs, not vice versa. Two firms, New Enterprise Associates and the Mayfield Fund, had refused to give Clark any money when he went to see John Doerr, a partner at Kleiner Perkins. At forty-six, Doerr was already well known in Silicon Valley. Born and raised in St. Louis, he had a master's degree in electrical engineering from Rice University and an MBA from Harvard. In the 1970s, Doerr worked at Intel. He went on to co-found a chip company that was eventually sold for $125 million. He joined Kleiner Perkins in 1980 and was responsible for investing in a number of spectacularly successful companies, including Lotus, the creator of the spreadsheet, Compaq Computer, the world's largest PC manufacturer, and Sun Microsystems, which pioneered PC workstations. But in the early 1990s Doerr's luck changed. He backed GO, a company that lost a lot of money trying to market pen computers, and he became involved in the abortive attempt to build the information superhighway. Doerr was badly in need of another big success when Clark, whom he had known for many years, walked in the door.

In some ways, the two men couldn't have been more different. Clark is six feet two, with broad shoulders, a sailor's vocabulary, and a hot temper. Doerr is short, thin, and intense. He wears plastic-framed glasses and speaks in business-school jargon. A profile by John Heileman in *The New Yorker* described him as "a highly caffeinated Clark Kent."[22] But Clark and Doerr did have some things in common. They were both engineers; they both knew technology could create vastly profitable enterprises from nothing; and they were both impressed by the popularity of Mosaic. (In the summer of 1994, more than a million copies were in use.) Bill Joy, the chief scientist at Sun Microsystems, demonstrated Mosaic to Doerr, saying, "This is so big the only thing to do is dive right in."[21] Doerr took Joy's advice. Without further ado, he agreed to give Clark $5 million on the terms he demanded. Clark would remain the largest shareholder in Mosaic Communications, and Kleiner Perkins would become the second biggest. If the Mosaic replacement proved as successful as Doerr hoped, Kleiner Perkins would do very well; but Clark would do even better.

The irascible engineer had got the deal he wanted, and he had also shifted the balance of power in Silicon Valley. From now on, the VCs would have to pay the entrepreneurs what they demanded. A couple of decades earlier, the same thing had happened in the film industry, with power shifting away from the financiers (the studios) and toward the talent (the actors and directors). The consequences in Hollywood were soon apparent—vast sums invested in increasingly dubious ventures. Before long the pattern would be repeated in Silicon Valley.

## IV

**In the summer of 1994, *Time* ran the first of its many cover stories on** the Internet, describing it as "the nearest thing to a working prototype of the information superhighway," and adding that it was "growing faster than O.J. Simpson's legal bills."[23] By the time the story appeared Mosaic Communications was starting to look like a real company. Work on the new Web browser was going well, and more employees were being hired. They weren't all software writers who slept under their desks. Some were marketers, some were support staff, some even had titles like Executive Vice President. In September, Mosaic Communications did its first deal, with MCI, the long-distance telephone company, agreeing to provide the software for an online shopping mall. Greg Sands, a marketing hire, was asked to come up with a name for the firm's main product, ("Mozilla" was considered too lighthearted.) After soliciting ideas from the engineers—"info-suck" and "info-nipple" were two of their helpful suggestions—Sands came up with one of his own that stuck: Mosaic Netscape.[24]

The next task was to decide how much to charge for the new browser. Mike Homer, a former Apple Computer executive who was head of marketing, wanted to charge $99 for each copy. Andreessen disagreed vehemently. He knew that people expected things to be free on the Internet, but that wasn't his only consideration. He had been studying the history of Microsoft, the most profitable firm in the computer industry, which had always priced its software cheaply to build market share. Andreessen believed that for Mosaic Netscape to take over the Web browser market from rivals like Spyglass it would have to give its browser away for nothing, or close to nothing, and make money elsewhere. "It's basically a Microsoft lesson, right?" he explained. "If you get ubiquity you have a lot of options, a lot of ways to benefit from that. You can get paid by the product that you are ubiquitous on, but you can also get paid on products that benefit as a result. One of the fundamental lessons is that market share now equals revenue later, and if you don't have market share now, you are not going to have revenue later."[25] In the end, Andreessen and Homer settled on a compromise. Netscape would be "free but not free." Students and educators would be allowed to download the browser for nothing. Everybody else would get a ninety-day free trial, after which they would supposedly pay $39. Mosaic Communications would also try to make money from the specialized software, known as server software, that it sold to people who wanted to set up their own Web sites. It was a new version of an old business strategy made famous by Gillette: give away the razors but charge for the blades.

On October 13, 1994, Mosaic Communications posted the beta version of Mosaic Netscape on its Web site. The unveiling turned into a repeat of what had taken place twenty-one months earlier in Illinois. The first person to download Mosaic Netscape was in Japan. Within the hours, thousands of computer users all around the world were trying to download it. After that, the demand never slackened. Mosaic Netscape looked similar to its elder sibling, but it was faster, fancier, and less prone to crashing. It also supported more complicated page layouts, and it allowed users to exchange encrypted messages, such as credit card numbers, which was crucial for the future development of online commerce. The media reviews were generally positive. "It blew us all away," *Business Week* quoted a user as saying.[26] The same article argued that software like Mosaic Netscape could "make the Internet a mass medium for home shopping, banking, and a host of other services." The only hiccup came when the University of Illinois threatened to sue, claiming it deserved a licensing fee for each copy of Mosaic Netscape. Clark and Andreessen insisted that the code was completely new, but after a couple of months of legal wrangling, they agreed to pay $1 million to the university and to change the name of their company to Netscape Communications Corporation in order to settle the dispute.

In December 1994, Netscape released the alpha version of Netscape Navigator 1.0. During the following three months, more than 3 million copies were distributed, making it one of the most popular pieces of software ever launched. Most of these browsers were given away free, but some were sold. Companies inundated Netscape with requests to license the new Web browser and the server software that accompanied it. By March 1995, Netscape had governed revenues of about $7 million. Meanwhile, the extraordinary growth of the Web continued. According to a *Business Week* survey published in early 1995, there were now more than 27,000 Web sites, and the number was doubling every two months. At that rate of growth, by the end of the year there would be more than a million Web sites. Even the old media companies, which had been fixated on the information superhighway, were forced to sit up and take notice. In February 1995, a group of them that included Hearst, Times Mirror, and TCI bought an 11 percent stake in Netscape Communications for $17 million, valuing the entire company at more than $150 million.

A month later, with demand for the Netscape Navigator still increasing, Clark gave an interview to *The New York Times* in which he said: "I'm astonished. I've never seen anything like this in my life."[27] Clark's surprise was probably genuine, but he had good reason to play up the Netscape phenomenon. Although his company was less than a year old, he was already thinking about floating it on the stock market.

# chapter 5  the stock market

I

**Stock markets are like electricity and sewage systems: extremely** useful inventions that can sometimes go haywire. Stock markets transfer resources from people who have savings they don't know what to do with to businesses that have investment projects they don't have enough money to finance. This may sound trivial, but it isn't. Economic systems that have relied on other methods of mobilizing savings for investment, such as government fiat (the Soviet bloc) or the banking system (Germany), have run into problems. And stock markets don't just allocate resources; they also provide incentives for innovation and hard work. If an entrepreneur sets up a company that does well, he or she can issue stock to investors in an IPO, a process known as "going public." The promise of striking it rich in the stock market gets a lot of people out of bed in the morning.

The first stock market, as far as we know, was in ancient Rome, at the Forum, where men of means gathered to trade all sorts of things: land, houses, ships, cattle, slaves, stocks, and bonds. The stocks (*partes*) and bonds were issued by the *publicani*, companies that carried out many of the functions of the Roman government, such as collecting taxes, building temples, and dredging rivers. As the British historian Edward Chancellor points out in his highly informative book, *Devil Take the Hindmost: A History of Financial Speculation*, it is no surprise that the first stock market should have been in Rome.[1] The Roman Empire had a system of laws that protected private property and allowed it to be freely traded. In the dark era that followed the collapse of Rome there was no rule of law and little trade beyond barter. It wasn't until the Middle Ages that financial markets reappeared, with the issuing of government bonds by Italian states, such as Venice, Florence, and Genoa. The Italian city-states also created companies with tradable shares, but it was in Antwerp, Belgium, in the sixteenth century, that the first modern stock market appeared. After Spanish troops invaded Belgium in 1585, most of the traders moved to Amsterdam, which became the financial capital of its era, with banks, double-entry bookkeeping, joint-stock companies, and a stock market where people could invest in companies of all kinds.

Speculation—buying things in the hope that their price goes up before they are sold—is at least as old as stock markets, and so is the feverish mind-set that speculators invariably fall victim to. The speculators of sixteenth-century Amsterdam were "full of instability, insanity, pride and foolishness," a contemporary testified. "They will sell without knowing the motive; they will buy without reason." Even on their deathbeds, "their last worries are their shares."[2] It was in Holland that the first recorded speculative craze occurred—in tulip bulbs. During the "Tulipmania" of the 1630s, the price of Gouda bulbs went from 20 guilders to 225 guilders. Croenen bulbs went from 20 guilders to 1200 guilders. (The average annual wage at the time was about 300 guilders.) In February 1637, the tulip market crashed, and many speculators went broke.

The first recorded stock market mania occurred in London, in 1720, when the South Sea Company, which had been granted a government monopoly on trade with the Spanish colonies in South America, issued stock. In six months, the price of South Sea Company shares went from 128 to 1,050. A great wave of speculation took over London, and everybody from Alexander Pope to Isaac Newton to King George I got caught up in it. Enterprising men looked at the buoyant market and rushed to found new speculative vehicles. These "bubble companies," as they were known, would post notices in the newspaper laying out their business plans and offering to take subscriptions at coffee shops in the City of London. There were technology companies, such as Sir Richard Steele's Fish-Pool Company, which claimed to have invented a new fishing boat that would keep the catch alive until it reached port. There were financial services companies, such as Matthew West's "Company for buying and selling South Sea stock and all other public stocks." And there were exploration companies, such as the "Company of London Adventurers for the carrying on a trade to and settling colonies in Terra Australis." (This half a century before Captain Cook discovered Australia.)

As the boom continued, the number of new issues multiplied—from five in January 1720 to eighty-seven in June. Some of the bubble companies were clearly fraudulent, such as the company for "extracting Gold and Silver from Lead and other sorts of ore." One cheeky soul even set up a company "for carrying out an undertaking of great advantage but nobody to know what it is." After gathering up the subscriptions, he fled to the Continent.[3] In September 1820, the bubble burst. Stock in the South Sea Company fell by more than 75 percent, and many people, Newton among them, were ruined. Amid a public outcry, the Chancellor of the Exchequer (the British equivalent of the Secretary of the Treasury) and several directors of the South Sea Company were sent to the Tower of London. Lamented Pope: "The universal deluge of the S. Sea, contrary to the old deluge, has drowned all except a few Unrighteous men."[4]

## II

**The United States came late to the game of stock market speculation.** The New York Stock & Exchange Board opened for business on Wall Street in 1817, but it wasn't until the Civil War and the development of the railroads that large-scale capital raising began. The banker Jay Cooke was the first person to demonstrate that ordinary Americans would part with their savings in return for pieces of paper issued by governments and businesses. During the Civil War, Cooke successfully organized the sale of $500 million worth of federal government bonds. Some of his later ventures were less successful. In 1869, he took over the Northern Pacific Railway, which linked Lake Superior to Puget Sound, and tried to sell $100 million worth of railway bonds. This proved impossible and on Thursday, September 18, 1873—the first "Black Thursday"—Cooke's bank failed while he was paying a visit to President Ulysses S. Grant. Fear swept Wall Street, and creditors rushed to withdraw their deposits. Several other banks collapsed. "Dread seemed to take possession of the multitude," *The New York Tribune* reported.[5] Panic was so widespread that the New York Stock Exchange was forced to close down for ten days. Public faith in the financial markets was destroyed for a generation. Mark Twain captured the popular attitude in *Pudd'nhead Wilson* when he wrote: "October. This is one of the peculiarly dangerous months to speculate in stocks in. The others are July, January, September, April, November, May, March, June, December, August and February."[6]

It wasn't until after the First World War that Americans returned to the stock market in large numbers, a development that coincided with unprecedented confidence in the economy and in the efficacy of American business. Following the invention of the Federal Reserve System in 1913, there were few lasting recessions, and many economists came to believe that the new science of monetary policy had rendered them obsolete. Meanwhile, industrialists like Alfred Sloan, the head of General Motors, were applying novel methods to corporate management, with sterling results. In 1927, *Barron's*, the financial weekly, hailed a "new era without depressions."[7] (In September 2000, the same publication would carry the front-page headline, "Can Anything Stop This Economy? Despite Recent Signs of a Slowdown, Expect the Economy to Remain Robust, with No Recession in Sight.")[8] The mood of optimism spread to the stock market, and millions of people bought shares for the first time—only to be caught out in October 1929. Groucho Marx and Irving Berlin were among the neophyte speculators who lost most of their money during the Great Crash. Charlie Chaplin was another keen investor, but he had liquidated most of his portfolio by the time the market collapsed.

During the Internet boom it became almost unpatriotic to compare the 1990s to the 1920s. People who did so were accused of carping. But for all but the willfully blind, the similarities between the two eras were legion, no more so than in the popularity of technology stocks. Among the speculators' favorites during the 1920s were issues like Wright Aeronautics, Boeing, and, especially, Radio Company of

America, RCA, or Radio, as it was then known, the most glamorous and fastest-growing corporation of the 1920s. Commercial radio was a revolutionary medium that shrunk the country like nothing before it, and Radio was the major player in the industry; it both manufactured radio sets and provided the programming they transmitted. In 1921 its stock hit a low of 1½. Thereafter, it climbed steadily until 1927, when it headed for the stratosphere. In April 1929, Radio hit a high, after adjusting for stock splits, of 570. During this stunning ascent, old-timers shook their heads in disbelief. Despite its rapid growth, Radio had never paid a cent in dividends, and many of its shareholders were professional gamblers. In October 1929, the stock lost 75 percent of its value. It recovered a bit during 1930, but then collapsed again, and remained collapsed for the rest of the decade. Despite the strong growth of commercial radio, RCA's stock didn't recover its April 1929 level until 1964—thirty-five years later.

For a generation after 1929, the stock market was once again discredited in the eyes of many Americans. There were occasional periods of speculation, but they tended to involve institutional investors and well-to-do people who could afford to take some losses. Middle-class families kept their money in the bank, in real estate, or in other investments. The speculative episodes that did occur tended to involve technology firms. In the early 1960s, for example, there was an electronics boom, and stocks like IBM and Texas Instruments took off. The space race had begun, and electronics and computers were inextricably linked with the rocket technology that, it was hoped, would soon propel man to the moon. As stock prices rose, there was a rush of IPOs, many of them involving firms with names that played on words like "electronics," "dynamics," and "space." There was Astron, Dutron, Vulcatron, Transistron, as well as Circuitronics, Supronics, Videotronics, and even Powertron Ultransonics. In one particularly egregious (and prescient) example related by the Princeton economist Burton G. Malkiel in his book *A Random Walk Down Wall Street*, American Music Guild, a firm whose business involved selling phonographic records and players door-to-door, changed its name to Space-Tone before going public. The shares were issued at $2 each, but quickly rose to $14.[9] Almost four decades later, another music company, K-Tel International, would adopt a strikingly similar tactic, with strikingly similar results. In K–Tel's case, the magic phrase would be "the Internet."

## III

**Stocks confer ownership in a corporation, which, in turn, confers** the right to receive some of the profit that the firm generates. Usually, most profits are plowed back into the firm to pay for future investment, but some money is also distributed to shareholders in the form of dividend payments. It seems reasonable to expect that a stock's price should reflect the value of the dividends that the firm is likely to pay over the foreseeable future, which, in turn, depends on its earnings growth. That, indeed, is what countless generations of MBA students were taught. A number of mathematical equations have been developed to relate stock prices to dividends and earnings. As long ago as the 1930s, John Burr Williams, a Harvard-trained economist, came up with what is still the most widely used valuation formula: the "dividend discount model."[10] To use this formula, which Benjamin Graham and David L. Dodd popularized in their famous textbook *Security Analysis*, three facts about a company need to be known: its current dividend, the growth rate of its earnings, and the interest rate it faces in financing investments.[11] Once these numbers are in hand, the student can plug them into the formula, which will produce an estimate of the stock's "intrinsic value." If the stock price is higher than the intrinsic value, the stock is overvalued and investors should sell it. If the stock price is less than the intrinsic value, the stock is undervalued and investors should buy it.

The dividend discount model is a bit complicated to explain to the general public, so Wall Street analysts also rely on simpler rules of thumb to assess whether stocks are cheap or expensive. The most famous of these is the price-to-earnings ratio, or "PE ratio," which is calculated by dividing a company's stock price by its earnings-per-share. If company X's stock is trading at $100, and it made $10 per share in its latest financial year, its trailing PE ratio is 10. (Analysts also employ forecasts of future earnings to create advance PE ratios.) Companies with rapidly growing earnings tend to have high PE ratios, reflecting their bright prospects. Slow-growing companies tend to have commensurately low PE ratios. There is no "right" value for the PE ratio, but over the past century the average figure for U.S. stocks has been about 14. Among other ratios that stock analysts look at are the "dividend yield," which is the annual dividend payment a stock yields divided by its current price, and the "price-to-book ratio," which is a company's stock market valuation divided by the accounting value of its assets.

None of these mathematical formulas is infallible: stock prices often bear little, if any, relation to what the formulas say they should be. Uncertainty about the future is one reason for this discrepancy. Just because a company's profits have risen at an annual rate of 25 percent during the past five years, this doesn't mean they will grow at that rate during the next decade. They might grow faster. More likely, they will grow more slowly. But nobody knows for sure. Depending on the growth rate that is assumed virtually any PE ratio or stock price can be rationalized. During the 1950s and the 1970s, many stocks had PE ratios in the single digits. During the 1960s and 1980s, many of the same stocks had PE ratios in the twenties. In the 1990s, PE multiples rose to levels never seen before, in many cases triple digits. During each one of these periods the majority of Wall Street analysts insisted that stock prices were reasonable.

When a firm is issuing stock for the first time in an IPO, the valuation problem is even trickier. Such firms are forced to publish their financial history in the IPO prospectus, but if they have only been operating for a year or two, as was often the case in recent years, that information isn't much of a guide to what will happen in the future. With few hard numbers to go on, investors have to rely on guesswork and emotion. When the economy is doing well they tend to be optimistic about the future and attribute generous growth rates to companies, even to those that don't deserve them. Stock prices tend to be high and rising, and IPOs plentiful. During an economic downturn, on the other hand, pessimism tends to be widespread, and even the stocks of fast-growing firms trade at low levels. As for the IPO market, it often shuts down completely in a recession.

During the Internet boom analysts and investors would be forced to invent new ways to value stocks. The vast majority of Internet companies made no profits and paid no dividends, so the methods taught in Graham and Dodd didn't apply to them. If the old formulas were used, they produced an "intrinsic value" of zero for most Internet stocks. Since Wall Street was busy trying to sell these stocks to the public, it didn't advertise this fact, but instead looked for more flexible valuation methods. Given the boundless nature of human ingenuity, especially financially motivated human ingenuity, it was sure to come up with one. Ultimately, it came up with several, but they all shared one attribute: whatever prices investors were paying for Internet stocks, the new valuation methods made them appear reasonable (or almost reasonable).

## IV

**Corporate earnings and crowd psychology apart, the other big influ**ence on the stock market is the policy stance of the Federal Reserve. Generally speaking, when the Fed is cutting interest rates, or keeping them low, stock prices go up. When the Fed is raising rates, or keeping them high, stock prices go down. The bull markets of both the 1980s and the 1990s occurred during periods of low and falling interest rates. In both 1929 and 1987, a rise in interest rates preceded a stock market crash. The historic relationship between monetary policy and the stock market explains why Wall Street watches Alan Greenspan's comments so closely. If the Fed chairman even suggests that he and his colleagues on the Federal Open Market Committee (FOMC), the Fed's policy-making arm, might be considering a hike in interest rates, stock prices tend to fall in anticipation. If Greenspan drops the merest hint of lower rates ahead, the market tends to rally.

There are several reasons why the Fed should have so much influence on the market. The most straightforward is that when interest rates drop, the returns on savings accounts and CDs drop with them, and the stock market looks more attractive. When CD rates are down around 3 percent or 4 percent, as they often have been during the past decade, many households go searching for higher returns on their money, even if that involves taking on a higher level of risk. A fall in interest rates also reduces the borrowing costs that firms and consumers face, which leads to more spending on everything from factories to homes to automobiles. Other things being equal, this rise in spending will lead to higher demand for goods and services throughout the economy, and higher corporate earnings. When earnings are rising, individual stocks are worth more. When the Fed raises interest rates the logic works in the opposite direction. Rates on bank deposits and CDs increase, which makes them a better deal for savers. Simultaneously, consumers and firms find it more costly to borrow, which prompts them to cut back on their spending, leading to a reduction in overall demand and lower corporate profits. When earnings are falling, stocks tend to fall with them.

In raising or lowering interest rates, the Fed also controls the amount of money and credit circulating in the financial system. This is an unavoidable consequence of how it operates. The most important interest rate that the Fed controls is the federal funds rate, which is the rate that commercial banks charge each other for overnight loans. When the Fed wants to reduce the federal funds rate, it buys U.S. government bonds from Wall Street firms, paying them with freshly minted currency that is then deposited in the banking system. This increase in the money supply allows the commercial banks to make more loans, which produces an expansion of credit throughout the economy. If the Fed wants to raise interest rates, it sells some of its portfolio of U.S. government bonds to Wall Street firms. The cash that the firms use to pay for the bonds is then withdrawn from circulation, and the money supply falls. With less cash on their balance sheets, banks can make fewer loans, and the amount of credit in the economy declines. On Wall Street, the amount of money and credit available is often referred to as "liquidity." When liquidity is plentiful the price of assets (stocks especially, but also real estate) tends to rise. When liquidity dries up, as happened in many Asian countries during 1997 and 1998, asset prices fall sharply. In the United States during the second half of the 1990s, there was an unprecedented amount of liquidity in the financial system, and this was an important factor underpinning the stock market's rise.

Through all of these channels, the Fed can influence the rate at which the U.S. economy grows, although it often takes several interest rate moves for a policy change to have the desired effect. In normal times, the Fed restricts itself to interest rate changes of a quarter percentage point or a half percentage point, but when it wants to impact the economy quickly it introduces a succession of interest rate moves, often adding up to 2 percent or 3 percent. Whether interest rates are 5.5 percent or 5.25 percent doesn't make that much difference to the economy, but there is an enormous difference between interest rates of 3 percent and 8 percent. At 3 percent, the cost of borrowing is so cheap that it acts as a big stimulus to spending. At 8 percent, borrowing is so expensive that spending will be sharply curtailed. The Fed doesn't like to admit it publicly, but by raising interest rates sufficiently it has the power to push the economy into recession. Every recession since the Second World War has followed a tightening of monetary policy—in most cases one intended to head off inflation. During the second half of the 1990s, the biggest danger facing investors was that Greenspan and his colleagues would decide to repeat this treatment and bring the long economic expansion to an end.

# chapter 6 ipo

I

**In January 1995, the Dow Jones Industrial Average was lingering**
around 3,800, about the same level it had been at a year earlier. During
1994, Alan Greenspan and his colleagues at the Federal Reserve Board
had raised short-term interest rates from 3.5 percent to 6.5 percent to
slow down the economy and head off a possible revival of inflation.
This policy shift prompted Wall Street analysts to reduce their forecasts
of corporate earnings, which contributed to the stock market's sluggish
performance. The big political story of early 1995 was the rise of Newt
Gingrich following the Republicans' victory in the 1994 midterm
congressional elections. As the new Speaker of the House of Representatives, Gingrich was eager to present himself as a national leader
for the information age. The former history professor frequently held
court about the technological changes sweeping the nation and the
political implications thereof. During Gingrich's orations, the Internet
often featured prominently—another indication that going online and
surfing the World Wide Web was no longer the preserve of scientific
researchers, computer buffs, and sex addicts. It was now a mainstream
pastime, enjoyed by millions of ordinary Americans.

Part of the growth in online traffic came from commercial online
services, such as CompuServe, America Online, and Prodigy, which
were grudgingly starting to provide their customers with access to the
Internet. CompuServe, which had been in business since 1969, was
the oldest online service. Now owned by H&R Block, the accounting firm, it had more than 500,000 subscribers, who paid $9 a month,

plus an hourly usage fee, for access to a range of proprietary content that included news, chat, and information. Most of CompuServe's customers were business users, and they provided a steady if unspectacular stream of profits. America Online, which was third in the market with about 200,000 subscribers, had been losing money ever since 1982, when it started out as a distributor of online video games under the name Control Video Corporation. In March 1992, America Online did an IPO, which, despite the firm's troubled history, succeeded in raising $23 million. A year later, Microsoft, which was preparing to start its own online service, tried to buy America Online, but Steve Case, the firm's young chief executive, turned down the deal.

Prodigy, which IBM and Sears had launched with great fanfare in 1990, was in even worse shape than America Online, having run through hundreds of millions of dollars. Although it didn't operate on the Internet, Prodigy was in many ways the prototype Internet business. In return for $14.95 a month, subscribers received unlimited access to expensively produced news and information sites that featured Howard Cosell on sports, Liz Smith on Broadway, and Evans and Novak on politics. There were also video games and online shopping. "We had a belief that goods will be sold electronically, so why not establish dominance in the marketplace," Ross Glazer, a senior Prodigy executive, explained. "You could make the case that eventually there would be no need for malls."[1] In the event, Prodigy's customers turned out to be more interested in communicating with each other than in buying CDs and airline tickets. Unfortunately, Prodigy limited free e-mails to thirty a month, and it didn't introduce chat rooms until 1994. Advertising revenues were a lot lower than expected, and Prodigy learned a lesson that many Internet start-ups would learn years later: in the online world, large numbers of users, easy-to-use software, and high-quality content don't necessarily add up to a profitable business.

The World Wide Web's rapid growth presented a threat to the online services, which depended on subscribers paying for proprietary content. In March 1994, America Online allowed its members limited access to the Internet. A few months later, Prodigy said it would provide full access at the start of 1995, and America Online was forced to follow suit. In preparation, America Online acquired a firm called Booklink Technologies, which made its own Web browser, and another called NaviSoft, which produced software for publishing on the Web. Case even tried to buy a stake in Netscape Communications, but he was rebuffed. CompuServe also moved toward the Internet. In February 1995, it paid an eye-popping $100 million for Spry Inc., a Seattle-based company whose Web browser had a market share of less than 10 percent.

Despite the exponential growth of traffic on the Internet and the World Wide Web, online commerce was still in its infancy. In April 1994, two Arizona lawyers, Laurence Cantor and Martha Siegel, posted an advertisement for their firm on more than five thousand Internet bulletin boards. Sending people unwanted commercial messages like this, a practice known as "spamming," was *verboten* on the Internet. Cantor and Siegel found themselves deluged with so many angry messages that their local Internet service provider closed their account. But the traditionalists were fighting a losing battle. According to Cantor and Siegel, their spam generated $100,000 in extra business. Discreet advertising was already an established feature on the Internet. Bookstores advertised on literary bulletin boards, sex companies advertised on sex sites, and florists advertised at florist.com. O'Reilly & Associates, a California publishing company, had set up an Internet service called Global Network Navigator, which included "GNN Marketplace," a primitive online shopping mall.

Corporate America was slowly realizing that through the Internet it could reach millions of customers, most of them affluent and educated. Marty Nisenholtz, an executive at Ogilvy & Mather, a New York advertising agency, drew up a set of guidelines for online advertising. (Nisenholtz's first rule was that intrusive e-mails were unwelcome.) In November 1994, AT&T and Zima, a beverage company, placed the first "banner" advertisements on the Web, at Hotwired. com, the online arm of *Wired*. The advertisements were interactive, which was claimed to be their great virtue. Whenever somebody clicked on a banner, he or she was transferred to another Web site that provided more information about the advertiser. (Of course, people could simply ignore the banners, but this aspect of interactivity wasn't stressed at the time.)

All of this activity didn't go unnoticed on Wall Street, where hordes of investment bankers were busy searching for deals. Investment bankers are basically realtors. The properties they sell are companies, and securities in companies. Like real estate agents, they charge a hefty commission for their services. Managing an IPO is a particularly lucrative business. When an investment bank issues $100 million in stock from a new company, it usually keeps about $7 million of the proceeds for itself, and that is only the start of the payoff. Most young companies are forever in need of money, and they end up doing a lot of follow-on stock and bond issues, which generate more commissions. Another thing that investment bankers share with real estate agents is that they are always on the lookout for the next trendy area, where big money can be made in fixing up old properties and building new ones. The Internet was just such a neighborhood. During the early 1990s, it was widely seen as a bohemian enclave, but during 1994 and 1995 this attitude changed, and the rich started to move in. "It's like the land rush in Oklahoma," Larry Ellison, the chairman of Oracle, said in February 1995. "The best spot in the valley goes to the one who gets there first."[2]

With demand for Internet-related companies increasing, the investment bankers set about increasing the supply. The first candidates were the Internet service providers, which were enjoying strong growth. In December 1994, Netcom On-Line Communications Services, an ISP based in San Jose, issued 1.85 million shares in a stock offering organized by Volpe, Welty & Company, a small investment bank based in San Francisco. The media didn't pay much attention to the Netcom IPO, but Wall Street did. The stock was issued at $13, valuing Netcom at more than $85 million. Since Netcom didn't make any profits or pay any dividends, its stock was priced on the basis of a new formula: value per subscriber. Netcom certainly had subscribers—about 41,500 of them—and they had to be worth something. At $13 a share, each one of them was valued at about $2,100—more than twice the value that the stock market was attributing to cable television subscribers. This was despite the fact that Internet service providers charged about $20 a month, while cable companies charged upwards of $30 a month. There was no obvious reason why Internet users should be valued so highly, but even at this early stage Internet stock valuation wasn't based on reason. It was based on hope and hype. The new valuation formulas were primarily an attempt to rationalize the fervor of investors. "This is a rocket that has been launched," Eric Schmidt a senior executive at Sun Microsystems, declared shortly after the Netcom IPO. "There's no one who can stop it."[3]

Within a few months of going public, Netcom's stock price had doubled, thereby justifying the new valuation formula, at least in the eyes of its progenitors. In the spring of 1995, two more ISPs went public at outlandish prices. PSINet, a Virginia company that had lost more than $10 million during the previous year, sold 3.8 million shares at $12 each, valuing the company at $431 million. UUNet, which was also based in Virginia, sold 4.725 million shares at $14 each, and its stock price almost doubled on the first day. Goldman Sachs, the most prestigious firm on Wall Street, underwrote the UUNet offering, and the sight of the mighty Goldman giving its imprimatur to Internet stocks raised the industry to a new level of respectability.

Many Wall Street veterans looked askance at these events. Even in Silicon Valley, where companies tend to go public quicker than elsewhere, there had been a custom that IPO candidates should have two or three years of profit-making behind them. Some of the new Internet companies had hardly been in business for three years, let alone made profits for that long, but their stocks were being snapped up like Impressionist paintings. "Anything that even sounds like it's an Internet play can go public without much on the books," Cristina Morgan, a senior executive at Hambrecht & Quist, a San Francisco–based investment bank, commented. "Investors want to be on board."[4]

## II

**Jim Clark, the founder of Netscape, was watching these events** closely. Back in 1986 his first firm, Silicon Graphics, had carried out a successful IPO after being in business for five years, which was then considered fast. Netscape was barely a year old, but its revenues were growing rapidly, and its browser was spreading like one of the filthy jokes that Clark liked to tell. By the end of May 1995, more than 5 million Netscape Navigators had been distributed, and Netscape's market share had gone from zero to more than 60 percent.

Clark stood to make a lot of money if Netscape went public, but that wasn't his only consideration. He was hearing rumors that Spyglass, the company that had licensed the Mosaic browser from the University of Illinois, was preparing to do an IPO, and he didn't want to be left behind. A successful stock offering would produce a lot of publicity, which would be immensely valuable to a young company like Netscape. In the old days, firms went public because they needed the money to expand, but in the 1990s IPOs had turned into marketing events. "I continued to preach the gospel, assuring the unsaved that the Internet was their salvation," Clark later wrote. "But we needed something else to get the world's attention. More marketing bullshit! For a tiny little company with modest but exploding revenues, what was the biggest marketing event of all?"[5]

There was yet another reason to move quickly, which Clark didn't like to acknowledge publicly. At some point soon, Microsoft was bound to react to Netscape's growing popularity, which was a potential threat to its grip on the PC desktop. Microsoft monopolized the market for PC operating systems with Windows 95, and the market for PC applications with Microsoft Office. Bill Gates had been slow to realize the importance of the Internet, but he was finally coming to his senses. Earlier in 1995, Microsoft had licensed Spyglass's technology in order to ship a Web browser with the Windows 95 operating system and the Microsoft Network, both of which were due to be launched in August. Netscape Navigator was a superior browser to Spyglass's Mosaic, but Clark knew that Gates was unlikely to stop there. Before very long, Microsoft was sure to attack the Web browser market in a more serious manner. If Netscape was going to issue stock, it made sense to do so while the competition was sparse.

In early June 1995, Clark called a board meeting and invited Frank Quattrone, an investment banker at Morgan Stanley, to make a presentation. At thirty-nine, Quattrone was not a typical Wall Street preppie. He had grown up in an Italian-American family in Philadelphia, and he still spoke with a strong accent. After getting his MBA at Stanford Business School in 1981, Quattrone chose to stay in California. He joined Morgan Stanley's San Francisco office as an associate working on technology IPOs. At that time, the Silicon Valley investment-banking industry was largely detached from Wall Street. Three San Francisco–based firms—Hambrecht & Quist, Montgomery Securities, and Robertson, Stephens—handled most of the deals. Quattrone saw an opportunity for his new employer to move in on a rapidly growing business. With its strong links to institutional investors and its famous name, which emerged from the breakup of J. P. Morgan's financial empire during the Great Depression, Morgan Stanley could offer Silicon Valley companies instant credibility on Wall Street. The strategy worked. During the late 1980s and early 1990s, Quattrone helped some of Silicon Valley's most successful companies to go public, including Cisco Systems and Silicon Graphics, which is when he met Clark. After Clark founded Netscape, Quattrone got back in touch with him. In early 1995, Quattrone helped organize the deal that saw several big media companies take stakes in Netscape, an experience that convinced him other investors would be willing to back Netscape despite its youth.

At the Netscape board meeting, Quattrone argued that an IPO would be a big success, especially if it was done before Windows 95 appeared. Given all the necessary paperwork, the earliest possible date was August, a month when many people on Wall Street decamp to the Hamptons and Martha's Vineyard. "With this company, and in this market, I think people will give up their vacations to see the road show," Quattrone said.[6] The venture capitalist John Doerr was willing to go along with an immediate IPO, but Jim Barksdale, a courtly southerner whom Clark and Doerr had brought in as Netscape's chief executive earlier in the year, thought it was too early to go public. The firm's revenues in the second quarter of 1995 were only $12 million, and it was still losing money. Barksdale, who had previously held senior positions at Federal Express and McCaw Cellular Communications, was also worried that an IPO might distract Netscape's staff and attract more attention from Microsoft. He asked for some time to think things over, and the board meeting broke up.

Clark was relentless. As Netscape's founder, chairman, and biggest shareholder he couldn't be ignored for long. A couple of weeks later, Spyglass held its IPO, issuing two million shares at $17. The stock closed above $21. Clark became even more insistent. "If Spyglass could score a successful IPO, we had to get our asses in gear," he later wrote.[7] A couple of days after the Spyglass offering, Clark called another board meeting, this time via telephone. When everybody was on the line, he asked Barksdale what he had decided. "Okay," Barksdale said. "Let's do it."

The process of taking a company public takes place in three stages. The first task is to prepare a wealth of financial information about the firm and file it with the Securities and Exchange Commission. Fortunately, Morgan Stanley had gathered many of the relevant figures earlier in the year. In mid-July, Netscape published its prospectus and said it intended to sell 3.5 million shares at $12 to $14 each. This was only a provisional estimate the actual price of a stock issue is never decided until a day or two before the IPO—but it indicated that Morgan Stanley believed Netscape was worth about $500 million, more than three times the valuation placed on it earlier in the year. In other circumstances, such a valuation would have been considered excessive, but in this instance it turned out to be too low.

This became clear during the second stage of the IPO process: the investor road show. In late July and early August, Barksdale and Andreessen crisscrossed the United States and Europe to meet the fund managers and other institutional investors who would be bidding for Netscape's stock. In theory, an investor road show is an occasion for skeptical investors to take the measure of the company's management and ask some tough questions. In practice, most of the people who attend have already decided to buy, and the main reason they show up is to impress the underwriters who control the stock allocations. At stop after stop, Barksdale and Andreessen were treated like visiting dignitaries. In New York, so many people tried to get in that some were turned away. During the presentations, Andreessen regaled the audience with his views about the future of the Internet, while Barksdale played the part of the southern minister. "It's just like church," he would say in his Mississippi drawl. "Come on down the front and be saved."[8]

After the road shows finished, Quattrone and his colleagues at Morgan Stanley gathered for the third and final stage of the IPO process—the pricing of the stock. They were facing a dilemma. The number of shares to be issued had already been increased to 5 million, but judging by the expressions of interest during the road shows 50 million could easily have been sold. The IPO price would have to be raised, but by how much? Pricing a stock issue is as much an art as a science. Ideally, the price would be low enough for the stock to enjoy a decent "bounce" when it started trading but high enough to ensure that Clark and Barksdale didn't feel like they had left too much money on the table. After some debate, Morgan Stanley recommended an issue price of $31 a share. Barksdale thought that figure was too high, and he insisted on a price of $28, which would value Netscape at more than a billion dollars.

## III

**On the morning of August 9, 1995, Clark woke up at his usual time** in his home in Atherton, a small town a few miles north of Palo Alto. "The weather at seven A.M. was typical for a summer morning in the semimythical part of California known as Silicon Valley," he wrote in *Netscape Time*, a memoir published in 1999. "While the rest of the country sweltered, in my neighborhood thirty miles south of San Francisco the clouds lay so low they verged on fog. The temperature hovered in the mid-fifties. Had this been almost anywhere else, the dull light coming through the bedroom windows would have suggested a day of rain, but I knew that within two hours the sun would burn away the clouds and the temperature would climb into the nineties. Rain still was months away."[9]

While Clark contemplated meteorology, the men and women on the Equity Capital Markets trading floor at Morgan Stanley's global headquarters, high above the north end of Times Square, were in a frenzy of activity. Even at $28 a share, the demand for Netscape stock was easily outstripping the supply. The stock had been due to start trading at 9:30 A.M. E.S.T., but at 10:30 it hadn't opened. So many investors were bidding for the stock that Morgan Stanley's traders were finding it impossible to establish a floor for the first trade. Whatever price they indicated, investors seemed willing to bid more. Everybody on Wall Street, it seemed, wanted in on the Netscape offering. Many of the bidders were mutual fund managers, but there was also heavy demand from individual investors. The Netscape IPO had captured the public imagination in an unprecedented manner. At Charles Schwab, the discount brokerage, the recorded phone message had been changed to say, "Press one if you're calling about Netscape."[10]

Back in Silicon Valley, Clark was getting nervous. After having breakfast and calling Morgan Stanley a couple of times, he drove to Mountain View, where his secretary had rigged up an electronic ticker tape to display Netscape's stock price in real time. It was now after 8 A.M. on the West Coast, and after 11 A.M. on the East Coast, but the electronic display said $28. Trading still hadn't opened. Clark thought of swinging by Andreessen's office but decided against it. Andreessen wasn't in yet anyway. Having worked late the previous night, he was in bed. At about 8:30 A.M., Clark's secretary finally put through a call from somebody at Morgan Stanley to tell him the stock had opened at $71. "Unbelievable," the voice said. "Congratulations."[11] After putting the phone down, Clark did some arithmetic in his head. His 9.7 million shares were now worth $663 million. A little later, Andreessen finally woke up and logged onto Quote.com, a financial Web site, to find out what was happening. When he saw the stock price and realized he was worth about $70 million his eyes widened. Then he got back into bed and went back to sleep—at least that is what he later claimed he did.

Over the course of the day, Netscape's stock climbed as high as $74. Almost 14 million shares were traded, which meant that each one of the 5 million shares changed hands nearly three times, on average. At the close, the stock stood at 58¼, valuing Netscape at $2.2 billion, almost as much as General Dynamics, the giant defense contractor. On its first day of trading, Netscape's stock had risen by 108 percent. As *The New York Times* noted the following morning: "It was the best opening day for a stock in Wall Street history for an issue of its size."[12] Pretty much everybody involved in the IPO had gotten seriously rich. Clark's shares were worth $565 million, not as much as they had been earlier in the day, but enough to make him one of the wealthiest men in the country. Kleiner Perkins's stake, which had cost it $3.5 million sixteen months earlier, was now worth $256.3 million. Doerr's decision to give into Clark's demands had turned into the most successful venture capital investment in history. Barksdale's shares, which he had received on taking the CEO job, were worth $244.7 million—a handsome return for eight months of work. Andreessen was worth $58.3 million. As for the rest of the University of Illinois team—Bina, Mittelhauser, Totic, *et al.*—they were each worth at least $20 million. Clark had come through on the promise he had made in Illinois a year and a half earlier. He couldn't help seeing what had happened as a personal triumph. For the past year or more he had been preaching the Internet gospel to anybody who would listen. "People started drinking my Kool-Aid," he told Michael Lewis. "Netscape obviously didn't create the Internet. But if Netscape had not forced the issue on the Internet, it would have just stayed in the background. It would have remained this counterintuitive kind of thing. The criticism of it was that it was anarchy. What the [Netscape] IPO did was give anarchy credibility."[13]

Clark's statement contained a lot of truth, but it wasn't anarchy in the usual sense of the word that had been legitimized. Some of the early Internet enthusiasts harbored anti-authoritarian, anticapitalist instincts, but they were now in a small minority. Anarchy in the post-Netscape sense meant that a group of college kids could meet up with a rich eccentric, raise some more money from a venture capitalist, and build a billion-dollar company in eighteen months. Anarchy was capitalism as personal liberation. To a country based on the twin pillars of free enterprise and individualism, this was an intoxicating vision, and it goes a long way toward explaining the extraordinary enthusiasm shown for the Internet in the ensuing years. From the moment of Netscape's IPO onward, going into the business world didn't necessarily mean putting on a suit, killing your teenage dreams, and working for a stultifying corporation. It could just as easily mean pulling on an old T-shirt, hooking up with some friends, and striking out on your own.

The Internet had turned into the new American frontier—an argument made explicitly by John Perry Barlow, the rancher, writer, and co-founder of the Electronic Freedom Foundation. "Today another frontier yawns before us, far more fog-obscured and inscrutable in its opportunities than the Yukon," Barlow declared. "It consists not of unmapped physical space in which to assert one's ambitious body, but unmappable, infinitely expansible cerebral space. Cyberspace. And we are all going there whether we want to or not."[14] As this passage indicates, Barlow is something of a hippie. As a young man he wrote song lyrics for the Grateful Dead. In one of history's bizarre coincidences, Netscape went public the same day that Jerry Garcia, the lead singer of the Dead, died of a heart attack. As the cultural icon of one era left the scene, a new one replaced him: Andreessen, the Wisconsin farm boy who had turned himself into an "Internet billionaire."

But as was the case with the hippie movement, there was always something slightly suspect about the notion of the Internet as a capitalist nirvana. For one thing, Andreessen wasn't a billionaire. Clark, Doerr, and Barksdale, three men who were already wealthy, made a lot more money from the Netscape IPO than he did. Since Andreessen came up with the idea for Mosaic in the first place, this was hardly fair, but it reflected an eternal verity: most of the rewards of capitalism—Internet capitalism or any other form of capitalism—go to the well-to-do. For another thing, it was far from clear that the money that had been made in the Netscape IPO was the real folding stuff. Only 5 million shares had been issued. Most of Netscape's 38 million shares, including all of those owned by Clark and Andreessen, were not yet trading. The stock price had been boosted by an artificial shortage of stock that would gradually be eliminated as more shares were issued over the coming months and years. Finally, it was by no means certain that Netscape was capable of withstanding the challenges that it would inevitably face. Despite the startling success of its IPO, this was still a business that gave away its main product and that faced imminent competition from Microsoft.

For now, none of these things seemed to matter. America was moving into a different realm—one where the restrictive laws of economics and gravity had been temporarily suspended. "This frontier, the Virtual World, offers opportunities and perils like none before," Barlow declared. "Entering it, we are engaging what will likely prove the most transforming technological event since the capture of fire. I have a terrible feeling that your children, by the time they are my age, would be barely recognizable to me as human, so permanently jacked in to the Great Mind will they be."[15]

## IV

**The media reaction to the Netscape IPO was mixed.** *The Financial Times,* Europe's leading business newspaper, compared Netscape to Boston Chicken, a fast-food chain that went public amid a blaze of publicity in November 1993 but quickly ran into trouble. *Time* pointed out that Microsoft was only two weeks away from launching Windows 95, which would come packaged with a new Web browser that "like other Microsoft programs, may smother all competitors."[16] George Gilder, who had finally discovered the World Wide Wed and adopted it with the zeal of a convert, was much more positive. Writing in *Forbes*, he anointed Marc Andreessen as the new Bill Gates and claimed that the Internet would "displace both the telephone and the television over the next five years or so."[17] Gilder's article caused amusement in Internet circles, because hitherto he had expressed little interest in the World Wide Web. "George, George, George—what took you so long?" Howard Anderson, a well-known technology consultant, commented wryly.[18]

Microsoft released Internet Explorer 1.0 at the end of August, but it turned out to be a barely improved version of the Mosaic browser. The Microsoft Network, which was launched at the same time, was equally uninspired. A month later, Netscape released the beta version of Netscape Navigator 2.0, which was far more impressive. It included space for "plug-in" applications, such as music players, and it also featured the "Java" programming language, which enabled users to download software from the Internet. The incorporation of Java made Netscape even more of a threat to Microsoft. If computer users could download word processing programs and spreadsheets from the Internet, they might no longer need Microsoft Windows and Microsoft Office. In November, Rick Sherlund, an analyst at Goldman Sachs, removed Microsoft's stock from his recommended list, and it fell sharply. Netscape's stock continued to astonish. In early December 1995, it reached $170, at which point Netscape was worth almost $6.5 billion.

# chapter 7 yahoo!

I

**From the early days of the Mosaic browser, one of the most popular**
sites on the Web was "Jerry's Guide to the World Wide Web," a listings page maintained by David Filo and Jerry Yang, two graduate students in the Stanford computer science department. Filo and Yang,
who were both in their mid-twenties, shared a trailer, where they
were supposed to be writing a Ph.D. dissertation on computer-aided
design, but they spent much of their time trawling the Web for sites
they liked. Filo, a quiet and intense fellow, was born in Wisconsin and
brought up in Louisiana; Yang, the more outgoing of the two, was
born in Taiwan and arrived in San Jose at the age of ten. By late 1993,
the list of favorite Web sites had grown to more than two hundred
and was getting out of hand. The Mosaic browser included a primitive "bookmark" facility, but it didn't allow much sorting. Filo and
Yang wrote some simple software that allowed them to group the
sites as they wished and posted it on the Web. Before long, they
found themselves inundated with e-mails suggesting new sites to
include. With their thesis supervisor overseas, they decided to cover
the entire Web. Throughout 1994, they surfed obsessively, often visiting a thousand sites a day. They renamed their enhanced guide
Yahoo!, a word chosen from the dictionary that was also Filo's nickname growing up. (The exclamation point was "pure marketing
hype," according to Yang.)[1]

By the summer of 1994, Yahoo! had tens of thousands of regular
users, many of whom called up a number of different pages. In the

fall, the Yahoo! site had its first million-hit day, which translated into about 100,000 individual users, and Filo and Yang started to think about turning their hobby into a business. Early in 1995, they went to see some venture capitalists. Several of them showed interest in Yahoo!, but they also expressed concern about potential competition. While Filo and Yang were indexing the Web by hand, other scientists were writing software programs called "Web crawlers," or "search engines" that did the job electronically, taking a phrase and scanning millions of Web pages to find every place it was mentioned. Michael "Fuzzy" Maudlin, a computer programmer at Carnegie-Mellon, had developed a search program he called Lycos. Steve Kirsch, a Silicon Valley entrepreneur, was backing a program called Infoseek. Christine and Isabel Maxwell, two daughters of the late British press baron Robert Maxwell, were behind the Magellan search engine. Kleiner Perkins was backing a firm called Architext, which soon changed its name to Excite. Kleiner Perkins encouraged Filo and Yang to merge with Architext. They refused, turning instead to Sequoia Capital, a venture capital firm that had financed Apple Computer, Atari, and Oracle.

In March 1995, Filo and Yang incorporated Yahoo! Soon after, Michael Moritz, an Englishman and former journalist who was a partner at Sequoia, visited them in their trailer. It struck him as "every mother's idea of the bedroom that she wished her sons never had."[2] The blinds were down; it was noisy; and there were golf clubs, pizza cartons, and unwashed clothes strewn around. Yahoo!'s popularity impressed Moritz, nonetheless, and he particularly liked the name. He did worry about the site being free, but he convinced himself that it would be able to sell advertising if it kept growing at current rates. Moritz offered Filo and Yang $1 million for 25 percent of Yahoo! on two conditions: they keep the same name and allow him to hire an experienced chief executive. If it had been six months later, after the Netscape IPO, Filo and Yang would have been able to demand a much higher price. But in April 1995 $1 million was still considered a lot of money. They accepted Moritz's offer.

Yahoo! rented an office in Mountain View, a short distance from Netscape. One of the first people the firm hired was Srinija "Ninj"

Srinivasan, a friend of Yang's from Stanford. Srinivasan reorganized the Yahoo! guide to make it more flexible, while maintaining its basic character. Yahoo! was popular because it made the Web seem human and manageable. Before any Web site could be listed it had to have been inspected and approved by a Yahoo! employee. The guide was organized in a hierarchical fashion. At the top of the hierarchy were a set of broad categories, such as entertainment, business, and health. Below these were smaller subcategories. A Yahoo! user who typed in "The Beatles" might receive a list of twenty Web sites under the heading: "Entertainment: Music: Artists: Rock: The Beatles." Other search engines provided more extensive listings, but they were electronically generated and contained a lot of irrelevant entries. Yahoo! was more selective. "If you've got thirteen Madonna sites, then you probably don't need a fourteenth," Yang explained.[3]

The chief executive that Moritz insisted on hiring turned out to be Tim Koogle, an angular forty-three-year-old who had spent nine years at Motorola and three years as president of Intermec, a Seattle-based technology company. Koogle had long wavy hair, collected electric guitars, and drove fast cars, but he was meant to be the reassuring adult presence at Yahoo! During the early summer of 1995, he arrived in Mountain View. "The office was in the right-hand corner of a little industrial building," he later recalled. "We had about a thousand square feet. Everybody was crammed in there with borrowed desks, and there was a hole in the roof that leaked every time it rained."[4]

Koogle's first task was to fire some management consultants that Moritz had hired, who were "charging too much money and getting too little done."[5] After doing that, he set about writing a business plan that would explain how Yahoo! could make money despite giving away its product. Filo and Yang had already ruled out charging people to use their site. With some justification, they believed Yahoo!'s popularity was due to the fact that it reflected the values of the Internet, including free access. "We really wanted to keep the service free—that was a fundamental goal," Yang explained. "It was a process of saying, 'How do we keep it free and develop a business model?'"[6] This question would torment many Internet companies. Netscape's answer had been to charge for ancillary products, but Yahoo! didn't have any ancillary products. The only other option, as Moritz had realized, was to rely on advertising.

Advertising-sponsored media companies can be immensely profitable, as the television networks have shown, but turning Yahoo! into a successful media company would be a challenge. In 1995, the Internet was widely viewed as a technology industry, and Yahoo! was commonly seen as a technology product. Koogle set out to change this perspective. He hired Karen Edwards, a marketing executive formerly at Twentieth Century Fox, to seduce the media buyers that dominate the advertising industry. Edwards pitched Yahoo! as a cheap and effective vehicle for targeting specific groups. When General Motors places an ad on CBS, millions of people who aren't interested in buying a new car see it. The Internet seemed to eliminate this wastage. In theory, Web sites like Yahoo! had three great advantages over traditional media companies. They could monitor precisely which Web pages a user called up; they could serve up different Web pages to different readers; and they could count how many people clicked on the ads. Advertisers could then compare click-through rates to gauge the appeal of different ads. If people were ignoring a certain ad, it could be replaced with a new one in days, or even hours. By the end of 1995, Yahoo! had attracted about $1 million in advertising revenues. This wasn't a great sum, but it was a start, and Koogle believed there would be much more to come given that Yahoo! was already delivering about 3 million Web pages a day to users. "In spite of no real marketing spending and no infrastructure in the company, there was a lot of organic take-up," Koogle recalled later. "That usually speaks volumes."[7]

## II

**With the benefit of hindsight, the benefits of Internet advertising** were grossly exaggerated. Even in the early days, there were studies showing that the average click-through rate was about 2 percent, which meant that 98 percent of people were ignoring the ads. When this mass boycott was taken into account, advertising on the Web, far from being cheap, was extremely expensive. The average cost of an Internet ad was about $4 per hundred page views, which meant that advertisers were paying about $2 for every person that clicked on their ad. Glossy magazines like *Vogue* charged about $50,000 for a full-page ad. Assuming that half of *Vogue*'s 2 million readers looked at the page, the advertiser was being charged about five cents per set of eyeballs.

In late 1995 and early 1996, few were willing to consider the possibility that Internet advertising might prove to be a bust. Kevin O'Connor, a Michigan-born engineer and entrepreneur, had recently started DoubleClick, the first Internet advertising agency, in New York's Flatiron District, which was rapidly becoming known as Silicon Alley because of the large number of Internet-related companies that were springing up there. DoubleClick was a joint venture between O'Connor and his partner, Dwight Merriman, and the advertising agency Bozell, Jacobs, Kenyon & Eckhardt. Its software allowed ads to be targeted to specific groups, based on occupation, geographic origin, and several other characteristics. DoubleClick sold banner ads on most of the popular Web sites, including Netscape, America Online, and Yahoo! To begin with, Netscape's home page, the default home page for anybody who had a Netscape Navigator browser, was the most popular ad buy. DoubleClick's success prompted other agencies to set up Internet divisions. Disappointing results from the earliest online advertising were either ignored or reinterpreted in a positive manner. Forrester Research, a company that was making a name as a bullish interpreter of Internet trends, estimated that online advertising would increase from an estimated $37 million in 1995 to $700 million in 1998. (Later in 1996, Forrester would raise its 1998 forecast to $1 billion.)

The growth of service firms like DoubleClick and Forrester Research demonstrated how the growth of Internet industry was starting to feed on itself. Every new Internet venture employed a new group of people with a vested interest in boosting the online economy. The most powerful boosters were on Wall Street, where the Netscape IPO had legitimated a new business model—one in which earnings and balance sheets didn't matter. In the new Internet era, the game was to raise money from investors, clamber aboard an exponential growth curve, and worry about revenues and profits later. Mary Meeker, a thirty-five-year-old stock analyst at Morgan Stanley, was one of this strategy's strongest defenders. Meeker was supposed to provide Morgan Stanley's clients with objective advice about the technology companies she covered and about the wider trends affecting the computer industry. Traditionally, stock analysts came pretty low down the Wall Street pecking order, since they didn't bring in any money directly, but Meeker would help change that.

Like Marc Andreessen, Meeker grew up in a small farming town: Portland, Indiana. After attending DePauw University, she worked briefly for Merrill Lynch in Chicago, then did her MBA at Cornell. She arrived on Wall Street in 1986 and took a job at Salomon Brothers. In 1991, she moved to Morgan Stanley to cover the PC industry, where she became a protégée of Frank Quattrone. Through her work on companies like Microsoft and Compaq, Meeker was well placed to observe the development of online communication, and she saw parallels between the rise of the PC and the rise of the Internet. "If you looked at Microsoft and believed Bill Gates when he said, 'A personal computer on every desktop. A personal computer in every home,' it was easy to extrapolate and see that Microsoft was going to become a big company someday," she explained. "The lesson I learned was to apply the same reasoning to America Online. Simple as it sounds, I believed in 1993 that everyone would use e-mail someday."[8]

Meeker enjoyed an inside view of the Netscape IPO, and it got her thinking about how the online economy would fit together. In February 1996, she and one of her research associates, Chris DePuy, circulated The Internet Report, a three-hundred-page tome that included everything from a history of the ARPANET to a list of recommended Web sites. Meeker believed the Netscape IPO was a "world-changing event" that had created "a new way of financing companies."[9] The days were gone when start-up firms had to spend years building up a track record of profitability before going public. In the post-Netscape world, stock market investors were willing to play the role of venture capitalists, funding companies much earlier in their development in the hope of making high returns. Meeker and DePuy said the growth of the Internet was "still at the very early stages" and represented "a big market opportunity for lots of companies." They went on: "Consider this report our puck on the ice at the beginning of a very long game."[10] Most Wall Street research reports are quickly and justly forgotten, but *The Internet Report* became a standard reference, and more than 100,000 copies were distributed. Marc Andreessen said the report "offers critical insight into both the Internet and the markets it will affect."[11] Steve Case described it as "a fabulous history, encyclopedia, reference guide and road map rolled together." John Doerr called it the "definitive Internet report," adding, "Burn all the others."[12] HarperCollins turned *The Internet Report* into a paperback book, which sold for $22. In an earlier era, the sight of a major book publisher rushing out what was essentially a Wall Street stock circular might have raised some eyebrows, but not in 1996. Instead, the HarperCollins editors were widely praised for being so clued in.

*The Internet Report* was important for two reasons: it made buying Internet stocks seem like a respectable activity; and it contained the genesis of a new valuation model for Internet stocks. Investors could read the report and tell themselves they were contributing to an industrial revolution, not just speculating wildly. Meeker and DePuy lamented the fact that "the number of pure-play investment vehicles related to the Internet is shockingly short."[13] Their recommended Internet portfolio consisted of just five companies: three equipment makers (Cisco Systems, Ascend Communications, and Cascade Communications); a software company (Intuit); and an online service (America Online). They omitted the Internet service providers because they faced too much competition, and they excluded Netscape because of the stock's volatility and its strong performance since the IPO. ("Investors should hold off in the near term until it becomes more seasoned," they warned.) The analysts acknowledged being "nervous about the valuation levels" of some Internet stocks, but they argued that traditional valuation methods could be misleading.[14] Four of the five stocks they recommended had PE ratios greater than 50, and the other, Cisco Systems, had a PE of 25. The key to valuing Internet stocks was not current earnings, Meeker and DePuy argued, but earnings potential, which was vast. "For now, it's important for companies to nab customers and keep improving product offerings: mind share and market share will be crucial. While skeptics like to say

that America Online loses money on a cash flow basis (excluding subscriber acquisition costs), once it obtains 5–10 million subscribers, it
will be able to harvest the cash flow. If a company can build subscribers in a small but rapidly growing market with a compelling economic model and maintain that market share when the market gets
bigger, it should reap good profit margins."[15]

This argument would soon be picked up elsewhere on Wall Street
and used to justify the unprecedented prices being paid for Internet
stocks. Instead of concentrating on earnings and revenues, many analysts would promote "mind share" and "market share" as key valuation indicators. The only way to quantify these concepts was to look
at the traffic on a company's Web site. If this appeared to be increasing dramatically, the company was worth more, even if its losses were
also rising, as was often the case. The new valuation methodology
provided the owners of Internet companies with a peculiar set of
incentives. Instead of being rewarded for cutting costs and increasing
revenues, like most managers are, they were rewarded for increasing
the number of page views. Not surprisingly, many of them would end
up spending as much money as possible on marketing and promoting
their sites, regardless of the cost.

Meeker, having been involved in the Netscape IPO (she helped
set up one of the first meetings between Quattrone and Clark), was
hardly a neutral observer of the Internet industry. She knew many of
the key players personally. "I remember that in 1995 I would speak
with Marc Andreessen and we would try to count up how many people understood this stuff," she recalled later. "We thought it was about
four hundred."[16] In the following few years, the members of this
informal network, some of whom referred to themselves as the "class
of '95," would socialize together, attend each other's conferences,
and make pots of money together. Meeker's access to the Silicon Valley inner circle was one of her great selling points. She would become
the public voice of the Internet establishment—the person who
helped to define and spread its collective wisdom. In doing so, she
would turn herself into a media celebrity and also attract many lucrative IPOs and secondary stock offerings to Morgan Stanley. As one
Silicon Valley figure, Roger McNamee, a partner at the investment
firm Integral Capital, noted: "Morgan Stanley's great insight was that

the analyst could be used as a competitive weapon—not only to analyze IPOs but to cause them to happen. Mary's thought leadership in
the industry helped Morgan Stanley to line up many of the most
exciting Internet deal."[17] What this meant, of course, was that
Meeker would no longer be just a stock analyst. Her main role would
be as an investment banker.

## III

**Morgan Stanley was just one of many investment banks trying to**
capitalize on the growth of the World Wide Web. Many of the ventures that they marketed were "concept" stocks—companies that
seemed to encapsulate a big idea. In February 1996, Hambrecht &
Quist and Robertson, Stephens, issued 2 million shares in a Silicon
Valley company called CyberCash at $17 each. Within a week the
shares were trading at more than $50. William Melton, the man
behind CyberCash, had already made a fortune by cornering the
market in the electronic terminals that stores use to verify credit card
numbers. In August 1994, Melton came out of retirement and
founded CyberCash, which developed software to protect the security of online credit card transactions. With its catchy name, Cyber-
Cash had no shortage of media attention, but it did have a shortage of
customers. In the seventeen months between its incorporation and its
decision to go public, the firm's total revenues were zero—though it
did manage to accumulate losses of more than $10 million. This
record presented something of a challenge to stick-in-the-mud stock
analysts that liked to go by the numbers. After Standard & Poor's
refused to recommend CyberCash's stock, Mark Basham, an analyst
at the ratings agency, explained apologetically: "The lack of any sales
was a major negative in our rating."[18]

Internet telephony was another concept that investors could relate
to. By using the Internet, people on different continents would soon
be able to talk to each other for the cost of a local call. That was the
theory, anyway. In practice, the packet-switching technology that the
Internet was built on was unsuitable for two-way conversation. But
that didn't prevent VocalTec, an Israeli company, from issuing stock

in the same month that CyberCash went public, also through Hambrecht & Quist.

The most popular concept was the "search engine." With about 200,000 Web sites already in existence, even the most devoted online surfer needed help in keeping up with all the new stuff that was appearing. By the spring of 1996, Yahoo! was serving up about six million Web pages a day, and it was being touted as a possible IPO candidate, along with Lycos, Excite, and Infoseek. The desire for a marketing coup, rather than the need for money, was the driving force behind the rush to Wall Street. Most of the big search engines had enough cash to fund their operations for a good while longer. CMG Information Services (CMGI), a Boston-based venture capital company, was backing Lycos. Excite's investors included the Tribune Company, the owner of *The Chicago Tribune*. As for Yahoo!, it had just raised $100 million from Softbank, a Japanese financial company. But Netscape had demonstrated the publicity value of an early stock offering.

In January 1996, Montgomery Securities issued shares in a little-known search engine company called Open Text Corporation at $15 each. The Open Text IPO was small, but it demonstrated that investors were willing to buy into the search engine concept. In March, Lycos, Excite, and Yahoo! all announced plans to go public. Lycos went first. On April 2, with Hambrecht & Quist acting as the lead underwriter, it issued 3 million shares at $16. The shares opened at 29¼ before falling back to $21.94 at the close, valuing the company at close to $300 million. Two days later, Excite issued 2 million shares through Robertson, Stephens. The stock was priced at $17. It rose to 21¼, before falling back to 16¹¹⁄₁₆. Despite closing below the issue price, Excite, whose total revenues in 1995 were $434,000, was valued at about $175 million.

Tim Koogle, Yahoo!'s CEO, hadn't wanted to go public yet. He harbored old-fashioned ideas about firms making steady profits before issuing shares. "I really wanted a few more quarters," he told *Fortune*. "I wanted to be sure we could deliver our numbers consistently and ahead of expectations."[19] The investment from Softbank meant that Koogle didn't have to worry about financing Yahoo!'s growth. The firm was still adding features to its site, and it had just launched a television marketing campaign, which the Black Rock agency in San Francisco had created. One ad showed an angler calling up Yahoo! for baiting tips then landing one giant fish after another. It was a clever attempt to demonstrate Yahoo!'s usefulness without putting off technophobes. Still, Koogle knew that Yahoo! couldn't afford to ignore the IPOs by Lycos and Excite. There was a strong belief on Wall Street that firms gained a big advantage by going public early, and these perceptions could easily become self-fulfilling. "We couldn't afford to be boxed in," Koogle said. "So we took the risk."[20]

Koogle approached Morgan Stanley. To his surprise the firm proved reluctant to help. Mary Meeker argued that it was too soon for Yahoo! to go public. Privately, Meeker doubted that Yahoo! was a real business. "I was, like, Yahoo!, you know, just a search engine—a little hard to figure out," she would later admit. "We'd just taken Netscape public and we felt like the next thing we would do had to be the next Netscape. So we didn't take Yahoo! public, which in hindsight was a brain-dead mistake."[21] With Morgan Stanley out of the picture, Koogle turned to its biggest rival, Goldman Sachs, the last of the great Wall Street partnerships.

The very name Goldman Sachs had connotations of wealth and prestige. Acquiring a partnership at Goldman was one of the top prizes in American finance, and the firm's top executives moved freely in the highest echelons of business and politics. Robert Rubin, the Treasury Secretary, had spent most of his career at Goldman, ending up as the firm's co–senior partner. Goldman liked to maintain a low profile, but rivals knew it as a fierce competitor that often resorted to aggressive tactics in order to win business. During the late 1920s, the Goldman Sachs Trading Corporation organized two of the biggest and most speculative investment trusts, Shenandoah and Blue Ridge. When the stock market crashed in October 1929, many of the firm's clients were ruined. In the late 1980s and early 1990s, Goldman did a lot of business with Robert Maxwell, the crooked British media baron who looted his employees' pension funds.

Goldman was eager to catch up with Morgan Stanley in the technology business. It opened an office in Silicon Valley and promoted its own stars, Bradford Koenig and Michael Parekh, as rivals to Frank Quattrone and Meeker. When the opportunity to take Yahoo! public came along, Goldman seized it. At the end of March, Koogle and Yang, together with a number of people from Goldman, departed on an investor road show. Yang, who was now twenty-eight but still looked a lot younger, proved almost as popular with investors as Marc Andreessen had been the previous summer. The environment could hardly have been friendlier, with investors snapping up technology companies of all kinds. In early April, Lucent Technologies, the former equipment-making arm of AT&T, which supplied telecommunications gear of all kinds, raised $3 billion in the biggest IPO yet. A few weeks later, Lucent's market value topped that of AT&T.

On the morning of April 12, 1996, 2.6 million Yahoo! shares started trading under the symbol "YHOO." The stock was issued at $13. It opened at $25, rose to $43, and closed at $33, a first-day "pop" of more than 150 percent. This was bigger even than Netscape's first-day gain, and it was the second biggest gain ever for an IPO on the Nasdaq. Despite having just sixty-eight employees, Yahoo! was now valued at about $850 million. Yang and Filo each owned shares worth more than $150 million. "The valuations are into the sphere of surrealism," David Menlow, president of the IPO Financial Network, commented.[22]

## IV

**At this point, with investors' appetite for Internet stocks apparently** insatiable, Louis Rossetto, the founder of *Wired*, decided to cash in on the buoyant IPO market. His publication had proved a big editorial success, acquiring close to 300,000 subscribers and a National Magazine Award. But Rossetto's ambitions ranged well beyond print. He had also launched a Web site called Hotwired.com, a search engine called HotBot, and a television division. In May 1996, Wired Ventures, Rossetto's holding company, announced it was going public, with Goldman Sachs acting as the lead underwriter. The prospectus described Wired Ventures as "a new kind of global, diversified media company for the 21st century" and placed a provisional value on it of about $450 million.[23] If all went well, Rossetto and his partner, Jane

Metcalfe, would each end up with stakes worth about $70 million. Nicholas Negroponte's stock would be worth about $30 million.

Things didn't go well. A number of commentators pointed out that, despite Rossetto's grandiose claims, Wired Ventures wasn't really an Internet company at all: it was a publishing company. More than 90 percent of its revenues came from its print magazine. Publishing companies tend to sell for between one and three times their revenues. Applying this principle to Wired Ventures, the company was worth perhaps $75 million, and even this valuation was generous. Despite its growing popularity, *Wired* magazine appeared to have lost about $10 million in 1996. Allan Sloane, a financial columnist at *Newsweek*, said he "wouldn't touch Wired at anything resembling" the asking price. *The New York Observer*'s Christopher Byron described the Wired offering as "a piece of junque du jour."[24] If Internet stocks had still been soaring, these comments could have been dismissed as the demented grumblings of jealous hacks. But just as Rossetto and his colleagues were preparing to set out on the pre-IPO road show, the stock market entered one of its periodic snits, and Internet stocks tumbled. Goldman was forced to postpone the stock offering.

The market's downturn also hit other Internet companies that were planning to go public. A few of them, such as CNET, which operated a number of Web sites devoted to computers and the Internet, slipped through the IPO window before it closed. Others weren't so lucky. Magellan, the search engine owned by the Maxwell sisters, Christine and Isabel, found itself desperate for cash. In *Burn Rate*, a deliciously honest memoir of his years as an Internet entrepreneur, Michael Wolff described the abortive merger negotiations between Magellan and his own similarly cash-strapped company, Wolff New Media. At one point during the talks, the chief executive of Magellan admitted that his firm desperately needed money to meet its next payroll. Wolff writes:

> Mistake. Big mistake. I knew it. It was the utterance that would change everything.
> You can't say to investors, I have a problem, I have a big problem.

You can't say, I need your money to feed the mouths I have to feed. I need your money to pour down the maw.

You can't say, Hey, what did you think was going on? There's a fire burning like crazy and we have to keep throwing the dollar bills on.

And that was, unmistakably, what (the Magellan chief executive) was saying.

And while that was true of his business and of every other business in the new Internet industry and while everybody knew it was true—that is, that cash was being consumed at a rate and with an illogic that no one could explain, much less justify—you must never, never admit it.[25]

Neither Magellan nor Wolff New Media survived 1996. The slump in Internet stocks lasted through the summer. As Labor Day arrived, Excite and Lycos were both trading at less than half their IPO prices; Yahoo! had fallen from its first-day close of $33 to less than $20. The IPO market was still virtually closed down. "The honeymoon is over," *Upside*, a San Francisco–based technology magazine, declared in its October issue. "The window has closed for the 'concept' deals that brought frenzied hype like we've never seen before."[26]

None of this prevented Goldman Sachs from trying once more to sell Wired Ventures to the public. In a revised prospectus, Goldman valued Rossetto's company at $293 million—$157 million less than it had been valued at just a few months earlier.[27] The discrepancy disturbed many people on Wall Street, and Rossetto received a lukewarm reception when he set out on the investor road show. Rumors began to spread that the IPO might have to be aborted. The sight of the mighty Goldman pulling an issue once was rare enough; for it to pull one twice was practically unheard of. Rossetto wrote an angry memo to his staff attacking the "clueless" mainstream media that had misrepresented the company. The memo was leaked, but it didn't do any good. In late October, the day before the IPO was due to take place, Goldman canceled it. Rossetto tried to put a brave face on things, but he couldn't avoid the embarrassment of his company being one of the first big Internet failures. If Wired Ventures had gone public in the spring of 1996, at a more modest price, Rossetto could easily have been worth $20 million or $30 million on paper. Now, his moment had passed. He managed to raise some more money from private investors, but not enough to finance the expansion he had planned. Wired Ventures went into decline. Within twelve months of the IPO's collapse, Rossetto had stepped down as chief executive. In early 1998, *Wired* magazine was sold to Condé Nast.

# chapter 8  battle for the 'net

**I**

**As the Internet economy grew, several distinct markets developed**
within it, and in each of them there was intense competition. The
markets were arranged in horizontal fashion, one on top of the other.
At the bottom was the market for telecommunications gear, with
firms like Cisco Systems, Ascend Communications, and Lucent Technologies as the major players. On top of this was the market for Web
browsers, which Netscape dominated, with Microsoft trying hard to
get a foothold. On the next level up was the market for Internet
access, which included dozens of Internet service providers, as well as
online services such as America Online and CompuServe. Finally,
there was the market for content, which attracted hundreds of
entrants every week. The new Web sites offered news, shopping,
entertainment, and anything else that could be reduced to ones and
zeroes.

Each market was different. The fiercest battle was in the Web
browser market, where Microsoft was trying to protect its unparal-
leled profit margins against encroachment from the Internet. For
years, Bill Gates's company had been making things for a dollar and
selling them for ten dollars, thereby demonstrating the vast potential
for any company that could combine digital technology with market
power. Both Microsoft Windows and Microsoft Office benefited
from economies of scale and monopoly positions. Once they had
been developed, the cost of replicating them and putting them on
CDs was negligible. Yet Microsoft was able to charge hundreds of

dollars for some versions of Microsoft Office, having seen off most of its competitors.

This business model had turned Gates into the world's richest man, and he took a surprisingly long time to realize how the Internet challenged it by threatening to make Microsoft's products obsolete. Nathan Myrhvold, a Cambridge University–trained physicist who was Microsoft's technology guru, influenced Gates. Like many technically adroit people, Myrhvold was beguiled by the information superhighway, and he was slow to shift his gaze to the Internet. In the first edition of Gates's 1995 book *The Road Ahead*, the Internet hardly featured at all. In May 1995, Gates finally woke up. He e-mailed his colleagues about the coming "Internet Tidal Wave" and the possible creation of "something far less expensive than a PC which is powerful enough for Web browsing."[1] But even at this point, Gates still seemed to think he could seize control of the Internet by creating the Microsoft Network, an online network with its own set of technical standards that would replace those laid down by the inventors of the Internet and the World Wide Web. It wasn't until the Netscape IPO and the failure of the Microsoft Network to make much of an impact that Gates realized he had lost control of events.

In the fall of 1995, Marc Andreessen said that Windows might soon be reduced to a "poorly debugged set of device drivers."[2] Baiting Gates was unwise. On December 7, the anniversary of Pearl Harbor, the Microsoft chairman told hundreds of reporters and analysts who had gathered at the Seattle Convention Center that from now on Microsoft would be "hard core about the Internet."[3] The Internet Explorer, Microsoft's struggling Web browser, would be improved, expanded, and distributed free. Microsoft would also give away the accompanying Web server software, for which Netscape was charging more than $1,000. It would license the Java programming language and generally do everything in its power to grab market share from Netscape. Andreessen and Jim Barksdale, Netscape's chief executive, tried to laugh off Microsoft's counteroffensive, but Wall Street wasn't amused. In one day, Netscape's stock fell by almost $30. The "Browser Wars" had begun.

A couple of months later, in February 1996, Andreessen appeared barefoot on the cover of *Time*, the first Internet entrepreneur to be accorded this honor.[4] *Time* portrayed Andreessen as a modest tycoon, who rushed home from work at five every evening to walk his dog. As is often the case, the cover story proved to be a sell signal for investors. When somebody makes the cover of *Time*, he or she is usually at or past his peak. Andreessen was already stumbling in his battle with Gates, who had virtually unlimited resources to call upon. Microsoft's research budget alone was almost five times the size of Netscape's annual revenues, and the software giant had more than eight hundred people working on an upgraded Web browser. Microsoft isn't the most creative company in the world, but it is expert at taking other firms' products and improving them. When Internet Explorer 3.0 appeared in August 1996, most independent experts agreed that it was at least as good as Netscape Navigator 3.0.

Microsoft's strength isn't based on money and resources alone. More than nine out of ten PC users see a Windows screen when they switch on their machines. In the past, Microsoft had ruthlessly exploited this monopoly to cripple competing products like Word-Perfect and Lotus 1-2-3. After Gates's Pearl Harbor Day speech, it did the same thing to Netscape. In March of 1996, Microsoft persuaded America Online to choose Internet Explorer as its default browser. Steve Case, America Online's chief executive, was no friend of Gates—just a few months earlier Microsoft had tried to put AOL out of business by setting up the Microsoft Network—but he couldn't resist the offer of an AOL icon on every Windows desktop. "I could never have imagined myself standing there with Gates because of our history with Microsoft, but I thought it was best for AOL, so we did it," he said.[5]

Two days after the deal with America Online, Microsoft signed a similar one with CompuServe, the second largest online service. Gates also exerted pressure on the PC manufacturers, especially Compaq Computer, which had previously agreed to install Netscape Navigator on its popular Presario models. When Microsoft started shipping Internet Explorer with its Windows 95 operating system, Compaq replaced the Microsoft Web browser with Netscape Navigator. Gates found this intolerable. Early in 1996, Microsoft sent Compaq a letter threatening to end its agreement to license Windows 95 unless it agreed to keep the Internet Explorer on the desktop. This was effectively a threat to put Compaq out of business. Without Windows loaded onto its machines, no PC manufacturer could hope to survive. Compaq quickly buckled and restored the Internet Explorer to its desktops. For a few months, it shipped the Presario with both Internet Explorer and Netscape Navigator. Then it dropped Netscape Navigator.

Partly as a result of these tactics, Internet Explorer's share of the browser market increased sharply. In August 1996, Netscape's lawyers contacted the Justice Department and claimed that Microsoft was once again using anticompetitive tactics. In 1995, Microsoft had signed a consent decree with the government relating to previous misbehavior in other areas. Netscape had a strong case to make, but even if it succeeded in attracting the Justice Department's attention, which it did, any legal action would likely take years. Netscape didn't have years. It was loosing market share every day. Forced onto the defensive, it tried to reposition itself as a supplier of software to companies setting up internal computer networks known as Intranets. This was a reasonable strategy—businesses were already Netscape's biggest customers, and unlike private users they tended to pay for their Netscape Navigators—but it was also an admission of weakness. Netscape was no longer trying to displace Microsoft: like everybody else in the computer industry, it was merely trying to survive alongside the beast of Redmond. And survival was by no means assured.

In December 1996, Jim Allchin, a senior Microsoft executive, sent an e-mail to his boss, Paul Maritz, arguing that "we must leverage Windows more" to defeat Netscape.[6] The best way to do this, Allchin went on, was to "think about an integrated solution," by which he meant making the Internet Explorer a part of the Windows operating system, so that every customer who bought a Windows PC would automatically get a Microsoft Web browser. If Microsoft was allowed to do this, Netscape would be forced to persuade computer buyers to download a second Web browser, which is a bit like trying to sell people a second CD player to go with their stereo system. After some internal discussion, Gates agreed to go along with the integrated solution, a decision that would soon lead to a major antitrust case.

**II**

**The competition in the market for Internet access had already pro-** duced a clear winner: America Online. In April of 1996, Steve Case, America Online's thirty-seven-year-old chairman, appeared on the front of *Business Week* lying atop a pile of America Online diskettes, which were fast becoming as familiar to Americans as Nike sneakers and Oreo cookies. "It is Case's America Online that has shown how to turn a community of cybernauts into a mass market and how to successfully turn a computer network into a new medium for enter- tainment and news," the accompanying article declared. "With more than five million customers and 75,000 joining every week, AOL is the most potent force in cyberspace."[7]

It hadn't always been thus. For years, the digital cognoscenti had looked down on Case's firm. "I never knew anybody who took AOL seriously as an Internet company," Michael Wolff wrote in a fairly typical comment.[8] The Internet insiders sneered at America Online for many reasons. It was based in Vienna, Virginia, an unfashionable suburb of Washington, D.C. It didn't have much proprietary technol- ogy. It relied on others for content. It was slow providing access to the Internet. And many of its customers were computer neophytes who liked its blandly reassuring features, such as the recorded voice that said, "You've got mail." But Case wasn't seeking to impress Sili- con Valley. He was trying to create a mass-market product, and when people referred to America Online as the "Kmart network," he took it as a compliment.

If Marc Andreessen and Jerry Yang represented the frontiersmen in American history, Case represented the merchants and lawyers who followed in the settlers' wake. He was born and raised in Honolulu, where his father was a corporate attorney. As a teenager, Steve and his elder brother, Dan, set up a mail-order company that sold everything from greeting cards to watches. At Williams College, in Massachu- setts, Case was a B-minus student. He majored in political science— "the closest thing to marketing," he said later—and his least favorite subject was computer science.[9] (He was also a disc jockey on the col- lege radio station and sang in new wave bands.) After graduating, Case joined Procter & Gamble as a management trainee. Two years later, he moved to Pizza Hut, where his job involved trying to come up with appetizing new pie toppings. At twenty-three, Case was just another corporate grunt, seemingly destined for a life of schlepping around the country from sales meeting to sales meeting. If anybody in his family was heading for the top, it seemed to be Dan, who had become a Rhodes scholar and an investment banker at Hambrecht & Quist in San Francisco.

In 1983, Dan invited Steve to the annual Consumer Electronics Show in Las Vegas and introduced him to Bill Van Meister, a flamboyant entrepreneur who was starting an online video game company. Bored by his job and sick of living in Wichita, Kansas, Case decided to join Van Meister's venture, which was called Control Video Corporation. It was a fateful decision. Control Video Corporation ran into trouble, resulting in Van Meister's ouster, but another firm, Quantum Computer Services, arose from its ruins to provide online services for two PC companies, Commodore and Apple. In 1989, Quantum changed its name to America Online, a name that Case, who by now was president of the company, had dreamed up.

Case's humdrum character was arguably the key to America Online's subsequent success. As a nontechnologist, he knew the fear of computers that lurked inside most ordinary mortals. His motto was "make it easy and make it fun."[10] America Online was the first online service to adopt the point-and-click technology pioneered by Apple, and it introduced other user-friendly features, such as the "key word" system that eliminated the need to type in Internet addresses. Case's model was television, a complicated technology that had been reduced to a few buttons. America Online presented its content in channels, such as Today's News, Personal Finance, Travel, Education, and Entertainment. The most popular channel, by far, was Personal Connection, the electronic doorway to hundreds (and later thousands) of online chat rooms.

America Online marketed itself as a family service, but some of the activities on its network were hardly family fare. Among the names of the chat rooms that its subscribers created were "submissive men," "married but flirting," and "crossdressers2." The Internet, which allowed people to communicate with one another while retaining their anonymity, was ideally suited to sexual fantasy, and from the early years a good proportion of the traffic on it was taken up by pornography. America Online quietly encouraged some of this traffic to migrate to its network. Certain members of Congress criticized America Online for allowing sexual activity on its system, but in this aspect, too, Case was in tune with the majority of his countrymen. In public, Americans tend to be puritans. In private, as the success of the adult video industry had already demonstrated, there are few activities that they won't enthusiastically countenance.

According to an article in *Rolling Stone* in October 1996, up to half of all the chat on America Online was sex-related, and the sex chat rooms were bringing in more than $80 million a year in revenues.[11] The popularity of the sex chat rooms was a major reason that America Online overtook Prodigy, the online service owned by Sears and IBM. Prodigy didn't allow sex chat rooms, and it checked all notices posted on its message boards for inappropriate content. America Online had no such compunctions. "That's why AOL has eight million members and Prodigy failed to a shadow of its former self," a senior executive at Prodigy told Kara Swisher, the author of *aol.com*, an informative history of America Online published in 1998.[12]

Clever marketing also played an important role in America Online's success. Case's experience at Procter & Gamble and Pizza Hut had taught him that AOL couldn't be sold like soap powder and pizza. Going online is what economists call an "experience good," which means that people only know if they like it when they try it. Many consumers were put off online services by the initial cost of the software. In 1993, Jan Brandt, America Online's marketing director, suggested distributing the AOL software for nothing, along with a few free hours of service. Case approved Brandt's plan, and America Online started sending out free diskettes. They were sent to people's homes; they were given away with magazines; they were given away on airlines, in football stadiums, even in frozen steaks. Eventually, about 250 million discs would be distributed—almost one for each person in the country. The marketing campaign was expensive, but it was also phenomenally successful. In July 1993, America Online had about 250,000 subscribers. A year later, there were a million of them. In February 1996, the number reached 5 million. Along the way,

America Online raced past Prodigy and CompuServe, and also defeated the threat from the Microsoft Network.

A steadily rising stock price accompanied this rapid growth. Although many of America Online's subscribers didn't get full access to the World Wide Web until 1996, the company traded as an Internet stock. Between March 1992 and March 1996, its market value rose from $70 million to $6.5 billion. Support from Wall Street enabled Case to finance his ambitious expansion plans. Following its successful IPO in 1992, America Online sold more stock in 1993, and again in 1995. The latter issue, which raised more than $100 million, demonstrated how far perceptions of the company had changed. America Online's IPO was underwritten by Alex Brown & Co. and Robertson, Stephens. In 1995, the underwriters included Morgan Stanley, Goldman Sachs and Merrill Lynch. Mary Meeker, Morgan Stanley's Internet analyst, was one of Case's biggest supporters. From 1993 onward, she retained a buy recommendation on America Online's stock. In *The Internet Report*, she wrote that "nobody does a better job of making general information available for a mass market audience than America Online," and argued that the firm should be viewed not just as an online service provider but as a "consumer media/entertainment company."[13]

Despite its remarkable growth, American Online faced some serious problems. In the spring and summer of 1996, these problems came into open view. The firm's network hadn't been built to deal with the traffic it was handling, and delays in connecting became so lengthy that it acquired the nickname "America On Hold." In August, the network crashed for nineteen hours, prompting headlines such as "America Goes Offline," and "CHAOS@AOL." Case apologized, but many subscribers, who had been unable to retrieve their e-mails for a full day, were furious. Somebody set up an Internet newsgroup, alt.aol-sucks, where people could vent their anger toward the company. Web sites such as AOL Watch and Why AOL Sucks appeared. The vitriol shocked Case, but there wasn't much he could do about it in the short term. The only solution was to invest in upgrading the system.

On Wall Street, too, criticisms surfaced, and America Online's stock price suffered. Between May and September it fell from above $70 to below $30. For years, America Online had been bolstering its profits by using suspect accounting practices. The firm treated its marketing expenditures as an investment, the cost of which could be written off over a number of years, instead of being counted immediately against profits. Given that America Online was deluging the country with free diskettes, the sums involved were far from trivial. Case initially tried to ignore the Wall Street critics, but in October 1996, with the stock price still sagging badly, he finally faced up. America Online wrote off $353.7 million in what it called "deferred subscriber acquisition costs." This was more money than the firm had made in its entire existence. With proper accounting introduced, America Online looked suspiciously like every other loss-making Internet firm that had raised a lot of money in the stock market and blown it on a big marketing campaign. "The Emperor hath no Pants, AOL hath no profits," one wag posted on The Motley Fool.[14]

The most serious threat to America Online came from its outdated pricing structure. While most Internet service providers were providing unlimited access to the Internet for $19.95, Case's company was still charging its subscribers by the hour if they stayed online beyond a certain time limit. Many heavy users, who could easily run up monthly bills of hundreds of dollars, were switching to cheaper alternatives. America Online's "churn rate"—the percentage of its subscribers who left every month—reached 6 percent, a development that alarmed investors. If it continued, the majority of AOL subscribers would leave within a year. Case had to do something. He first introduced a slightly less restrictive pricing plan—twenty hours for $19.95, with additional charges after that—but that didn't satisfy subscribers. Unlimited access was becoming the Internet standard. America Online couldn't resist the trend and hope to maintain its leadership position. Case, who spent a lot of time online gauging the attitudes of his customers, was aware of this, but he also knew that moving to flat-rate pricing would be a tremendous challenge; America Online had found it hard enough to make a profit when it was charging heavy users by the hour. In October 1996, Case had his hand forced. The Microsoft Network adopted a $19.95 unlimited usage plan. Case couldn't allow Bill Gates to steal his customers. A couple of weeks later, America Online announced that it, too, would henceforth charge its subscribers a flat rate of $19.95.

Case coupled the pricing change with an internal reorganization. He hired Robert Pittman, the cofounder of MTV, to run America Online's service. Pittman was known in New York media circles as an ebullient and ambitious figure. Despite losing an eye while he was growing up in Mississippi, he flew his own plane. He also socialized with celebrities, and employed a slick public relations adviser, Ken Lerer, who had helped to mastermind disgraced financier Michael Milken's public defense during the 1980s. After joining America Online, Pittman compared the Internet to the early days of cable television, when most of the cable networks lost money. Eventually, networks like MTV and Nickelodeon developed powerful brands and made big profits. Pittman insisted that the same thing would happen on the Internet, and that America Online would be one of the big winners.

Pittman had a point. America Online's success was based on what economists call vertical integration. It provided both access to the World Wide Web and its own Web content. This allowed it to exploit the self-reinforcing network effects that had spurred the growth of the Internet in the first place. As its subscriber base grew, America Online could afford to provide more features, which in turn attracted more subscribers. Moreover, the new subscribers provided a wealth of content of their own, in the form of chat room messages. America Online was a media company that got much of its programming for nothing. If its subscriber base kept growing, this was a business model that was likely to generate profits before too long.

## III

**Men such as Gerald Levin, the chairman of Time Warner, Michael** Eisner, the chairman of Walt Disney, and Rupert Murdoch, the chairman of News Corporation, looked jealously at America Online's growth. Walt Disney, Time Warner, and News Corporation each owned a broad range of assets—newspapers, magazines, television stations, broadcast networks, film studios, cable networks—but many of these properties were now widely regarded as antiquated. The old media was itself full of pieces about how the old media was doomed. Many of these pieces were ill considered, but they prompted the media barons into action.

In September of 1993, News Corporation bought Delphi Internet Services, a Massachusetts-based firm that provided access to the Internet to scientists and researchers. The purchase took place well before the incorporation of Netscape, a testimony to Murdoch's sharp eye, but it never had much chance of working out. The News Corporation executives, who were responsible for *The Simpsons* and *The New York Post*, didn't know what to make of the Internet folk, with their strange customs; and the feeling was reciprocated. "We backed the wrong people," Murdoch said philosophically some years later. "They were very clever, very nice, but they were not very commercial. And we didn't put enough resources into it."[15] In May 1996, News Corporation sold Delphi back to its founders. By then, Murdoch had also abandoned his second Internet venture—a much more ambitious and expensive project called I-Guide.

The idea behind I-Guide seemed plausible: a *TV Guide* for the Web. News Corporation already owned *TV Guide*, so why not replicate its success in cyberspace? Murdoch dispatched Anthea Disney, *TV Guide*'s editor, to Silicon Alley, where she set up a 75,000-square-feet newsroom staffed with hundreds of young recruits, along with some more seasoned journalists from Murdoch's Fleet Street newspapers. From start to finish, I-Guide was a fiasco. Initially, it was going to be a subscription-based online service, much like America Online and Prodigy. Then the focus shifted to the Internet. The launch date was repeatedly delayed. By the time that I-Guide finally launched, in February 1996, Yahoo! and other search engines had taken the market it was aimed at. A few days before I-Guide started operating, News Corporation restructured it and fired most of its employees.

Murdoch could console himself that his rivals weren't faring any better. In October 1994, Time Warner launched Pathfinder, a Web site that featured online editions of *Time, People,* and several other magazines that the company owned. Pathfinder provided Levin with an escape route from the disastrous interactive television experiment in Orlando; its ambitious launch indicated that Time Warner had decided the Internet was the future. Paul Sagan, a cousin of Carl Sagan, the scientist and author, was hired as president of Time New Media. Walter Isaacson, a well-known *Time* journalist, was placed in charge of creating content for Pathfinder. Dozens of staff were hired. Technology was purchased. Consultants were retained.

To begin with, Pathfinder appeared to be a success. Compared to most Web sites, it provided a cornucopia of features—more than ninety of them, including the "Netly News," question-and-answer sessions with Time Inc. journalists, and details of upcoming products from Warner Music and the Warner Bros. film studio. Practically overnight, Pathfinder turned into the most popular site on the Web; and it also became the first site to take in appreciable advertising revenues (about $2.5 million in 1995). Unfortunately, the early promise soon faded. Pathfinder's share of the Web audience shriveled, and its ad response rates remained disappointing. It tried to introduce user charges—about $5 a month—but shelved them in the face of resistance from users. In its first year, Pathfinder lost more than $10 million. In its second year, Don Logan, the head of Time Inc., referred to it as a "black hole."[16] In early 1996, Isaacson returned to *Time* as managing editor, and the editor of Pathfinder was ousted. Later in the year, Sagan resigned. Levin had a second new media embarrassment on his hands.

In normal circumstances, the failure of Pathfinder and I-Guide would have persuaded other media companies to steer well clear of the Internet. But circumstances were far from normal. With the country increasingly fixated on the World Wide Web, every self-respecting media executive—even the most old-fashioned ones, such as the owners of *The Washington Post* and *The New York Times*—was forced to come up with an "Internet strategy." In part, this reflected a crisis of confidence on the part of the old media. Many people who worked on newspapers and at broadcast networks tacitly accepted the idea that the Internet would eventually put them out of business. In fact, the old media's prospects remained good. Newspaper readership and the share of the television audience captured by the broadcast networks were both declining, but that had been true for decades. There was little sign that the Internet was accelerating the declines. Indeed, a strange thing was happening on the way to the graveyard: the old media was making more money than ever before. Newspapers like *USA Today* and *The Wall Street Journal* were fat with advertising, much of it from technology companies. On prime-time television, the cost of thirty-second spots on popular shows like *Seinfeld* and *E.R.* was reaching unprecedented heights, in some cases as much as half a million dollars.

This didn't happen by accident. As audiences splintered under the impact of the new media, the remaining mass-market mediums became more valuable, even if their numbers were falling. When Ford wanted to launch a new car, or Paramount Pictures wanted to promote an upcoming movie, they needed to reach the entire country, which wasn't possible via the Internet. The major networks, while they didn't deliver as many eyeballs as they had done in the 1970s, still had tens of millions of viewers. *USA Today* sold more than 2 million copies a day. Herbert Simon, a Nobel Prize–winning economist at Carnegie Mellon University, captured what was happening when he wrote, "A wealth of information creates a poverty of attention."[17] For this reason, anything that could hold the attention of a large part of the population was practically priceless. As a result, the Super Bowl and the Oscars, two quintessentially old media events, were turning into advertising extravaganzas, with dozens of expensive commercials specially created for them.

The media executives could see all this happening, but still they refused to sit out the Internet frenzy. In July 1996, NBC teamed up with Microsoft to launch MSNBC, a round-the-clock interactive news service that would compete with CNN on television and with Pathfinder and other Web sites on the Internet. Each side committed $200 million to MSNBC, with no clear idea how the money would ever be repaid. "We'll be doing our best to get advertising income, and we expect the Internet to expand dramatically, and that's partly why we see this as a profitable venture," was the best explanation that Bill Gates could offer.[18] Jack Welch, the chairman of General Electric, which owns NBC, was even more vague. "This is a big deal for GE because commerce is never going to be the same again in the next decade," he said. "Commerce in the next decade will change more than it's changed in the last hundred years. Business will be done differently. Distribution will be done differently. People will buy products differently."[19]

Welch's statement may have been inane, but he had a well-earned reputation as one of the shrewdest businessmen in America. The launch of MSNBC allowed NBC (and General Electric) to align itself with the Internet, while having somebody else, Microsoft, pick up part of the cost. The cable channel that MSNBC replaced—America's Talking—had been struggling anyway, so there wasn't much to be lost by switching formats. From Welch's perspective, the real audience for the MSNBC deal was Wall Street, which was agog about the coming "convergence" of media, computers, and telecommunications. By joining up with Microsoft, NBC appeared to be positioning itself for this convergence.

There was no reward for being financially conservative. When News Corporation turned its back on the Internet after the failure of I-Guide, its stock price lagged behind its competitors'. The perception that Rupert Murdoch didn't "get" the Internet was much more damaging to News Corporation's stock price than the earnings write-offs from Delphi and I-Guide had ever been. Eventually, Murdoch was forced to do more Internet deals in order to keep investors happy. A similar thing happened to Michael Eisner. For years, Disney avoided making big investments in the Internet. In August 1995 it spent $19 billion on an old media asset, ABC. The merger of Disney and ABC created an immensely powerful company, but it also helped create the impression on Wall Street that Disney had been left out of the multimedia age. In order to counter this impression, Disney would eventually spend hundreds of millions of dollars to launch its own updated version of Pathfinder, Go.com, with similarly dismal financial returns. But by that stage losing money on the Internet would be nothing to be ashamed of. To the contrary, it would be viewed as the inevitable and, indeed, desirable cost of moving into the twenty-first century. In such an environment, Eisner, Levin, *et al.* would have a fiduciary duty to their shareholders to waste large sums on dubious online ventures.

# chapter 9 irrational exuberance

I

**The rise of stocks like America Online, Netscape, and Yahoo! was**
part of a broader phenomenon. In the first four months of 1996 alone,
American households deposited about $100 billion in stock mutual
funds.[1] As recently as 1990, these funds had taken in just $12 billion
during the entire year. With all this money pouring into the stock
market, prices were rising sharply. Between the beginning of 1995
and the end of May 1996, the Dow climbed from 3,837.10 to
5,643.20, a rise of 45 percent. Meanwhile, the Nasdaq rose by about
65 percent, from 751.31 to 1,243.43. A fierce debate developed on
Wall Street about whether a speculative bubble was emerging, not
just in Internet stocks but in the market at large. On one side were the
traditionalists, who believed that stock prices had already risen well
beyond levels that could be justified on economic fundamentals. On
the other side were the "New Economy" enthusiasts, who argued
that the time-honored methods of valuing stocks no longer worked
and should be discarded.

Two of the most prominent bears, Barton Biggs, the chairman of
Morgan Stanley Asset Management, and Byron Wien, Morgan Stanley's chief U.S. investment strategist, could have been typecast for the
role of skeptical elders. They were both sixty-three years old, with
gray hair, lined faces, and fashion clocks that appeared to have stopped
during the Eisenhower presidency. At the start of 1996, Wien predicted a thousand-point decline in the Dow, and Biggs advised
investors to lighten up on U.S. stocks. Given that the market had

climbed so sharply during 1995, these calls were understandable, but they were also ill timed. In the first two months of 1996, the Dow rose another 500 points. Wien and Biggs refused to change their views. "I believe that U.S. stocks are overheated, overvalued and vulnerable to a cyclical bear market," Biggs wrote to his clients. "The longer the craziness in the United States goes on, the higher the price we will have to pay." Both Biggs and Wien were willing to accept that there were gradations in the collective insanity they spied around them. The rise in technology stocks, such as Microsoft, Dell Computer, and Intel, they saw as bordering on irrational. The rise of Netscape, Yahoo! Excite, and the rest of the Internet sector they viewed as inexplicable.

"You've got stocks selling at absolutely unbelievable multiples of earnings and revenues," Biggs told a visitor to his office in May 1996. "You've got companies going public that don't even have any earnings. You've got people setting up Internet pages to reinforce each other's convictions in these highly speculative stocks. This is wild stuff out of the past. In every market where it has happened—from the U.S. to Japan to Malaysia to Hong Kong—it always ends in the same way."[2] Biggs pulled out a set of charts to support his case. They showed the history of stock prices relative to profits, dividends, accounting values, and several other things. According to every single one of the charts, valuations were higher now than at any point since the 1920s. In several cases, they appeared to be higher than they were in 1929. "The sociological signs are very bad too," Biggs continued. "Everybody's son wants to work for Morgan Stanley. Worthless brother-in-laws are starting hedge funds [risky, unregulated investment funds]. I know a guy who is fifty and he's never done anything. He's starting a hedge fund. He's sending out brochures to people. I've got one here somewhere."[3]

Biggs and Wien worked at the same firm as Mary Meeker and Frank Quattrone, two of the leading promoters of Internet stocks, a fact that hadn't gone unnoticed on the rest of Wall Street. It hadn't gone unnoticed inside Morgan Stanley either. As one of the leading underwriters of stocks in the country, Morgan was making vast profits from the bull market. In the second quarter of 1996 alone, Wall Street firms earned about $3 billion in underwriting fees. "Believe me, the investment bankers would love me to be wildly bullish," Wien admitted. "But I do this job because I can express the truth as clearly as I can understand it. That's the strength of the product."[4] To Morgan Stanley's credit, Wien appears to have been speaking the truth. The firm's senior executives apparently took the view that its clients were intelligent enough to appreciate a range of views, even if some of them were diametrically opposed. Biggs, Wien, and Meeker often wrote for the same investment circular. In the same issue, a reader might well find a doom-laden essay by Biggs, a note of measured caution from Wien, and a buy recommendation for Netscape or America Online from Meeker.

Elsewhere on Wall Street, the environment was less liberal. One by one, most of the bears either changed their views or found themselves shunted aside. David Shulman, an investment strategist at Salomon Brothers, was one of those to recant. Throughout most of 1995 Shulman warned that stocks were dangerously overvalued, but in December he admitted that he had been mistaken and advised investors to buy more stocks. "The powerful 1995 rally in stock prices is not a bubble but rather a signal that the valuation paradigm has changed," Shulman wrote.[5] The crux of his argument was that investors were now willing to pay more for stocks because they no longer feared a resurgence of inflation. This was a reasonable argument, as far as it went, but Shulman's conversion also had a lot to do with the old Wall Street truism that trying to resist a strongly rising (or falling) market is folly. "The tape has a way of telling you," Shulman said a few months later. "If the tape keeps going up every day, something's wrong with the bear's case."[6] Shulman conceded that he was worried about speculation in Internet stocks, and that he still believed the stock market to be overvalued on economic grounds, but he added: "We are going to go higher before we go lower."

Abby Joseph Cohen, Shulman's opposite number at Goldman Sachs, didn't harbor any such ambivalence. A short woman with brown curly hair who favored conservative gray suits, Cohen had been bullish since 1991. The grounds for her long-standing optimism, she explained in the spring of 1996, were "the wonderful things going on in the U.S. economy," such as lower inflation, corporate restructuring, and the aging of the baby boomers.[7] The most important development, Cohen argued, was that American workers and firms had become a lot more productive, thereby dramatically increasing the economy's capacity to generate higher wages and profits. If Cohen was correct, it was a truly monumental change, and not only for shareholders.

Productivity determines standards of living. If a tailor makes two suits a day and sells them for $200 each, his productivity is $400 a day. If he raises his output to three suits a day and sells them for the same price, his productivity increases to $600 a day. The rate of productivity growth determines how fast living standards increase. Between 1948 and 1973, productivity grew at an annual rate of more than 3 percent. After 1973, for reasons that were never fully explained, the growth rate fell to about 1.5 percent. When compounded over long periods, even small discrepancies in productivity growth rates add up to big differences in living standards. Between 1948 and 1973 the standard of living of most American families doubled. Between 1973 and 1995, living standards stagnated.

In early 1996, the productivity figures tracked by the Commerce Department and the Bureau of Labor Statistics were showing little signs of improvement, but that didn't worry Cohen, who knew her way around the official statistics, having once worked as an economist at the Fed. "I believe that the government's productivity figures are wrong," she said bluntly. "Take a look at Goldman Sachs, for example. We have invested heavily in sophisticated voice-mail systems and word processing systems and so on. I know that the productivity of the technical staff is multiples of what it used to be. I just know that to be the case, but it doesn't get measured anyplace."[8]

Cohen's optimistic views would eventually make her famous, but at this stage she was still largely unknown. She wasn't even a partner at Goldman Sachs. Nonetheless, she displayed the certitude of a math teacher instructing her pupils in calculus. When it was put to her that the good economic news might already be reflected in stock prices, she replied that the positive changes in the economy were "so dramatic that one cannot expect them to be quickly incorporated by investors."[9] In the long term the only thing that mattered for stock prices was growth in corporate profits, Cohen insisted, and profits were rising faster than anybody had thought possible. "The people who say the stock market is up x percent and therefore is overpriced are not looking at the right thing. Stock prices should reflect growth of earnings or some other fundamental standpoint. Our conclusion is that the market is reasonably priced; in fact, I would argue that it is undervalued."[10]

## II

**The debate about the stock market continued throughout 1995 and 1996.** Toward the end of that period, it seemed clear that the bulls had won. Every time the stock market took a tumble, as it did several times, it came back stronger than ever. The market's rise silenced most of the remaining voices of caution on Wall Street; anybody who persisted in questioning it was seen as hopelessly antiquated. Some of the most famous investors in the land found themselves cast into this category. In April 1996, Warren Buffet, "the Sage of Omaha," issued a new class of stock in his company, Berkshire Hathaway. Regular Berkshire Hathaway shares were trading at $34,000 each—Buffet had always refused to split the stock—and the new stock, which was priced at $1,100, was designed to appeal to small investors. In a letter to shareholders, Buffet warned that neither he nor his longtime partner, Charlie Munger, "would currently buy shares" in Berkshire Hathaway, "nor would they recommend that their families or friends do so."[11]

Jeffrey Vinik, the manager of the biggest mutual fund in the country, Fidelity's Magellan Fund, was another stock market skeptic. During 1995, Vinik placed a big bet on technology stocks, which paid off handsomely, but at the end of the year he became concerned by what he saw as "euphoria" among investors and shifted some money into bonds.[12] In early 1996, the Magellan Fund's performance suffered compared to rival funds that had remained fully invested in the stock market. In May, Vinik announced that he was resigning from Fidelity and setting up his own money-management company. He insisted that he hadn't been fired, but the lesson other fund managers took from Vinik's departure was unambiguous: taking money out of the stock market could be a career-ending mistake. "It sent a message that you had better be right or else your job is on the line," Barton Biggs commented. "He was early, and there's no difference between being early and being wrong."[13]

Many mutual fund managers carried on buying stocks even though they believed them to be overvalued, which was not necessarily irrational. At the end of every quarter, fund managers are assessed relative to their peers in a series of published league tables. In this environment, following the herd is often the optimal strategy, especially during a bull market. If stock prices continue to rise during a given quarter, the fund manager who keeps all his money in the market will look clever at the end of it. Even if the market crashes, and the fund manager's stocks do badly, most of his competitors will look equally stupid so he will probably retain his job. Only by stepping out of line and selling, which is what Vinik did, does the fund manager risk his position. Trapped in this logic, the vast majority of fund managers tend to keep buying stocks regardless of their prices, which makes the market even more overvalued.

The idea that rational behavior on the part of individual investors can lead to an irrational outcome—a speculative bubble—dates back at least to Charles Mackay's *Memoirs of Extraordinary Popular Delusions and the Madness of Crowds*. In his account of the South Sea bubble of 1720, Mackay stressed that most of those involved knew that the promise of riches from the South Sea trade was a myth, and that many of the bubble companies were fraudulent, but they saw the chance to make some quick money and took it. In the memorable words of an English banker who took part in the bubble: "When the rest of the world is mad, we must imitate them in some measure."[14]

Until the middle of the twentieth century, most economists took it for granted that stock markets were dominated by herd behavior. Keynes's "beauty contest" model of investing is a good example of how economists used to think. But following the Second World War, a new economic theory became popular, which viewed investors as ultrarational and financial markets as ultraefficient. According to the so-called Efficient Markets Hypothesis, the stock market is an enormous calculating machine, which always sets the "right" prices, taking account of all the relevant information available. Between the mid-1960s and the mid-1980s the vast majority of American financial economists believed in the Efficient Markets Hypothesis. It wasn't until the stock market crash on October 19, 1987, that they started to question it seriously. If stock prices are always right, why did the Dow fall by 508 points in a single day for no apparent reason? According to most of the evidence, the only reason that many investors were selling on Black Monday was because they saw other people doing the same thing—a classic case of herd behavior.

During the 1990s, building mathematical models of herd behavior turned into a growth industry among economists. The models vary in detail, but they share one important attribute: at some point, people stop thinking for themselves and start copying others because they have decided it is in their self-interest to do so. It is this behavior that generates speculative bubbles. And once the bubbles get going, they tend to feed on themselves, with the increases in stock prices drawing ever more people into the market. "A fad is a bubble if the contagion of the fad occurs through price; people are attracted by observed price movements," Robert Shiller, an economist at Yale, explained in his 1989 book *Market Volatility*. "In the simplest bubble model, price increases themselves thus cause subsequent price increases until price reaches some barrier; then the bubble bursts and price drops precipitously, since there are then no further price increases to sustain the high demand."[15]

Models of herd behavior are not confined to the stock market. They have been used to explain everything from crime waves to fashion fads to the collapse of the communist regime in East Germany. (In the latter case, millions of people copied each other and took to the streets.) One economist used a model of herd behavior to explain why so many television shows look the same: network programmers, instead of trying to make the best shows they can, simply copy the most successful shows on the other networks. Another economist pointed out how, during the middle of the nineteenth century, herd behavior led to the construction of more than 10,000 miles of plank roads. The first wooden road was built in Salina, a small town in upstate New York, where an entrepreneur named George Geddes had persuaded people that the planks would last about eight years. Word of the exciting innovation quickly spread, and almost three hundred plank road companies were incorporated, many of them claiming that the planks would last between ten and fifteen years. After just four years, however, the wooden road in Salina had decayed to such an extent that the entire idea was discredited. Construction elsewhere came to a rapid halt.

The models of herd behavior predict that large numbers of people, in a wide variety of circumstances, will coverage on the same actions. This is exactly what happened during the Internet boom. Those mutual fund managers that eschewed Internet stocks, and there were many of them to start with, found their funds sliding down the performance league tables. Even the most cautious fund managers couldn't ignore what was happening. "We're all looking at the performance of Internet companies that have come out since Netscape," Lise Buyer, an analyst at T. Rowe Price Associates, a Baltimore-based mutual fund company that is famously conservative, told *The New York Times* shortly after Excite's IPO. "While they have been incredibly volatile, people who participated in the initial public offerings are better off than those who didn't."[16] Every quarter, the pressure grew on fund managers to find the Internet religion. In the end, few were able to resist the call.

## III

**The real coup was marketing Internet stocks to individual investors:** doctors, dentists, cab drivers, and all sorts of other people. A critical element in individual investing in Internet stocks was the Internet itself, which created a virtual community of risk takers where none had existed before. In the past, the typical individual investor was a fellow sitting at his kitchen table with a copy of *The Wall Street Journal* and, perhaps, an annual report. If he wanted to discuss his portfolio, he would call his broker, who, assuming he was honest, would advise against dramatic gestures. In the Internet era, this picture was as outdated as black-and-white television. Armed with an account at E*Trade, Ameritrade, or any of dozens of other online brokerages, the individual investor had the information, the technical capacity, and the moral support to become a professional speculator. A click of the mouse and he could display his portfolio. Another few clicks and he could buy and sell stock, with electronic confirmation of his trades dispatched within seconds. If he wanted reassurance about his investment strategy, or simply to swap gossip about his trades, he could go to financial Web sites like The Motley Fool and Ragingbull.com, where he could exchange notes with thousands of like-minded souls.

E★Trade, which was based in Palo Alto, pioneered online trading. Compared to most Internet companies, it had a long history. Bill Porter, a physicist and inventor with more than a dozen patents to his credit, founded the firm in 1982. In its formative years, E★Trade then called TradePlus, provided electronic quote and trading services to other brokers, including Fidelity, Charles Schwab, and Quick & Reilly. In July 1983, a Michigan doctor placed the first online trade using E★Trade's technology; but in commercial terms Porter proved ahead of his time. It wasn't until the early 1990s that online trading started to catch on. In 1992, Porter adopted the name E★Trade and started offering accounts through CompuServe and America Online. As the online services grew in popularity, so did E★Trade. By the end of 1995, it had about 40,000 accounts and was handling more than 4,000 trades a day. Unlike most online firms, E★Trade was even making profits: $2.6 million in 1995.

In February 1996, E★Trade moved to the Internet, allowing investors to buy up to 5,000 shares for less than twenty dollars. (The exact fees were $14.95 for stocks listed on the New York Stock Exchange and the American Stock Exchange, and $19.95 for stocks on the Nasdaq.) This was a fraction of the commissions levied by full-service brokers, such as Merrill Lynch, and it was also considerably less than discount brokers, such as Charles Schwab, were charging. By May 1996, E★Trade was processing about 11,000 Internet trades a week, and it announced plans for an IPO. In its prospectus, filed in early June, it pointed to the ongoing "shift in demographic and societal norms" that was transforming American finance. "Increasingly, consumers are taking direct control over their personal affairs, not simply because they are able to, but because they find it more convenient and less expensive than relying on financial intermediaries."

E★Trade hired Robertson, Stephens to be its lead underwriter, filling out the roster of investment bankers with Hambrecht & Quist and Deutsche Morgan Grenfell. The latter firm was new to the Internet scene. A few months earlier, it had poached Frank Quattrone from Morgan Stanley, reportedly agreeing to pay him at least $20 million over three years, plus a big share of any profits he made. Quattrone took most of his fellow investment bankers with him from Morgan Stanley, but Mary Meeker stayed behind. Despite Quattrone's efforts, the E★Trade IPO was far from trouble free. In the run up to the offering, the online brokerage's trading system crashed, rival Charles Schwab cut its prices, and Internet stocks fell sharply. The IPO had to be postponed, but on August 16, 1996, E★Trade finally issued 5 million shares at $10.50. The stock opened at $11.75 and closed at $11.25, valuing the firm at more than $300 million. This was hardly a repeat of the Netscape or Yahoo! IPOs, but it opened the way for other online trading firms to follow E★Trade's lead and go public.

By the summer of 1996, about 800,000 Americans had online trading accounts, and the number was increasing daily. Online investing wasn't just cheaper than traditional investing; it was a lot easier. Investors could place orders twenty-four hours a day, seven days a week. They could also get access to up-to-the-minute news, real-time stock quotes, and analysts' reports—the sort of information that used to be restricted to Wall Street professionals. If they had the time and the inclination, they could also do their own stock research. The Securities and Exchange Commission's Web site contained earnings reports, proxy statements, and other legal filings from every public company in the country. Before the advent of the Internet the only way to see these reports was to trek to the SEC's reading rooms in Washington or New York and grapple with a microfiche reader. Many companies also set up their own Web sites and posted all of their press releases and financial reports for shareholders to look at.

The financial chat rooms were important because they placed individual investors in a group setting, where they were more likely to take risks and act like copycats. Many online traders frequented The Motley Fool on America Online. David and Tom Gardner, two twenty-something brothers from Alexandria, Virginia, started the site in August 1994, taking its name from Shakespeare's *As You Like It*. The Gardners had a refreshingly irreverent approach to investing. They poked fun at the Wall Street establishment and the financial press, whom they dismissed as the Wise. Just like in a medieval court, they argued, the only people who could be relied on to tell the truth were the outsiders, the Fools. The Gardners set up their own model stock portfolio, which more than doubled in the first eighteen months. They advocated investing in companies with strong market positions and holding for the long term, but many of their followers took a more short-term approach.

In April 1995, The Motley Fool set up a bulletin board devoted to Iomega, a small firm based in Roy, Utah. Iomega wasn't an Internet start-up, but from an investor's perspective it was the next best thing: a technology company with a nifty new product, the Zip drive, a storage device with many times more capacity than a floppy disc. Between May 1995 and May 1996, Iomega was one of the best-performing stocks on the Nasdaq, going from less than $5 to more than $50. The Motley Fool chat room wasn't the only factor behind this precipitous rise—Iomega's Zip drive received strong reviews from the computer press—but it surely played a role. The bulletin board provided a forum for investors to exchange news and discuss Iomega's future. Whenever anybody had the temerity to post a message questioning Iomega's valuation, or mentioning the fact that bigger, better-financed competitors were moving into the same market, they were quickly drowned out with upbeat counterarguments. The Iomega fad provided a textbook case of how a speculative bubble can form. The stock became one of the most talked about in the country. Even journalists were not immune to the hype. One New York magazine writer, a seasoned reporter with enough gray hairs to know better, was talked into investing a good deal of his savings in Iomega by a fellow commuter on the Metro North. The bubble burst in June 1996, when, in just a few days, and for no apparent reason, Iomega's stock fell by more than half. "Is there a reason for concern here that some of us don't know about? HELP," an anguished investor wrote on The Motley Fool.[17]

Iomega wasn't the only stock with a bulletin board of its own. Before long, Netscape, Yahoo!, and many other speculative issues had similarly devoted bands of followers. People read about Internet stocks on the Internet, talked about Internet stock on the Internet, and bought Internet stocks on the Internet. The technology at the center of the speculative boom helped to facilitate and sustain the speculation. It was almost as if the Dutch tulips had doubled as personal digital assistants, allowing the Amsterdam speculators to key in their trades. The only historic parallel was the development of radio technology in the 1920s, which allowed people traveling on transatlantic liners to wire in their buy orders for Radio. In the Internet age, anyone with a computer and a modem could behave like a passenger on a luxury liner—at least for a while.

## IV

**Responsibility for supervising the U.S. stock market is split between** the Securities and Exchange Commission and the Federal Reserve, the nation's central bank. The SEC is supposed to look after the interests of individual investors, while the Fed oversees monetary policy and the behavior of financial institutions. Traditionally, senior officials at the SEC and the Fed have avoided comment on the level of the stock market. Since 1913, when the Fed was founded, only twice has its chairman publicly warned about excessive speculation. In early 1929, then-chairman Roy Young criticized commercial banks for lending too much money to stock speculators. In June 1965, William McChesney Martin referred to "disquieting similarities between our present prosperity and the fabulous twenties"—a statement that caused the Dow to fall sharply. McChesney Martin also came up with the most famous definition of the Fed's role in the economy, which he said was to "take away the punch bowl just when the party gets going."[18]

By the middle of 1996, many senior people in Washington were concerned that the party on Wall Street might be getting too riotous. Robert Rubin, the Treasury Secretary, was one of the worrywarts. In his long career on Wall Street, which began in the early 1960s, Rubin had never seen anything like what was happening in the stock market. To Rubin, it appeared that investors were ignoring one of the basic laws of finance: the only way to achieve high returns is to take on high risks. Despite his concerns, Rubin was reluctant to say anything publicly. The Treasury Secretary didn't have formal responsibility for the stock market, and Rubin's boss, Bill Clinton, was running for reelection. Trying to talk down the stock market in an election year would hardly be a smart political move. Arthur Levitt, another Wall Street veteran, who headed the SEC, was also getting nervous. Levitt believed it was his job to speak out. "I think investors can accommodate themselves to a 7 percent gain rather than a 30 percent gain, but can they accommodate themselves to a 20 percent loss or 30 percent loss?" he said to a reporter.[19] A fall of the magnitude Levitt was talking about would have taken the Dow down by somewhere between 1,100 and 1,600 points. When this was pointed out to Levitt, he replied: "I'm not going to suggest that a 20 percent loss or a 30 percent loss is looming on the horizon. But what I am suggesting is that if there can be gains of that amount there obviously can be losses of that amount too."

Levitt's warnings didn't have much impact. Investors were far more concerned about the attitude of Alan Greenspan, the Fed chairman. After nine years in office, the seventy-year-old Greenspan was a revered figure, widely credited with rescuing the economy after the 1987 stock market crash and engineering the long period of noninflationary growth during the 1990s. Greenspan and his colleagues on the Federal Open Market Committee (FOMC), which meets eight times a year to set short-term interest rates, certainly had the power to sink the stock market if they so wished. In early 1994, when they raised the federal funds rate for the first time in several years, the Dow fell sharply. At the next meeting of the FOMC, Greenspan congratulated his colleagues, saying: "I think we partially broke the back of an emerging speculation in equities."[20]

In the summer of 1996, Greenspan was reluctant to repeat the trick. During the past year, the Fed had cut the federal funds rate from 6.0 percent to 5.25 percent, which had helped boost the market. While stock prices were now undoubtedly high, the Fed chairman, who had recently been nominated for another four-year term, was far from convinced that a speculative bubble had developed. Like many on Wall Street, he was coming to believe that higher stock prices were at least partially justified by the economy's sterling performance. Many of the old rules of thumb didn't seem to work anymore, especially the one that said unemployment and inflation move in opposite directions. Unemployment had fallen to about 5.5 percent, but there was still no sign of the rising prices that many economists had predicted. Some of Greenspan's colleagues believed it was only a matter of time before inflation picked up, and they wanted to raise the federal funds rate in order to slow down the economy, but Greenspan refused to go along with this argument. Like Abby Joseph Cohen, he believed that American firms and American workers were becoming a lot more productive, even if the official statistics were failing to pick this up. If this were indeed the case, the economy should be able to grow a good deal faster than in the past without sparking inflation.

Greenspan's willingness to challenge the conventional wisdom was the product of a lively and independent mind. He was born in March 1926 in Washington Heights, an upper Manhattan neighborhood then known as Frankfurt-on-the-Hudson because of the large number of German Jews that lived there. Greenspan's parents separated when he was a young child, and his mother, Rose, brought him up. Economics wasn't his first love: that was music, especially jazz. After graduating from high school, Greenspan went to Juilliard, the famous conservatory, but he dropped out and joined Henry Jerome and His Orchestra, a swing band that performed at, among other places, Childs restaurant in Times Square. Greenspan played the tenor sax and the clarinet. In 1945, he started taking evening classes in economics and business at New York University, which was then known as the School of Commerce. After getting his bachelor's degree he did some postgraduate courses at Columbia, then took a job on Wall Street as an economic analyst. He stayed there for twenty years, creating a profitable consulting firm, Townsend Greenspan, whose clients included Alcoa, U.S. Steel, and J. P. Morgan. In the 1968 presidential campaign, Greenspan served as Richard Nixon's economic adviser. Six years later, Nixon, shortly before he resigned, invited Greenspan to chair the White House Council of Economic Advisers. After Gerald Ford became president, Greenspan took up the post.

Shortly after Labor Day of 1996, Greenspan called some Fed economists together and asked them to reexamine the productivity figures.[21] He wanted the aggregate numbers that the Bureau of Labor Statistics reports every quarter broken down by individual industries. Perhaps by looking at these figures—for automobile plants, aircraft production, banking, retailing, and so on—it would be possible to figure out why the government was missing the productivity upturn. A couple of weeks later, the staff economists confirmed what a number of academic studies had already found: the reason that the overall figures were so low was that the service sector, which employs about two-thirds of the workforce, had seen virtually no productivity growth at all in three decades. In some service industries, such as grocery stores, productivity had actually fallen. Greenspan thought this was incredible. How was it possible that productivity growth had stagnated in the banking industry, for example, despite the spread of automated teller machines and telephone banking?

The staff study made Greenspan ever more convinced that the official productivity figures were misleading.[22] At an FOMC meeting in late September, he persuaded his colleagues to keep the federal funds rate on hold. After the Fed's decision, the stock market resumed its upward climb. In October, the Dow raced past 6,000. A couple of months later—after Bill Clinton had been reelected to the White House in a landslide—it reached 6,500. In just two years, the Dow had risen by nearly 3,000 points. Many stocks had doubled in twelve months. Even if productivity growth had accelerated, a jump of this size was difficult to justify on economic grounds. Inside the Fed, worries about a possible speculative bubble increased.

In early December, Greenspan hosted an informal seminar on the stock market at the Fed's art deco headquarters on C Street in Foggy Bottom. The Wall Street attendees included Byron Wien, Abby Joseph Cohen and David Shulman. Yale economist Robert Shiller, the specialist on speculative bubbles, and his coauthor, Harvard's John Campbell, were also there. They had brought some charts to support their argument that the stock market was grossly overvalued. Shiller ran through some psychological evidence he had been collecting, which implied that crowd behavior had a lot to do with the market's rise. Greenspan seemed interested in Shiller's presentation but remained noncommittal. After the seminar finished, he and some of his fellow governors had lunch with the participants.

A couple of days later, on December 5, 1996, Greenspan attended a reception at the American Enterprise Institute, a conservative think

tank in Washington. He was there to receive the Francis Boyer
Award for notable contributions to American society. Previous recip-
ients included Henry Kissinger, Gerald Ford, and Ronald Reagan.
After receiving his award, Greenspan delivered a long address entitled
"The Challenge of Central Banking in a Democratic Society." Most
of the speech was taken up with a historical discussion going back to
Alexander Hamilton and William Jennings Bryan, but the Fed chairman also slipped in a brief reference to the current situation: "Clearly,
sustained low inflation implies less uncertainty about the future, and
lower risk premiums imply higher prices of stocks and other earnings
assets. But how do we know when irrational exuberance has unduly
escalated asset values, which then become subject to unexpected and
prolonged contractions as they have in Japan over the last decade?
And how do we factor that assessment into monetary policy?"[23]

Amid the economist's jargon, the phrase "irrational exuberance"
stuck out prominently—just as Greenspan had intended it to. Even
before he got up to speak, the Reuters news agency sent out a one-
line alert based on an advance text: "Fed must be wary when irrational exuberance affects stocks, assets—Greenspan." In Japan and
Australia, where the following day's trading session had already
begun, stock prices fell sharply. When trading started in Europe, the
selling continued. The German market fell by more than 3 percent.
When the New York Stock Exchange opened, the Dow slid 140
points. Shiller was driving his child to school in New Haven when
he heard the news about Greenspan's speech and its impact on the
markets. I wonder if I had anything to do with that, he thought to
himself.[24]

Greenspan had issued what was, by his opaque standards, a clear
warning to investors, but it didn't prove very effective. Later in the
day, stock prices recovered. The Dow closed down just 55.16 points,
a loss of less than one percent. On Wall Street, after the initial shock,
the Fed chairman's statement was interpreted as a sign of weakness.
"The Fed has no intention of tightening monetary policy simply to
push the equity market down," Bruce Steinberg, an economist at
Merrill Lynch, told The New York Times. "It will only tighten when it
believes the inflation climate requires it."[25] Other analysts were even

more dismissive of Greenspan's intervention. "Instead of raising rates, he is going to make speeches," Christopher Quick, a senior executive at the Quick & Reilly discount brokerage, commented.[26]

Wall Street had taken the measure of its man. Greenspan was concerned about the stock market, but not concerned enough to raise interest rates. A few weeks later, at the start of 1997, the Dow took off again. By the second week of February, it had topped 7,000.

# chapter 10  amazon.com

I

**By the spring of 1997, e-commerce companies were proliferating** like bacteria. With a little money, practically anybody could set up a Web site and try to sell things. Jason and Matthew Olim, two teenagers in Amber, Pennsylvania, founded CDNOW in the basement of their parents' home and did $6 million worth of business in 1996. Before long, the Olims faced competition from many other music sites, such as CD Universe. Despite all of this entrepreneurial activity, it was far from clear how much money was being spent online. Estimates ranged from $300 million a year to more than $1 billion, but most of the figures being bandied about were produced by commercial research organizations with a vested interest in the growth of e-commerce. The lower estimates were probably more accurate. Despite the hoopla surrounding online shopping, most people still preferred to make their purchases in bricks-and-mortar stores. "In the three years since the Internet has taken off, the slow growth of electronic commerce has been one of its big disappointments," *The Economist* commented in a May 1997 survey article. "The software bugs, baffling interfaces and limited selections in the average online shop make even the corner grocery shop look like a miracle of organization and choice. And most online stores are losing a fortune."[1]

If e-commerce had been subject to the regular discipline of the market, the early setbacks would have proved fatal. But consumers were not driving online commerce; Wall Street was driving it. A few days after *The Economist*'s piece appeared, the IPO market, which had been in the doldrums for months, perked up. On May 14, Rambus, a microchip maker, went public. Its stock was issued at $12 and closed at 30¼, a rise of more than 150 percent. The following day, Amazon.com, the online bookseller, issued 3 million shares at $18. The stock opened at $27 and closed at 23½. By the standards of Netscape and Yahoo!, it wasn't much of a debut, but one of the most controversial capitalist ventures of the twentieth century was now a public company.

Jeff Bezos, Amazon.com's founder, was born in Albuquerque, New Mexico, on January 12, 1964. His parents separated before his birth, and he never knew his biological father. Bezos's mother remarried a Cuban immigrant, Miguel Bezos, a petroleum engineer for Exxon. From an early age, Bezos was an overachiever. At Palmetto High School in Pensacola, Florida, where he was the valedictorian of the class of 1982, he wrote a term paper entitled "The Effect of Zero Gravity on the Aging Rate of the Common Housefly," which won him a trip to NASA. His valedictorian speech was a call for man to colonize space. He also got a place at Princeton, where he entered the honors physics program but switched to electrical engineering and computer science after he discovered that other students were even smarter than he was.[2]

Bezos graduated summa cum laude in 1986 with a grade-point average of 3.9 and took a job at Fitel, a small New York firm that was building a computer program for carrying out international financial transactions. In 1988, he moved to Banker's Trust, a big Wall Street bank, where he quickly became a vice president. He helped set up BTWorld, a software program that allowed clients of the bank to track their corporate retirement plans. Two years later, at the age of twenty-six, Bezos switched jobs again, this time to a hedge fund founded by David Shaw, a Stanford-trained computer scientist who helped pioneer the application of computers to finance. Shaw's fund, D. E. Shaw, used high-powered PC workstations to seek out and make profitable trades.

After a couple of years, Shaw put Bezos in charge of drumming up new business. In early 1994, he asked him to investigate the possibilities for making money on the Internet. Bezos was immediately struck by the growth of traffic on the World Wide Web, which was running at an annual rate of about 2,300 percent. "You have to keep in mind that human beings aren't good at understanding exponential growth," Bezos told Robert Spector, the author of *Amazon.com*, a history of the company. "It's just not something that we see in our everyday life." A phenomenon growing as fast as the Web is "invisible today and ubiquitous tomorrow."[3] At the time, few businesses were operating on the Web, but Bezos thought it was only a matter of time before capitalism conquered the new medium. He put together a list of twenty items that could be sold online, including computer software, office supplies, books, magazines, and music. After narrowing the choices to books and music, he settled on the former for a couple of reasons. There were more books to sell than music titles, and, unlike the music industry, which is dominated by a handful of big companies, there were "no eight-hundred-pound gorillas in book publishing and distribution."[4]

Despite evolving into a major business with an annual turnover of more than $25 billion, the book industry had remained fragmented, with more than 50,000 different publishers, ranging from famous names like Random House and Simon & Schuster to tiny imprints that published one or two titles. On the retail side of the business, the biggest players were Barnes & Noble and Borders, two national chains that had grown rapidly during the 1980s and now controlled about a quarter of the market. The rest of the market was split between mail-order clubs, department stores, and independent bookstores, which still numbered in the hundreds of thousands. Bezos saw the chance to build an online retail business that could dwarf its rivals in selection, convenience, and geographic reach. The biggest Barnes & Noble stores stocked about 175,000 books, which was only a fraction of the 1.5 million English-language books in print. Such stores were expensive to build and operate. By eliminating the cost of real estate and sales staff, Bezos believed it should be possible to offer customers cheaper prices than they could get in traditional bookstores while offering a broader selection and making higher profit margins.

Bezos recommended that D. E. Shaw set up an online bookstore. When Shaw rejected the idea, he decided to quit and start his own. Bezos didn't make this decision lightly. In the spring of 1994, top Ivy League graduates didn't give up good jobs on Wall Street to take a gamble on the Internet. Bezos justified taking the risk using what he called a "regret minimization framework." He told Spector: "I knew that when I was eighty there was no chance that I would regret having walked away from my 1994 Wall Street bonus in the middle of the year. I wouldn't even have remembered that. But I did think there was a chance that I might regret significantly not participating in this thing called the Internet that I believed passionately in. I also knew that if I tried and failed, I wouldn't regret that. So, once I thought about it in that way, it became incredibly easy to make that decision."[5]

Bezos and his wife, Mackenzie, whom he had met while she was working as a research associate at D.E. Shaw, packed up their Manhattan apartment, flew to Texas, then drove to Seattle. Bezos chose Seattle, the home of Microsoft and Boeing, as his new company's location for several reasons. He had friends there. It had a large community of computer scientists. It was in a state that didn't have a sales tax. And it was close to Roseburg, Oregon, where the country's biggest book distributor, Ingram Book Group, had a major distribution center. On July 5, 1995, Bezos incorporated his new company under the name Cadabra Inc. (as in "abracadabra"). One of his first tasks as an Internet entrepreneur was to come up with a better name. Since Web sites were often listed alphabetically, he wanted one beginning with the letter "A." After perusing the dictionary, he settled on Amazon, the world's largest river. The name was instantly recognizable but also vague enough to stand for anything, which was useful from a branding standpoint. Bezos insisted on calling the company Amazon.com, the first such use of the ".com" suffix. Some of his friends considered this a mistake, but it turned out well, helping to differentiate the new firm and also creating a new collective noun for Internet companies: "dotcoms."

## II

**Bezos rented a house in Bellevue, a suburban city on the other side** of Lake Washington from Seattle. Amazon.com started out in the garage, which had been converted into a recreation room. The firm's first two employees were both computer scientists: Sheldon Kapham, an expert in databases who had worked for Kaleida Labs, a failed multimedia joint venture between Apple and IBM; and Paul Barton-Davis, an Englishman who had helped to set up a Web site at the University of Washington. For months, Kapham and Barton-Davis concentrated on building a reliable and easy-to-use retail Web site. Bezos insisted that they keep it as simple as possible. Some early e-commerce sites took minutes to load and froze whenever a customer tried to buy anything. Bezos ruled out any data-intensive graphics. He paid Kapham and Barton-Davis out of his own pocket. When he ran out of money, his parents invested about $250,000. At this early stage, raising money from outside investors wasn't really an option. Amazon.com was just a clever name for a business idea that wasn't even original.

Books had been sold online for years. As far back as 1991, Computer Literacy Bookshops, a Silicon Valley company that specialized in technical books, set up clbooks.com and accepted orders over the Internet. Three years later, BookStacks Unlimited, a Cleveland company, started Books.com, which offered more than 400,000 titles at discounted prices. The Books.com Web site included a number of features designed to make users feel like part of a community of readers: reviews, excerpts, discussion groups, and a daily radio show covering literary news. Amazon.com would adopt many of these features and add a few of its own.

Amazon.com's Web site launched on July 16, 1995. Its home page featured the firm's logo, the letter "A" with a river running through it, and the slogan "Earth's Biggest Bookstore." A search box allowed users to browse through a million books by author, title, subject, and publication date. Amazon.com encouraged its users to submit reviews, which it posted online. Just as Bezos had wanted, the site was simple, quick, and functional. The prices were cheap, but not astonishingly so. Non–best-sellers were discounted by 10 percent, best-sellers by 30 percent; and a group of featured books by 40 percent. Amazon.com promised to ship books in anything from twenty-four hours to six weeks, depending on how obscure they were. In the first week, customers submitted about $12,000 worth of orders.

Six months later, at the start of 1996, sales were big enough that

Bezos and his colleagues, who had already moved to a grungy office building in downtown Seattle, needed more space. Amazon.com was acquiring a following, albeit at a cost. During 1995 it had lost more than $300,000, on revenues of $511,000. Bezos tried to raise some more money from people he knew in the Seattle business community but found it tough going. The ambitions for Amazon.com that he laid out to potential investors were pretty modest. He was aiming to break even in 1997 on annual sales of somewhere between $10 million and $20 million. After much arm-twisting, he managed to secure outside investments totaling nearly $1 million.

It was the media that transformed Amazon.com from an interesting small business story into a multibillion-dollar corporate thriller. On May 15, 1996, *The Wall Street Journal* published a front-page story under the headline "How Wall Street Whiz Found a Niche Selling Books on the Internet." The article, written by G. Bruce Knecht, was overwhelmingly positive. It related how Bezos had quit his job on Wall Street and tapped out a business plan for Amazon.com on a laptop computer as his wife drove him across country. "Though it hasn't yet posted a profit, the company is on its way to ringing up more than $5 million in sales this year—better than most Barnes & Noble Inc. superstores," Knecht wrote. "Its site on the World Wide Web has become an underground sensation for thousands of book lovers around the world, who spend hours perusing its vast electronic library, reading other customers' amusing online reviews—and ordering piles of books."[6] *The Wall Street Journal* sells nearly 2 million copies a day and is required reading in the corporate world. Being featured on its front page is, quite literally, the sort of publicity that money can't buy. The day the piece came out, Amazon.com's business doubled. Then it doubled again, and again.

From Bezos's perspective, the timing couldn't have been better. He had just started talking to venture capital firms about financing his expansion plans. One firm, General Atlantic Partners, had offered to invest $1 million in a deal valuing Amazon.com at about $10 million. After the article appeared in *The Wall Street Journal*, and other VCs inundated Bezos with calls, he raised the valuation he was demanding to $100 million. General Atlantic agreed to a valuation of $50 million, but Bezos, who could now have his pick of suitors, refused its offer.

Instead, he invited John Doerr, of Kleiner Perkins, up to Seattle. Having Doerr behind Amazon.com would impress Wall Street. Doerr accepted the invitation. After looking around Amazon.com's headquarters, he thought Bezos's valuation excessive, but he nonetheless offered $8 million for a 13 percent stake, valuing the company at about $60 million. Bezos had by now been offered better terms elsewhere, but he agreed to the deal. "If we'd thought all this was purely about money, we'd have gone with another firm," Bezos told *The New Yorker*. "But Kleiner and John are the gravitational center of a huge piece of the Internet world. Being with them is like being on prime real estate."[7]

The cash infusion from Kleiner Perkins was more than enough to pay for a nationwide advertising campaign. Bezos was now getting a lot more ambitious. He had been studying the history of the Walt Disney Company, and he wanted to turn Amazon.com into an equally powerful brand. Great brands are what distinguish successful companies, such as Disney, Nike, and Coca-Cola, and allow them to charge premium prices. On the Internet, there were no strong brands, with the possible exception of America Online. If Amazon.com could exploit the publicity it was receiving to create a distinctive brand identity, it would have some protection when, as many people expected to happen, Borders and Barnes & Noble launched their own Web sites. The first Amazon.com ads appeared in *USA Today*, *The Wall Street Journal*, and *The New York Times Book Review*. Bezos also did advertising deals with *The New Yorker*, *Atlantic Monthly*, and *Wired*.

Bezos also realized the importance of promoting himself, and the media was happy to cooperate. Newspaper and magazine editors were desperate to put a human face on the Internet story, and writing about Bezos was an obvious way to do it. With his baby features and his infectious cackle, he could all too easily be portrayed as the goofy boy next door. Bezos stories multiplied. Most of them focused on his discovery of the World Wide Web, his fateful drive across country, and the origins of Amazon.com in a Bellevue garage. Few mentioned that he was ordered to research Internet commerce, that he flew from New York to Texas, and that he rented a house with a garage precisely so he could say that Amazon.com had started out in one. The media presented Amazon.com as a radically new type of business—

one that wasn't hemmed in by the physical constraints facing other companies. "Amazon.com is truly virtual," *Fortune* informed its readers in December 1996. "Though it has become a multi-million-dollar business that employs 110, there's still no storefront and little inventory."[8] Even the normally skeptical *Economist* fell for this line, describing how "three floors above an art gallery on a slightly seedy street in Seattle, the world's biggest bookstore, Amazon.com, hums inside a refrigerator-sized box in the corner of a humble storeroom."[9] In reality, the computer in the corner was only a small part of Amazon.com's business. The rest of the company was a lot more old-fashioned than Bezos liked to admit.

Whenever a customer placed an order for a book, Amazon.com ordered it from a distributor, usually Ingram, which trucked it to Seattle. Once there, the book was packed, addressed, and shipped to the customer. Apart from the actual ordering of the book, each step of this process involved manual labor. Far from being "truly virtual," Amazon.com was a labor-intensive business. In the beginning, it didn't stock many books of its own, but it soon realized that ordering the same books repeatedly made no sense. In November 1996, Amazon.com rented a 93,000-square-foot warehouse in South Seattle, where it stocked copies of frequently ordered titles, such as the Dilbert series. Bezos hired a senior executive from Federal Express, the overnight delivery service, to run the warehouse and distribution operations, which employed hundreds, and later thousands, of people. Many of these workers were hired on temporary contracts, so they didn't appear on Amazon.com's payroll, but they were an essential part of the firm's operations.

### III

**The slogan "Earth's Biggest Bookstore" was also questionable.** Although Amazon.com's Web site listed more than a million titles, only a few hundred of these books were in stock and ready for immediate delivery. The rest had to be ordered from the distributors, or from the publishers direct, which is just what happens when a customer walks into a regular bookstore and asks for a book that isn't in stock. In a rare piece of journalistic enterprise, two journalists at *Slate*, an online magazine started by Michael Kinsley, a former editor of *The New Republic*, tested Amazon.com's claim to be the fastest and most convenient bookstore. The *Slate* journalists simultaneously ordered a best-seller and an obscure textbook from Amazon.com and two regular bookstores. The regular stores both beat Amazon.com by a week in delivering the bestseller, although the online firm was the quicker to deliver the textbook.[10]

Reality was less important than perception. Amazon.com had established itself in the public mind as a quick and convenient place to buy books. In the final quarter of 1996, its sales came to more than $8 million. *Time* magazine named Amazon.com as one of its ten "Best Web sites of 1996." Buying books online had now turned into a fashionable activity, and it introduced countless people to the Internet. In many American households, opening the brown corrugated packages from Amazon.com was a regular ritual. The books ordered from Amazon.com were often obscure. When people wanted the latest John Grisham or Stephen King novel they tended to go to the nearest bookstore; but when they were searching for a biography of Napoleon or a computer textbook they often went online. This thrilled many publishers. Michael Lynton, the head of Penguin Putnam, told *The New York Times* that selling books over the Internet would bring "enormous benefit to the [publishing] business because it's not about selling big, best-selling authors. It's about selling our back list, and it's very rare that opportunity comes along."[11]

Amazon.com's growing popularity didn't please everybody in the book business. Toward the end of 1996, Leonard and Stephen Riggio, the New York brothers who owned Barnes & Noble, visited Bezos in Seattle. Accounts of the meeting differ. *The Wall Street Journal* reported that the Riggios offered to purchase Amazon.com outright, a claim they denied. Another version of events had the Riggios expressing interest in a joint Web site that would sell books from both Amazon.com and Barnes & Noble. Stephen Riggio confirmed to the *Journal* that he and his brother were also thinking about setting up their own Web site. "We have to be a player," Riggio said. "Online bookselling is going to be a very big thing."[12] In January 1997, Barnes

& Noble agreed to become the exclusive bookseller on America Online.


## IV

**The Riggios' interest in the Internet reinforced Bezos's belief that** Amazon.com had to establish its dominance of the market quickly. He had the slogan "Get Big Fast" emblazoned on T-shirts and gave them to employees at the company picnic. In March 1997, Amazon. com announced plans to introduce software that would make book recommendations to customers based on past purchases and the buying patterns of others that had bought the same titles. Such "collaborative filtering" software, which was first used by the online music store Firefly, was being widely hailed as the next big thing in e-commerce, because it exploited the interactivity of the Internet to offer customers something that offline stores couldn't match. Bezos liked to claim that Amazon.com was not just a retailer, but a "technology company," or an "artificial intelligence company." This wasn't strictly true—firms like Wal-Mart were heavy users of information technology, but they were still classed as retailers—but there were sound business reasons for the hyperbole. Retailing is a highly competitive industry, with low profit margins. On the stock market, even successful retailers trade at modest prices, while most technology companies trade at a premium. Bezos was already thinking about taking Amazon.com public. A few months earlier he had taken an important step in that direction by hiring Joy Covey, a former chartered accountant at Ernst and Young, as his chief financial officer. Covey had exactly the sort of experience that Wall Street insisted upon for IPO candidates. In 1993, she had been the chief financial officer at DigiDesign, a Boston software company, when it did a successful IPO.

In February 1997, shortly after joining Amazon.com, Covey invited a number of investment banks to a "bake-off" for the prize of managing the anticipated IPO. Goldman Sachs, Deutsche Morgan Grenfell, Hambrecht & Quist, Alex Brown, and Robertson, Stephens were among the firms that made presentations. Morgan Stanley was a conspicuous absentee. Mary Meeker and the rest of Morgan's technology department were keen to pitch for the Amazon.com business, but they were overruled by the bank's top executives out of loyalty to Barnes & Noble, which was a longtime client. Meeker was so angry that she considered resigning, but she decided against it. Covey chose Deutsche Morgan Grenfell, Frank Quattrone's firm, to be the lead underwriter, with Hambrecht & Quist and Alex Brown as the comanagers. The decision was a coup for Quattrone, whose investment banking team was still seeking to establish itself in its new location. Quattrone and his colleagues started work on a prospectus, which Amazon.com filed with the SEC at the end of March, revealing that it planned to issue 2.5 million shares at $12 to $14 each.

The prospectus was a schizophrenic document. Its opening passage stressed the purported advantages of online commerce, including "virtually unlimited online shelf space" and "lack of investment in expensive retail real estate and reduced personnel requirements."[13] This section was followed by a list of "risk factors" facing the company. All prospectuses contain such a section, but Amazon.com's lawyers had clearly insisted on full disclosure, lest investors subsequently claim they had been misled. After revealing that it had lost $6 million since its inception, the company said it "believes that it will incur substantial operating losses for the foreseeable future, and that the rate at which such losses will be incurred will increase significantly from current levels." The reasons for this dire prediction were spelled out in detail. "The online commerce market, particularly over the Internet, is new, rapidly evolving and intensely competitive, which competition the Company expects to intensify in the future. Barriers to entry are minimal, and current and new competitors can launch new sites at a relatively low cost."[14]

Any objective person reading the prospectus would have been forced to conclude that Amazon.com's prospects were poor. In any business, from a hot dog stand to the auto industry, the keys to generating profits are selling a popular product and avoiding ruinous competition. The first step is a lot easier than the second one, as a glance at the hot dog industry makes clear. Fast-food stands are cheap to set up, so they often attract competitors, which limits their profitability. If competitors are barred, as is often the case at sporting stadiums, for example, where one firm gets the entire concession, the hot dog business can be immensely profitable. The principle is a universal one: if the barriers to entering an industry are high, profits tend to be high. When barriers to entry are low, so are profits.

Amazon.com was openly admitting that in e-commerce the barriers to entry were low. If they stayed this way, the chances of any online retailer making sustainable profits were slim, and e-commerce would represent a return to the "perfect competition" envisioned by Adam Smith. In perfect competition, all goods sell at cost, and profits are zero. Bill Gates was among those who believed that the Internet would turn out this way. In the second edition of his book, *The Road Ahead*, Gates said the Internet would lead to a "new world of low-friction, low-overhead capitalism, in which market information will be plentiful and transaction costs low. It will be a shopper's heaven." If investors had accepted Gates's argument, the Internet stock boom would have come to a rapid end. But Wall Street analysts came up with a competing economic vision that was much more favorable to Internet companies. In this "winner-takes-all" model, the Internet economy would end up looking more like a television quiz show in which the victorious contestant takes home all the prizes.

Economists developed the winner-takes-all theory to explain the success of technology companies like Microsoft and Intel. In technology markets, consumers tend to settle on one or two dominant products, such as Microsoft Windows, which generate big profits. One reason why this happens is that technology goods are complicated. After people have learned how to use them they are reluctant to incur the financial and psychological costs of adopting a rival technology. When the music industry switched from vinyl to CDs, listeners had to spend heavily to convert their record collections, and they refused to switch again to mini-discs. "Switching costs" of this nature represent one major barrier to entry. "Positive feedback loops," which reinforce the dominant product's position, represent another. In the early 1990s, Microsoft Windows was already by far the most widely used PC operating system. Seeing this situation, independent software developers, such as video game companies, neglected Macintosh and other Microsoft rivals, preferring to write their applications for Windows. Before long, computer buyers had many more Windows applications to choose from, which further increased Microsoft's market share.

The Internet stock promoters, such as Mary Meeker, applied the winner-takes-all model to e-commerce. Barriers to entry on the Internet were low to begin with, they conceded, but this situation wouldn't last. Once companies like Amazon.com established themselves as market leaders, online shoppers would get used to using them, and it would be extremely difficult for other firms to challenge. In the language of game theory, firms that took an early lead would enjoy a big "first mover advantage," and many of them would end up dominating their markets. From Wall Street's perspective this argument had a welcome corollary. Since investors were being offered the chance to pick the big winners of the future, they couldn't expect to get them cheap. High stock prices made sense.

Like many Internet companies, Amazon.com's business plan was predicated on the winner-takes-all model. Bezos's strategy was to raise a lot of money from investors and use it to build market share. Once market dominance had been achieved, hefty profits would follow automatically. That was the theory anyway. In practice, it wasn't clear if switching costs and positive feedback loops really applied to e-commerce. A visitor to Yahoo!'s home page could switch to Lycos's home page with one click. Similarly, an Amazon.com customer could check the prices on offer at a rival online bookstore in a few seconds. As for positive feedback loops, they were also hard to find. If anything, firms like Amazon.com seemed to suffer from negative feedback. The more money they spent, the more money they lost.

Amazon.com was already facing competition, and more was on the horizon from Barnes & Noble. As its prospectus admitted, "many of the Company's competitors have longer operating histories, larger customer bases, greater brand recognition and significantly greater financial, marketing and other resources than the Company."[15] The only way that Amazon.com could steal an edge was to slash its prices, but this was a costly strategy. The financial accounts published in the prospectus showed that Amazon.com was paying about $16 to buy and ship each book that it sold at $20. On top of this, it was spending about $8 in advertising and $1 in overhead, bringing its total cost per book to $25. If a regular firm followed this business model, it would go bankrupt in a few months. The only justification Bezos could offer was that if Amazon.com kept growing, profits would appear at some (unspecified) point in the future. The early losses were presented as a deliberate strategy. "If we're profitable in the next two years, it will be an accident," he told *Fortune*.[16]

## V

**A few weeks after Amazon.com published its prospectus, Barnes &** Noble unveiled plans for its own Web site, Barnesandnoble.com, and sued in federal court to prevent Amazon.com from calling itself "Earth's Biggest Bookstore." Amazon.com's warehouse "stocks only a few hundred titles," the suit claimed. "Barnes & Noble stocks more books than Amazon and there is no book which Amazon can obtain that Barnes & Noble cannot."[17] The Barnes & Noble counteroffensive came as Bezos and Covey were completing an exhausting three-week road show that took in twenty-four cities. Thanks to all the publicity that Amazon.com had received, the road shows were packed with eager investors, but Bezos and Covey refused to tell them how quickly Amazon.com would turn a profit. Instead, they stressed its rapid growth. Sales in the first quarter of 1997 were $16 million, more than revenues in all of 1996. Losses had also jumped dramatically, to almost $3 million, but Bezos had already explained that heavy losses were part of his strategy, and investors seemed willing to take him at his word. The investment bankers, as they moved from city to city, carried a book in which they recorded how much stock each investor was interested in buying. At the end of the three weeks, the entries in the book showed that there would be more than enough buyers for Amazon.com's stock.

A couple of days before the IPO, Deutsche Morgan Grenfell increased the size of the issue to 3 million shares and raised the price to $18. At that price, Amazon.com would be valued at about $420 million. Bezos, who owned almost 10 million shares, would be worth about $180 million. Kleiner Perkins's $8 million investment would be valued at $60 million. On May 15, 1997, the stock started trading on the Nasdaq under the symbol "AMZN." From the beginning, it was volatile, often rising or falling several points a day. These gyrations were partly a reflection of the fact that only 3 million of Amazon.com's 23 million shares were trading. With so few shares available for investors to buy and sell, even small orders could move the stock price significantly. It was the same artificial shortage of stock that had distorted the valuations of Netscape and every other Internet company. A firm's market capitalization is equal to the total number of shares outstanding multiplied by its stock price. In order to arrive at the $420 million valuation figure for Amazon.com that appeared in the newspapers, journalists multiplied the $18 issue price by 23 million. This calculation was based on the tacit assumption that the 20 million Amazon.com shares that weren't yet trading would have received the same price on the open market, which was questionable. If another 20 million shares had been issued in the IPO, the stock price would almost certainly have been a good deal lower.

The investment bankers knew about this discrepancy, but they didn't publicize it, and they were delighted to see more headlines about Internet stocks. The publicity would help them to unload the backlog of IPOs that had been building up for months. The Rambus and Amazon.com stock offerings "caused every investment banker and every venture capitalist in Silicon Valley to just go absolutely nuts," Roger McNamee, the well-known Silicon Valley investor, told CNNfn in late May. "They were just hoping for a big IPO to get things going again."[18]

# chapter 11  the new economy

I

**The Silicon Valley–Wall Street production line swung back into** action. In June 1997, Mary Meeker issued another Internet report—this one devoted to online retailing. "The Net provides a powerful, efficient new channel of retailing to more than 35 million Web users (we expect more than 150 million by 2000), who are just a mouse click away from consummating transactions 24 hours a day, seven days a week," the report enthused.[1] Meeker argued that online commerce would allow new companies, such as Amazon.com, to create powerful new brands in a low-cost environment, and she identified financial services, computer goods, travel, and books as the most promising areas.

Meeker didn't mention food as a potential market, but June also saw Peapod, an online grocer based in the Evanston, Illinois, area, go public. Peapod wasn't a new company. Andrew and Thomas Parkinson, two brothers, had founded the firm in 1989. The Parkinsons were graduates of Wesleyan University in Middletown, Connecticut, and, like Steve Case, they had both worked for Procter & Gamble. "I saw a lot of research that kept saying people disliked grocery shopping, but I couldn't see how to make a (home-shopping) model work," Andrew Parkinson explained to *Progressive Grocer* magazine.[2] To begin with, Peapod supplied customers with its own software to use to place orders. In 1996, it started operating on the Internet. Customers in seven major metropolitan areas could select a wide range of goods, from fruit and vegetables to soap powder. After an order was placed, Peapod's employees would pick up the supplies from a nearby grocery store and deliver them to the customer. The service wasn't cheap. There was a monthly membership fee of $6.95, plus $4.95 for each delivery, plus a commission of 5 percent.

Other Internet companies also rushed to go public, including At Home, a Silicon Valley start-up that provided fast access to the Internet via cable television wires. At Home's planned debut on Wall Street marked the return of the "concept" IPO. The company could boast neither a popular product nor much name recognition. All it had was a big idea—"broadband"—and the backing of the same team that had brought the world Netscape: Kleiner Perkins and Morgan Stanley. In early 1995, John Doerr and one of his partners at Kleiner Perkins, William Randolph Hearst III, the grandson of the legendary press baron, invited Milo Medin, a NASA computer scientist, to visit them in Northern California. Medin, who was only thirty-two, had led the team that built the NASA Science Internet, a high-capacity computer network linking researchers in sixteen countries. When Medin arrived in Palo Alto, Doerr asked if he would like to transform the regular Internet into a similarly high-capacity network by exploiting the cable wires that passed nine out of ten homes in the United States.

The vast majority of Internet users connected to the network via a modem attached to regular a telephone line, which was often a slow and tortuous process, especially if they were trying to download audio and video files. Cable wires have a lot more bandwidth than telephone wires, and connecting to the Internet through them is several hundred times faster. Doerr and Hearst believed that Web users would pay handsomely for a better connection, while companies like CNN and ABC would readily provide voice and video content. Medin agreed to move to Silicon Valley, and in March 1995 At Home incorporated itself, with Hearst as its interim chief executive and Medin as its first employee. Kleiner Perkins invested $2.3 million to get the firm going, and TCI, the cable television company, invested $7.7 million.

Even by Internet standards, At Home was an audacious venture. From the beginning, it swallowed cash at an alarming rate. Medin decided that merely giving people cable modems wouldn't suffice for At Home's purposes. If the firm really wanted to supply reliable fast access to the Web, it would have to build its own nationwide data network, which could bypass the bottlenecks on the Internet. This would cost a lot of money. With Kleiner Perkins's reputation behind it, At Home raised more than $90 million in outside investment. Much of this cash came from TCI and other cable companies that saw providing Internet access as a way to generate extra revenues from their cable systems. At Home agreed to split its monthly subscription fee, upwards of $40 a month, with the cable companies. Netscape, one of Kleiner Perkins's previous triumphs, also invested $5 million in At Home, in return for which At Home adopted a modified version of the Navigator browser.

With help from the media, Hearst and his successor as chief executive, Tom Jermoluk, who was recruited from Silicon Graphics, promoted broadband as the next-generation Internet experience. In January 1996, Hearst told *Wired* that At Home could gain a million subscribers inside a year.[3] This proved a tad optimistic. In May 1997, when At Home announced that it was going public, with Morgan Stanley as the lead underwriter, it had a just 5,000 subscribers. The only impressive numbers in At Home's prospectus were its losses. In less than two years, it had run through more than $50 million. Hearst and Jermoluk didn't try to hide this figure: they presented it as a measure of At Home's ambition. By now, some cynics on Wall Street were starting to suspect that the stock market values of Internet companies were correlated with their losses. At Home seemed intent on providing more evidence to support this theory. It warned of losses "for the foreseeable future," and also acknowledged that its future depended on its cable partners' willingness to roll out its service, and on the willingness of customers to pay more than double the price of regular Internet access. "Because of the foregoing factors, among others, the Company is unable to forecast its revenues with any degree of accuracy," the prospectus said. "There can also be no assurance that the Company will ever achieve profitability."[4]

Once again, investors ignored these warnings. On July 11, 1997, Doerr, Jermoluk and several other At Home executives gathered in Morgan Stanley's Times Square headquarters to watch the firm's stock start trading. At Home was issuing 9 million shares at $10.50

each. By this stage, Doerr was something of a public figure. A month earlier, he had appeared with Vice President Al Gore at a Nashville conference on the family, where he unveiled a new venture capital fund designed to rescue failing public schools. On the day of the IPO, John Heilemann, a writer for *The New Yorker*, was trailing Doerr for a profile in which he described what happened:

> Now, as Doerr and a handful of At Home's bosses and boosters hovered anxiously over a blue computer screen, the Nasdaq symbol "ATHM" flashed for the first time, and, with it, the stock's opening price of nearly twenty-five dollars—more than double the offering price, and an amount giving At Home a market value, however fleeting, of almost three billion dollars. With mock solemnity, Doerr announced: "America's capital markets are a national treasure," and everyone burst into a chorus of grateful laughter.[5]

Later in the day, the stock fell back a little. It closed at $17, which valued At Home at about $2 billion—only slightly less than Netscape was worth at the end of its first day of trading. Kleiner Perkins and Morgan Stanley were starting to make a habit of creating sensational Internet IPOs.

## II

**The wave of Internet stock issues accompanied a renewed rally in the** broader market. In the first six months of 1997, the Dow rose by another 7 percent, to above 6,800. On Independence Day, Louis Rukeyser, the host of *Wall Street Week*, a long-running show that goes out on PBS every Friday evening, celebrated the Dow's push toward 7,000. "My-oh-my, you talk about a joyous Fourth of July!" he told his viewers. "The world of money hasn't had such a festive celebration since Alexander Hamilton was arguing with Thomas Jefferson."[6] Rukeyser, a courtly white-haired figure who looked and sounded as if he had stepped out of Calvin Coolidge's cabinet, was an exception to the generation gap on Wall Street. He was just as bullish as any twenty-eight-year-old mutual fund manager. *Wall Street Week* wasn't his only stock market venture. He also published a monthly investment newsletter and organized investment conferences that attracted thousands of paying visitors.

> So let's make it three cheers for the red, white, and green. Red stands, not necessarily for the Communist takeover of free-market Hong Kong—we'll have to wait and see on that one—but for the faces of all those wiseguys who have been telling us for years that the U.S. stock market couldn't possibly keep on going higher. You betcha! White stands for ashen faces of all those alleged experts who kept telling us that a nation couldn't keep on creating jobs and increasing profits without reigniting a terrible inflation. And green stands for you know what: all the money that's still being made by those wise enough to keep the faith.[7]

Rukeyser had reason to crow about the U.S. economy. In the first quarter of 1997, the Gross Domestic Product grew at an annual rate of more than 5 percent, its best performance in more than nine years. The Consumer Price Index rose at an annual rate of just 2.2 percent. In April, the unemployment rate fell to 4.9 percent, its lowest rate since 1973. Americans were understandably optimistic. In June, consumer confidence reached its highest level since 1969. Even the official productivity figures finally seemed to be picking up. In the second quarter of 1997, output per hour in the non-farm business sector of the economy, which means most of it, grew at an annual rate of 2.7 percent, more than twice the average rate over the previous two decades. This was the second quarter out of four that productivity growth had topped two percent. "I remember when we held a press conference around this time in 1972 and I said what we had was the best combination of economic numbers in history—and then I amended that to say I meant the Christian era of history," Herbert Stein, chairman of the White House Council of Economic Advisers in the Nixon administration, told *The New York Times*. "I think the numbers are even better now."[8]

Of course, the news wasn't all positive. Despite a recent up-tick, the average hourly wage of production workers, after adjusting for inflation, had hardly increased at all since 1973. (According to some measures it had fallen.) Credit card payments and other forms of consumer debt were growing strongly, as many families took out extra loans to finance their spending. The media didn't linger over these trends. Instead, it produced a glut of articles arguing that there was a "New Economy"—one in which the old rules of economics no longer applied. *Business Week*, the weekly bible of corporate America, led the way in popularizing this argument. In December of 1996, Michael Mandel, a Harvard Ph.D. in economics who served as *Business Week*'s economics editor, wrote an article entitled "The Triumph of the New Economy." A few months later, Mandel returned to the theme in a long cover story on "The New Business Cycle," in which he argued that high-technology was now the driving force in the U.S. economy, accounting for a third of overall growth in the previous year. "The unique nature of an expansion led by high-technology explains why the U.S. has been able to sustain a lower unemployment rate with faster growth and less inflation than economists ever believed possible," Mandel wrote. "Despite strong demand and rising wages for programmers, network technicians, and other high-tech workers, inflationary pressures are counteracted by constantly falling prices for such products as computers and communications equipment."[9] Mandel was careful to say that recessions hadn't been abolished, but a few weeks later he appeared to change his mind. In yet another cover story, "The New Growth Formula," he argued that the recent productivity upturn, if sustained, could lead to good times "for the foreseeable future."[10]

Mandel's argument was similar to those being made by Abby Joseph Cohen and other Wall Street bulls. Since the early 1980s, American firms had been spending heavily on computers and other forms of information technology, investments that should have led to higher productivity growth throughout the economy. The failure to find such a link was known to economists as the "productivity paradox." Mandel claimed that the United States was now finally receiving the payback for the investments it had made in computers. The "productivity paradox seems to be over," he wrote. "The big change is not in the computers themselves, but in how they are being used. With networks connecting anyone to anyone else, it's now easier to use computers to streamline all sorts of business processes—and create totally new ones, such as letting your customers order goods from your electronic catalogue on a Web site."[11]

All mass movements need an ideology to rally around. The idea that the Internet was transforming the American economy provided a seductive one for stock market bulls. Wall Street analysts began to pepper their investment circulars with references to the "New Economy" and the economic benefits of technology. Internet investors adopted the same language and assured themselves that they were helping to change society for the better by buying stocks like At Home and Amazon.com. This rationalization helps to explain why the anti–Wall Street bias of the 1980s disappeared. When Michael Milken and Ivan Boesky were plying their trade, the stock market was widely associated with selfishness, greed, and criminality—an attitude captured in Oliver Stone's *Wall Street*. A decade later, there was no stigma attached to speculating in the stock market, especially if the object of speculation had anything to do with the Internet. Buying Internet stocks was almost a patriotic activity. Entrepreneurs like Steve Case and Jeff Bezos symbolized the old American values of individualism, hard work, and enterprise. How could there be anything morally suspect in financing their attempts to turn themselves into the next Rockefeller?

From a historical perspective, none of this was surprising. Speculative bubbles and idolization of businessmen invariably go together, as do speculative bubbles and talk of a "new era." The New Economy arguments of the 1990s replicated those made during the 1920s, when they were known as the "new economics."[12] In the fall of 1928, Herbert Hoover, soon to become the nation's thirty-first president, declared that the end of poverty was in sight. Around the same time, John Moody, the head of Moody's ratings agency, published an article in *Atlantic Monthly* entitled "The New Era in Wall Street." Moody didn't restrict himself to finance. "Civilization is taking on new aspects," he wrote. "We are only now beginning to realize, perhaps, that this modern, mechanistic civilization in which we live is now in the process of perfecting itself."[13] Within a few years of these words being written, the "civilization" that Moody referred to had given rise to the Great Depression and Adolf Hitler.

## III

**It was one thing for journalists and Wall Street stock strategists to** argue that technology had transformed the economy. But New Economy thinking also penetrated to the highest reaches of the American government. In July 1997, when the Group of Seven nations held their annual economic summit in Denver, it was widely interpreted as an opportunity for the United States to teach the rest of the world how to run a successful economy. "America in the world: still on top, with no challenger," a headline in *Fortune* announced.[14] President Clinton tried not to gloat about the economic problems facing Europe and Asia, but many of his subalterns were not so polite. They advised anybody who would listen that the route to economic success was to copy the American example and open up their economies to competition and technological change. Many foreign delegates were furious at what they saw as U.S. arrogance.

The summer of 1997 also saw the Clinton administration publish its long-awaited policy paper on e-commerce. Ira Magaziner, who had masterminded Hillary Clinton's ill-fated proposal to reform health care via extensive government intervention, was in charge of shaping the administration's policy toward the Internet. In the case of e commerce, he advocated a "non-regulatory, market-oriented approach."[15] Magaziner wasn't just buckling to Silicon Valley campaign contributors, although the policy he recommended was the one they had been demanding. The Clinton administration had decided that a hands-off attitude to the Internet was in the country's strategic interest. Online commerce was shaping up to be one of the biggest industries of the twenty-first century, and American companies dominated it. The only threat to this American hegemony was the possibility that foreign governments would seek to boost their own firms under the guise of imposing national standards on online commerce. As long as the Internet remained a government-free zone, it would be difficult to introduce this sort of protectionism.

The most influential proponent of the New Economy doctrine, although he carefully avoided using the phrase, was Alan Greenspan, who had continued to resist pressure from his colleagues at the Fed to raise interest rates beyond a quarter-point rate hike that was introduced in March 1997. On July 22, 1997, Greenspan went up to Capitol Hill to deliver his semi-annual report on monetary policy. These appearances are the only political accountability that a Fed chairman faces. Once nominated by the president and confirmed by the Senate, he can set interest rates as he sees fit, as long as he can persuade a majority of his fellow members of the FOMC to back him. In Greenspan's case, this was seldom a problem. After ten years at the Fed, he dominated the FOMC like few of his predecessors.

In a wide-ranging presentation, Greenspan told the Senate Banking Committee that the economy's recent performance had been "exceptional," so exceptional that it might represent a "once or twice in a century phenomenon that will carry productivity trends nationally and globally to a new higher track."[16] As always, the Fed chairman hedged his statements with qualifications, but he clearly indicated his agreement with those economists and journalists who had argued that the benefits of computer technology were finally feeding through to the economy at large. He specifically mentioned the research of two Stanford economic historians, Paul David and Nathan Rosenberg, which suggests that even revolutionary inventions, such as the electric dynamo, often take a long time to produce sizeable increases in productivity. Other complementary technologies have to be developed before the benefits of the first one can be fully exploited. "What we may be observing in the current environment is a number of key technologies, some even mature, finally interacting to create significant new opportunities for value creation," Greenspan said. "For example, the applications of the laser were modest until the later development of fiber optics engendered a revolution in telecommunications. Broad advances in software have enabled us to capitalize on the prodigious gains in hardware capacity. The interaction of both of these has created the Internet."[17]

Wall Street traders reacted joyously to Greenspan's testimony, concluding correctly that, despite the stock market's continued rise, he had no intention of raising interest rates. The Dow jumped more than 150 points to close above 8,000 for the first time. Previous Fed chairmen would have been alarmed at such a reaction, but Greenspan didn't seem concerned. Since his "irrational exuberance" speech the previous December, he had hardly mentioned the stock market publicly. Privately, he still regarded the question of whether there was a speculative bubble as an open one. After making the famous speech, Greenspan had ordered the Fed's staff economist to determine whether there was any objective way to tell when a rising market had turned into a speculative bubble. After an extensive survey of past speculative episodes, the best economic brains in the Fed concluded that there wasn't any reliable method. Speculative bubbles could only be identified definitively in retrospect.

Even if what was happening on Wall Street was a bubble, Greenspan was far from sure that the Fed should try to let the air out. While it may have been possible in theory to raise interest rates just enough to deflate stocks gently, he seriously doubted that such a policy would be feasible in practice. Falling stock prices—like rising stock prices—tend to feed on themselves; and the process can easily spiral out of control. In trying to preempt a crash, the Fed could just as easily cause one. Given this danger, Greenspan believed the Fed should stick to its traditional role: running the economy at the maximum rate consistent with stable or falling inflation. It couldn't completely ignore what was happening on Wall Street, but the stock market should only affect monetary policy insomuch as it affected the economy at large.

In taking this position, Greenspan committed himself to a policy stance that had proved untenable for one of his predecessors during an earlier speculative boom. At the start of 1929, Roy Young, the then chairman of the Fed, turned down a senior colleague's request for "sharp, incisive action" to quell the speculation that had caused the Dow to double in two years.[18] Fearing that raising interest rates might cause a crash rather than prevent one, Young instead pleaded with the big banks to lend less money to speculators. This policy, which was known as "direct pressure," proved ineffective. As stock prices continued to rise in the spring and summer of 1929, Young became demoralized. The Fed could only brace for the "inevitable collapse," he said.[19] But this hands-off policy didn't last. It is a property of speculative booms, from tulip mania to the Japanese stock market and real estate bubbles of the 1980s, that they don't remain contained in one sector. Eventually, they go to such extremes that they distort behavior throughout the economy. This is what happened in 1929, and it forced the Fed to act. In August, Young, against his better judgment, raised the interest rate that the Fed charges commercial banks for loans. A couple of months later the stock market crashed, and Young's reputation was destroyed.

Greenspan was well aware of Young's fate. In deciding to let the stock market boom take its course, he took an educated gamble that even if the stock market did eventually crash he would be able to deal with it. This decision was largely based on his experience following the stock market crash of October 1987, when the Fed pumped more money into the economy and successfully prevented a recession. If there was another crash, the Fed could do the same thing again. Its big mistake in 1929, Greenspan believed, had come *after* the stock market crash, when it failed to cut interest rates aggressively enough to revive the patient. "There's no guarantee that even if you get a 1929, you'll end up with a 1932," he told a former colleague.[20]

Greenspan's flexible approach to economics was partly a reflection of his age. He started studying the subject before much of its modern orthodoxy was established. This was especially true of macroeconomics, the field that relates to the economy at large. Most students who studied macroeconomics during the 1970s and 1980s were taught three basic theories: the economy has a natural speed limit, known as the "potential growth rate"; unemployment cannot fall below a certain level without inflation picking up; and an expansion in the money supply causes inflation. Greenspan didn't have much faith in any of these theories, all of which had been invented well after he left school. In fact, he wasn't really a macroeconomist at all. Ever since the early 1950s, when he took his first job at the Conference Board, an economic research organization, he had preferred to look at ground-level data from throughout the economy and work from there. When he became an economic consultant, he continued to focus on individual industries, such as steel, agriculture, and automobiles. He never had much time for the elaborate mathematical models that economists constructed during the 1960s and 1970s, with the help of computers, to forecast the economy as a whole. Even now, as Fed chairman, he preferred to burrow down and find out what was happening on the shop floor. Every day, he spent several hours alone in his office overlooking Constitution Avenue, making his way through page after page of numbers from all sectors of the economy.

Greenspan had a famous head for details. On one occasion recounted by Lawrence Lindsey, a former Fed governor who went on to become President George W. Bush's senior economic adviser, the Mississippi had sprung its banks, interfering with road and rail links. "At the time of the weekly Board of Governors meeting, the U.S. economy was literally linked together by a single bridge," Lindsey recalled. "Greenspan not only knew the location of the bridge, but also the various reroutings that could be used to get merchandise there."[21] In the summer of 1997, as Greenspan scoured the recent statistics from various sectors of the economy, he saw a pattern developing. Heavy investment in information technology was giving firms more timely information about their customers' demands and their own production processes, enabling them to reduce inventories and eliminate spare capacity. As a result, corporate profits were rising sharply, which went some way, at least, toward justifying current stock prices. The exuberance of investors was not necessarily "irrational."

But Greenspan's reluctance to second-guess the judgment of investors was not purely a result of economic reasoning: it was also a matter of ideology. Although often portrayed as a moderate pragmatist, he is, in fact, a fervent free-market conservative. He has been one since the early 1950s, when he fell under the influence of Ayn Rand, the Russian-born libertine and philosopher who wrote *The Fountainhead* and *Atlas Shrugged*. "What she (Rand) did—through long discussions and lots of arguments into the night—was to make me think why capitalism is not only efficient and practical, but also moral," Greenspan once explained.[22] For many years, he was a member of Rand's coterie of admirers, which she dubbed the Collective. Rand's descriptions of capitalism in *Atlas Shrugged*, which she read out to the Collective, struck the young Greenspan as inspired. "Ayn, this is *incredible*," he blurted out on one occasion. "No one has ever dramatized what industrial achievement actually means as you have."[23] Even in later years, when many of Rand's former associates turned against her, Greenspan remained loyal. "She did things in her personal life which I do not approve of, but ideas stand on their own," he said in early 2000. "What was a syllogism back then is a syllogism today."[24]

To a Randian like Greenspan, the Internet provided fresh confirmation of capitalism's infinite capacity to re-create itself. (He rarely dwelled on the central role that the federal government had played in the network's development.) Guided by the profit motive, entrepreneurs like Marc Andreessen and Jeff Bezos were creating vital new industries and shaking up the tired corporate establishment, much as the heroic figures in *Atlas Shrugged* had done. Wall Street was playing a central role in this process of national renewal, channeling valuable resources from investors to entrepreneurs. Far from being a casino, as Keynes had once claimed, the stock market was acting as the creative hub of the economy. Its judgment had to be taken seriously. If millions of investors were saying that At Home was worth $2 billion, what business of the Fed chairman was it to say they were misguided?

## IV

**One of the oldest sayings on Wall Street is, "Don't fight the Fed."** Once it became clear that Greenspan had aligned himself with the forces of the New Economy, even more of the bears retired from the battlefield. "Everybody is tired of being bearish and being wrong," Barton Biggs told a reporter who caught up with him while he was puttering around his Connecticut garden in the summer of 1997. Earlier in the year, Biggs had once again advised his clients to sell stocks and raise cash, a recommendation that few of them had heeded. "The clients don't want to raise cash," he said. "And the portfolio managers who are competing against the market index don't want their superiors telling them to raise cash."[25] Biggs and many of his friends, who had been on Wall Street since the 1960s, were feeling like dinosaurs. "I was at a dinner the other night," he went on. "There were a lot of older people there who are very bearish, like Larry Tisch [the former chairman of CBS]. But Larry Tisch doesn't run money anymore. The guys who have the cash flow, the ones who are running the money, are between twenty-eight and thirty-eight."[26]

As stock prices kept going up, more renowned investors were publicly embarrassed. In July 1997, George Soros told a German magazine that the presence of so many inexperienced investors could lead to an "international stock market crash."[27] On the day that Soros's comments appeared in the American press, the Dow rose by another 108 points. With the bears' credibility in tatters, the public's attention and respect had shifted to the likes of Abby Joseph Cohen and Ed Yardeni, the chief economist at Deutsche Morgan Grenfell. A few weeks after Soros's gloomy comments, Yardeni said that based on "rational exuberance about profits and near-zero inflation" the Dow could reach 10,000 by 2,000 and 15,000 by 2005.[28]

The growing optimism about the economy at large only added to the enthusiasm for technology stocks. Between March and September 1997, the Nasdaq rose by almost 800 points. After Labor Day, Internet stocks rallied further. At Home was one of the big gainers. The cable venture still had only 7,000 subscribers, but the word broadband was being uttered in reverential tones on Wall Street. "[At Home] has built an outstanding platform that I think will in three to five years lead to some fairly significant profits," Shaun Andrikopoulos, of Alex Brown & Sons, commented.[29] (The fact that Alex Brown had helped to underwrite At Home's IPO may have had something to do with Andrikopoulos's support.)

Amazon.com also rallied. On September 22, it hit a new high of 55½, which meant it had risen by more than 200 percent from its IPO price of $18. Thanks to some clever publicity stunts, the media was still providing the online bookseller with invaluable exposure. In July 1997, John Updike, the veteran novelist, agreed to supply the beginning and end of a story to be posted on Amazon.com's Web site. Members of the public would be invited to write the intervening narrative, with a prize of $1,000 for each successful entry. Updike, the author of *Rabbit Is Rich* and *The Witches of Eastwick*, was hardly an obvious choice to promote online technology. At sixty-five, he composed most of his fiction by hand, and his personal computer didn't have an Internet connection. Updike didn't need the $5,000 that Amazon.com offered, but his publisher advised him to do it. He dug out a mystery story that he had started and abandoned thirty years ago,

"Murder Makes the Magazine," which revolved around Miss Tasso Polk, the founder and editor of *The Magazine*. By September 1997, when Updike sat down to write an ending, *USA Today*, *The South China Morning Post*, and the *BBC World Service* had all done stories about his venture online, prompting him to comment wryly: "This has gotten more ink than my last six books."[30]

Mary Meeker also contributed to Amazon.com's cause. Analysts at firms not involved in an IPO don't usually start covering the new company until it has firmly established itself. Meeker, still outraged by her bosses' refusal to do business with Amazon.com decided to flout this custom. In late September, she initiated coverage of the online bookseller with an "outperform" recommendation, telling her clients: "We are making a long-term bet on this company—we do not want to miss this one."[31] Despite Amazon.com's heavy losses, Meeker argued that it satisfied the three most important criteria for investing in young companies: a big potential market, a sound management team, and an exciting product. Turning to the company's heady stock price, and adopting the royal "we," she provided her most detailed argument yet for discounting old valuation methodologies.

> We have one general response to the word "valuation" these days: "Bull market." We have been in the technology sell-side trenches for about a decade and simply—we believe that we have entered a new valuation zone. In addition to valuations being a function of a happy market, this zone is also a function of the Internet.
>
> As we have said again and again—the world has never experienced as rapid/violent a commercial evolution of a fundamental business change as that being caused by the acceptance/usage of the Internet as a communications and commerce tool. Never before have companies like Netscape and Yahoo! gained so much mind share and market share (and market capitalization) so quickly. Anyway, it has all introduced a brave new world for valuation methodologies and it is a time of especially high risk/reward, in our view.
>
> When you overlay the high valuation of many "start-ups" with the relatively high valuation of the general market, well, we are where we are, just trying to do our jobs and find some early stage great companies. If they execute, the valuations will take care of themselves. Again, it's about monster markets, great management teams, and good products.[32]

Following Meeker's plug, Amazon.com's stock rose even further. In October it reached $60. The same month, Jeff Bezos announced that his firm had attracted its millionth customer, a Japanese reader who ordered a biography of Princess Diana, and flew to Asia to deliver the book personally.

America Online, another of Meeker's stock picks, was also doing well, having recovered from the problems it faced in 1996. On September 2, 1997, the company announced that it now had 9 million subscribers, and its stock hit $70, up from a low point of $25 the previous fall. America Online's revenues were now rising strongly, partly due to a sharp jump in advertising. Bob Pittman, the former MTV executive whom Steve Case had hired the previous year, was promoting America Online as the dominant media company of the Internet age, and advertisers appeared to be listening to him. In October, the stock hit an all-time high of $90. Investors were looking forward to America Online booking its first quarter of real earnings, and they weren't disappointed. In the fourth quarter of 1997, the company made $20.8 million, giving at least some credence to Meeker's argument that Internet companies, if they kept growing rapidly, would eventually generate big profits.

With stock prices soaring, the number of publicly funded Internet companies continued to increase. In October, N2K, an online music store based in New York, sold 3 million shares at $19 each, with Paine Webber acting as the lead underwriter. N2K had lost $10.1 million in the first six months of 1997 on revenues of just $2.9 million, and it wasn't even the market leader. CDNOW, which was also preparing for an IPO, dwarfed N2K's market share. Nonetheless, N2K's IPO went well, and within a few weeks the stock hit $30. In November, Goldman Sachs took public Real Networks, a Seattle firm whose Real Player software allowed people to play music and video files downloaded from the Internet. The Real Player helped to bring the Internet to life, but Real Networks was in the same position that Netscape had been in a couple of years earlier—giving away its main product and facing imminent competition from Microsoft. At least Rob Glaser, the founder of Real Networks, knew what he was facing. He was a former Microsoft executive.

# chapter 12 a media bubble

I

**Every weekday, from early morning, a steady stream of town cars** made their way from lower and midtown Manhattan up the West Side Highway and across the George Washington Bridge. Once in New Jersey, the cars took the Fort Lee exit, hooked a couple of right turns, and deposited their passengers in front of an ugly gray office building that is home to CNBC. With more than twelve hours of programming to fill each day, the CNBC producers couldn't be too picky about whom they put on screen, but they did have some standards. Their ideal studio guest was a former beauty queen who covered technology stocks, spoke in short declarative sentences, and dated Donald Trump. Since there weren't many of these women available, the producers generally had to settle for balding, middle-aged men who revered Alan Greenspan and tried their best to speak in English. The vast majority of CNBC's guests were bullish. Bears weren't exactly banned, but they weren't exactly welcome either. They tended to come off as crotchety, and the viewers didn't like them. But when the market was plummeting they couldn't be avoided.

Monday, October 24, 1997, was one such occasion. By midafternoon the Dow was down almost 400 points, and pain was etched into the faces of the CNBC anchors. The network turned to Barton Biggs, hardly a CNBC favorite. As well as being congenitally bearish, Biggs had an annoying tendency to speak over the heads of the viewers. But on this occasion he was on his best behavior. He avoided gloating and warned investors not to panic. "I don't think anybody should do anything right now," he said. "Within twenty-four hours this thing could be going in the opposite direction."[1] While Biggs was speaking, the Dow's fall passed 500 points. At three-thirty, with the Dow down 554 points, its biggest-ever points drop, the New York Stock Exchange halted trading and closed for the day. It was the market's first early close since the shooting of President Reagan in 1981.

Remarkably enough, Biggs turned out to be correct. The following day, the Dow jumped 337 points, its biggest points gain ever. CNBC's reporters didn't hide their delight. "It's great to see all those arrows pointing up," Susie Gharib gushed. A couple of days later, the excitement and tension in Fort Lee was still palpable. "Asia's down; Latin America's down; Brazil has allowed two banks to be taken over by foreign firms; it's a backdoor bailout," Ron Insana, a CNBC anchorman who had worked for sixteen hours on the day of the big sell-off, told a visitor.[2] While Insana went off to prepare for his daily show, Bill Bolster, CNBC's aptly named president, pointed out that the network's ratings had quadrupled, to almost one million, in the past few days. "We caught on to a Gulf War that's going to last forever," Bolster declared. "An event like this happens and Ron Insana becomes Norman Schwarzkopf."[3] Jack Welch, the chairman of General Electric, which owns NBC, had personally congratulated Bolster. It is not every day that Welch calls up his underlings to praise them. Bolster, a strapping Iowan who generally keeps two packs of Merits on his desk, was as pleased as punch. "We had a chance to define our brand, and we took it," he said, beaming. When it was suggested to him that CNBC had been cheerleading for the stock market during the downturn, Bolster didn't flinch. "That is an observation that I am very comfortable with," he replied.[4]

NBC started CNBC in 1989 as a hedge against the declining ratings of its broadcast network. The new network, which was situated in New Jersey so it could utilize cheap, nonunion labor, started life as the Consumer News and Business Channel, presenting a combination of shopping tips and financial advice. In 1991, NBC purchased the assets of the rival Financial News Network, which had recently gone bankrupt, and folded its assets into the renamed CNBC. FNN had been a pioneer in business television. It was founded in 1981 by Glen Taylor, a former minister and children's television producer, and it started air-ing on three UHF stations in California with a stock ticker running across the screen. FNN never made any money, but it managed to get distributed to 30 million homes, which is why CNBC bought its remains. Many of CNBC's reporters, including Insana, Bill Griffeth, and Sue Herera, started their careers at FNN. Insana would later call FNN's launch the "seminal moment" in the democratization of the financial markets, since "it was the first time you didn't have to call a broker to get a stock price."

After the merger, CNBC added a stock ticker and shifted its focus from consumer news to Wall Street. Over the next few years, it turned itself into something between a notice board for investors and a fan club for corporate America. Chief executives loved to go on CNBC. When they had good news to impart, they could deliver it directly; when they had bad news, they could sugarcoat it for investors. Either way, they were assured of a respectful hearing. Between the corporate bigwigs, CNBC filled its airtime with the town car passengers. When the stock market took off in the mid-1990s, this strategy paid off. In 1996, when Bolster arrived from WNBC-TV Channel 4 in New York, he found that he was sitting on a printing press. CNBC's audience wasn't very big—a couple of hundred thousand on an average day—but it was affluent enough to attract major advertisers. Compared to other networks, CNBC's production costs were minimal. Its reporters were paid less than their NBC colleagues, and its guests appeared for nothing. No wonder that Jack Welch became such a big fan of the network.

CNBC didn't create the stock market boom, but it did help to perpetuate and amplify it. To borrow a term from biology, the network acted as a "propagation mechanism" for the investing epidemic. All across the country—in bars, banks, health clubs, airports, and doctors' waiting rooms—televisions were permanently switched to CNBC. The network's reporters didn't hype stocks directly. Rather, they helped to create a populist investing culture in which adulation of the stock market was the norm. The word "adulation" is not an exaggeration. CNBC treated the stock market as a sport, and there was never any doubt which side was the home team. The network's daily schedule was set up like the coverage of an NFL game. In the morning, there were pregame shows, detailing the latest team news (overnight corporate announcements, market activity in Europe and Asia) and focusing on key match-ups ahead (economic statistics to be released, earnings announcements, important speeches). Throughout the trading day there was live coverage, with a revolving cast of announcers and color commentators. And after the market closed, a lengthy postgame show reviewed the day's action, focusing on the big winners and losers.

On all but the darkest of days, an upbeat tone was maintained. CNBC's reporters were enthusiastic, perky, and well informed. Together, they produced smart, entertaining television, which was all the more impressive for being largely unscripted. What they didn't produce was objective news. The vast majority of CNBC's guests were analysts and fund managers who "talked their book"—pumped up the stocks that their firms owned. CNBC's reporters were more than content to let them do so. "A lot of financial journalists seem to hate capitalism," Joe Kernen, CNBC's stocks editor, himself a former Wall Street broker, complained. "It would be like having sportscasters who hate sports. I love capitalism."[5] Unlike other journalistic organizations, CNBC allowed its journalists to trade the stocks of the companies they covered, as long as they held on to them for several months. This policy wasn't advertised to the public, but most viewers probably wouldn't have minded even if it had been. CNBC's appeal was largely based on the fact that it seemed to be willing the stock market higher. Why should its employees be deprived of the chance to get rich along with everybody else?

CNBC wasn't the only stock market booster. If viewers tired of Maria Bartiromo, the "Money Honey," on the floor of the New York Stock Exchange, they could switch to CNNfn, where similar, if less appetizing, fare was being served up. Bloomberg Television provided a third source of financial news. The major networks were much slower to catch on to the stock market story. Their evening news reports rarely went beyond recitations of that day's closing prices, and during trading hours they were showing soap operas. As the boom continued, NBC News began to use CNBC reporters on its evening broadcast; CBS News and ABC News didn't have that option. The networks' problems went well beyond the fact that they were primarily geared up to cover the White House and the State Department. In many ways, they had lost control of the nation's news agenda to cable television and the Internet. As a result, for the first time since the dawn of commercial television, they missed the biggest story of the decade.

## II

**The October 1997 sell-off proved to be a hiccup—another chance for** investors to "buy on the dips." In January 1998, the month *Newsweek* revealed the Whitewater prosecutor was investigating charges that President Clinton had had a sexual relationship with a White House intern, the Dow moved back above 8,000. The stock market and the Monica Lewinsky story would dominate the news for the rest of the year, with some of the biggest headlines reserved for Internet stocks. Nineteen ninety-eight was the year that Internet fever turned into an epidemic, with investors of all types succumbing. In just twelve months, America Online's stock rose by 593 percent, Yahoo!'s stock rose by 584 percent, and Amazon.com's stock rose by an astounding 970 percent. Old media companies sought desperately to clamber aboard the Internet bandwagon. The Walt Disney Company took a stake in Infoseek, the search engine, and also created the Go network as a potential rival to Yahoo! and America Online. NBC invested in C–Net's Snap site.

The number of Internet IPOs continued to increase. In late January, VeriSign, a Silicon Valley company that provided digital identification cards to facilitate online commerce, went public in an offering underwritten by Morgan Stanley. On the first day of trading its stock rose from $14 to 25½. CDNOW quickly followed VeriSign's example, selling 4 million shares at $16 each. In February, DoubleClick, the online advertising agency, became the first Silicon Alley firm to go public. Its stock jumped from $17 to 27⅜, and Kevin O'Connor, its founder, saw his stake rise to $76 million. Mere mention of the word "Internet" was now enough to send investors into conniptions. In April, the Dow broke through 9,000, and K–Tel International, the mail-order music business best known for its "Hooked on Classics" series, announced that it would soon start distributing its compilations of old hits over the Internet. Before the announcement, K–Tel's thinly traded stock was below $7. During the next ten days, it quadrupled. On April 21, after K–Tel announced a stock split to "further enhance the availability and affordability" of the stock, it jumped another $12, to 41⅝.

At this point, two prominent British publications called on Alan Greenspan to bring the stock market back to earth before it crashed of its own accord. "America is experiencing a serious asset-price bubble," *The Economist* announced in an editorial. "The Fed needs to raise interest rates now. Uncertainty is no excuse for Mr. Greenspan to sit on his hands."[6] A week later, *The Financial Times* compared the U.S. economy to Japan in the 1980s, saying: "This is unquestionably a bubble."[7] It is just conceivable that if the American media had taken up these arguments and pressured the Fed, Greenspan would have responded. But the American media was no longer an objective observer of events: increasingly, it was itself part of the bubble. In response to the carping from London, *The New York Times* published an editorial defending the nation's amour propre. "America today is nothing like Japan eight years ago," it insisted. "The American economy today is nearly a mirror opposite."[8] Economic downturns hadn't been abolished, the *Times* conceded, distancing itself from the more extreme New Economy enthusiasts, but "a recession that might start now would reflect the ordinary ups and downs of a complex economy, and not the inevitable implosion following speculative excess."

*Newsweek* also did its bit for national pride, reporting that Greenspan had privately poked fun at the *Economist* article.[9] Few American publications queried Greenspan's wisdom. This wasn't just a matter of hero worship—although there was some of that. Questioning the stock market's rise had already embarrassed many newspapers and magazines. In April 1996, *Fortune* published a cover story, "How Crazy Is This Market?" which said a "confidence-shattering crash" was inevitable at some point.[10] In July 1997, with the Dow 2,000 points higher, *Fortune* ran another alarmist cover story, this one posing the question: "Time to Cash In Your Blue Chips?"[11] Readers who sold out after either of these articles missed another big run-up in stock prices. Not surprisingly, *Fortune*'s coverage of the stock market became notably less questioning as time went on—and this was true of a lot of publications.

A few individual curmudgeons remained: Alan Abelson, of *Barron's*; Allan Sloan, of *Newsweek*; Jim Grant, the editor and publisher of *Grant's Interest Rate Observer*, a Wall Street newsletter. These writers maintained a steady supply of skeptical interpretation, but bearish journalists, like bearish analysts, were largely ignored. The truth was that few Americans wanted to read negative pieces about the stock market. Journalism, like all commodities, is subject to the laws of supply and demand. As the demand for skeptical reporting dropped, the supply fell back to match it. Similarly, as the demand for upbeat coverage increased, the supply expanded to meet it.

In July 1998, *Money* magazine addressed the boom in stocks like Amazon.com, Yahoo!, and K-Tel. "Seeing such price gains, you may have two questions," *Money* noted. "One, is Internet mania based on nothing more than hype? And, two, is it too late to get it on the action?" The answers were reassuring—at least to Wall Street: "First, the Internet boom is for real," and "Second, you are not too late." The article went on: "It's true that eager investors have bid up many Internet stocks to astonishing prices. Yahoo!, for instance, trades at more than 40 times sales; by comparison, even premium-priced Microsoft goes for less than 15 times sales. But the Internet's potential is so great that even today's rich prices will likely be justified for many companies in the long run"[12]

It is unfair to single out *Money*—many other magazines ran similar articles—but the fact that such a conservative publication could recommend Yahoo!'s stock demonstrated how far American journalism had been compromised. A few weeks later, *Time*, which had been running boosterish articles about the Internet for years, surpassed itself with a cover picture of Jerry Yang above the headline "Kiss Your Mall Goodbye: Online Shopping is Faster, Cheaper, and Better." Of all the dubious articles published about the online economy, this was one of the most hysterical. "In our 20th century consumer culture, it may seem almost too good to be true: the latest and greatest products, custom-made and delivered whenever you want!" writer Michael Krantz gushed. "And how to pay for all this online bounty? We hope you've bought some Yahoo! stock."[13]

Yahoo! was the latest media darling. A week earlier, its stock had surged to more than $200, making paper billionaires out of Yang and David Filo. In September 1998 both *Business Week* and *Upside* published cover stories on the company. A few months later, *Advertising Age* made Filo and Yang their "People of the Year." Most articles about Yahoo! parroted the company's line that it had transformed itself from a mere "search engine" into a "portal," or even a "broadcast network of the Web," and that this strategy would prove highly profitable. There was even some evidence to support this story. In the first quarter of 1998, Yahoo! recorded its first profit: $4.3 million. By the summer, its Web site was attracting about 40 million visitors a month—"more than the 30 million who tune in weekly to NBC's top-rated TV show, *ER*," *Business Week* pointed out—and only America Online was receiving more traffic.[14]

But Yahoo!'s future was far from assured. Unlike America Online, it had no subscription income, so it was totally dependent on advertising, which was little more effective on Yahoo! than elsewhere on the Internet. Overall click-through rates—the percentage of people who click on banner ads—refused to rise above 2 percent; often they were lower. Conversion rates—the percentage of people who make a purchase after seeing an ad—remained minuscule. Yahoo! nonetheless charged its advertisers premium prices, which it was able to get away with because most of them were other Internet companies desperate for publicity. This was a highly questionable business model. For Yahoo! to succeed in the long run, investors would have to keep pouring money into Internet companies indefinitely, so they could keep spending it on marketing. Should Internet stocks ever falter, most of Yahoo!'s revenues would surely dry up.

The media tended to ignore such subtleties. Like Yahoo!, it was reveling in all the advertising that the Internet generated. Many publications put on new sections to accommodate the extra ads they were receiving. *The New York Times* added a weekly "Circuits" section, which was stuffed full of computer ads. *The Wall Street Journal* added a weekend section and sometimes split its first section in two. *Enter-*

*tainment Weekly* added an Internet section. *Business Week, Fortune,* and *Forbes* all expanded their coverage of technology and personal finance, the two main sources of additional advertising. Even *The New Yorker* started publishing special issues devoted to technology. Generally speaking, and with some honorable exceptions, the reporting in the new sections was tame and business-friendly, which suited the advertisers and the Internet companies just fine. For any start-up, a favorable mention in the media was valuable; for loss-making Internet companies, whose futures depended on raising more money from investors it was essential. "We happened to launch on the same day that the Communications Decency Act was dealt a fatal blow, which was great timing," Rufus Griscom, the founder of Nerve.com, later recalled. "As a result, the day that we launched it was on CNNfn; a week later we were in *Newsweek*; a month after that there was a full page on us in *Time*, and off we went. We had almost immediately several hundred thousand readers. And, in retrospect, arguably the single largest benefit of being online has been the press hype."[15] In many cases, the Internet start-ups could pick and choose which newspapers and magazines they wanted to cover them. "It was unbelievable how traditional media fell over themselves to praise and cover Internet companies," Nicholas Butterworth, the founder of SonicNet, an online music site, said. "Every day we all got streams of visitors from traditional media trying to write positive things about Web companies because their readers were demanding it. It sold magazines and made them look hip."[16]

## III

**The most enthusiastic proponents of New Economy journalism were** the technology and business magazines that sprung up in the wake of *Wired*. Louis Rossetto failed to become a media mogul, but he started a trend. By the end of the 1990s, the nation's magazine racks were groaning under the weight of magazines covering the New Economy from every conceivable angle.

In November 1995, Alan Webber and William Taylor, two editors at the *Harvard Business Review*, founded *Fast Company*, a monthly lifestyle magazine that promoted itself as a *Rolling Stone* for MBAs. Webber and Taylor started out with $200,000 of their own money, and they persuaded Mortimer Zuckerman, the owner of *Atlantic Monthly* and *U.S. News & World Report*, to back them. Their publication was a glossy incarnation of the pro-business but bomb-the-corporation ideology taught by management gurus like Peter Drucker and Tom Peters. It was devoted to the proposition that "a new generation of businesspeople is changing how people work and what work stands for; that as a result, companies are changing in fundamental ways; and that business, in turn, has become the most powerful force changing the world."[17] *Fast Company* turned Marxism on its head. In its view, workers, far from being oppressed, were being given a chance to express their individuality through their roles in the production process. In its first-anniversary issue, *Fast Company* published an article entitled "John Doerr's Startup Manual," which described the Kleiner Perkins VC as "an avatar of the Web" and highlighted some of the character traits that had made him such a success: "his unrelenting drive and competitiveness, his willingness to take huge risks and go beyond standard procedure to achieve success," and his "superhuman energy." Clearly, Doerr was *Fast Company*'s type of business executive. "There's never been a better time than now to start a new business," he told the magazine. "America honors, supports, and encourages new business. Not that it's easy. But part of the American dream is building a new business that creates jobs and financial independence."[18]

The spring and early summer of 1998 saw the appearance of two new magazines devoted exclusively to the online world. In April, the first issue of *The Industry Standard*, a San Francisco–based title that described itself as the "weekly newsmagazine of the Internet economy," hit newsstands. International Data Group (IDG), the owner of *PC World* and *Macworld*, was behind the new venture, and John Battelle, a thirty-two-year-old editor who was formerly Rossetto's deputy at *Wired*, served as its president and publisher. Battelle said *The Industry Standard*'s intended audience was "the senior-level person who wakes up at night and wonders how the Net affects my business," and he guaranteed advertisers a circulation of 60,000.[19]

*The Industry Standard* started out as a semiweekly, with plans to go weekly in 1999. Battelle hired an able and experienced staff. Jonathan Weber, a veteran technology editor at *The Los Angeles Times*, became the editor in chief. Michael Wolff, the New York Internet entrepreneur who had by now reverted to journalism, signed on as a columnist, as did Carl Steadman, the founder of Suck, an influential early Web site. James Ledbetter, *The Village Voice*'s media critic, became the new magazine's New York bureau chief. Under Weber's steady hand, *The Industry Standard* quickly established itself as a reliable and comprehensive source of reporting on the people, deals, and technological developments that kept the Internet economy humming. Its first cover story, "Domain Games," described how speculators were buying up addresses on the World Wide Web and then selling them to corporations at a big profit.

*Business 2.0*, a glossy monthly whose first issue appeared in July, was very different from *The Industry Standard*.[20] Published by Imagine Media, the owner of *PC Gamer* and several other technology magazines, it described itself as the "oracle of the New Economy," but "courtier of the New Economy" would have been more accurate. The magazine set up an "advisory board" that included Jeff Bezos, Halsey Minor, the founder of C-NET, and Jeff Mallett, the chief operating officer of Yahoo! *Business 2.0*'s editor was James Daly, another veteran of *Wired*. "The New Economy—decentralized and antihierarchical—is the most promising opportunity in years and the biggest business story of the next decade," Daly declared. "Other magazines touch on this point, but none are inspired by it." *Business 2.0*'s editorial content was dutifully reverential. In the first issue, there were profiles of "The 25 most intriguing minds of the new economy."[21]

The new Internet magazines had little trouble attracting advertising. The advertisers in the first issue of *The Industry Standard* included IBM, Anderson Consulting, Hewlett-Packard, and Silicon Graphics. In the first issue of *Business 2.0*, Netscape and IBM bought space, and so too did BMW and Absolut Vodka. This was another indication of how the Internet's reputation was changing. In the early days it had been viewed as an obscure preserve for computer nerds and other eccentrics. Now it was being promoted as a sexy and fashionable destination for affluent young things—an online Club Med.

The surge in Internet-related advertising also benefited a number of existing magazines that focused on technology, such as *Upside* and *Red Herring*, both based in San Francisco. By the beginning of 1998, *Upside* had 150,000 subscribers, and its ad-heavy issues usually ran to more than two hundred pages. *Red Herring*—the name was the slang term for an IPO prospectus—was sometimes even fatter.

The appearance of so many magazines devoted to the same subject was a classic sign of a speculative boom approaching its peak. During the mania for railways in 1840s England, the railways press expanded to include fourteen new weekly papers and two new daily papers, one for the morning and one for the evening. The list of railway titles included: *The Railway World, The Railway Express, The Railway Examiner, The Railway Globe, The Railway Standard, The Railway Mall, The Railway Engine, The Railway Telegraph, The Railway Register, The Railway Director*, and *The Railway Review*. Following the financial crash of 1847, most of these publications perished.

## IV

**The media bubble also spread to the Internet itself, despite the fact** that many early attempts to launch online magazines, such as *Slate* and *Salon*, had struggled to overcome the reluctance of Internet users to pay for editorial content. The only newspaper that enjoyed much success in attracting online subscribers was *The Wall Street Journal*. Financial information and pornography were the two items that people seemed willing to pay for online. By the start of 1998, there were tens of thousands of pornography sites, offering material catering to every taste imaginable. The Internet pornography companies pioneered a number of business tactics that later spread to mainstream Web sites, such as disabling the "back" button so people couldn't leave their site and utilizing pop-up advertisements. Two of the online sex firms were even listed on the Nasdaq: Metro Global Media, which was based in Rhode Island, and Private Media Group, a Swedish company. They reported 1998 revenues of $34 million and $20.5 million, respectively.

The market for financial information was somewhat less well served. Emboldened by the popularity of The Motley Fool and the success of the online *Wall Street Journal*, James Cramer, a journalist and investor who was a frequent guest on CNBC, decided to set up his own financial Web site, TheStreet.com, to cater to the growing number of individual investors who wanted to trade like the Wall Street professionals. "The personal computer is the communications tool that has made all the difference," Cramer wrote in his weekly column in *New York* magazine. "It has become the equalizer between amateur and professional."[22]

Cramer's multifarious activities demonstrated the blurring of the lines between journalism and Wall Street. Basically, he was a professional speculator, but he was also a prolific writer, a would-be media mogul, and an energetic self-promoter. The son of a gift-wrap salesman, he grew up in the suburbs of Philadelphia and won a scholarship to Harvard, where he edited the student newspaper, the *Crimson*. After graduating, Cramer worked for *Congressional Quarterly* in Washington, then did reporting stints at the *Tallahassee Democrat*, the *Los Angeles Herald Examiner*, and *American Lawyer*. In 1981 he returned to Harvard to attend law school, but spent much of his time watching the Financial News Network and investing in stocks. Every week, he would leave a stock pick on his dorm-room answering machine. One day, Marty Peretz, a Harvard lecturer who owns *The New Republic*, called to ask Cramer to write a book review and heard the message. After taking Cramer's stock tips for several weeks, Peretz demanded to see him at a local coffee shop, where he handed over a check for $500,000. (Peretz's wife is an heir to the Singer sewing machine fortune.) In two years, Cramer tripled Peretz's money.

After leaving Harvard, Cramer joined Goldman Sachs, where he traded stocks for wealthy clients. In 1987, he quit Goldman, and a few months later, he co-founded a hedge fund, Cramer, Berkowitz & Company, with Peretz as one of the original investors. Between 1988 and 1996, Cramer's fund made an annual return of 22 percent, compared to 15 percent for the S&P 500. Cramer made a fair amount of money, but he wasn't content to be just another Wall Street rich guy. He also wrote financial columns for a variety of publications, including *GQ, New York*, and *Worth*. Being a journalist and an investor at the same time presented obvious conflicts of interest, but Cramer shrugged them off, and he was rarely called to account. In 1995, in *Smart*

*Money*, he recommended four stocks without disclosing that his fund owned significant stakes in the companies (almost 10 percent in two cases). After the piece was published, Cramer's stock jumped in value by more than $2 million. The SEC cleared Cramer of any illegality, but the *Columbia Journalism Review* questioned his ethics. That didn't stop other magazines from continuing to employ him.

With $3 million each from Cramer and Peretz, TheStreet.com launched in November 1996. In order to placate the SEC, Cramer agreed to have nothing to do with its news coverage and to stay away from its offices. He recruited David Kansas, a reporter from *The Wall Street Journal*, as TheStreet.com's editor. The site offered financial news, online chat, and a daily column by Cramer called "Wrong!" Subscribers were charged $12.95 a month. The prospect of writing a daily column while he was running a hedge fund didn't disturb Cramer, an insomniac who arose at 3:45 A.M. each day. "We'll have stuff that will blow your mind," he told *Fortune*. "I intend to make a fortune on this."[23]

TheStreet.com didn't live up to either of those promises, but Cramer's column provided an entertaining insight into the mind of a speculator. "I am a big believer in the Internet," he said in March 1998. "I am always looking for stocks in that field."[24] Three months later, his enthusiasm for Internet stocks remained undiminished. "We simply don't have enough pieces of paper that represent the right to own future profits from the Net," he wrote.[25] Most of TheStreet.com's readers seemed to appreciate Cramer's blunt arguments, and the fact that he was backing them up with real money, but not everybody was convinced. "For the most part all we have are pieces of paper representing the right to own future losses from the Net," a subscriber named Jonathan Magulies complained in an e-mail posted on the site. "Most of these companies are bloody with red ink." To Cramer, that was the sort of antediluvian thinking that kept people poor. "There are companies whose business wouldn't exist if it weren't for the Net, and a lot of them are good businesses," he insisted a while later. "AOL is a great business: they have thirteen million subscribers. Thirteen million of anything is good. [Robert] Pittman is a genius. I think Yahoo! has a possibility of being a good business if they can execute. . . . Amazon, by virtue of the inefficiencies in our capitalist system, has a model that works. Whoever thought Amazon would be crushed by Barnes & Noble and Borders massively misjudged the market."[26]

In former times, Cramer might well have been dismissed as an engaging tout. In the late 1990s, he was invited to appear on Fox, CNN, CNBC, and ABC's *Good Morning America* to dispense investment advice to the masses. He even appeared in an advertising campaign for Rockport shoes. President Clinton wrote him a congratulatory note on his fortieth birthday, which he framed and hung in his office. (Cramer was a big contributor to the Democratic Party.) "He's on track to enter Wall Street's hall of fame for ubiquity, right alongside Brooks Brothers ties," the *New York Post* commented.[27]

Cramer portrayed himself as the embodiment of the new stock market populism—the fast-talking Jewish boy who crashed his way into Wall Street—but he wasn't quite the outsider he pretended to be. From his Harvard days onward he was friendly with plenty of powerful people, including a number of prominent journalists. Some of these journalists invested money with Cramer. The investors included Michael Kinsley, the editor of *Slate*, Kurt Andersen, a former editor of *New York*, and Hendrik Hertzberg, a senior editor at *The New Yorker*. The fact that illustrious journalists were speculating with Cramer rarely appeared in print, although it was well known in New York media circles. Many of those who knew didn't consider it newsworthy. At book launches and magazine parties, it was rare to meet anybody who wasn't heavily invested in the stock market. The gossip on such occasions often centered on how so-and-so had got in early on such-and-such a stock. Jason Epstein, the editor in chief of Random House, was said to have made a small fortune on Amazon.com Kinsley and the other *Slate* journalists had certainly made a lot of money from their Microsoft stock. The notion of journalists as observers maintaining an Olympian detachment, an idea that had always been questionable, was now a quaint myth. Like so many of their countrymen, America's journalists were enveloped in the speculative bubble up to their necks.

During previous speculative episodes, journalists and writers, unless they knew something about gold mining or biotechnology, had

enjoyed scant opportunity to get in on the action. In such circumstances, it was easy to remain aloof from the money-grubbing throng.
But the Internet boom was centered on the media industry. The sight
of Jim Cramer and others creating online businesses that seemed
headed for successful IPOs set minds racing. Many journalists came to
see themselves not as mere artisans hired to fill up the space between
advertisements but as "content providers" and would-be entrepreneurs. With the normal constraints of founding a business removed—
e.g., the requirement that the venture should have a realistic chance of
making money—the possibilities were endless. Why not set up a Web
site for women? For angry consumers? For pet owners? For space
enthusiasts? For journalists? For people who don't want to stand in
line at the Department of Motor Vehicles? Before long, all of these
businesses would exist—and journalists would write favorable articles
about many of them.

# chapter 13  greenspan's green light

## I

**In late July 1998, Alan Greenspan delivered his semi-annual report**
on monetary policy to the Senate Banking Committee. Since his previous report, in February, the Fed had kept the federal funds rate
steady, at 5.5 percent. In fact, the rate had been the same since March
1997, and it hadn't shifted by more than 0.25 percent for three years.
This do-nothing policy, which was sometimes referred to as "watch-
ful waiting," had accompanied an unprecedented economic expansion, but it had also facilitated a speculative boom that even
Greenspan, with his laissez-faire inclinations, now found disturbing.
On June 10, 1998, Goldman Sachs issued stock in Inktomi, a Silicon
Valley search engine. Inktomi operated in a crowded market, and
during the past two years its losses had outstripped its revenues. On its
first day of trading, the stock doubled. The following day,
Amazon.com announced plans to sell CDs as well as books. Its stock,
which earlier in the month had been trading at $40, raced to $100; a
few weeks later, it hit $140. Investors' appetite for Internet stocks
seemed to have no bounds. On July 17, Broadcast.com, a Dallas start-
up that posted audio and video feeds on its Web site, went public in
an IPO managed by Morgan Stanley. Broadcast.com didn't have any
of its own programming, and its site was free. For revenues, it relied
on advertising and corporate video conferencing. In 1997, the firm
had lost $6.5 million on revenues of $6.9 million. After being issued at
$18, Broadcast.com's stock closed at 62¾. This was a first-day gain of
250 percent, the biggest IPO "pop" yet.

Even on Wall Street, these events caused astonishment. It was one thing for professional investors to dabble in risky stocks, but the most aggressive speculators now appeared to be regular Americans. *The New York Times* reported that, on the streets of Manhattan, UPS drivers and taxi drivers were trading technology stocks on laptop computers and portable quotation machines. CNBC claimed its audience had increased by 75 percent in a year. The speculative mania was starting to spiral out of control. Only Greenspan had the capacity to restrain it, but his eyes were fixed on the ongoing financial upheaval in Asia. The Asian crisis began in Thailand in 1996, when the Thai government devalued the Baht, and it quickly spread to Hong Kong, Indonesia, South Korea, Malaysia, Singapore, and Taiwan. Most of these countries entered deep recessions. In the middle of 1998, Greenspan was worried that a rise in U.S. interest rates might lead to renewed chaos in Asia, which could spill over into Japan, the world's second largest economy, and, from there, to the United States. The Asian crisis had placed Greenspan in an awkward position. After sitting on the fence for a couple of years in the debate about whether there was a speculative bubble, he had now concluded that what was happening on Wall Street did, indeed, represent a bubble, at least in part. But he still didn't accept that it was the Fed's duty to burst the bubble, and his concerns about Asia reinforced this reluctance.

Some of the nation's most famous economists were calling on Greenspan to change course. "I think there is a good deal of comparison between the market in 1929 and the market today," Milton Friedman, the University of Chicago Nobel laureate, told *The New Yorker*. "I think both of them are bubbles. Whether the magnitudes are the same I don't have any idea. If anything, I suspect there is more of a bubble in today's market than there was in 1929."[1] Paul Samuelson, of MIT, who has also been to Stockholm, was equally blunt. "I define a bubble as a situation in which the level of stock prices is high because of a self-fulfilling prophecy in which people believe the market is going to go up," he said in July. "On that basis, I think there has been an element of bubble in the market for at least two years, possibly longer." By refusing to raise interest rates, Samuelson argued, Greenspan had "painted himself into a corner. He's now dealing with the physics of avalanches."[2]

Inside the Fed, Greenspan was coming under pressure from his previously quiescent colleagues. At an FOMC meeting in May 1998, there was a lively debate about whether the rise in the stock market was affecting behavior elsewhere in the economy. "Some members expressed concern that the widespread perception of reduced risk or complacency that had bolstered equity prices beyond levels that seemed justified by fundamentals were beginning to be felt in a variety of other markets as well, including commercial and residential properties, business ventures, and land," the official minutes recorded.[3] Two FOMC members—Jerry Jordan, president of the Federal Reserve Bank of Cleveland, and William Poole, president of the Federal Reserve Bank of St. Louis—voted to raise interest rates immediately. Jordan and Poole were both monetarists who believed that the recent rapid growth in the money supply was a signal of higher inflation on the way. Greenspan argued against any immediate action. The FOMC backed him by ten votes to two, but, as recorded in the official minutes, "a number of members indicated that the decision was a close call for them."[4]

Between May and July, the pace of economic growth had moderated a little, but the stock market had continued to rise. Wall Street was watching Greenspan's appearance on Capitol Hill closely for signs of what the Fed would do next. After being introduced by Al D'Amato, the chairman of the Banking Committee, Greenspan delivered a detailed presentation on the "cross-currents" affecting the economic outlook. The economy was growing too strongly, he said, but there was a reasonable chance that it would slow down of its own accord. "Failing that, firming actions on the part of the Federal Reserve may be necessary to ensure a track of expansion that is capable of being sustained." At the same time, Greenspan continued, "We need to be aware that monetary policy tightening actions in the U.S. could have outsized effects on very sensitive financial markets in Asia."[5] This was typical Greenspan: hinting at higher interest rates, but hedging his bets. The following day, the Fed chairman appeared before the House Banking Committee, where he was asked about the possibility of a stock market crash. "History tells us that there will be a correction of some significant dimension," he replied. "What it doesn't help you on very much is when."[6]

Despite the studied ambiguity of Greenspan's remarks, Wall Street decided that higher interest rates were finally on the way. The Dow fell three days in a row, slipping back below 9,000. A week later, it slumped 299 points in one session. The run-up in Internet stocks also faltered. Amazon.com fell back to below $120. Yahoo! dipped below $180. It is interesting to speculate what might have happened next if happenings overseas hadn't intervened. The stock market boom was posited on the belief that Greenspan would keep interest rates low, an assumption that had now been challenged. The next meeting of the FOMC was scheduled for late August. If the Fed had raised interest rates at that meeting, stocks would undoubtedly have fallen. It is impossible to know just how severe the sell-off would have been, but the bullish sentiment would have been badly dented. It is conceivable that the Internet stock boom would have come to an end then and there. More likely, several interest rate hikes would have been necessary to burst the bubble. Either way, the next two years would have looked very different.

## II

As it was, international events prompted Greenspan to hold off from raising interest rates, and the parade of Internet IPOs continued. On August 11, 1998, GeoCities, an online community based in Santa Monica, California, went public. GeoCities encouraged people to use its Web site to publish home pages, which it then grouped into forty different "neighborhoods," each with its own chat room. About 2 million people had already set up pages on the site, many of them containing pictures of their families and pets, and GeoCities had turned into the sixth most popular destination on the Web. In June 1998, it had 14 million visitors. The company had lost $8.9 million on revenues of just $4.6 million in 1997, but that didn't concern most investors. In Internet terms, GeoCities had a solid pedigree. CMG Information Services, the Boston venture capital firm that had financed Lycos, was one of its big investors, and Goldman Sachs was underwriting the stock issue. The financial chat rooms were full of speculation that GeoCities' IPO would be another Broadcast.com.

This didn't quite happen, but the stock went from $17 to $37, and that on a day when both the Dow and the Nasdaq fell.

Six days later, on August 17, President Clinton testified to the grand jury investigating the Lewinsky affair and went on television to admit misleading the public earlier in the year. In Moscow, the Russian government, led by Sergei Kiriyenko, the youthful prime minister, devalued the ruble and reneged on some of its debts. The move shocked international investors and angered ordinary Russians, who saw the value of their savings slashed by half. A few days later, Boris Yeltsin, Russia's president, fired Kiriyenko and recalled Victor Chernomyrdin, whom he had fired a few months earlier. The Russian devaluation sparked an international financial crisis that President Clinton, speaking a month later, would describe as the "biggest financial challenge facing the world in a half-century."

All around the world, financial markets shuddered, stabilized, then shuddered again. On Tuesday, August 31, the Dow fell by 513 points—its second-biggest points drop. The Nasdaq dropped 140.43 points—its biggest points fall. Internet stocks were particularly hard hit. Excite and Amazon.com both fell by more than 20 percent, Yahoo! and America Online by about 15 percent. Stocks bounced back the next day, as investors followed their usual pattern of buying the dips, but then fell again for three days in a row. At the week's end, *Time* published a cover showing figures falling off a cliff-shaped stock chart, with the headline: "IS THE BOOM OVER?" With Asia already in a slump, Russia in turmoil, and Latin America teetering, there were widespread fears of a global depression developing.[7]

All eyes turned to Greenspan. After being pressed for months to raise interest rates, he now found himself being urged to cut them in order to calm the markets. Political leaders seemed powerless to act. Bill Clinton flew to Moscow to meet Boris Yeltsin, but the summit turned into near farce, with the American president being heckled by Vladimir Zhirinovsky, the ultranationalist Russian politician. "Clinton, you are an idiot!" Zhirinovsky roared. "Your dollar is dirt." On Wall Street, there were many who could feel Zhirinovsky's pain. Investors had taken massive losses as stock and bond markets the world over slumped. The biggest victims were hedge funds like George Soros's Quantum Fund, which had lost $2 billion in a few weeks, and Long Term Capital Management, a Greenwich-based fund, which had lost a similar amount.

On September 4, Greenspan said in a speech that it was "just not credible that the United States can remain an oasis of prosperity unaffected by a world that is experiencing greatly increased stress."[8] This was a clear suggestion that lower interest rates were being considered, but Wall Street was too addled to be reassured by hints. The financial markets were in chaos. Currencies and bond prices that usually moved together were racing apart. Lenders were cutting off funds to borrowers. On September 20, Long Term Capital Management, which had placed big bets all over the world that were now turning sour, informed the Fed that it was on the brink of bankruptcy and might have to unwind tens of billions of dollars' worth of investments. Bill McDonough, the chairman of the New York Fed, was worried that such a move might spark outright panic. Long Term was no ordinary financial firm. John Meriweather, a legendary bond trader, had set it up; two Nobel laureate economists were partners in it; and the Italian central bank, along with many wealthy individuals, had invested in it. Until its recent troubles, Long Term had been widely believed to be invincible. On Tuesday, September 22, McDonough summoned representatives from Wall Street's top firms, many of which had lent money to Long Term, and asked them to bail out the stricken fund. Many of the Wall Street chieftains were reluctant to help out a rival that had got itself into trouble, but under strong pressure from the Fed they agreed to come up with $3.5 billion in return for ownership and control of the firm.

Greenspan, meanwhile, gathered his FOMC colleagues on a conference call and told them he wanted to cut interest rates. Two days later, he went to Capitol Hill and all but announced that a policy easing was on the way. "I think we know where we have to go," he said.[9] The Dow, which had slipped below 8,000, immediately jumped 257 points. Wall Street was hoping that the Fed was ready to take dramatic remedial action. On September 29, the FOMC met and cut the federal funds rate from 5.5 percent to 5.25 percent. In a statement, it said the move was intended "to cushion the effects on prospective economic growth in the United States of increasing weakness in foreign economies and less accommodative financial conditions domestically."[10] After the announcement, the Dow fell by 100 points. Traders had been expecting a bigger interest rate reduction, and they were disappointed that the Fed had made no mention of further moves. During the next two weeks, the financial markets in the United States and abroad gyrated wildly. Internet stocks were some of the biggest losers. By the second week of October, Amazon.com and America Online were both 40 percent off their highs. Yahoo! was down 20 percent. GeoCities had fallen by 75 percent since its recent IPO. The new IPO market had virtually closed down, with more than twenty issues either postponed or canceled. Of more immediate concern to Greenspan, government and corporate bonds continued to be riled by unusual price movements, as investors fled from anything smacking of risk. For many pension funds and other institutional investors, bonds are just as important as stocks, maybe more so, because they are supposed to be safer. But amid the panic many investors were refusing to buy any but the safest of U.S. government bonds. In a speech to the National Association of Business Economics, Greenspan warned that uncertainty and fear were prompting investors to "disengage" from the financial markets, a development that, if sustained, could lead to a disastrous credit crunch.[11]

On October 15, in another conference call, Greenspan told his colleagues he intended to cut interest rates again. It was highly unusual for the Fed to change policy between FOMC meetings, but Greenspan thought the situation merited such a move. He didn't even ask for a vote. In a statement issued shortly after 3 P.M., the Fed announced another quarter-point reduction in the federal funds rate, saying it was a response to "growing caution by lenders and unsettled conditions in financial markets more generally." This time, investors were more impressed. The Dow jumped 200 points before the close. Wall Street interpreted the rate cut as a signal that the Fed would do whatever was necessary to restore stability to the markets. Stephen Slifer, an economist at Lehman Brothers, commented: "Without actually saying it, Greenspan is saying: 'We're going to supply liquidity to the system, and we're going to keep the U.S. economy out of recession in 1999.'"[12]

III

**The analysts had read Greenspan's mind correctly. In cutting interest** rates when there was little sign that the American economy was in trouble—GDP grew at an annual rate of more than 3 percent in the third quarter of 1998—Greenspan demonstrated the primacy of Wall Street interests in the Fed's deliberations. The financial troubles of George Soros and John Meriweather had little to do with ordinary Americans. Much of the money lost in Russia, Asia, and elsewhere had been invested in high-risk ventures by people who could afford to lose it. The losses in the U.S. stock market were more widely shared, but they were hardly catastrophic. Taking the past five years, the Dow was still up by more than 100 percent. In easing policy in such circumstances, Greenspan seemed to indicate that his policy of not letting the financial markets dictate monetary policy only applied while prices were rising. When prices had started falling, Greenspan had quickly changed policy. His actions added to the growing belief that the Fed would always be there to bail out investors if anything went wrong, and this made investors even more willing to take risks.

The tendency for people to act recklessly when they don't think they will suffer if things turn out badly is known to economists as "moral hazard." Moral hazard is often associated with insurance markets—car owners with insurance, for example, tend to drive less carefully than those without insurance—but it also applies to the financial markets. In allowing investors to look to him as a potential savior, Greenspan, however inadvertently, ended up further inflating the Internet bubble. The two interest rate reductions confirmed to many people on Wall Street that in a crisis the Fed chairman could be relied upon to take prompt and dramatic action to protect their interests. As Bill Dudley, the chief economist at Goldman Sachs, commented after the second rate cut: "This is a way of telling everyone, the lifeguard is back on duty; you can go back in the pool."[13]

The bulls hardly needed persuading. "We feel the cyclical bear market is over," Ralph Acampora, of Prudential Securities, announced on October 28.[14] Abby Joseph Cohen, of Goldman Sachs, reaffirmed her year-end target of 9,300 for the Dow. James Cramer said that it was time to start buying Internet stocks again. Prices might be crazy, he conceded, but they were going to get crazier. If the e-mails posted on TheStreet.com's Web site were any guide, most individual investors shared Cramer's view. Scott Worcester, an active Internet stock trader, wrote: "I agree, things are bound to get even crazier. After all, I sold my Excite at 39½ after thinking it hit major resistance at 40, and a few days later it goes through the roof! Yeah, probably now is the time to buy. The market makes suckers out of all of us." One J. B. Bauk was equally upbeat, declaring: "We are about to enter phase two of Internet stock mania."[15]

# chapter 14 euphoria

I

**The interest rate cuts in the fall of 1998 marked the transition from** the boom stage of the speculative bubble to euphoria. The peak of a speculative mania is a sight to behold. In the scramble to cash in before it is too late, all prior reasoning, sentiment, and knowledge count for naught. Only the twisted logic of the market matters. "I have enquired of some that have come from London, what is the religion there?" Jonathan Swift, who lived in Dublin, wrote during the South Sea bubble of 1720. "They tell me it is South Sea stock; what is the policy of England? the answer is the same, what is the trade? South Sea still; and what is the business? Nothing but South Sea."[1] Alexander Pope, when he wasn't lamenting this "miserable mercenary Period," was busy speculating with the rest.[2] Sir Isaac Newton, after selling his South Sea stock early in the year, reentered the market at a higher price and ended up losing twenty thousand pounds. Edward Harley, whose brother Robert founded the South Sea Company, described the atmosphere in London in colorful terms: "The demon stock jobbing is the genius of this place. This fills all hearts, tongues, and thoughts, and nothing is so like bedlam as the present humor which has seized all parties, Whigs, Tories, Jacobites, Papists, and all sects. No one is satisfied with even exorbitant gains, but everyone thirsts for more, and all this is founded upon a machine of paper credit supported only by imagination."[3]

The parallels between the South Sea bubble and the Internet bubble are striking. According to the historian Edward Chancellor, who supplied the quotes above, a total of 190 "bubble" companies were founded during 1720, of which four survived. The epic stage of the Internet bubble lasted from October 1998 to April 2000. During that period, more than 300 Internet firms did IPOs. At the end of 2001 most of them were still alive, but the attrition rate was high. During both speculative episodes, the sight of rising prices destroyed people's judgment. In 1720, Englishmen openly referred to the new companies as "bubbles," but that didn't prevent them from venturing to the City of London and handing over money. As the poet Edward Ward wrote:

> Few Men, who follow Reason's Rules,
> Grow Fat with South-Sea Diet,
> Young Rattles and unthinking Fools
> Are those that flourish by it.[4]

During the Internet bubble, similar reasoning was at work. Most people knew that Internet stocks were overvalued, but they couldn't resist joining the speculative horde, which, in many cases, included their friends, neighbors, and family members. All across the country, Americans who thought of themselves as sensible, upstanding citizens had watched their cousins and coworkers and even, in some cases, mothers-in-law making big profits on stocks like Excite, Yahoo!, and Amazon.com. "There is nothing so disturbing to one's well-being and judgment as to see a friend get rich," Charles Kindleberger, the MIT historian of financial manias, used to tell his pupils.[5] Refusing to buy Internet stocks, which had at first seemed to be a matter of mere common sense, was turning out to be costly and embarrassing. The most respected voices at the local parents association or poker group were those that had bought Internet stocks back in 1995 and 1996, while the voices of caution were being laughed at. Should there be another wave of speculative madness, as people like James Cramer were predicting, many people who had previously remained on the sidelines were determined to join in.

## II

**In late October and early November 1998, Internet stocks shot up,** none more dramatically than eBay. The online auctioneer had been the only Internet firm to go public during the international financial crisis. On September 24, 1998, Goldman Sachs issued 3.5 million eBay shares at $18, and the stock closed at 47⅜, a first-day pop of about 160 percent. This sterling performance amid an investor panic reflected the widespread fascination with eBay's Web site, on which everything from Beanie Babies to tropical islands was being sold to the highest bidder. EBay was one of the few online ventures that exploited the Internet to provide a service that couldn't otherwise have been provided; and it was also one of the few Internet IPO candidates to have recorded a profit: $215,000 on revenues of $14.9 million in the first half of 1999.

Pierre Omidyar, a thirty-one-year-old Silicon Valley entrepreneur who left France when he was six, founded eBay in September 1995. According to many media accounts of the firm's genesis, Omidyar was motivated by his girlfriend, who complained that she didn't have enough trading partners for her growing collection of Pez dispensers. Randall Stross, in his exhaustively researched book *eBoys*, tells a fuller and more convincing story.[6] During a previous incarnation, as the cofounder of Ink Development, a company that made software for pen-based computers, Omidyar oversaw the development of a back-end system to handle sales and accounting. In 1995, he decided, on a whim, to write some software that would allow people selling things online to conduct an electronic auction. He posted the service on a home page, which he called www.AuctionWeb, and let people use it for nothing. Omidyar didn't do any advertising, but word of his new site spread, and by the end of 1995 it was getting a couple of thousand hits a day.

In February 1996, Omidyar started charging sellers a small fee. Within a few months he was taking in $10,000 a month, which represented the commissions on the sales of fishing lures, coins, rare magazines, golf clubs, and all sorts of things. He left his day job, changed the site's name to eBay, and recruited a partner Jeff Skoll, a Canadian-born engineer, to help him run it. In the continued absence of any marketing, the number of listings was doubling every two months. In the fall of 1996, Omidyar approached Bruce Dunlevie, a VC he had worked with while he was at Ink Development. Dunlevie was now a partner at Benchmark Capital, a newish firm that had been founded in 1995. Dunlevie introduced Omidyar to one of his colleagues, Bob Kagle, who, after some initial reluctance, agreed to invest about $5 million for a 20 percent stake in eBay.

The $5 million turned into the best venture capital investment of all time. In early 1998, Meg Whitman, a senior executive at Hasbro, the toy manufacturer, agreed to join eBay as chief executive in preparation for an IPO later in the year. Whitman had never heard of eBay, but its growth rate impressed her, and so did its business model. Unlike Amazon.com and most other e-commerce companies, eBay had no inventory or shipping costs. It really was a purely virtual company. It brought the buyer and seller together, charged the seller a commission of between 1.25 percent and 5 percent, then left the two parties to sort out how to get the auctioned good from point A to point B. As a result, its gross profit margins were about 90 percent.

One of Whitman's first jobs was to hold a bake-off of investment banks for the job of managing eBay's IPO, which was scheduled for September 1998. After a lackluster presentation by Morgan Stanley's team, which was led by Mary Meeker, Whitman chose Goldman Sachs. In August, as Omidyar and Whitman set out on the inevitable investor road show, the Russian financial crisis erupted. There was some speculation that the stock issue would have to be postponed, as many others had been, but Goldman pressed ahead. EBay's story was so compelling that investors were willing to listen to it even during a panic. More than a million people had now used the auction site, and a dedicated community of users had grown up. At any one time, about 80 percent of the traffic on eBay came from repeat visitors. By the end of the road show, Goldman was confident it could sell the 3.5 million shares eBay was planning to issue several times over. On the evening of September 23, the shares were priced at $18, valuing eBay at $700 million.

The following morning, before Goldman had handled a single trade, Mary Meeker issued a strong buy recommendation for eBay, an unprecedented move for an analyst at a rival firm. In a report initiating coverage of the new stock, Meeker wrote: "EBay is defining a

new market that pulls together many of the key attributes of the best
Internet companies: content (created by users), community, commerce, unprecedented broad-based links between buyers and sellers of
goods, and, importantly, fun/entertainment/thrill of the hunt." And
Meeker went on: "EBay's market opportunity is huge."[7] When the
stock eventually opened, the first trade took place at $54. Later in the
day, the stock fell back slightly, but at the closing price of 47⅜ eBay
was valued at almost $1.7 billion. When the overall market stabilized
in late October, the stock rallied strongly, boosted by more buy recommendations. On October 26, Jamie Kiggen, of Donaldson, Lufkin
& Jenrette issued a twelve-month price target of $100. The stock sur-
passed that milestone in ten days. On November 10, Michael Parekh
and Rakesh Sood of Goldman Sachs raised their price target to $150,
and the stock jumped 27¹⁵⁄₁₆ to 130⅞. At this point, eBay had a market
capitalization of $4.6 billion, and Benchmark Capital's stake was
worth more than $900 million.

Also on November 10, stock in K-Tel International jumped 8⅝,
or 75 percent, to 20¼. After surging to over $40 earlier in the year
when it had announced plans to sell music over the Internet, K-Tel's
stock had collapsed during the summer. But investors were now snapping it up again because Microsoft Network had agreed to feature
K-Tel on its shopping channel. With Internet stocks rising again, the
investment bankers quickly relaunched some of the IPOs that they
had been forced to postpone over the previous couple of months.
Every big bank on Wall Street was now competing for Internet business. If Morgan Stanley and Goldman Sachs turned a company down,
it could go across town to Credit Suisse First Boston (where Frank
Quattrone and his team were now based, having moved on from
Deutsche Morgan Grenfell), Merrill Lynch, or any of a dozen other
firms.

On November 11, Veteran's Day, J. P. Morgan issued 2.1 million
shares in EarthWeb, a New York–based Internet company that published information online about the computer industry. Jack and
Murray Hidary, two brothers from Ocean Parkway, Brooklyn,
founded EarthWeb. In the first half of 1998, it had lost $5.3 million
on revenues of $1.9 million, but that didn't matter to investors. The
eBay offering aside, EarthWeb's Wall Street debut was the first chance

for investors to get in on an Internet IPO for months. The stock jumped from $14 to 48¹¹⁄₁₆, a rise of about 250 percent, the second biggest first-day gain ever, behind Broadcast.com. On paper, the Hidarys were worth $65 million each.

Two days after EarthWeb's IPO, Bear Stearns issued 3.1 million shares in TheGlobe.com, an online community that two Cornell science majors, Todd Krizelman and Stephan Paternot, formed in their dorm room in 1995. Like GeoCities, which had gone public earlier in the year, TheGlobe.com encouraged people to set up home pages on its site and hoped to make money by selling advertising. The first part of the strategy worked pretty well. When it filed to go public, TheGlobe.com had more than 2 million members. But advertising remained scarce. In the first nine months of 1998, TheGlobe.com's revenues came to just $2.7 million, and it lost $11.5 million. Even on the Internet, losing $4 for every $1 in revenue was notable.

Bear Stearns was a new name to Internet IPOs. The firm only got the opportunity to take TheGlobe.com public after several more established firms turned it down. Bear's investment bankers were determined to break into the Internet business, regardless of the risks. In October, they were forced to postpone the IPO because they couldn't find enough buyers for 3.1 million TheGlobe.com shares. A month later, after hurriedly resurrecting the stock issue, they were rewarded for their recklessness. This time, they had more than enough buying interest. On the morning of November 13, a Friday, Bear issued the shares at $9 each to its most favored clients. It then faced the tricky task of trying to maintain an orderly market when trading started. There was a massive imbalance in buy and sell orders. Tens of thousands of small investors had placed orders to buy TGLO "at market," which means at whatever price the stock is trading at when the order gets filled. Professional investors usually place "limit orders," which stipulate a price beyond which they won't trade, but many of the investors trying to buy TheGlobe.com's stock were new to the game, and they didn't realize the risks they were taking. In these circumstances, Bear's traders found it difficult to establish a floor for the first trade. Whatever price they indicated—$20, $30, $40, $50—was too low. CNBC reported that the first trade might be at $70, but even this proved to be a conservative estimate. After a lengthy delay, the first trade took place at $87—almost ten times the issue price. Even for an Internet stock, this was unheard of. Within an hour, the price had risen to $97. Everybody on Wall Street knew that this price couldn't be sustained, and the smart money started to sell. "I sold my TGLO at 88—who wouldn't?" Seth Tobias, a hedge fund manager, told TheStreet.com.[8] Another professional investor who sold at $90 and made a quick profit of $65,000 said: "I've had days similar to this, but this definitely feels good."[9]

As the professionals sold, the only purchasers were the individual investors who had placed orders to buy "at market" and were therefore buying blindly. By the close of trading, TheGlobe.com's stock had dropped back to $63.50. Even at this price, the stock had risen more than 600 percent, by far the biggest first-day gain in Wall Street history. *The New York Post* hailed Krizelman and Paternot as the latest "net geeks" to strike gold—their stakes were worth about $50 million each on paper.[10] This was true, but the real story was that the IPO market had veered out of control. On the following Monday, TheGlobe.com's stock fell to $48. Within a week, it was down to $32. Anybody who had bought shares on the first morning and held on to them had suffered a big loss.

## III

On November 17, 1998, just four days after TheGlobe.com's astonishing IPO, the Fed cut interest rates again, from 5.0 percent to 4.75 percent. It was the third rate cut in six weeks—the sort of policy shift usually reserved for recessions. The American economy was growing strongly, but Greenspan was still worried about the financial markets, in particular the bond markets, where prices hadn't fully returned to normal. "Although conditions in financial markets have settled down materially since mid-October, unusual strains remain," the FOMC said in a statement.[11] This was true, but in the stock market prices were straining in an upward direction, and Internet stocks were breaking free of any remaining ties. In cutting interest rates in such circumstances, Greenspan confirmed in the minds of many investors that he tacitly approved of what was happening.

Even the news that Netscape, the original Internet firm, had been forced to give up its independence didn't stop the rally in Internet stocks. At the end of November, America Online announced that it was acquiring Netscape for $4.2 billion in stock. The deal marked the final submission in Netscape's losing battle with Microsoft. In August 1995, at the time of Netscape's IPO, the Netscape Navigator Web browser had had a market share of about 80 percent; now it was trailing the Internet Explorer. As a firm, Netscape was concentrating on other areas of its business, including its Netcenter site and its e-commerce division. One of the main reasons that America Online bought the company was because of its popular Web site.

Since mid-October, the tactics that Microsoft had used to over-take Netscape Navigator had been the subject of daily jousts in a Washington courtroom, where Judge Thomas Penfield Jackson was hearing *United States v. Microsoft*, the Department of Justice's antitrust suit against Bill Gates's company. The government had filed suit back in May 1998, accusing Microsoft of illegally exploiting its Windows monopoly to strangle Netscape. The legal details and ramifications of the Microsoft case have already filled several books, but its economic significance can be summarized quickly. Internet Explorer's success demonstrated that many of the arguments used to rationalize the valuations of companies like Netscape, Yahoo!, and Amazon.com were deeply suspect. Microsoft had proved that in the Web browser part of the Internet economy, at least, the barriers to entry were low, and "first mover advantage" was a lot less important than deep pockets and overall clout in related markets. George Gilder's 1995 suggestion that Netscape was going to break Microsoft's grip on the computer industry now sounded like a bad joke, although Marc Andreessen tried to put a brave face on things. "This ought to be the preeminent Internet company over the next decade," he told *The New York Times* the day after Netscape's merger with America Online was announced.[12] As it happened, Andreessen was to be proved correct, but neither he nor Netscape would have much to do with the success of the merged company.

On November 28, the Nasdaq closed above 2,000 for the first time. Since the end of September, it had risen by more than 500 points. Five days later, the next Internet stock on the Wall Street conveyor belt, Ticketmaster Online–CitySearch, reached the Nasdaq. Earlier in the year, CitySearch, a publisher of online listings, had been planning to hold its own IPO, but the summer slump in Internet stocks put paid to that idea. In desperate need of money, it turned to Ticketmaster Online, the online arm of the well-known ticket agency. Ticketmaster was part of USA Networks, the owner of the USA cable channel. Barry Diller, the Hollywood executive who had tried to buy Paramount Pictures a few years back, was now the chairman of USA Networks, and he retained an eye for a deal. In September 1998, Diller merged Ticketmaster Online with CitySearch and hired some investment bankers from NationsBanc Montgomery Securities to offload the combined company to the public. In financial terms, it looked like a disaster area, with revenues in the first nine months of 1999 of $27 million and operating losses of $57.4 million, but, being an Internet company, this didn't matter much. The stock was priced at $14, and on the first day of trading it jumped to $40.25, a rise of 187.5 percent, valuing Ticketmaster Online–CitySearch at $2.7 billion. Given all of the recent competition, this was only good enough for fifth place on the all-time list of first-day gains, but it did lead some newspapers to resurrect their "Diller Sizzle" headlines.

It was getting difficult to keep track of all the Internet IPOs. During the two weeks after Diller's coup, there were another six of them; uBid, Internet America, Xoom, AboveNet, Infospace.com, and audiohighway.com. Some of these companies were little more than clever names. Audiohighway.com, a California provider of downloadable audio content, had garnered revenues of just $87,000 in the first nine months of 1998—less than a busy newsstand would have taken in. There were now so many Internet stocks that special stock indices were being set up to track their performance. Dow Jones launched the Dow Jones Internet Composite Index, which included a broad range of Internet issues. TheStreet.com set up TheStreet.com Internet Sector. "In an emerging and dynamic industry like the Internet, TheStreet.com Internet Sector gives investors the opportunity to track, trade, and invest in the aggregate performance of the Internet sector's biggest players," Keith English, TheStreet.com's chief executive, said in a statement.[13]

The new stock indices helped to maintain the illusion that the Internet was a regular business sector, just like the transportation sector or the drugs sector, with its own internal logic, metrics, and authorities. One of the latter was Henry Blodget, a thirty-three-year-old stock analyst at CIBC Oppenheimer, a small Wall Street brokerage owned by a Canadian bank. Blodget, a tall fellow with blue eyes and a shock of blond hair, was a Yale history major and a former fact-checker at *Harper's* magazine who only turned to Wall Street after his journalistic ambitions didn't pan out. He didn't have an MBA, but he did have a genius for publicity. On the evening of December 15, 1998, he issued a $400 price target for Amazon.com. The stock had just closed above $242, a price most old-timers considered outrageous. In attempting to justify his $400 target, Blodget admitted that he was on somewhat shaky ground, since Amazon.com's stock was already *"incredibly expensive."*[14] Nevertheless, he went on, "Amazon's valuation is clearly more art than science, and we believe that the stock will continue to be driven higher in large part by the company's astounding revenue momentum."[15] In its most recent quarter, Amazon.com's revenues had tripled compared to the same quarter in 1997. Since launching its music store earlier in the year, it had sold more CDs than all other online stores combined. Blodget interpreted this as evidence that Amazon.com could become the Wal-Mart of the Web. If Amazon.com could replicate Wal-Mart's 10 percent share of the discount retailing market in the $100 billion market for books, music, and videos, it would have annual revenues of $10 billion. Assuming it could also achieve a profit margin of 7 percent, it would earn $700 million a year. Applying to these earnings a PE multiple of 30, a relatively modest one for technology companies, Amazon.com would be worth about $21 billion, or about $400 a share.

Blodget's arithmetic was sound, but everything else about his valuation model was suspect. In its latest quarter, Amazon.com had lost $50 million. The company's capacity to generate any profit at all was questionable, let alone a net margin of 7 percent. Even the most profitable retailers, such as Wal-Mart, have net margins below 5 percent. Blodget's timing was excellent, however. Three months earlier, Amazon.com's stock had been trading below $100. Lately, it had rallied strongly as investors focused on its rapid revenue growth. On December 16, after Blodget's $400 price target hit the news wires, Amazon.com's stock jumped 46¼, to $289. At this price, Amazon.com was capitalized at $15.3 billion, almost as much as Sears. Things didn't stop there. With the media full of stories about holiday shopping online, Amazon.com was getting even more free publicity than usual. Mary Meeker added to the fervor when, in an interview with *Barron's*, she compared the firm's rapid growth to the early days of America Online. In the first week of the New Year—less than a month after Blodget made his seemingly outlandish prediction—Amazon.com's stock, which had just split three for one, topped $400 on a pre-split basis.

Blodget was hailed as a visionary. Jonathan Cohen, his rival at Merrill Lynch, looked more like a chump. A couple of days after Blodget's attention-grabbing move, Cohen had described Amazon.com as "probably the single most expensive piece of equity ever, not just for Internet stocks but for any stock in the history of modern equity markets." Unlike Blodget, who treated Amazon.com as a technology company, Cohen looked on it as a retailer, with the normal retailer's task of managing inventory, distribution, and marketing expenses. Even the most successful retailers have relatively low stock market valuations. Wal-Mart, for example, had a market capitalization that was equal to about 1.5 times its annual revenues. Cohen believed that Amazon, which had lower costs than a bricks-and-mortar retailer, should trade at a revenue multiple of somewhere between two and four. Using this valuation model as his guide, he predicted that within twelve months Amazon.com's stock would fall back to $50. Early in 1999, with the stock trading at more than $500 on a pre-split basis, Cohen resigned and moved to Wit Capital, an online brokerage. Blodget took Cohen's old job at Merrill Lynch, whose senior executives were now determined to break into the Internet IPO business. In hiring Blodget, they were hoping to create their own version of Mary Meeker.

## IV

**"If there must be madness," John Kenneth Galbraith wrote of Sep-**tember 1929, when the ill-fated Shenandoah and Blue Ridge investment trusts made their debut, "something may be said for having it on a heroic scale."[16] By the start of 1999, Galbraith, witty and articulate still at ninety, had his wish fulfilled. Henry Blodget's rise marked the final defeat for the already depleted ranks of reason and common sense. In the middle of January, CBS.Marketwatch.com, a financial news site, went public. After being priced at $17, its stock jumped to $130, before closing at 97½, a first-day gain of almost 500 percent. A few days later, At Home, the Kleiner Perkins start-up that offered high-speed access to the Internet, agreed to buy Excite, the Kleiner Perkins search-engine-turned-portal, for $6 billion in stock. Excite was the sixth most popular site on the Web, but it was still bleeding money. On January 28, Yahoo! announced that it was acquiring GeoCities for $3.6 billion in stock—a price that was more than 300 times GeoCities' 1998 revenues of $18.4 million.

If these events had given Alan Greenspan pause, he didn't let it show. At the end of January, during an appearance on Capitol Hill, Senator Ron Wyden, an Oregon Democrat, asked the Fed chairman how much of the Internet stock boom was "based on sound fundamentals and how much is based on hype?" This was how Greenspan replied to Wyden's question:

First of all, you wouldn't get "hype" working if there weren't something fundamentally, potentially sound under it.

The size of that potential market is so huge that you have these pie-in-the-sky type of potentials for a lot of different (firms). Undoubtedly, some of these small companies whose stock prices are going through the roof will succeed. And they may very well justify even higher prices. The vast majority are almost sure to fail. That's the way the markets tend to work in this regard.

There is something else going on here, though, which is a fascinating thing to watch. It is, for want of a better term, the "lottery principle." What lottery managers have known for centuries is that you could get somebody to pay for a one-in-a-million shot more than the value of that chance. In other words, people pay more for a claim on a very big pay-off, and that's where the profits from lotteries have always come from. So there is a lottery premium built into the prices of Internet stocks.

But there is at root here something far more fundamental—the stock market seeking out profitable ventures and directing capital to hopeful projects before the profits materialize. That's good for our system. And that, in fact, with all of its hype and craziness, is something that, at the end of the day, probably is more plus than minus.[17]

The language was awkward, but the meaning of "the Fed's gentle genius" (which is how *USA Today* described Greenspan a few weeks after he made this statement) couldn't have been clearer if he had been filmed buying a hundred shares of Amazon.com: investing in Internet stocks didn't just make sense; it was good for America.[18]

From an investor's perspective, the key question was for how long the rise in stock prices could be maintained. America Online was now worth more than Time Warner, the biggest entertainment company in the country. Even the most bullish Internet analysts didn't seriously attempt to defend this sort of valuation. The only way it could be rationalized was to think of Internet stocks as a parallel currency that was convertible to U.S. dollars on a one-to-one basis. When America Online paid $4.2 billion for Netscape, At Home paid $6 billion for Excite, and Yahoo! paid $3.6 billion for GeoCities, they didn't pay with cash: they used their stocks as currency. In U.S. dollars, the prices paid were beyond reason. In Internet dollars, they made a certain amount of sense. Investors were valuing online businesses on the basis of how many eyeballs their Web sites attracted. By joining together, Internet firms could claim a bigger audience and, thereby, give their stock prices yet another boost.

Any currency that is expanded recklessly—be it the German mark during the 1920s, or the U.S. dollar during the 1960s—is sure to be devalued at some point, because investors will eventually lose faith in it. In the case of U.S. dollars, the Fed bank controls the rate of expansion, and it usually does a decent job of retaining the currency's value. But the supply of Internet stocks was determined by VCs and investment bankers, both of whom had a strong incentive to speed up the printing presses, which is precisely what they were doing. If they were to keep this up, they would eventually flood the market, but for the moment this seemed like a remote danger. On February 10, 1998, there were three more Internet IPOs, each one representing a different aspect of the online dream.

Prodigy, the online service that IBM and Sears had launched with high hopes back in 1989, represented the inglorious past. In ten years, it had lost more than $300 million. Now owned by Global Telecom, an international telephone company, it could boast just 500,000 subscribers, and it had lost another $15 million in the latest quarter. Even in early 1999, marketing such a firm to the public was no trifling matter. Prodigy turned to Bear Stearns, which, following its success with the TheGlobe.com, was becoming known as the investment bank that did the deals others wouldn't. Once again, Bear didn't disappoint. It issued 8 million shares in Prodigy at $15 each, and the stock closed at $28.125.

VerticalNet, a Pennsylvania start-up that operated Web sites with names like adhesivesandsealants.com, testandmeasurement.com, and meatandpoultryonline.com, represented the boundless future. On Wall Street, and in the media, B2B (business to business) commerce was being touted as the next big thing. (Something had to be found to replace broadband communication, which hadn't lived up to the billing.) The ever-optimistic Forrester Research was predicting that B2B commerce, which included the online sales of everything from steel ingots to printing paper, would grow to $1.3 trillion by 2003. VerticalNet seemed poised to exploit this growth trend, despite the fact that its 1998 revenues came to just $3.1 million. Lehman Brothers issued 3.5 million shares in the company at $16, and they closed at 45⅜.

Healtheon, the third Internet IPO of the day, was very much of the present: it represented the IPO hat-trick attempt by Jim Clark, the founder of Netscape and Silicon Graphics. Clark started Healtheon in 1995 after he stepped down from running Netscape. From day one, it was a firm long on concept and short on marketable products. Michael Lewis, in his book *The New New Thing*, described how Healtheon started life as a blank piece of paper with a diamond on it.[19] At the corners of the diamond, Clark wrote four words: Payers, Doctors, Providers, and Consumers. In the middle, he placed an asterisk. The asterisk represented the new company, which would somehow link the corners, representing a sixth of the American economy, in an online network. Armed with his Magic Diamond, Clark went to see the VCs on Sand Hill Road and announced that he planned to "fix the U.S. health care system," a challenge that had recently bested Bill and Hillary Clinton.

Given Clark's success with Silicon Graphics and Netscape he could have announced that he was going to commercialize space travel and he would have been inundated with offers of money. The only question was which VCs he would allow to back him. He chose Kleiner Perkins, which had backed Netscape, and New Enterprise Associates, which had backed Silicon Graphics. Using the VCs' money, and some of his own, Clark hired some Indian software engineers and told them to get on with it. What the "it" was remained something of a puzzle, not least to Healtheon's own employees, many of whom had no idea how the U.S. health care industry worked. When the Indians wrote their first piece of software, Blue Cross Blue Shield of Massachusetts declined to buy it. Other customers proved equally reticent. Nevertheless, in the fall of 1998, Morgan Stanley tried to take Healtheon public. It was a reuniting of the Netscape team, but given the international financial crisis, the timing was off. *The Wall Street Journal* didn't help matters with a front-page story pointing out that many of the problems facing the health care industry, such as the rising cost of drugs, had nothing to do with the Internet—and, even if they did, Healtheon's software wasn't finished.[20] At the end of October, after Clark and Mike Long, Healtheon's chief executive, had traversed Europe and the United States on a disastrous investor road show, Morgan pulled the IPO.

Healtheon needed more money to meet its payroll. Clark was still convinced that investors would eventually see the magic in his diamond, and he put up another $20 million. At the start of 1999, with Internet IPOs soaring again, he was proved right. This time, Morgan Stanley didn't even bother with a road show. It simply invited some big investors to Silicon Valley, where Mike Long delivered his spiel. Despite the fact that Healtheon had by now run through almost $100 million, this proved more than enough of a marketing campaign for the 5 million shares the company was planning to issue. On February 10, when trading started, the stock jumped from the issue price of $8 to $33. It closed the day at 31⅜, valuing Healtheon at more than $2 billion and adding another chapter to the legend of Jim Clark.

# chapter 15  queen of the 'net

I

**Power corrupts, and absolute power corrupts absolutely, Lord**
Acton said. On Wall Street, financial success corrupts, and absolute
financial success corrupts absolutely. The corruption is not necessarily
venal: it affects people's judgment rather than their probity. In early
1999, the stock market was putting a negative value on caution and
common sense. Since everybody involved in the Internet bubble—
entrepreneurs, VCs, investment bankers, stock analysts, mutual fund
managers, ordinary investors, even journalists—was reacting to the
incentives provided by the market, these traits became harder and
harder to find. Mary Meeker witnessed this process firsthand. An
earnest and well-meaning woman, she found herself trapped in the
internal logic of a speculative bubble that she had helped to create.
Like many others, she eventually succumbed to this logic and did
things that she would later regret.

Since Frank Quattrone and his colleagues had quit Morgan Stanley in 1996, Meeker had become the firm's main weapon in the race
to attract Internet IPOs. Every week, dozens of venture capitalists and
Internet entrepreneurs got in touch with her, hoping that Morgan
Stanley would agree to take their firms public. With Meeker's reputation and Morgan Stanley's sales force behind it, an IPO was almost
guaranteed success. Inasmuch as Meeker was meant to be giving
objective advice to investors, her role as an investment banker, which
involved attracting and promoting Morgan-sponsored stock issues,
left her in a hopelessly conflicted position.

In order to avoid such conflicts of interest, investment banks at least pretend to maintain "Chinese Walls" between their research and investment banking departments. As a research department employee, Meeker was not supposed to have access to any inside information from public companies, such as their future acquisition plans, which investment bankers often know about. If she did obtain this sort of information, she would be considered "over the wall" and, therefore, unable to write about the company. But since Internet start-ups are not public companies until their IPOs, Meeker was not breaking any rules by visiting them, pitching for their business, and helping them go public. In a typical IPO, she would advise the Internet company how to position itself to investors, accompany its senior management on at least parts of the road show, and then, a few days before the IPO, lecture Morgan Stanley's sales staff about how to market the company's stock to investors. Twenty-five days after the stock started trading, the minimum period allowed by law, she would initiate coverage, almost always with a strong buy recommendation. Even after the IPO, Meeker usually kept in contact with the firm and, again in almost all cases, she maintained a buy rating on its stock.

Meeker defended her dual role by pointing out that she turned down at least nine out of ten IPO proposals. Although she was widely portrayed as the champion of Internet stocks, that was somewhat misleading. Her list of recommended stocks was still short, and it consisted mainly of Morgan clients: America Online, Amazon.com, Yahoo!, At Home, eBay, VeriSign, and several others. Before Meeker would consider backing a company, it had to satisfy the three conditions she had always insisted upon for Internet investments: big potential market, sound management, and original product. In the early days, maintaining this discipline was easy. Meeker was the first to admit that many Internet enterprises didn't deserve the public's money. (Though she somehow made an exception for Healtheon.) As the Internet boom progressed, maintaining high standards or, indeed, any standards, became a lot harder. TheGlobe.com's IPO was a turning point. Meeker refused to have anything to do with the company, then looked on astonished as Bear Stearns, a firm she didn't even consider a serious rival, not only took the firm public but engineered the biggest first-day gain in history.

IVillage's IPO, which took place in March 1999, was another milestone. The women's Web site, which had fourteen "channels" covering subjects like relationships, health, and astrology, had been racked by management turmoil since Claudia Carpenter, a former executive at QVC and Time Life, founded it in 1995. In three years, iVillage had burned through more than $65 million. In 1998 alone it had lost $43.7 million on revenues of just $15 million. When Morgan Stanley turned down the opportunity to take iVillage public, Goldman Sachs stepped in and placed its reputation on the line. This seemed to have been a dubious decision when, a week before the IPO, one of iVillage's four former chief financial officers accused the firm of using "inappropriate" accounting practices to boost its scant revenues. "Based on my experience at, and my knowledge of, iVillage, I would not be comfortable today being the chief financial officer taking this company public," Joanne O'Rourke Hindman, who had previously spent twelve years working for The Washington Post Company, said in a statement.[1] In other circumstances, such a charge, which iVillage strongly denied, could easily have derailed an unproven company's IPO. But investors ignored Hindman's allegations, and a relieved Goldman pressed ahead. A few days before the IPO was due to take place, the investment bank raised the estimated issue price to $22 to $24, from $12 to $14. On March 19, 3.65 million iVillage shares started trading on the Nasdaq. They jumped from $24 to $80, a rise of 233 percent, and at the end of its first day as a public company iVillage was valued at about $1.9 billion. Even by Internet standards, this was a stunning valuation for a troubled company that faced imminent competition from Oprah Winfrey and the Walt Disney Company. (Winfrey and Disney had both invested in a rival multi-media company aimed at women, Oxygen Media.) Carpenter was worth $80 million.

Meeker was stunned. "With every IPO the envelope is being pushed a little further and a little further," she told a reporter from *The New Yorker*, who was working on a profile of her, a few days after iVillage's Wall Street debut. "At some point you have to scream, Uncle."[2] These days, when Meeker went to see Internet entrepreneurs they weren't content to make tens, or even hundreds, of mil-

lions of dollars in an IPO: they wanted billions. Many of them compared their firms to Yahoo! or eBay, which were now valued at $35
billion and $20 billion, respectively. If Meeker expressed any doubts
about the prospects of achieving such a valuation, the entrepreneurs
would choose another investment bank to take them public. "We are
seeing the second generation of Internet entrepreneurs, and they have
market cap envy of the Jerry Yangs and Marc Andreessens," Meeker
complained. "Their expectations are starting at a much higher level.
The first generation was, like, 'Hey, isn't this great? I'm a billionaire.
Well, that's kind of embarrassing. What am I going to do with all this
stuff?' The next generation is saying, 'Well, if he's a billionaire, then
I've gotta be a billionaire too.'"[3]

It wasn't clear how far Meeker was willing to go in her criticism.
If she had really wanted to take a stand, she could have downgraded
some of the leading Internet stocks, such as eBay, which was trading
at about 1,600 times its revenues. This, Meeker wasn't willing to do.
Instead, she called up eBay's Web site on her office computer. "There
are 1.9 million items for sale," she said. "At the end of December
there were only a million. Not even three months, and traffic on the
site has nearly doubled." Meeker clicked on a few of the ongoing
auctions, pointing out some of the unusual items that were for sale.
"We've never seen companies grow this rapidly," she went on.
"There's no doubt in my mind that the aggregate market value of the
sector will be higher in two years than it is today. It's just a question
of which companies succeed and which fail. I think there will be only
a couple of handful of companies that really succeed."[4]

Meeker didn't believe that eBay's stock was worth 1,600 times
earnings on a valuation basis, but she didn't want to make the mistake
of downgrading the stock and then watch it rise further. She had done
that once before. Shortly after At Home went public, in 1997,
Meeker decided to give its stock a neutral rating because it had risen
so far so fast. When the stock kept on gaining, she looked silly. Things
were a lot crazier now. She was constantly getting calls from major
investors that wanted her advice about how to invest in the Internet.
Even Fidelity's Magellan Fund, the biggest mutual fund in the country, was buying Internet stocks. Henry Blodget, Meeker's opposite
number at Merrill Lynch, had just published a report in which he

conceded there was a speculative bubble in Internet stocks but never-theless advised investors to keep buying. "The overall Internet stock phenomenon may well be a 'bubble,' but in at least one respect it is very different from other bubbles: there are great fundamental reasons to own these stocks," Blodget wrote. "The companies underneath these stocks are (1) growing amazingly quickly, and (2) threatening the status quo in multiple sectors of the economy."[5]

Following his coup with Amazon.com, Blodget was now chal-lenging Meeker's position as the most widely quoted Internet analyst, and his report, which was entitled "Overview of Our Internet Invest-ment Philosophy," was an obvious attempt to challenge her intellec-tual leadership. Blodget conceded that Internet stocks had always seemed "absurdly expensive" on traditional grounds, but he argued that they were, nonetheless, valuable investments because of their practically unlimited potential. "When Yahoo! went public, it looked like the biggest joke in history—a list of Web sites with $1 million in revenue and a $1 billion valuation. Investors the world over (under-standably) crowed about manias and insanity, but it was actually trad-ing at an absurdly cheap 10X Q4 1998 annualized earnings. Investors who failed to ask themselves two questions—(1) how big the com-pany could actually be, and (2) how fast it could get there—missed the boat. With these types of investments, we would also argue that the real 'risk' is not losing some money—it is missing a much bigger upside."

As Blodget also pointed out, the laws of supply and demand, not revenues or earnings, were now determining the prices of Internet stocks. Despite the ongoing wave of IPOs, the supply of Internet stocks remained severely restricted. Most Internet companies still had only a small minority of their shares trading on the open market, with the rest still owned by the original investors. With so many people wanting in on the Internet stock boom and so few shares available to buy, there was only one way for prices to go: up. In such an environ-ment, Meeker was wary about standing in front of an oncoming train. "I don't want to be the Internet stock poster child," she said. "At the same time, though, it would be easy for me to say, 'Hey, based on tra-ditional valuation methodologies these stocks are overvalued.' They'd go down for two weeks and then go up again, because the money flows will continue to drive the sector."[6]


**II**


**In spite of her growing reservations, Meeker continued to play the** Internet IPO game at an unrelenting pace. She had breakfast meetings, lunch meetings, dinner meetings, and she often worked through the night on her research reports. Cabin crews on flights between New York and San Francisco got to know her personally. They were the lucky ones. Trying to see Meeker was like trying to get an audience with the Pope. Every day, she received hundreds of e-mails and phone calls requesting her presence at company meetings, Internet conferences, and media interviews. Sumner Redstone, the chairman of Viacom, wanted to talk about his company's Internet strategy. Morgan Stanley's London office wanted her to come to Europe to discuss Internet opportunities there. Barbra Streisand wanted her investment advice. As Meeker looked back over the last year, she realized that for the first time in her life she hadn't seen any of the films that won Oscars. She hadn't even had time to watch the Oscars ceremony.

To take some of the strain off Meeker's shoulders, Morgan Stanley had hired an investment banker from Robertson, Stephens, Andre de Baubigny, to act as her gatekeeper and emissary. While Meeker dealt mostly with Internet firms that were preparing for IPOs, de Baubigny sifted through the hundreds of hopefuls that were just getting off the ground. If a new venture showed sufficient promise, de Baubigny would advise Meeker to go and meet its management. As time passed, the quality of the firms that de Baubigny referred to Meeker went down. The reason for this was not hard to find. Most of the obvious ideas for doing business on the Web had already been exploited. Many second-generation Internet business plans were either derivative or downright loopy. Meeker knew this as well as anybody, but she wasn't willing to leave the field to Goldman Sachs, let alone Bear Stearns and Merrill Lynch.

Even if she failed to land an IPO for Morgan Stanley, Meeker tried to persuade the company to do business with the firm later on. After her superiors barred her from pitching for the Amazon.com IPO, Meeker publicly supported Jeff Bezos's "Get Big Fast" strategy and maintained a strong buy recommendation on Amazon.com's stock, despite its massive run-up. "If Amazon.com executes to its plan, it's a very powerful business," she insisted in March 1999. "They are the online leader in books, the online leader in music sales, the online leader in video sales, and they will soon be the online leader in online drugstores. The question becomes: how much of that business goes online? I am fairly confident that Amazon will have a market share in excess of 50 percent for online sales. It could become a super-retailing company."[7] Meeker's loyalty paid off. In late 1998 and early 1999, after finally jettisoning its allegiance to Barnes & Noble, Morgan Stanley landed the lucrative jobs of helping Amazon.com to sell $500 million in high-yield debt and $1.25 billion in convertible bonds. Both issues were the biggest of their type yet done by an e-commerce company, but Morgan Stanley didn't have any trouble selling them and earning its commissions.

Meeker also won over Meg Whitman, eBay's chief executive. Having blown the chance to take eBay public, Meeker asked for a chance to redeem herself. She flew to Boston's Logan airport, where she met Whitman, apologized for the poor IPO presentation, and showed her a draft of a glowing research report that she had written about eBay. Whitman stuck with her choice of Goldman Sachs to lead the IPO, but Meeker didn't give up. She went ahead and published her research report on the day that eBay's stock started trading. A few months later, when eBay was preparing for a $1.1 billion secondary stock offering, it chose Morgan Stanley to co-manage the issue, along with Goldman Sachs. "(Meeker) has been a terrific adviser in many ways," Whitman said in March 1999. "She has great ideas for the company. She's very thoughtful about what's going on in the space, and I always incredibly value what she has to say."[8]

Meeker's bosses supported her aggressive approach. Like their counterparts at other big securities firms, the men who ran Morgan Stanley took their firm's reputation seriously, but not as seriously as they took its profitability. Internet start-ups were an increasingly important source of Wall Street's revenues. The 7 percent IPO commission was only the beginning. It was usually followed by generous fees for underwriting secondary stock offerings and bond issues, and for advising on mergers and acquisitions, as the examples of Amazon.com and eBay had demonstrated. When all these deals were added together, an investment bank could make as much money from a small Internet company as it could from one of its blue-chip clients. This was the reason why nearly every firm on Wall Street was chasing Internet business.

Morgan Stanley's senior executives were just as determined as Meeker to retain the firm's premier position. But when pressed to explain how they justified selling companies with no earnings to the public, they absolved themselves of responsibility. "The people buying Internet stocks don't think they are buying Morgan Stanley, American Express, or Berkshire Hathaway," Joseph Perella, the head of Morgan's investment banking department, explained to a reporter in early 1999. "There has been a fundamental shift in American capitalism. Previously, venture capital was a private game. Now, the public is willing to fund the growth of companies that are almost start-ups. Basically, the public is saying, 'I want to own every one of these companies. If I'm wrong on nineteen and the twentieth one is Yahoo! it doesn't matter. I'll do O.K.' That's job-creating. That's wealth-creating. Yes, it is a lottery, as Greenspan said, but it's also fundamental to the evolution of this country."[9] Tall, bearded, and possessed of a preternatural calm, Perella had spent twenty-seven years on Wall Street. In the 1980s, he cofounded Wasserstein Perella, an investment bank that specialized in advising companies involved in hostile takeovers. The valuations being accorded to stocks like Yahoo! and Amazon.com surprised Perella, but he didn't let it disturb his equipoise. "Are they overvalued?" he said calmly. "Probably a lot of them are, but I don't know if I would use a word like 'excess.'" Perella regarded Meeker's emergence as a media celebrity with an equal measure of insouciance. "Mary is one of a kind, and that has to do with her personality, her dedication, and her space," he said. "If she were a steel analyst, you wouldn't be sitting there." And he went on:

"Mary is the right person in the right place at the right time. That's a very fortunate position to be in."[10]

## III

**One of the firms that Andre de Baubigny advised Meeker to visit** was Priceline.com. In the summer of 1998 de Baubigny drove up to Stamford to meet Richard Braddock, the company's chairman and chief executive. He was so impressed that on the way back to New York he called Meeker from the car and urged her to make a trip to Connecticut as soon as possible. Jay Walker, who founded Priceline.com in July 1997, had already been an entrepreneur for fifteen years. His most successful venture was NewSub Services, a direct marketing firm that sold magazine subscriptions by placing advertisements alongside credit card bills and turned into a $250-million-a-year business. Walker described Priceline.com as a "demand collection system." Stripped of the marketing jargon, the firm allowed airlines (and later hotels) to sell unfilled seats (and rooms) cheaply without undermining their overall fare structure. Tickets were non-changeable and nonrefundable. Customers had to be willing to fly on any airline and make a stop en route. Somebody flying from New York to Miami might end up going through Memphis. These restrictions were designed to prevent business travelers from using Priceline.com to buy cheap tickets. If the airlines thought that Walker's company would turn full-fare customers into bargain shoppers they would never agree to supply it with any seats.

Priceline.com's business model was undoubtedly clever; whether it would work was less certain. In order to boost revenues, the firm had resorted to buying tickets from the airlines at higher prices than customers had offered and making up the difference itself. The financial rationale for this behavior was the same one that motivated Amazon.com to sell books for less than it cost to buy them from the publishers and ship them to customers: if the top line grew sufficiently fast, the bottom line would eventually take care of itself. As one of Amazon.com's biggest supporters, Meeker could hardly argue with this strategy. Her basic view of the online economy had not changed much since she wrote *The Internet Report*. E-commerce would eventually look like the software business, with one or two dominant players in each market and everybody else extinct. In order to survive this process of digital Darwinism, it was essential to establish a grip on the market before any serious competitors emerged. Priceline.com was trying hard to do this. In addition to subsidizing its customers, it was spending heavily on advertising. In 1998, Priceline.com's sales and marketing expenditure came to almost $25 million, or about two-thirds of its revenues. To Meeker, this was a sign of strength, not weakness. "This is a time to be rationally reckless," she explained. "It is a time to build a brand. It really is a landgrab time."[11]

Just before Christmas of 1998, Priceline.com invited a number of investment banks to compete for the job of managing its IPO, which was scheduled for the spring. Morgan Stanley and Goldman Sachs both took part in the bake-off, and Meeker's reputation was the deciding factor. "We just think Mary is the best—that was the distinguishing reason we chose Morgan," Richard Braddock said.[12] "She has the credibility." Given the febrile state of the IPO market, there was never any doubt that Priceline.com's stock offering would be well received. Analysts were already comparing the company to eBay. Like eBay, Priceline.com didn't have any inventories, and it employed fewer than two hundred people. Moreover, its business model seemed to be adaptable to other markets. In the past few months, it had experimented with selling cars, hotel rooms, and mortgages.

On March 29, 1999, the day before Priceline.com was due to go public, the Dow closed above 10,000 for the first time, a timely reminder that the Internet stock mania was part of a much wider phenomenon. In January 1993, when Marc Andreessen had posted the Mosaic browser on the Web, the Dow was at about 3,000. In the summer of 1995, when Netscape went public, it was still under 5,000. Now that the Dow had reached five figures the Wall Street bulls saw no reason for it to stop there. "What we are looking at is confirmation in the stock market that the U.S. economy is in excellent condition," Abby Joseph Cohen told *The Washington Post*.[13] "I believe the bull markets continue until economic deterioration. I see no economic deterioration." Ralph Acampora was equally ebullient. "It's no longer a ceiling; it's a floor," he declared of the 10,000 threshold. "As time goes by, we'll be looking down at it."[14]

After the markets had closed, Morgan Stanley's IPO team got together to price the 10 million Priceline.com shares that would start trading the following morning. In the company's prospectus, the issue price had been estimated at $7 to $9, valuing Priceline.com at about $1.15 billion. The road show had been so successful that the price could now be increased substantially, but deciding how much to raise it wasn't easy. Since Priceline.com had no earnings, and revenues of only $35 million, the valuation formulas that the bankers had learned in business school were of no use, and neither were the new methodologies that Meeker, Blodget, and other Internet analysts had invented. The latter techniques depended on estimating the size of the total market and guessing how much of it the company in question could dominate. But in Priceline.com's case, the potential market was difficult to define. If it was restricted to airline tickets, it was too small to justify a billion-dollar valuation. If it was extended to hotels, mortgages, and cars, and maybe other goods, there was no way of knowing how much of the market Priceline.com could garner. The only obvious guideposts were the valuations of other Internet IPOs, but even these were of little help. Six months earlier, eBay had gone public at a value of $700 million; now it was worth almost thirty times that figure. One person who took part in the Priceline.com pricing meeting likened the process of valuing Internet companies to throwing darts. The aim was to set the price high enough for the company to be satisfied but low enough for investors to make a decent return. In the end, Morgan Stanley simply doubled the issue price, to $16. At $16 a share, Priceline.com would have a market capitalization of $2.3 billion—the highest value yet for an Internet IPO.

The next morning, when Priceline.com's valuation jumped to $10 billion, Mary Meeker was on a 7:35 A.M. flight to San Francisco. She was due to make a pitch for another IPO that afternoon, then meet a second Internet company in the evening and a third the following morning. After landing in San Francisco, she checked in with the office and learned what had happened. A couple of days later, she found a few minutes to mull things over with a reporter. The demand for Internet stocks was so frenzied that it now reminded her of tulipmania. "The difference is that the real values are being created. Tulip bulbs did not fundamentally change the way that companies do business."[15] But with every successive IPO Meeker's level of nervousness had increased, and the Priceline.com IPO had heightened her fears. The Internet stock boom was like a crescendo; it couldn't go on indefinitely. "I think we will have a big correction in Internet stocks sometime this year," she said. "I think a big correction would be very healthy. I personally would welcome it."

## IV

**Two days after Priceline.com's IPO, Yahoo! agreed to pay $6.1 bil-**lion for Broadcast.com. Appropriately enough, the deal was announced on April Fool's day. The previous summer, Broadcast.com had gone public at a valuation of $300 million, and its business hadn't changed much since then. It still didn't own any content. The sound on its audio feeds was still tinny; the pictures on its video feeds were still small and blurred; and its financial losses were still mounting. In 1998, Broadcast.com lost $16.4 million on sales of $22.3 million. The price that Yahoo! agreed to pay was about 275 times these revenues. It wasn't real money, of course. Yahoo! was paying for the deal in stock, just as it had paid for its $3.6 billion purchase of GeoCities earlier in the year.

The flood of Internet IPOs continued. On April 8, Value America, an online retailer based in Charlottesville, Virginia, went public at $23 a share, and the stock closed at $55, valuing the company at more than $2 billion. Craig Winn, Value America's founder, was a former salesman who had already led one public company into bankruptcy. These days, he flew around in a private jet and saw himself as a possible candidate for president in 2008. He promoted Value America as the Wal-Mart of the Internet, but a Wal-Mart without any inventories, a truly "frictionless" company. In Winn's vision, whenever a customer bought a television, or a personal computer, or even a bottle of aspirin, on Value America's Web site, the firm would pass the order onto the manufacturer, which would ship the goods to the customer direct. In reality, most manufacturers had neither the capacity nor the inclination to ship individual items. Winn and his backers, who included Paul Allaire, the cofounder of Microsoft, didn't seem disturbed by this discrepancy, and neither did investors.

Between the start of 1999 and the middle of April, the Dow Jones Internet Composite Index doubled. In its issue of April 12, 1999, *The Industry Standard* captured the mood of the moment with a cover featuring Priceline.com's Jay Walker and Mark Cuban, the founder of Broadcast.com, next to the headline "THIS WEEK'S BILLIONAIRES."[16] Inside the magazine, an article pointed out that America Online, which had been added to the S&P 500 at the start of the year, now had a market capitalization of $137 billion. A hundred thousand dollars invested in the stock eighteen months ago would now be worth $1.3 million. In a column entitled "I Want to Believe," Michael Parsons, the *Industry Standard*'s executive news editor, pointed out that investors were "wagering billions of dollars on complex business stories, and many might as well be putting their money on red or black in Las Vegas." Parsons continued: "A skeptic might find that a sad testament to human folly. A believer will point out that Las Vegas is the fastest growing city in America."[17]

On April 26, *The New Yorker* published its profile of Meeker, complete with her prediction of a big fall in Internet stocks sometime in the next year. The correction started immediately, with the Dow Jones Composite Internet Index falling more than 50 points, or almost 19 percent, to 224.85. Over the next two months, most of the big Internet stocks fell sharply. Amazon.com went from $209 to 110³⁄₁₆; eBay went from 209½ to $136; and America Online went from $151 to 102¹³⁄₁₆. At this stage, however, the mania for Internet stocks was too far advanced to be halted even by a sizable correction. Most investors regarded the sell-off as an inevitable hiccup. Unlike during previous corrections, the flow of IPOs continued.

Four days after the Meeker article appeared, Razorfish, a New York–based Internet company, went public. Credit Suisse First Boston issued 3 million shares at $16, and the stock more than doubled, to 33½. Razorfish made most of its revenues designing Web sites for companies like Charles Schwab, CBS, and Time Warner, but it described itself as a "global digital communications solutions provider." Craig Kanarick, the firm's cofounder, saw himself as a visionary. Speaking to *New York* magazine, he once described himself as a "Jewish guy with a lot of guilt, slightly misunderstood, trying to change an industry, somewhat brilliant."[18] Kanarick was one of many people, in New York and elsewhere, who were confusing good fortune with genius. During the following weeks and months, many more Silicon Alley firms went public. They included Star Media Network, which was trying to become the America Online of Latin America; Juno Online Services, which offered free e-mail; and Fashionmall.com, which sold clothes and beauty products. Few of these companies satisfied Meeker's criteria for a promising Internet start-up, but they all found willing investors, and so did another firm that Meeker had wanted nothing to do with: TheStreet.com.

James Cramer's financial news site was a case study in Internet economics. After two and a half years, it had gained just 50,000 subscribers, a good number of whom were lured in by cheap subscriptions. In 1998, TheStreet.com had racked up losses of $16.3 million on total revenues of $4.6 million. In the first quarter of 1999, things didn't improve any: TheStreet.com lost $7.2 million on revenues of less than $2 million. Parsing the numbers didn't help. During 1998, TheStreet.com spent more than $9 million on a marketing campaign that brought in about 20,000 paying customers, which meant it was paying $450 to acquire each of its $99.95 subscribers. The Web site also attracted some advertising, but almost half of it came from one company, Datek Online, the day traders' favorite online brokerage. When Meeker looked at TheStreet.com, she decided, sensibly enough, that its audience of investing enthusiasts was too narrow to support a viable business.

TheStreet.com's biggest asset was Cramer, who had turned into a garrulous emblem of the Internet era, despite a few scrapes along the way. Toward the end of 1998, a number of investors tried to pull their money out of his hedge fund, Cramer Berkowitz, which was having a bad year. Even Marty Peretz, TheStreet.com's cofounder, questioned Cramer's recent investment performance. About the same time, Cramer's media career stumbled. Shortly before Christmas, CNBC suspended him after he told viewers he wanted to sell short WavePhone, a tiny Dallas company, whose stock promptly collapsed. It turned out that Cramer hadn't actually shorted the stock, and eventually he was allowed back on the air. (The incident finally prompted CNBC to introduce stricter disclosure rules for its guests.)

Through it all, Cramer kept trading and writing at a frantic pace, and many traditional media companies remained eager to associate themselves with him. In January 1999, The New York Times Company paid $15 million for a minority stake in TheStreet.com. A couple of months later, Rupert Murdoch's News Corporation agreed to invest $7.5 million in a deal that included plans for a TheStreet.com television show on Fox. The investments gave TheStreet.com the credibility it needed to do an IPO, and Goldman Sachs agreed to underwrite the issue. On May 10, 1999, 5.5 million TheStreet.com shares started trading on the Nasdaq. Issued at $19, they shot up to $73 and closed at $60, a rise on the day of 216 percent. At the closing price, TheStreet.com was valued at $1.5 billion. Cramer's shares were worth $203 million. Peretz's stake was worth $182 million. Dave Kansas, the former *Wall Street Journal* reporter who was TheStreet.com's editor in chief, was worth $9.1 million. Cramer's sister and father came up from Philadelphia to help him celebrate. "I'm thrilled," he told *USA Today*. "TheStreet.com is like the people's choice. People vote for stocks these days. And they're buying into both the Web and the pioneers of the future."[19]

# chapter 16  trading nation

I

**Number fifty Broad Street is an old-fashioned office building just** around the corner from the New York Stock Exchange—the sort of place where each floor has several tenants, the elevator creaks, and the doorman gives you a tired look as you walk by. On a mild afternoon in the spring of 1999, forty people—all but two of them male—were sitting in a conference room on the seventeenth floor. There was one black and one Asian. The rest were white. Most looked to be around forty, but a few were in their mid-twenties, and a couple appeared to be of retirement age. They had come from Brooklyn and Queens and Long Island and New Jersey and Westchester—and one hopeful soul from as far as Iowa. The dress code was casual—polo shirts and jeans—but two Hasidic Jews were wearing white shirts, and one stickler had on a suit. Through the open windows, the sound of traffic and sirens wafted in, making it difficult to hear the two men at the front of the room who were describing their experience as professional day traders.

"As soon as I wake up in the morning, I turn on CNBC," Randy Guttenberg, a balding fellow with a goatee beard, who appeared to be in his early thirties, explained. "I look where the futures are. I listen to what they are talking about, what stocks are in play. And I look to see who the guests are going to be later in the day. Any time I hear that somebody's coming on CNBC, I say to myself, 'What's going on?' Michael Dell doesn't speak bad news. Bill Gates doesn't speak bad news. Every time they speak, they have something good to say. So I buy the stocks."[1] Guttenberg had worked at Lehman Brothers and Prudential Bache Securities. For the past two years, he had rented a desk and a trading terminal at Broadway Trading, the company that had organized the lecture. "I used to trade two or three stocks at a time; now I have ten or twenty stocks on my screen," he went on. "My time frame in trading can be anything from ten seconds to half a day. Usually, it's in the five-to-twenty-minute range."

The other speaker was a beefy young man in a T-shirt and jeans called Barry Slomiak. He had left Charles Schwab, where he was "getting bored to crap," to become a day trader. "To be honest, I got walloped for six or seven months," he said. "Then I started making some money. It's strictly a confidence game. It took time for me to have the confidence to trade a thousand stocks. Yahoo! still scares the crap out of me, because it's so volatile. If I have some Yahoo! I'm always thinking, 'How can I get out of it?'" A few members of the audience laughed nervously. They had each paid $1,500 for five days of coaching in the art of day trading.

After Guttenberg and Slomiak finished speaking, they took questions. A middle-aged man asked if they ever held on to stocks overnight. "In the beginning, I wouldn't recommend it," Guttenberg replied. "You don't need the extra risk. But when you are making money, sure. These days I tend to hold some positions overnight. Last night I took home E*Trade and Siebert because they had been beaten down so much." The questioner wasn't satisfied. He wanted to know the most that Guttenberg had lost by hanging on to stocks overnight. "When they devalued in Brazil, I came in and I was down $70,000," Guttenberg replied. "It was horrible. I've never been down that much." Around the room there were concerned looks. "Did you sell?" a voice asked. "No, I held on, and I ended up $15,000," Guttenberg said with a wry smile. "I know that sounds funny, but that's the way it is sometimes."

Marc Friedfertig, the founder of Broadway Trading, spoke next. He was a chubby man of medium height, with long dark curly hair and a friendly face. "Liquidity," he began. "That's why the stock market is the best place in the world to invest. You can buy at 50 and sell at 49⅞. Where else can you do that? Is your car liquid? No. If you had to sell it, it could take three hours or three months to get fair value."

Friedfertig set up Broadway Trading in 1995. A former futures trader and a member of the American Stock Exchange, he did his MBA at Columbia and worked at Morgan Stanley and First Boston before recognizing the trading possibilities that deregulation and technology had created. These went well beyond the services offered by firms like E★Trade and Charles Schwab. When a Schwab investor called up a stock quote on his computer, he saw the "bid"—the selling price—and the "ask"—the buying price. But these prices were only indicative. If the customer placed an order, he had to rely on Schwab to get the best price possible from the market makers in that stock. With stocks like Yahoo! and Amazon.com, which gyrated wildly, the actual price could bear little resemblance to the quoted prices.

Firms like Broadway Trading worked differently. Their computers linked traders directly to the Nasdaq market site and to several independent electronic exchanges that had sprung up in recent years, such as Instinet and Island. For any given stock, the trader could see the exact number of shares that were being offered, plus the prices being requested and the identity of the seller. By pressing a few buttons, the trader could accept one of the offers, or post his own offer on the screen for others to consider. For the first time in history, the ordinary investor really could trade alongside the professionals.

The goal of day trading, Friedfertig explained, was to dart in and out of the electronic marketplace, making a series of small profits. Buy at 50. Sell at 50⅛. Buy at 50⅛. Sell at 50¼. And so on. The two keys to successful day trading were money management and timing. "The number-one reason that people lose is because they don't know how to control their losses," Friedfertig said. "If things are working, keep trading. If things are not working, slow down. You've gotta be like a great quarterback." Until they got the hang of things, novices should limit themselves to blocks of 100 shares, priced somewhere between $5 and $55. They should avoid the top twenty movers "because that's where the sharks are," and they should always close out their trades if the market turned against them. "People who double up on their losses eventually get buried."

Listening to Friedfertig's presentation, day trading seemed like a reasonable way to spend days. It didn't sound easy—"The first six months are going to be hard, and I'm telling you that now"—but it did sound manageable, like learning a new sport. "So much of trading is about probabilities," Friedfertig said philosophically. "At any given moment supply and demand can change without you knowing it. Some guy at Fidelity can decide to dump all his Dell. The market is humbling. Everyone has setbacks." To explain his point, Friedfertig brought up the name of Serge Milman, Broadway Trading's star trader, a twenty-five-year-old Russian immigrant whom *Forbes* had featured on its front page a few months previously.[2] "Serge makes money nineteen days out of twenty, but when he loses he doesn't lose much," Friedfertig said. "The first goal is not to lose money. If you make $500 a day, that's $125,000 a year. Two hundred dollars a day is $50,000 a year. That's not too bad."

The audience members looked dubious. A few looked at their feet. They hadn't spent $1,500 to learn how to make $50,000 a year. They wanted to be like Serge, who, according to *Forbes*, had grossed $1.4 million the previous year and netted $800,000 after commissions. They wanted to be like Jeff Cooper, the author of *Hit and Run Trading*, who had a house in Bel Air and another in Malibu. Friedfertig knew this, of course, but he had to be careful. Lately, day trading had gotten some bad publicity. The attorney general of Massachusetts had sued one of Broadway Trading's rivals, claiming that it misled its clients about the likelihood of making profits. Arthur Levitt, the chairman of the Securities and Exchange Commission, had inveighed against day trading, warning investors that "investment should be for the long run—not for minutes and hours."[3] Friedfertig resented these attacks. He had written two books on day trading; he considered it a revolutionary development; but he had never claimed it was risk-free. "Nobody should take substantial risks unless you are making money consistently in trading 100 shares," he warned. "You guys have got to be able to play penny poker, and take it seriously, before you move to the big table."

## II

**Ironically, the SEC was partly responsible for the rise of day trading.** Until the middle of the 1990s, the big Wall Street firms dominated trading in Nasdaq stocks. In 1993, the Department of Justice launched an investigation, which concluded that the market makers were colluding to gouge the public, often by ignoring their orders. The SEC levied a billion-dollar fine and forced the Wall Street firms to agree to fill any order that improved on the quoted price and to display buy and sell offers from other electronic exchanges. These reforms allowed individual investors to see precisely what prices they were getting, and it also allowed them to trade with each other, rather than through the market makers. All they needed was a Nasdaq Level II trading screen and some trading software, both of which were provided by firms like Broadway Trading.

By early 1999, there were more than sixty day-trading firms, with almost three hundred offices, across the country. The biggest were Momentum Securities, which was based in Houston, and All Tech Investment Group, of Montvale, New Jersey. According to the SEC, the number of people trading full-time at day-trading firms was somewhere between 5,800 and 6,800. There were probably another few thousand people trading at home with software provided by the day-trading firms. Even counting these traders, day trading, properly defined, was the activity of a pretty small group of investors.

The main barrier to becoming a day trader was money. Most day-trading firms asked their customers to deposit between $50,000 and $100,000 before they could start trading. These deposits were necessary because the whole point of day trading was to buy and sell a lot of stocks, which takes a lot of cash. According to the Electronic Traders Association, a trade group for day-trading firms, the typical day trader placed thirty-five trades a day, each for an average of 700 shares. Although the number of day traders was small, the amount of trading they did was enormous. By the start of 1999, day trading accounted for about 15 percent of the total trading volume on the Nasdaq. This was an overall figure. For some Internet stocks, such as America Online and Yahoo!, the percentage was much higher.

Given the entry requirements, day trading was a game for rich people—or middle-income people who had mortgaged their futures. Unfortunately, there were a good number of the latter, drawn in by the prospect of giving up their jobs, their jackets and ties, and making money on their own time. Most day traders were well educated. It took a certain level of intelligence and arrogance to persuade yourself that you could trade successfully against Wall Street professionals who had been doing it all their working lives. Despite the large amounts of money at stake, the day-trading culture was casual. "Shop guys," the traders who sat shoulder to shoulder at firms like Broadway Trading, tended to be gregarious, swapping war stories, trading strategies, and gorging on pizza. (Some day-trading firms provided free lunch so the traders wouldn't have to stop trading.) "Remote guys," the traders who worked from home, were more isolated. They tended to spend a lot of time in chat rooms like mtrader.com and daytraders.com, where they picked up the latest gossip. Some of them frequented TheStreet.com, which had its own day-trading correspondent: Gary Smith, a freelance sportswriter who traded from his Connecticut home.

Like all forms of gambling, day trading was addictive. Some participants compared it to blackjack, others to compulsive video games. "Anyone who has ever played Space Invaders knows the drill," Steve Bodow, a writer and theater director who wrote about his day-trading experiences for *Wired* in early 1999, explained. "After a time, the little bastards take up residence behind your eyelids; the crimson bonus saucer floats across your field of vision while you're in a job interview. Day trading just subs numbers and ticker symbols for the marching pixel-goonies."[4] Some day-trading firms weren't as honest as Friedfertig about the risks their customers were taking. "If they follow the rules, they'll succeed," Sal Giamerese, a day trading coach at an All Tech Investment Group office in Fall Church, Virginia, insisted to *The Washington Post*. "It's like golf. If you're careful about how you place your feet, how you lift the club and follow through, you'll stand a far better chance of hitting the ball straight than hooking it. The same principle applies to day trading."[5]

In a way, the golf analogy was accurate. Like most amateur golfers, the vast majority of day traders did poorly. When the Massachusetts authorities investigated one day-trading firm in their state, they found that sixty-seven out of sixty-eight customers had lost money. Even if their trading strategies worked, day traders often ended up taking heavy losses after paying their hefty trading commissions. As more people got involved, tales of disaster multiplied. A Chicago waiter with no trading experience blew a $200,000 inheritance. A Boston retiree went through $250,000 of his wife's savings in a few hours. A California bank employee quit his job, borrowed $40,000 on his credit cards to start trading, and promptly lost the lot.

Mark Orrin Barton, a forty-four-year-old Atlanta man, was one of the losers. Barton was typical of the thousands of Americans who had given up their jobs to become day traders. A former chemist, scout leader, and Jehovah's Witness, he lived in Stockbridge, a modest suburb, with his second wife and two children, but he spent many of his days in the posh Buckhead section, where a number of day-trading firms had offices. Barton began day trading in 1998 at the offices of All Tech Investment Group. By April 1999 he had racked up big losses and his account was shut down. In early June, Barton started trading again at the nearby Momentum Securities. He claimed to be worth $750,000 and wrote a check for $87,500 to open an account.

Despite the change of venue, Barton's trading losses continued. Although Internet stocks were undergoing a correction, he kept buying them, particularly Amazon.com, in the hope of a turnaround. Ignoring the day traders' dictum, he refused to close out losing positions. In just eight weeks, he lost $105,000—his original stake plus $17,500 that he had borrowed on margin. On Tuesday, July 27, Momentum Securities issued Barton with a margin call: unless he came up with the money he owed, his account would be closed. That night Barton went back to Stockbridge and battered his wife to death with a hammer, bundling her body into a closet. The next day, Momentum informed Barton that a check he had written for $50,000 had bounced. This time, Barton went home and bludgeoned his nine-year-old daughter and twelve-year-old son. After placing their bodies in their beds, with their favorite toys beside them, Barton wrote a suicide note in which he said: "I don't plan to live very much longer. Just long enough to kill as many of the people that greedily sought my destruction."[6]

On Thursday, July 29, Barton put on the baggy shorts that he often wore to trade in and drove to Buckhead. He went first to Momentum Securities and asked for the manager, who, fortunately for him, was out to lunch. Barton walked onto the trading floor, commiserating with a few traders about the market, which was down steeply. "It's a bad trading day, and it's about to get worse," he said, pulling out a .45 automatic and a 9mm pistol.[7] He started firing wildly, killing four people and wounding several others. Then he went across the street to All Tech Investment Group, where the manager was in his office. After shooting him, Barton walked out onto the trading floor, said, "I certainly hope this doesn't ruin your trading day," and shot dead another four people before fleeing.[8] A few hours later, police pulled Barton over at a gas station, and he shot himself in the temple.

The Atlanta massacre brought home the risks, the losses, and the anguish of day trading. Harvey Houtkin, the founder of All Tech Investment Group, had once referred to day trading as "the best entertainment since television," but there was nothing entertaining about gullible investors losing their life savings.[9] The only people who consistently made money from day trading were Houtkin and his fellow owners of day-trading firms, who raked in enormous trading commissions. Taking the Electronic Traders Association's own figures, the average day trader bought or sold 6 million shares a year. Assuming that he paid two cents a share to trade, which was common, he spent $120,000 a year in commissions—more money than many day traders had in their accounts to begin with. Given these fees, the common perception that day trading was a relatively cheap business to operate was an illusion. Behind the marketing hype about personal empowerment, day trading was a business that any Wall Street old hand could appreciate: the customers risked their capital; the brokers made the profits.

## III

**If Barton had been able to hold on for a few more weeks, the mas-**sacre might not have happened. Amazon.com's stock, after falling for months, rebounded strongly in August, and the rest of the Internet sector did likewise. By then, Barton's shootings had largely disappeared from the media—widely written off as just another homicidal outburst by an angry white male. Barton was undoubtedly a disturbed individual. After the shooting spree, it emerged that he had been the prime suspect in the murder of his first wife and mother-in-law several years earlier. But in some ways he wasn't so untypical. In his decision to give up his regular career, his fascination with Internet stocks, and his belief that buying and selling stocks was a good way to get rich quickly, he was like countless other Americans.

Day trading, after all, was just an extreme form of online trading, which had developed into a national pastime. More than 5 million American households now had online trading accounts, and many had more than one. Charles Schwab, alone, had almost 6 million customer accounts, and it was adding another 100,000 every month. A third of all retail stock trades were being done online, and the percentage was increasing. In June, TD Waterhouse, the second biggest online brokerage, with almost 2 million accounts, went public in the biggest Internet IPO yet, raising more than $1 billion.

The established Wall Street firms, which had long subsisted on fat commissions, reacted to the growth of online trading by going through a cycle of shock, denial, and, finally, capitulation. In the summer of 1998, Launny Steffens, the vice chairman of Merrill Lynch, described online trading as "a serious threat to Americans' financial lives."[10] On June 1, 1999, less than twelve months later, Steffens stood alongside David Komansky, Merrill's chairman, as Komansky announced that the firm's customers would soon be able to buy and sell stocks online for $29.95—the same price that Schwab charged. "It's clear that there is a segment of the marketplace that wants access to Merrill Lynch and the markets through online trading," Komansky said. "We saw that as an inevitable market offer that we had to make."[11]

Day traders apart, the online investors could be divided into two groups. The first group, which numbered perhaps 200,000, comprised the most active traders, who bought and sold stocks every day, or almost every day. Many had turned investing into a first or second job. Unlike the day traders, they tended to hold on to stocks for days and weeks, sometimes even months. These people frequented TheStreet.com, RagingBull.com, and other financial Web sites. Many of them used no-frills online brokers, such as Datek, which charged as little as $10 a trade. They accounted for up to three-quarters of all online trades, and they were often responsible for the sudden spikes in Internet stocks. (Some Internet stocks became so volatile that firms like Schwab refused to deal in them.)

The second group of online traders was made up of people who bought and sold stocks on a regular basis, but didn't devote their lives to the market. This group included the vast majority of individual investors. They tended to favor firms like Schwab and Fidelity, which combined online trading with offices where customers could go and speak with real people. When Fidelity surveyed its online customers it found that they traded, on average, 5.5 times a month, compared with 2.7 times a month before they went online.[12] Not surprisingly, Internet veterans tended to trade most actively. Many newcomers reported themselves overwhelmed by all the financial information available online, and 37 percent of them admitted that they based their investment decisions on instinct.

Most online investors were men, but as time progressed more women took up the activity. By the end of 1999, about a third of Fidelity's new online customers were female. Many of these women learned about the stock market through investment clubs, which had sprung up all over the country. The growth of investment clubs is an aspect of the stock market boom that is often overlooked. In 2000, Robert Putnam, a professor of government at Harvard, published *Bowling Alone*, in which he claimed that the decline of bowling clubs and other groups where people have traditionally come together reflected an ominous decline in "civic society."[13] Putnam's was an interesting thesis, and it had some truth to it, but it ignored the proliferation of one type of voluntary association where millions of Americans gathered regularly, talked with each other, and acted in unison on an issue close to their hearts: money. In 1992, there were 7,200 investment clubs listed with the National Association of Investors Corp., a nonprofit organization based in Madison Heights, Michigan; at the start of 1999, there were more than 37,000. By then, the United States contained more investment clubs than movie houses. And this figure only included those investment clubs that had gone to the trouble of listing with the National Association of Investors. Probably half as many again hadn't bothered.

A typical investment club had about fifteen or twenty members, each of whom put about $40 a month into a kitty, which was then invested in stocks selected by all the members. More than two-thirds of the members of investment clubs were women. The model and inspiration for many of them was the Beardstown Ladies Club, of

Beardstown, Illinois, which in 1995 published a best-selling book, *The Beardstown Ladies' Common Sense Investment Guide: How We Beat the Stock Market and How You Can Too.* The Beardstown Ladies claimed to have made an annual return of close to 25 percent for a decade. An outside audit later revealed that the actual return was less than 10 percent, but that was after the group had appeared on the *Today* show and other television programs promoting their homespun approach to investing, which involved buying solid companies at decent prices. Not all of their imitators took such a conservative stance. When *The Daily News of Los Angeles* held a stock-picking contest for local investment clubs, the Wall Street Women of Granada Hills, a group of local hairdressers, came out on top with a portfolio that included America Online, eBay, EarthLink, and Yahoo![14]

There were investment clubs catering to blacks, Asians, college students, and even high school students. The National Association of Investors started a young membership program, with its own newsletter, *Young Money Matters.* CNBC organized a high school stock-picking contest, with the prize an appearance on its *Power Lunch* show, and received about 2,500 entries. There were Web sites, books, and summer camps for young investors. In the blighted South Bronx, teachers at Aquinas High School took their pupils on field trips to Wall Street.

As long as the stock market kept going up, few people questioned the underlying premise of all this activity—that buying and selling stocks on a regular basis was a profitable pursuit. Brad M. Barber and Terrance Odean, two economists from the University of California at Davis, did bother to look at the evidence, examining the trading records of a large discount brokerage between 1991 and 1996. During that period the firm's 12,000 most active investors earned an annual return of 10 percent, compared to 15.3 percent for all customers and 17.1 percent for the market. The main reasons why active traders did badly were commission costs and poor market timing. "Our central message is that trading is hazardous to your health," Barber and Odean concluded.[15] Their study confirmed what many others had shown before: for most people, the best way to invest is to buy a diverse portfolio of stocks, or a mutual fund, then forget about it for a decade or two. The worst way is to trade every day.

The only Americans who remained totally immune to the stock

market bug were those too poor or marginalized to be influenced by the dominant culture. It should be noted that this group was a lot bigger than is generally recognized. To talk of a "nation" obsessed with Yahoo! and Amazon.com was to ignore the fact that, despite the growth of a populist stock market culture, stock ownership in the United States remained heavily concentrated among the well-to-do. In 1998, the last year for which reliable figures are available, 48.8 percent of American households owned stocks in some form, up from 31.6 percent in 1989.[16] This was a big increase, certainly, but even after a decade and a half of rising stock prices the majority of American families still had no stake in the stock market at all. It is also worth noting that, regardless of the growth of day trading, online trading, and investment clubs, the majority of investors still didn't possess any individual stocks. In 1998, less than one-fifth of American households owned stock directly—that is, outside of mutual funds and retirement accounts. Most investors stuck to mutual funds. The mania for trading individual stocks, unprecedented as it was, remained a minority pursuit.

## IV

**In the summer of 1998, three economists published an article in** *The Journal of Economic Perspectives* entitled "Learning from the Behavior of Others: Conformity, Fads, and Informational Cascades."[17] Sushil Bikhchandani, David Hirshleifer, and Ivo Welch tried to explain why very different people often end up doing the same thing, such as wearing the same brand of shoes, watching the same television shows, or putting their money in Internet stocks. The key to such fads, the economists argued, is "social learning"—learning from the actions of others. When faced with a choice of actions, such as deciding whether to buy Yahoo! or eBay at a price equal to several hundred times its revenues, a person can react in one of two ways. The first option is to examine all of the alternatives, weigh up their costs and benefits, and make an independent judgment. "However, this can be costly and time-consuming, so a plausible alternative is to rely on the information of others," the article explained. "Such influence may take the form of direct communication and discussion with, or observation of, others."[18]

Imitating the actions of others is a trait deeply ingrained in many animals, not just humans. The economists speculated that it might be an evolutionary adaptation that has promoted survival by "allowing individuals to take advantage of the hard-won information of others."[19] Whatever the cause, once a few people decide to rely on others rather than thinking for themselves, the behavior can quickly spread. If this happens, the result may be an "informational cascade" in which, ultimately, nobody acts on his or her own judgment. "Public information stops accumulating," the economists wrote. "Any early preponderance toward adoption or rejection causes subsequent individuals to ignore their private signals, which thus never enter the public pool of knowledge." The result: "With virtual certainty, all but the first few individuals end up doing the same thing."[20]

By the summer of 1999, millions of Americans were trapped in an informational cascade. If they had been confined to a quiet room and asked whether they really believed that Yahoo! was worth more than Texaco, or America Online was worth more than Time Warner, most of them would have said no. But they were not confined to a quiet room. They were living in an environment where their friends and neighbors were buying stocks, Wall Street analysts and journalists were constantly reminding them that stocks were the best of all possible investments, and respected commentators were arguing that the Dow was heading for 20,000, 30,000, or even 40,000. In such an environment, as the sociologist Gustav Le Bon wrote in his classic book *The Crowd: A Study of the Popular Mind*, an individual "is a grain of sand amid other grains of sand, which the wind stirs up at will."[21]

Le Bon was writing during the 1890s, but his description of how people subjugate their own reasoning to the will of the crowd prefigured the work of contemporary economists. "The fact that (individuals) have been transformed into a crowd puts them in possession of a sort of collective mind which makes them feel, think, and act in a manner quite different from that which each individual of them would feel, think, and act were he in a state of isolation," Le Bon wrote. Once a crowd has formed, it has a natural tendency to go to extremes because "the individuals in the crowd who might possess a personality sufficiently strong to resist the suggestions are too few in number to struggle against the current."[22] Eventually, even the independent-minded give up the fight.

At the end of August, Charles Clough, one of the last remaining bears on Wall Street, announced his forthcoming retirement as Merrill Lynch's stock strategist. For several years, Clough had been advising investors to keep much of their money in cash and bonds. His cautious stance had become an embarrassment to himself and to his firm. In a recent *Wall Street Journal* survey of the performance of numerous stock strategists, he had come at the bottom in the one-quarter, one-year, and five-year categories. Clough's resignation was no surprise. What was surprising was that he had lasted so long. An ordained deacon in the Roman Catholic faith, he said he wanted to spend more time with his family and his church.[23]

# chapter 17  web dreams

**I**

**At the beginning of *startup.com*, an entertaining documentary that** tracks the rise and fall of Govworks.com, Khalil Isaz Tuzman, a handsome young investment banker, packs up his desk at Goldman Sachs and walks into the New York night, his arms full of boxes. It is May 1999. "I'm going to start an Internet company,"[1] Tuzman says, his sheepish grin betraying his disbelief. A few weeks later Tuzman finds himself on Sand Hill Road trying to raise money for a business with no assets, no experience, and no financial plan. All he has to pitch is the premise that people would prefer to go online to pay their parking tickets, update their driver's licenses, and otherwise deal with the government. Such services represent a "vertical market of $586 billion," he assures a group of VCs. "Parking tickets alone come to $500 million." A Kleiner Perkins representative tells Tuzman that Govworks.com is two years too late and located on the wrong coast, but he doesn't get disheartened. After more than a dozen meetings, in California and on the eastern seaboard, he and his childhood friend, Tom Herman, extract pledges for close to $20 million, enough to get them started. Another Web dream is under way.

What had started out as a novelty for computer science majors and Silicon Valley mavericks was now a staple of the MBA curriculum. The University of Michigan Business School started a course, "From Idea to IPO in 14 Weeks," in which students developed their own start-up proposals, and a venture capital firm paid $12,000 to sit in on the class. At Harvard Business School, a student poll indicated that of

880 students who would be graduating in the summer 1999, 343 were planning to join high-tech start-ups or venture capital firms, while only 308 were going into management consulting or finance. "I didn't want to miss the Big One," Patrick Mullane, a Harvard student who turned down a job at Arthur Andersen to join SupplierMarket.com, a B2B venture, told *Fortune*. "I didn't want to miss the next Industrial Revolution."[2] The students' role models were recent Harvard MBAs like Hope and Will Chen, who had sold their Internet billing company to eBay for $125 million, Stig Leschly, who had sold his start-up, Exchange.com, to Amazon.com for $200 million, and Anthony Tjan, who had raised $100 million for his Internet firm, Zefer. "There's never been a time in contemporary history when there's been a chance like this to leave your mark on the world," Tjan said to *The Boston Globe*.[3]

Ivy League MBAs weren't the only ones who saw the Internet as an escape from the routine and the bureaucratic. A survey carried out in the spring of 1999 suggested that one in twelve Americans was at that moment trying to found a new business. Many more were thinking about it. The exploits of Internet entrepreneurs like Jerry Yang and Jeff Bezos had turned them into icons. The media was full of stories about the demise of the corporation and the rise of small businesses. In a cover story celebrating the rise of a "Free Agent Nation," *Fast Company* calculated that there were now about 25 million people who worked for themselves in the United States.[4]

While the Internet was undoubtedly spawning a lot of start-ups, much of what was being written about them didn't make economic sense. The wave of individual enterprise, while commendable on some levels, was really an artifact of the speculative bubble, which was directing unprecedented sums of capital toward the venture capital industry. Enterprise without capital is like a Cadillac without gas. It may look impressive, but it isn't going anywhere. In 1996, there were 458 venture capital firms in the United States, with $52 billion under management. By international standards, these were impressive figures; no other country in the world had a venture capital industry on anything like the U.S. scale. But in just three years the industry more than doubled in size. By 1999, there were 779 venture capital firms, with $164 billion to spend. Everything about the industry was getting bigger. At the start of the 1990s, a $100 million venture capital fund was considered large. Now, Kleiner Perkins and other Silicon Valley firms were raising billion-dollar funds. Much of the money that went into these funds was hardly speculative capital in the classic sense. The investors included university endowments, such as those at Harvard and Stanford, and charitable trusts, such as the Ford, Hewlett, and Wellcome foundations. Many of these institutions saw investing in venture capital funds as a less risky way to participate in the Internet boom than picking individual stocks.

With their coffers bulging, the VCs had the capacity and the incentive to fund a lot more start-ups. In 1996, they gave $11.2 billion to 2,123 new ventures. In 1999, 3,957 companies received a total of $59.4 billion. The average investment in 1999 was $15 million, but some of them were much larger. In one round of financing, Datek Online Holdings, the online trading firm, raised $195 million. In another, Planet Rx, an online drugstore, raised $59.3 million. The range of companies that received funding was startling. E-Stamp, a business that planned to sell stamps over the Internet, raised $31.5 million.

Each of these companies was heading for an early IPO, which is why they were able to raise so much money. The days when VCs nurtured investments for five or ten years before selling them to the public were over. These days, twelve months was a long-term investment horizon. Many VCs had reservations about what was happening, but they were just as trapped in follow-the-leader logic as the investment bankers and the mutual fund managers were. Before the advent of the Internet, VCs had often demanded that entrepreneurs put a third of their own net worth into their companies. By the middle of 1999, the VCs were competing with one another for the privilege of financing the next Internet business plan that came through the door, and all prior rules had been suspended. "It was absurdly easy," a young Harvard Business School graduate who helped raise several million dollars for an Internet start-up in the fall of 1999, recalled. "You would walk into offices in New York and people would immediately offer money to you if they thought you looked smart. We didn't have any data on the market; we didn't have a product demo; we didn't have anything. We had a business plan, but that was it."[5]

Even the old-line venture capital firms, which were more conservative than their Silicon Valley and Silicon Alley brethren, were lured into the Internet industry. For the partners at the Mayfield Fund, an East Coast firm that had been going since the 1960s, it was Amazon.com's $30 billion stock market valuation that proved the turning point. In the spring of 1999, they made more than a dozen investments in e-commerce companies, including an online invitation company, an online retailer of college textbooks, and a gay and lesbian portal. The Mayfield Fund also invested in Govworks.com.

## II

**The biggest venture capital deal of the year was for $275 million,** and it closed in July, shortly after the Atlanta day-trading massacre. The company that received this massive cash infusion was Webvan, an Oakland-based start-up that was planning to build a nationwide chain of online grocery stores. Of all the follies of the Internet boom, Webvan was arguably (but not indisputably) the grandest. Louis Borders, the founder of the Borders bookstore chain, which Kmart bought from him in 1992, was the man behind Webvan. In his Internet venture, Borders originally wanted to target the entire American retail market—more than $2 trillion a year—selling everything from fresh fish to designer clothes over the World Wide Web. In 1997, when Borders went to see the partners at Benchmark Capital, they were skeptical about this plan, but his intelligence and ambition impressed them. After persuading him to start out with groceries, they agreed to invest $3.5 million in seed money. Sequoia Capital, which had financed Yahoo!, invested the same amount. One of Benchmark's partners told Borders that he was setting up a billion-dollar company. "Naw," Borders replied. "It's going to be ten billion. Or zero."[6]

By early 1999, Borders had raised another $150 million from a varied group of investors that included Yahoo!; CBS; Knight-Ridder, the newspaper chain; and LVMH, the French luxury goods conglomerate. (Bernard Arnault, LVMH's suave chairman, was the latest old-economy bigwig to fall for the Internet.) Webvan used some of this money to build a 330,000-square-foot warehouse in Oakland, which would serve as a laboratory for testing Borders's theory that he could undercut bricks-and-mortar competitors like Safeway and Kroger. As the existing online grocers, such as Peapod and Streamline, had discovered, selling groceries over the Internet was challenging. Grocery items are bulky, heavy, and, in many cases, perishable—all of which makes them expensive to store and transport.

Borders, a math major in college, believed the key to success was clever technology. When he set up his first bookstore, he wrote his own software to manage its inventory. The Oakland warehouse, which opened for business in June 1999, looked like something out of a Fritz Lang movie. A vast array of computerized conveyor belts delivered grocery items to specially designed "pods," or assembly areas, where an employee packed them into bags. Webvan offered more than 300 varieties of vegetables, 350 types of cheese, and 700 wine labels. Once an order had been assembled, it was loaded onto a truck and taken to one of twelve docking stations in the Bay Area. There it was transferred to one of Webvan's sixty small vans, which delivered it to the customer's home in a predesignated thirty-minute time slot.

Despite its modern machinery, Webvan quickly ran into some old-fashioned logistical problems. The cold temperatures necessary to preserve fresh produce made the conveyor belts malfunction; the celery didn't fit into the produce bags; the soft cheeses got crushed; and the delivery vans got stuck in the San Francisco traffic. Webvan also discovered what Peapod and other competitors had learned long ago. Most people prefer to drive to their local grocery store and pick out their own tomatoes. It had taken Peapod ten years to build a customer base of 100,000. Webvan needed a lot more customers than that to justify its heavy investment, and the early signs weren't encouraging. On any given day, the Oakland facility, which was designed to handle eight thousand orders, was getting just three hundred or four hundred. And more than half of the customers who bought groceries from Webvan never returned.

By any objective standards Webvan's launch was a failure, but that wasn't reflected in most of the press coverage that the company received. A month or so after it started making deliveries, a report in *Business Week* said Webvan "may be the most innovative E-commerce venture to date."[7] The article quoted Kevin Czinger, a former investment banker at Goldman Sachs who served as Webvan's chief financial officer, saying: "This is the first back-end re-engineering of an entire industry."[8] Also in July, Webvan signed a billion-dollar deal with Bechtel, the company that built the Hoover Dam, to construct twenty-six more warehouses across the country, starting with Atlanta. To pay for this expansion, it closed the $275 million financing round, with investors that included Sequoia Capital, Softbank (the Japanese investment company headed by Masayoshi Son), and Goldman Sachs, Webvan's financial adviser. In return for the $275 million, the participants received just 6.5 percent of Webvan, which was already valuing itself at more than $4 billion. The presence of Goldman Sachs on the list of investors was particularly notable. No longer content to earn tens of millions of dollars in investment banking fees, the eminent Wall Street firm had decided to join the real action: acquiring Internet equity.

In early August, just two months after it started selling groceries, Webvan filed for an IPO. This was a new record, beating Drugstore.com, which had just gone public after five months in business. Webvan's prospectus revealed that in the first six months of 1999 it had lost $35 million on sales of $395,000. Borders and his backers realized that they needed a reassuring front man to interpret these figures for Wall Street. They found him in George T. Shaheen, the fifty-five-year-old chief executive of Andersen Consulting, a leading technology consulting firm, with 65,000 employees in nearly fifty countries. Shaheen gave up a retirement package worth tens of millions of dollars to join Webvan. In return, he got 1.25 million Webvan shares, which weren't yet trading, and options to buy another fifteen million at $8 each. Assuming that the IPO went off as planned, this signing-on package would be worth at least $100 million. Shaheen's move demonstrated that just about anybody would join an Internet company if they received enough stock and options.

After a Labor Day lull, the IPO market picked up again in mid-September, with stock issues by, among others, Gardens.com, Ashford.com, and Perfumania.com. Webvan, meanwhile, released its prospectus. Shaheen told *Forbes* that Webvan would "set the rules for the largest consumer sector in the economy."[9] This was an innocuous enough comment, but it came during the pre-IPO "quiet period" when companies are supposed to remain silent. At around the same time, Adam Lashinsky, a columnist for TheStreet.com, published details from Webvan's investor road show, which are usually off-limits to journalists. According to Lashinsky, the firm's senior executives had said it would boast profit margins of 12 percent, compared to 4 percent for normal supermarkets, and that each of its warehouses could generate annual revenues of $300 million. This was wishful thinking—the Oakland warehouse was still operating way below capacity—but it should have been disclosed in the prospectus, which it wasn't.

The SEC forced Webvan to postpone the IPO and file an amended prospectus. In the new document, which appeared in October, the firm revealed that Goldman Sachs, its own financial adviser, expected it to lose $78.3 million in 1999, $154.3 million in 2000, and $302 million in 2001. Even in the fall of 1999, selling a company that was expected to lose half a billion dollars in its first three years was no trifling matter. Fortunately for Webvan, the forced delay worked in its favor. During October, technology stocks continued to rally strongly, and the IPO market roared along. PlanetRx.com, Women.com, and E-Stamp were among the many Internet companies that went public. On November 2, the Nasdaq closed above 3,000 for the first time, a milestone that received a lot of media attention. Goldman Sachs seized the moment. Three days later, it issued 25 million Webvan shares at $15 each. The stock opened at $26 and closed at $24.875, for a first-day gain of 66 percent. This valued Webvan at almost $8 billion, the biggest first-day valuation for an Internet company since Priceline.com. Goldman Sachs and the other investors that had put up $275 million in July had doubled their money in less than four months. Shaheen, seven weeks into the job, had seen his recruitment package rise to almost $300 million. And Borders was now worth more than $2 billion.

## III

**Webvan's IPO offered encouragement to other Internet companies** that were spending money like Imelda Marcos on a shoe-shopping spree. Clearly, no online business was too dubious to be packaged and sold to investors as long as it had some prestigious names behind it. In the weeks following Webvan's stock offering, TheKnot.com, a wedding site, went public, and so did many other e-commerce start-ups, including eGreetings.com, MotherNature.com, SmarterKids.com, and eCollege.com. Several big Internet companies filed to do IPOs early in 2000, including Homegrocer.com, Webvan's rival, and Pets.com, a San Francisco–based start-up that was targeting the $20 billion a year market for pet food and pet accessories.

The battle of the pet sites represented the *reductio ad absurdum* of the Internet bubble, but it was no laughing matter to those involved. In the spring of 1999, more than half a dozen online pet stores were looking for outside financing, and more than two dozen venture capital firms were vying to fund them. The pet market was one of the few big chunks of consumer spending that remained untapped by Internet retailers. Nearly two-thirds of American families owned pets, and many of them would rather have gone hungry than deprive their canine and feline loved ones.

Greg McLemore, a Pasadena entrepreneur who had registered hundreds of Internet addresses, including Toys.com and Pets.com, founded Pets.com in November 1998 and moved it to San Francisco. In early 1999, he persuaded Hummer Winblad Venture Partners, a well-known Silicon Valley venture capital firm, to back the company, and he also sold a 50 percent stake to Amazon.com. Jeff Bezos, the devoted owner of a golden Labrador, had once offered a job to Julie Wainwright, Pets.com's chief executive, and she negotiated the deal with Amazon.com. "We invest only in companies that share our passion for customers," Bezos said. "Pets.com has a leading market position, and its proven management team is dedicated to a great customer experience, whether it's making a product like a ferret hammock easy to find, or help in locating a pet-friendly hotel."[10]

Amazon.com's involvement with Pets.com came as a blow to the other online pet store entrepreneurs who were busy making presentations up and down Sand Hill Road. It didn't stop them, though. In May, Paw.net, another San Francisco–based start-up, changed its name to Petopia.com and raised $9 million from Technology Crossover Ventures, of Palo Alto. "There is a huge potential for growth in the pet category as an e-commerce play," Jay Hoag, a partner at

Technology Crossover Ventures, said. "Currently, the pet food and supply market is highly fragmented. As more customers turn to the Internet to make purchases, Petopia.com will leverage its distribution and manufacturer relationships and its brand to create a nationally recognized virtual store and community for consumers."[11] This was a hopeful statement. PetsMart and Petco, each with hundreds of stores, dominated pet food retailing across the country, and neither had any intention of allowing its market to be taken away. PetsMart teamed up with an online firm called Petjungle.com to create PetsMart.com. Petco, after hiring Morgan Stanley to advise it how to go online, decided to invest in Petopia.com. When Petstore.com, yet another online venture, raised almost $100 million from a group of investors including Discover Communications, the owner of the Animal Planet cable network, the stage was set for a costly four-sided battle.

Pets.com fired the first shots. In the summer of 1999 it raised another $50 million from Hummer Winblad, Amazon.com, and Bowman Capital, a hedge fund. With money in the bank, it slashed its prices by almost 50 percent and hired TBWA/Chiat Day, an advertising agency, to create an expensive marketing campaign. This dual offensive was premised on the now-familiar argument that the only way to succeed on the Internet was to gain market leadership and establish a strong brand. By the end of 1999, Pets.com had racked up losses of $61.8 million on revenues of just $5.8 million. Most of this money went on advertising. TBWA/Chiat Day, which numbered Apple Computer and Levi-Strauss among its clients, created the Pets.com Sock Puppet, a chatty "spokesdog" that quoted Joseph Conrad, asked housecats out on dates, and objected to the use of socks as Christmas stockings. The Pets.com sock puppet quickly became a popular symbol of e-commerce, but it didn't generate much business. At the start of 2000, Pets.com was attracting fewer than a million visitors a month to its Web site, and its revenues were lower than both Petsmart.com and Petopia.com.

The other pet sites, which had been forced to compete with Pets.com's price cuts, weren't faring any better. Most of them were selling goods at a loss. Pets.com even introduced free shipping, a big expense for twenty- and forty-pound bags of dog food. Insofar as there was any business logic at work, it was that the pet sites, after attracting customers with cheap dog chow, would then be able to sell them higher-margin products, such as ornate leather collars and down-filled cushions. Each site promoted itself as the one true community of pet lovers. Pets.com sponsored "Canine Couture" fashion shows and offered free veterinary advice. Petopia.com built an aviary and doggy pound at its headquarters and also entered an alliance with the American Society for the Prevention of Cruelty to Animals. Petstore joined forces with the American Animal Hospital Association. PetsMart bought AcmePet.com, a popular online community of pet owners.

At the core of all this activity was the race to do on IPO. The online pet stores provide a classic example of how the Internet boom had inverted the traditional order of business. Instead of using the stock market to build companies, VCs and entrepreneurs were now using companies to create stocks. Costly marketing campaigns were launched not only to attract customers but, more important, to grab the attention of potential shareholders. The task of building the company was secondary—a chore that had to be performed before the IPO, but not the real reason why Harvard MBAs like Andrea Reisman, Petopia's chief executive, were giving up promising careers elsewhere. Pet food is only pet food, even to a Harvard MBA.


## IV

**The American public was the main beneficiary of the venture capital** glut. In cities like New York, Boston, and Seattle, couch potatoes could now log on to their computers and order beer, videos, and ice cream—all of which would arrive within the hour free of delivery charges. Joseph Park, a twenty-seven-year-old Korean American, was one of the philanthropists providing this service. In 1997, Park quit his job at Goldman Sachs. (With so many of its employees leaving to become Internet entrepreneurs it is hardly surprising that the investment bank turned itself into an Internet investor.) Park and a friend, Yong Kang, set up Kozmo.com, an online convenience store that they named after the character on *Seinfeld*. After convincing Flatiron Partners, a New York venture capital firm that had financed many Silicon Alley companies, to provide initial financing, they rented a warehouse in the East Village and recruited dozens of bicycle messengers to deliver orders as small as a packet of gum. Taking a page from Price line.com's book, they hired Lee Majors, from the show *The Six Million Dollar Man*, to tout Kozmo.com in a series of commercials.

Kozmo.com proved popular, particularly with teenagers, college students and other nocturnal creatures. Park boasted that he was feeding "half the potheads in New York,"[12] but marijuana users weren't his only customers. Videos and computer games were the most popular items, and Kozmo.com also did a brisk trade in AA batteries and condoms. Henry Kravis and David Rockefeller, two of the richest men in the country, agreed to put some money behind Park's vision, and so did Jeff Bezos. At the end of 1999, Amazon.com, which was buying stakes in a number of Internet companies, invested $60 million in Kozmo.com. A month later, Kozmo.com signed a cross-promotion agreement with Starbucks. Park and Yong were now making plans to expand to thirty cities by the end of 2000. There was even talk of launching in Tokyo. Such plans were posited on the successful completion of an IPO. In preparation for a stock issue, Kozmo.com recruited a chief financial officer from Federal Express, a marketing director from Ethan Allen, a chief technology officer from Coca-Cola, a logistics expert from United Parcel Service, a specialist in supply chain management from Ernst & Young, and a vice president of corporate development from Blockbuster.

What these veterans of the old economy really thought about Kozmo.com is an interesting question. The options they received, while it may have salved their doubts, surely didn't vanquish them. If Kozmo.com hadn't had ".com" attached to its name, it would have had trouble raising any money from outside investors, let alone $100 million. According to a subsequent study done by the consulting firm of Booz, Allen & Hamilton, each delivery that Kozmo.com made cost $10 in labor and overhead. This sum didn't include Kozmo.com's marketing expenditures or the cost of the goods it delivered. Since the average customer order was for about $12, it was mathematically impossible for the company to turn a profit. Changing the business model wasn't really an option, either. Park had promised from the outset that delivery wouldn't cost anything, and several competitors—notably Urbanfetch.com—were also offering free delivery. Park's best hope was to take Kozmo.com public before its shortcomings became glaringly apparent, then try to find a deep-pocketed buyer, like Amazon.com or Webvan. As long as Internet stocks continued to defy economic fundamentals, a successful completion of this strategy was not out of the question.

Internet start-ups now constituted a major industry, with a broad range of ancillary businesses to support it, including venture capital firms, investment banks, management consultants, publicists, marketers, and lawyers. There were even "Internet incubators," firms that brought all of these functions under one roof. CMGI, the Boston-based firm that had invested in Lycos and several other early Internet companies, had now turned itself into an Internet incubator, and its founder, David Wetherell, was now being hailed as an investing genius. Internet Capital Group, which went public in August 1999, was another Internet incubator. Idealab, a California-based firm that helped to create eToys, an online toy store that went public in May 1999, was a third. By now, the Internet start-up craze had spread to every conceivable sector of the economy—and a few inconceivable ones too. In *The Monk and the Riddle*, the veteran Silicon Valley investor Randy Komisar described meeting a young entrepreneur who was trying to raise money for an online venture called Funerals.com.

> "We're going to put the fun back into funerals."
> With that declaration, the meeting began. It was a curious elevator pitch.
> "The fun back into funerals?" I asked.
> "Absolutely. We're going to make it easy to make choices when someone dies. You know, the casket, the liner, flowers, that kind of thing."[13]

Journalists were particularly prone to the start-up bug. Michael Elliot, the editor of *Newsweek*'s international edition, quit his job and set out to raise money for e-Countries, a Web site devoted to geopolitics. Peter Gumbel, the *Wall Street Journal*'s Los Angeles bureau chief, became the editor in chief of *Business.com*, a new financial information site. The entrepreneurial spirit also spread to the staff of fashion magazines like *Vogue* and *Elle*, a group not previously noted for their devotion to the bottom line. Several prominent editors gave up their chauffeured town cars for fashion sites with names like Eve.com, Beautyscene.com, and Beautyjungle.com.

The two best-known journalists-turned-Internet-entrepreneurs were Kurt Andersen and Michael Hirschorn, former colleagues from *Spy*, the satirical magazine that had skewered the money culture of the 1980s. Andersen, a former editor of *New York* magazine and columnist at *The New Yorker*, had just finished his first novel, *Turn of the Century*, which bravely, if not entirely successfully, tried to capture the uneasy convergence of money, media, and ambition that contemporary New York represented. Hirschorn, a popular and rumpled figure, had recently been fired as editor of *Spin* magazine. Together, the two Harvard graduates decided to set up what their business plan described as "a must read online site for the cultural elite." The name they landed on was Insidedope.com, which was eventually shortened to Inside.com. "It wasn't just about the money—not for me anyway," Hirschorn would later recall. "It was about creating something new, something not trapped in the dead-end culture of print magazines, something where the staff owned part of the company."[14] There is no reason to doubt Hirschorn's motives, but he and Andersen were hardly oblivious to the immediate financial possibilities. At one point in *The Turn of the Century*, Lizzie Zimbalist, the main female character, consults an investment banker, Nancy McNabb, about floating her software company on the stock market. McNabb tells her:

> "I think we can end up north, nicely north [of $75 million]. The KillerWare offering Thursday and the Be-My-Friend.com IPO tomorrow will tell us a lot about the weather we're facing out there, microcap-valuation-wise." She pauses. "You have earnings, yes?" The question is an afterthought."[15]

Andersen no doubt appreciated the irony of fictionalizing the Internet boom at the same time he was becoming a player in it. "No one feels guilty about being rich anymore and not caring about anything except money," he told the London *Times*. "Unemployment is at a historic low. The kids come pre-sold out. A twenty-one-year-old today knows only the post-liberal Reagan philosophy, the free market won. They come into a landscape where their college friends make

$5 million overnight. They see the rewards of capitalism directly—
and they look good."[16]

College graduates weren't the only ones with a benign view of
what was happening. In the media circles where Andersen and
Hirschorn circulated, most people no longer thought of capitalism as
an oppressive system crying out for critique, or as a comic farrago ripe
for satire; rather, they looked upon it as something akin to a Las Vegas
slot machine with the barrels stuck on jackpot. Until the management
got wise to it and did some repairs, they'd continue feeding quarters
in the slot.

# chapter 18 warning signs

I

**George Soros is one of the most successful investors of the modern** era. In 1987, he published *The Alchemy of Finance*, in which he introduced the concept of "reflexivity" to explain why financial markets go to extremes.[1] In a bull market, Soros argued, the very fact that stock prices are rising appears to improve the economic outlook, which prompts investors to become even more optimistic. This leads to more buying, and the market rises further, thus restarting the cycle. Soros used the word "reflexivity" to describe this self-reinforcing process because the rise in stock prices reflects the apparent improvement in the economic outlook, and the improvement in economic outlook reflects the rising stock prices. With each oscillation of the cycle, investors' expectations about future profits and economic growth ratchet upward. Eventually, their expectations move so out of line with reality that they are impossible to fulfill. At this point, the market becomes vulnerable to a correction. Disappointed expectations have a negative effect on stock prices, and falling stock prices make the economic fundamentals look worse. Unless more good news arrives quickly, reflexivity starts to work in the opposite direction. The drop in stock prices feeds on itself, eventually leading to a collapse.

Professional economists, who tend to see financial markets as omniscient calculating machines, gave Soros's book a cool reception, but he is a lot richer than they are. Certainly, his theory fits the Internet boom. Rising stock prices boosted consumption and investment, which boosted economic growth, which, in turn, underpinned further rises in stock prices. The reflexive process was most powerful in the technology sector, which generated perhaps a third of all the growth in the economy between 1995 and 1999. Technology component manufacturers like Cisco Systems, Lucent Technologies, and Nortel Networks expanded at unprecedented rates. Their biggest customers were upstart telecommunications companies, such as Qwest, Williams Communications, and 360 Networks, that owed their existence to the buoyant financial markets. Some of these firms were building national networks to challenge long-distance carriers like AT&T and Sprint. Others were building local networks to compete against the Baby Bells. But they all depended on the financial markets to raise the vast sums of money needed to finance their expansion. In attempting to justify the prices investors were paying for Cisco, Nortel, and other technology favorites, Wall Street analysts looked at their current growth rates and extrapolated them into the indefinite future. This valuation method conveniently ignored the fact that the high growth rates were themselves a product of the stock market's rise. Should the market falter, they would almost certainly disappear.

Most technology investors didn't query the upbeat analysis that Wall Street was peddling. With a stock market downturn unthinkable, there wasn't much point in worrying about the consequences should one arrive. In fairness, it is always difficult to tell when the market has left reality so far behind that a downturn is imminent. History isn't much of a guide. In early 1929, legend has it, Joseph P. Kennedy liquidated his portfolio after a shoe shine boy gave him a stock tip. If Kennedy had been alive in the 1990s he would have sold out years before the peak. With confidence in the economy and the Internet practically unbounded, more and more Americans were getting into the market. According to one story, unconfirmed but from a reliable source, even the surgeons at New York's Mount Sinai Hospital were taking time out from their regular jobs to trade stocks. Between patients, they were reportedly using a computer in the operating room to place buy and sell orders.

**II**

**In the summer of 1999, Barton Biggs traveled to Sun Valley, Idaho,** where he had been invited to present his dyspeptic views in a debate with James Glassman, an economics columnist at *The Washington Post*. Glassman had coauthored *Dow 36,000*, a new book that was receiving a lot of attention. In it, Glassman and his co-author, Kevin Hassett, argued that stocks are no riskier than bonds over the long term and should be priced accordingly. Traditionally, investors have demanded a "risk premium" for holding stocks. Glassman and Hassett calculated that if this premium were eliminated the Dow, which was then hovering around 11,000, would more than triple. This argument didn't make much sense—the whole point of bonds is that they are safer than stocks—but it showed how far New Economy thinking had progressed. In the fall of 1929, Irving Fisher, an eminent Yale Professor, earned a place in the history books when he suggested, a few weeks before the Great Crash, that stock prices had reached "a permanent and high plateau." Glassman made Fisher sound like a pessimist. During the debate with Biggs, he argued that the Internet was the transcending invention of the twentieth century, more important than the jet aircraft, the contraceptive pill, and nuclear fission. Biggs considered Glassman's argument to be ridiculous. Even the humble air conditioner had altered history more than the Internet, he said. Without air conditioning, Atlanta would be a small town and modern Singapore wouldn't exist. After the speeches were over the issue was decided by a show of hands. Glassman won by 180 votes to 2. One of the people who voted for Biggs was his wife.

Biggs flew back to New York and brooded. Morgan Stanley was underwriting more Internet IPOs by the week. (It would end up doing twenty-seven Internet IPOs in 1999, more than it had done in the previous four years combined.) Mary Meeker and her colleagues were still being more discriminating than some of their rivals, but nobody could pretend that drugstore.com and Ask Jeeves, two of Morgan's latest Internet IPOs, were future members of the Fortune 500. In trying to justify her buy recommendation on stocks like these, Meeker was being forced to rely on increasingly suspect valuation methods. In a report on drugstore.com published in October, she pointed to the fact that the average user of its Web site viewed 14.9 pages a month in August, compared to 10.3 on its rival's, PlanetRx, site. "Additionally, drugstore.com maintained a level of 48 percent engaged shoppers (a unique user who views at least three minutes of content within the category) ahead of PlanetRx, which had 45 percent."[2] There was little mention of whether "engaged shoppers" actually bought anything, or when either drugstore.com or PlanetRx, both of which were taking heavy losses, would turn a profit.

Few of the Internet companies that Morgan Stanley was preparing for IPOs satisfied the criteria that Meeker had once insisted to met before she would even consider taking a firm public: big potential market, sound management, and clever products. Biggs privately suspected that the investment bankers, at Morgan and elsewhere, would keep pumping up the bubble until it burst. He could understand why, and he even had some sympathy for the investment bankers given the competitive pressures they were facing. In asset management, his part of the business, the competition was equally intense. If you renounced the latest investment craze too early, and fell down the performance league tables, you placed the future of the firm at risk.

After Labor Day, as traders returned to their desks, stocks of all kinds were trading at levels never before seen relative to earnings and dividends. The PE ratio on the S&P 500 index was 33, compared to a previous high of 22.3 in August 1987, two months before Black Monday. Ray Fair, a Yale economist, tried to answer a question that was on many minds: Did current stock prices make any sense? In order for the answer to be "yes," Fair calculated, corporate earnings would have to grow at an annual rate of 14.5 percent for ten years, and the ratio of after-tax profits to GDP would have to double—from 6 percent to 12 percent.[3] This wasn't impossible, but it would involve an unprecedented redistribution of income from workers to corporations. Much more likely, with unemployment at its lowest level in thirty years, was a profit squeeze, as workers demanded higher wages.

Lending from brokerage houses, another time-tested sign of excessive speculation, was rising sharply. Since Alan Greenspan's "irrational exuberance" speech in December 1996, margin debt had almost doubled. As a percentage of GDP, it was now at its highest level in more than sixty years. Other types of borrowing, including bank loans, credit card loans, and home-equity loans, were also rising fast. Total household debt stood at 102 percent of personal disposable income, compared to 85 percent in 1992. There were increasing signs that all of this extra debt was having an effect. Amid the ongoing boom, more people than ever were defaulting on their debts. Personal bankruptcies were running at record levels.

These indicators strongly suggested that the American economy was in a credit-driven speculative bubble of the sort Japan went through in the 1980s, but investors preferred to believe the upbeat explanations provided by Glassman and others. This, too, was typical of the late stages of a speculative mania. The September issue of *Wired* contained a number of articles on the coming age of "ultra-prosperity." Kevin Kelly, the magazine's executive editor and the author of *New Rules for the New Economy*, sketched an America in 2020 where the average household income was $150,000, middle-class families had their own personal chefs, and the Dow was north of 50,000 and heading for 100,000. Such a scenario "looks more plausible all the time," Kelly wrote. "How many times in the history of mankind have we wired the planet to create a single marketplace? How often have entirely new channels of commerce been created by digital technology? When has money itself been transformed into thousands of instruments of investment?"[4]

Kelly also interviewed George Gilder, who was now himself an Internet entrepreneur of sorts. Gilder published the monthly *Gilder Technology Report*, which, for $295 a year, alerted investors to the latest developments in science and technology and provided a list of stocks that stood to benefit. Qualcomm, which rose more than 2,500 percent in 1999, was one of Gilder's favorites. JDS Uniphase was another. "I don't think Internet valuations are crazy," Gilder declared. "I think they reflect a fundamental embrace of huge opportunities. Virtually all forecasts estimate something like a thousand-fold increase in Internet traffic over the next five years. . . . In ten years, at this rate, there would be a million-fold increase."[5] It is to be hoped, for the sake of his subscribers, that Gilder's prognostications about technology were more firmly grounded than his arithmetic. According to most estimates, there were at that time about 150 million Internet users. A millionfold increase from there would have produced 150 trillion Internet users. The world's population is only about 8 billion.

Kelly also contacted another name from the past, Harry Dent Jr., the baby-boomer theorist, who back in 1992 had predicted that the Dow would reach 8,500 sometime between 2006 and 2010, a forecast that turned out to be too conservative. Dent now had his own advisory firm, and he was giving speeches. A few months previously, AIM Management Group, a mutual fund company, had paid him the ultimate tribute by setting up the AIM Dent Demographic Trends Fund, which invested in companies that looked set to exploit the aging of the baby boomers. Dent had just published a paperback version of his latest book, *The Roaring 2000's Investor*, in which he predicted that the Dow would reach 41,000 in 2009. "For the past ten years I have been one of the most bullish forecasters about the future, and yet even I have underestimated the market," he told Kelly. "We did not really account for the international growth—we now have five billion new consumers to sell to. And historically, at about the middle part in a boom, you get a transition to higher valuation levels when people understand the boom is here to stay. The investment cycle kicks in and floods the market with money. That's where we are now."[6]

## III

**"Face it: Out there in some garage an entrepreneur is forging a bullet** with your company's name on it," Gary Hamel, a Harvard Business School professor, warned the nation's CEOs in the September 1999 issue of the *Harvard Business Review*. "You've got one option: you have to shoot first."[7] Across the country, companies were heeding Hamel's advice, and, as a result, the dividing line between the old and new economies was becoming blurred. The Walt Disney Company, which already owned Go.com, the fifth most visited site on the Web, was buying the rest of Infoseek. Time Warner, which had finally shuttered its Pathfinder portal after years of heavy losses, had teamed up with Sony to buy CDNOW. NBC had issued its own Internet tracking stock, NBCi. News Corporation had set up a $300 million venture capital arm, which took a stake in Healtheon. The melding of the old and the new wasn't confined to the media. Barnes&Noble. com, which went public in the spring of 1999, was expanding into music retailing. Wal-Mart and Toys "R" Us were both launching online divisions. Jack Welch, the chairman of General Electric, had decreed that the Internet was GE's number-one priority. Ford and General Motors were preparing to move their vast purchasing operations online.

The inspiration for much of this activity was Amazon.com, which was now "Earth's Most Talked About Company." In just four years, the Seattle start-up had reached $1 billion in revenues, and Jeff Bezos had turned into what his hometown paper, *The Seattle Times*, called "The Internet's Ultimate Cult Figure."[8] When he appeared at company events his own employees asked for his autograph. Bezos was no longer just a businessman. To many, he was a totem, a messianic savant to whom the divine truth had been revealed. "When we try to comprehend something as vast, amorphous, and downright scary as the Internet, it's no wonder we grope for familiar historical precedents—the railroads, the interstate highway system, the telephone network," a *Business Week* cover story on "The Internet Age" declared in October 1999. "But none of those really captures the Internet's earthshaking impact on the business world. For that, we must take the advice of Internet commerce pioneer Jeffrey P. Bezos."[9]

The Gospel According to Jeff, which he proclaimed to *Business Week* and anybody else who would listen, was that capitalism had entered its Cambrian era, the equivalent of the period 550 million years ago when multicelled life first appeared on earth. "It was the greatest speciation ever seen, but it was also—which people forget— the greatest rate of extinction ever seen," Bezos said. "We're going to see all kinds of ideas tried, and the majority of them are probably going to fail." One of the businesses whose survival was rarely called into question these days was Amazon.com. "It's not only the dominant bookseller (valued at $22 billion, while Borders, with 260 physical superstores, is worth a bare billion), but has quickly become the biggest music retailer on the Net, as well as a seller of toys and consumer electronics," *Newsweek* reported. "Amazon.com is the flagship for Internet commerce, living proof of the viability of its business model—selling goods directly to customers on the Net."[10]

The scale of Bezos's ambition was stunning. Some commentators said he wanted to create an online Wal-Mart, but that was an understatement. Wal-Mart doesn't compete directly with Toys "R" Us, Nobody Beats the Wiz, Home Depot, and Tower Records. Amazon.com now competed with all of these stores, and that was just a start. Bezos wanted to dominate the entire online shopping market. At the end of September, he announced the formation of zShops, an online shopping mall where Amazon.com's 12 million customers would be able to buy everything from jam to sailboats. When a customer typed in something she wanted—a fishing rod, say—the software would check if Amazon.com carried it. If the item wasn't in stock, the customer would be directed to the home page of an affiliate store that did stock it. "Sixteen months ago, we were a place where people came to find books," Bezos said. "Tomorrow, we will be a place to find anything, with a capital 'A.'"[11]

Unlike some Internet zealots, Bezos never claimed that traditional retailing would go away. He knew that human beings were active and gregarious creatures that liked to go out and shop. But he believed about fifteen percent of retail spending—more than $500 billion—would eventually go online, and he wanted to grab a large part of that for Amazon.com. Bezos insisted that his strategy was based not on a Napoleonic ego, but on increasing returns to scale. As Amazon.com expanded into new areas, its revenues would grow faster than its costs, he argued. Unlike regular retailers, it didn't have to build new stores and staff them up in order to grow. The zShops initiative was a good example of this strategy. Whenever an online customer bought something in a store that he or she had entered from Amazon.com, Amazon.com received a commission. If Amazon.com also handled the billing, which it often did, the commission was 5 percent of the purchase price. "It's a completely new model," Bezos insisted.[12] Investors seemed to believe him. The day of the zShops announcement Amazon.com's stock jumped $15, to 80¾.

Bezos was a persuasive talker, but Amazon.com's costs weren't as fixed as they looked. In addition to its existing distribution centers in

Seattle and Delaware, the company was building another five huge warehouses across the country. These facilities employed thousands of blue-collar workers, who earned $7.50 an hour, more when they worked overtime, as they often did in busy periods. As its business grew, Amazon.com also had to hire a lot more customer service representatives, plus computer technicians and marketing and sales people. Advertising costs were growing strongly too. In 1997, Amazon.com had spent about $30 for each customer it acquired; in 1999 it was spending more than $35 for each new customer.

Companies that really exploit increasing returns to scale, such as Microsoft, make more money the faster they expand. The faster that Amazon.com grew, the more money it lost. At the end of October 1999, it reported a third-quarter loss of $197 million, on revenues of $356 million. Compared to the same quarter in 1998, sales had increased by 130 percent, but losses had risen by 437 percent. Even Henry Blodget was shocked by this development. If Amazon.com didn't move toward profitability soon, he warned, investors would become "as tired as we are of endless postponement of gratification."[13] Blodget downgraded Amazon.com's stock from "strong buy" to "accumulate," and four other analysts also issued downgrades. In a week, the stock dropped from $76 to $63.

Fortunately for Bezos, Christmas was approaching. Some analysts were predicting that online sales during the holiday season could top $10 billion. Amazon.com, which had purchased 181 acres of wrapping paper and 2,500 miles of red ribbon in anticipation of packing about 15 million gifts, stood to be the major beneficiary of this shopping bonanza, and its stock recovered strongly. On December 9, it hit an all-time high, on a split-adjusted basis, of $113, before falling back on profit taking. The following day, it closed at 108$^{11}$/$_{16}$, valuing the company at about $37 billion. Amazon.com's stock, like its founder, was now larger than life. No longer a mere paper claim to the prospective profits of a single company, it had turned into a barometer of the public's faith in the high-tech future. With the new millennium approaching, that faith seemed limitless. The same day that Amazon.com's stock reached $113, VA Linux, a small computer company, went public amid a welter of publicity about the Linux operating system, which was being touted as a possible challenger to

Microsoft Windows. VA Linux's stock soared from $30 to 239¼, a rise of almost 700 percent. This was an even bigger jump than The-Globe.com's stock enjoyed on its first day, and it set a new IPO record.

While all this was happening, the editors of *Time* magazine were settling on their "Man of the Year." Previous choices had included Joseph Stalin, Mohandas Gandhi, and Martin Luther King Jr. This year, the pick was Bezos, the cackling thirty-five-year-old embodiment of e-commerce. A few days before Christmas, Bezos's smiling face appeared on the newsstands. Inside the magazine there was a five-thousand-word profile, which revealed that Bezos's role models were Thomas Edison, an obvious choice, and Walt Disney, not an obvious choice at all. "The thing that always amazed me was how powerful his vision was," Bezos explained. "He knew exactly what he wanted to build and teamed up with a bunch of really smart people and built it. Everyone thought it wouldn't work, and he had to persuade the banks to lend him $400 million. But he did it."[14] The implication was clear: Bezos had struggled against similar odds as Walt Disney to build Amazon.com, and his vindication was approaching.

On Friday, December 29, 1999, Muhammad Ali rang the opening bell on the New York Stock Exchange. When the closing bell rang a few hours later on a session shortened for the holiday, the Dow was at an all-time high of 11,497.12. For the year, it was up 25.22 percent. The Nasdaq, which only the previous day had closed above 4,000 for the first time, was also in record territory, at 4,069.31. Since the start of 1999, it had risen by 85.6 percent, the best performance ever by a major American stock index, surpassing the Dow's 81.7 percent surge in 1915. Some narrower indexes had performed even better. The Dow Jones Internet Composite Index had climbed 167 percent on the year.

## IV

**On the morning of Monday, January 10, Steve Case, the chairman of** America Online, walked onto a stage at the Equitable Center in midtown Manhattan and announced that America Online was buying Time Warner for $165 billion. "We are pleased to have you with us today as we announce the merger to create the first global media and communications company of the Internet century," Case said. The fourteen-year-old "Cockroach of Cyberspace" was taking over the world's largest media company, a sprawling behemoth whose antecedents dated back to Henry Luce and Jack Warner. Case, the Internet entrepreneur, had put on an expensive blue suit and a yellow power tie for the occasion. Gerald Levin, the chairman of Time Warner, was casually dressed in an open-necked shirt and khakis. Case presented the deal as a "merger of equals," but there was no doubt which side would be in charge. Case would be AOL Time Warner's chairman. The new company's stock symbol would be "AOL." America Online's shareholders would own 55 percent of the merged company. While Case was speaking, Time Warner's three top executives—Levin, Ted Turner, and Richard Parsons—were sitting behind him like ornaments.

America Online was planning to pay for the acquisition with its stock, which a month earlier had reached an all-time peak of $91.75. Time Warner's shareholders, in return for surrendering their company's independence, would receive a premium to the current stock price, but they would end up owning just 45 percent of the combined company. In agreeing to accept America Online's stock as payment, Levin and his colleagues were declaring their faith in America Online's stock market capitalization of $163 billion. "The new media stock market valuations are real," Levin insisted. "Not in every case of course. But what AOL has done is get first position in this New World. Its valuation is real, and I am attesting to that."[15]

This was a remarkable claim. America Online had made a lot of progress since 1996, when the company's survival had been called into question. It now had 20 million subscribers, and more than half of all Internet users in the United States were its customers. Its new instant messenger service was extremely popular. In the last four quarters, it had made a profit of $879 million, far more than any other Internet company. In short, America Online had demonstrated that providing mass-market access to the Internet on a subscription basis was a viable business model. But this was a long way from saying it was worth $163 billion.

Time Warner, which was valued at $83.5 billion before the merger announcement, had revenues of more than $26 billion from its cable systems, film studios, and publishing operations. This was more than five times America Online's revenues of $5.2 billion. Time Warner also had heavy debts to service, which kept its earnings down, but it was generating about $6 billion a year in cash flow, four times as much as America Online was producing. Moreover, Time Warner was far from a neophyte when it came to technology. Many of its cable systems had already been upgraded to provide high-speed access to the World Wide Web. In terms of preparing for the next generation of Internet technology, Time Warner was much better placed than America Online, which still relied on slow telephone connections.

Despite this obvious imbalance, most media observers accepted Levin's argument that the merger represented a sensible vote of confidence in Internet stocks. "The Internet boom looks less ephemeral today," the editorial page of *The New York Times* opined.[16] Peter Huber, a fellow at the Manhattan Institute, was even more emphatic. The merger "marks the beginning of the end of the old mass media, and the end of all serious debate about the triumph of the new," he wrote in *The Wall Street Journal*.[17] Huber went on: "Time Warner chairman and CEO Gerald Levin has grasped what many casual observers, especially older and wealthier ones, just can't yet believe: For the old media, now, it's go digital or die."

Such reactions were predictable and confused. A year earlier, when Lycos had tried to merge with USA Networks, its shareholders had refused to accept the deal. Case was repeating the Lycos–USA Networks strategy, but on a much grander scale. Clearly, *he* didn't think that the old media was doomed. "Traditional media assets have a vibrant future if they can be catapulted into the Internet age," he explained. After merging with America Online, Time Warner would be able to promote its magazines, films, and television shows online. At the same time, America Online could create more content based on Time Warner's properties, which would attract more people to its service. In the new media world, more than ever, companies needed famous brands like *People*, CNN, and *Bugs Bunny* to attract people's attention.

The real significance of the merger between America Online and

Time Warner was the confirmation it offered that the old media and the new media were converging—a convergence that had devastating implications for Internet stocks. After all, the main rationale put forward for the high prices of these stocks was that Internet companies were completely unlike ordinary businesses, so standard methods of valuation didn't apply. In using America Online's inflated stock to buy Time Warner, Case held this argument up to the light, where it could be examined. Once there, it didn't look very convincing. America Online and Time Warner, it turned out, were both media companies that sold editorial content to the public and charged for it, largely, by subscriptions. True, America Online's chat rooms were accessed via phone lines, whereas Home Box Office movies were sent down cable wires, but that wasn't a big difference, especially if such distinctions would soon be obliterated with the arrival of high-speed Internet connections. The only big differences between America Online and Time Warner were in the size of their businesses and, most especially, the valuations accorded to their stocks. Before the merger announcement, Time Warner was valued at about twenty times its annual cash flow. Applying this multiple to America Online, the company was worth about $30 billion, less than a fifth of its current stock market capitalization. Case was well aware of this discrepancy, which helps to explain why he had called Levin in October 1999 and suggested a merger. In joining with Time Warner, Case exploited the stock market bubble to convert his company from an Internet service provider with uncertain prospects in a future where broadband access to the Internet would eventually become the norm into a global media colossus that could survive and prosper in any environment. At least one old media mogul looked on in admiration. "It was a brilliant piece of financial engineering," Rupert Murdoch commented. "He jumped in and bought something with $6 billion in cash flow."[18]

The day after the merger announcement, America Online's stock fell by almost 10 percent, to $64.50. Investors were starting to focus on the fact that it was no longer solely an Internet company, with Internet growth rates. After the merger, it would be a new media–old media hybrid, growing at 20 percent or 25 percent a year instead of 50 percent. With America Online's stock falling, Time Warner's stock was dragged down too, because the company's shareholders were being paid in stock. This went on for several weeks. By the end of January, America Online was trading below $60, down more than a third from its December peak. Case had torpedoed his company's stock, but he had secured its long-term future.

## V

**Few Internet entrepreneurs were as shrewd as Case. Many of them** mistakenly believed that the Internet was a viable business in itself, rather than a distribution vehicle that worked for some products (financial information, music, pornography, auctions) but didn't work for others (food, clothes, and anything that people liked to touch). No firm guarded its status as an Internet company more zealously than Yahoo! In the four years since it went public, the Silicon Valley company had transformed itself into a full-service online network, offering everything from online shopping to auctions to stock quotes. Yahoo! now had more than 40 million users, making it the second most popular site on the World Wide Web after America Online. It operated sites in fourteen foreign countries (in twelve languages), including the United Kingdom, France, Germany, Korea, Ireland, and Mexico.

Yahoo!'s financial strategy, which relied on advertising for revenue, also seemed to be paying off. The day after the America Online–Time Warner press conference, it announced profits of $44.7 million for the fourth quarter of 1999. For the year as a whole, Yahoo! earned $61.1 million on revenues that had jumped 140 percent to $588.6 million. More than three thousand companies were now advertising on Yahoo! In anticipation of the earnings release, Yahoo!'s stock broke through $500, a new all-time high, valuing the firm at $131.6 billion. There is a lot of competition, but this may well have been the most exaggerated valuation ever placed on an American company. Yahoo! was now worth more than Walt Disney and News Corporation combined. Its stock market valuation was 224 times its 1999 revenues and 2,154 times its 1999 earnings.

On Wall Street people were speculating that Yahoo! would soon follow America Online's lead and buy Disney or News Corporation. Jerry Yang, Yahoo!'s cofounder, had been talking to a number of media companies, including News Corporation, but only about set-ting up some joint ventures. Yang and his colleagues had decided to remain independent. "We really believe in saying, 'Hey, these are the opportunities that are ahead of us,'" Yang explained a few weeks after the America Online–Time Warner announcement. "'We are purely on the Internet. We are anchored in Silicon Valley. We believe in partnering so that consumers end up having the best experience.' Does that mean that ultimately we will have to combine with a big media company? I think that is a conclusion that people rush to get to."[19] In some ways, Yang's determination to remain independent was commendable. If any company still represented the Internet's freewheeling tradition it was Yahoo! But from a business perspective, the failure to buy a Disney or a Viacom, or another big cash-generating asset, was a grave error. Before long the opportunity to do a transforming deal would be gone. By the end of January, Yahoo!'s stock had already fallen back to below $325.

# chapter 19 the fed strikes

I

**On January 4, 2000, Alan Greenspan made the five-minute trip from** the Fed's headquarters in Foggy Bottom to the White House, where President Clinton nominated him for another four-year term of office. The president boasted about the records that the U.S. economy was setting—unemployment at a thirty-year low, poverty at a twenty-year low, welfare rolls at a thirty-two-year low—and paid tribute to Greenspan's intellect. The Fed chairman had been one of the first economists to recognize "the power and impact of the new technologies on the New Economy, how they changed all the rules and all the possibilities." In fact, the president went on, Greenspan's "devotion to new technologies has been so significant, I've been thinking of taking Alan.com public; then, we can pay the debt off even before 2015."[1]

The joke was closer to the truth than the president imagined. Greenspan's policies had played a central role in the stock market boom. The biggest danger to any bull market is the possibility that the central bank will raise interest rates sharply, stopping the economy in its tracks and decimating corporate earnings. Greenspan had been resisting pressure to tighten monentary policy for several years. During 1999, the Fed did raise rates on three occasions, by a quarter percentage point each time, but these hikes only reversed the emergency rate cuts it had introduced in the fall of 1998 following the collapse of Long Term Capital Management. At the start of 2000, short-term interest rates stood at 5.5 percent—almost exactly where they had been in the summer of 1995, when Netscape went public.

Low interest rates weren't Greenspan's only contribution to the stock market boom. His frequent references to the benefits of new technology, and his refusal to criticize excessive speculation, also played an important role. In August 1999, Greenspan said stock prices reflected "judgments of millions of investors, many of whom are highly knowledgeable about the prospects for the specific companies that make up our broad stock price indexes."[2] Instead of second-guessing these educated judgments, the Fed ought to stick to monitoring inflation pressures in the economy, he concluded. Most commentators accepted Greenspan's reasoning, but it wasn't wholly supported by history. The very reason the Fed was founded in 1913 was to prevent a repeat of the speculative busts that had become increasingly common in the previous half century. If investors were always rational and sensible, there would be no need for an authority figure to oversee the financial markets. (A central bank *would* still be needed to manage the money supply.) Unfortunately, investors are not always on their best behavior. Sometimes they succumb to greed and the herd mentality. In these instances it is up to the Fed chairman, invested with all the intellectual and political authority of his office, to try to restrain them.

Raising interest rates is the usual way to restore sanity, but it isn't the only option. Greenspan could have tried to limit margin lending, which the Securities Exchange Act of 1934 empowered him to do. After growing rapidly during 1999, margin debt reached $243.5 billion in January 2000. At that level, it amounted to 1.57 percent of the stock market's total value, which equaled the previous peak in the fall of 1987. The Fed already regulated margin lending by forcing investors to pay for half of their stock purchases in cash, meaning the "margin requirement" was 50 percent. Senator Charles Schumer and others were calling for the margin requirement to be raised to 60 percent or higher, but Greenspan refused to act. He considered such a move unfair to small investors. Professional investors could often lend money to buy stocks without resorting to margin loans; small investors couldn't. Plus, the basic idea of regulating lending decisions offended Greenspan's free market principles. If investors wanted to put their money into the stocks of Amazon.com or 1-800-FLOW-ERS.com, that was their business. As he had frequently pointed out, the act of taking calculated risks is the essence of capitalism.

All the same, even Greenspan was increasingly worried about what was happening in the stock market. Since his speech in August 1999, the Nasdaq had risen another 1,000 points, and day trading had become more popular. It was hard to classify people buying and selling stocks whose names they hardly recognized as calculating, well-informed investors. To the Fed chairman, they looked more like day trippers to Atlantic City plunging on red or black. Privately he joked that he would like to introduce a law prohibiting day traders from buying a company's stock unless they could identify the product it produced. Greenspan still believed it was impossible to identify a speculative bubble definitively, except in retrospect, but he was now pretty much convinced that one had developed, at least in parts of the stock market. When he looked at the prices that investors were paying for Internet stocks, he found them bizarre.

Moreover, the real economy and the financial economy were now intertwined—a classic symptom of a late-stage speculative bubble. The rising stock market had fueled an unprecedented spending spree on the part of consumers and firms, which, in turn, had caused economic growth to accelerate. In 1998, the economy expanded by 4.8 percent, about twice its long-term growth rate. In 1999, the rate of expansion rose to 5.0 percent, well above the rate that even most proponents of the New Economy thesis believed to be sustainable. Early in 2000, there was no sign of growth slowing. If anything, it seemed to be accelerating further. In December 1999, the U.S. economy created another 315,000 jobs, automobile manufacturers announced that they had their best year ever, and retailers reported a strong Christmas season. American consumers were now spending every dollar they earned, and then some. According to some measures, the personal savings rate had dipped into negative territory, which meant that people were borrowing, or running down their assets, to finance their spending. Greenspan had been proceeding on the assumption that the Fed could concentrate on the real economy—inflation, unemployment, and productivity growth—and ignore the ups and downs of the stock market. This assumption was no longer tenable. As a result of the stock market boom, the economy was threatening to spiral out of control.

On January 13, 2000, Greenspan outlined his latest thinking about the economy to the Economic Club of New York. He began with his now-familiar theme that "awesome changes" were taking place in "the ways goods and services are produced and, especially, in the way they are distributed to final users."[3] The development of information technology, including the Internet, had provided firms with much more timely information about their markets and their suppliers. This had enabled them to reorganize production, cutting out unnecessary labor and inventories. Between 1995 and 1999, labor productivity had grown at an annual rate of 2.8 percent, double the 1.4 percent rate recorded between 1973 and 1995. "In short, information technology raises output per hour in the total economy principally by reducing hours worked on activities needed to guard against the unknown and the unanticipated," Greenspan said.[4]

On this occasion, he didn't linger on the productivity debate. His main purpose wasn't to praise the New Economy, but to point out its dark side. Accelerated productivity growth had two effects. On the supply side of the economy, it encouraged firms to expand capacity. On the demand side, it sparked a run-up in stock prices, as investors looked forward to the higher profits that the new technology would generate. The rise in stock prices, in turn, led to an increase in consumer spending through the "wealth effect." People felt richer, so they spent more. The argument so far was familiar to anybody who has taken Econ. 101, but here Greenspan introduced a twist. The expansion in firms' capacity took time to come on line, he explained. Building factories and getting all the new technology to work together was no simple matter. By contrast, the rise in stock prices, and the concomitant increase in consumer spending, was immediate. Consequently, overall demand in the economy rose faster than overall supply. It was this "imbalance between growth of supply and growth of demand that contains the potential seeds of rising inflationary and financial pressures that could undermine the current expansion."[5] For the past few years, the gap between supply and demand had been met by drawing more people into the workforce, many of them immigrants, and by importing more goods from abroad. But this couldn't go on forever. When these buffers were exhausted, the excess demand would be filled by rising prices.

It was a convoluted argument, which attracted criticism from academic economists when they began to study it, but its internal logic mattered less than its practical consequences. Greenspan had finally come up with an economic rationale for interfering with the stock market. To reduce the risk of inflation, the wealth effect would have to be attenuated. This "does not mean that prices of assets cannot keep rising," Greenspan explained, "only that they rise no more than income."[6] With personal income growing at about 6 percent a year, this implied that stock prices could grow by 6 percent too. In the current environment, such a return was piddling. The Nasdaq had just returned almost 90 percent. Most investors weren't expecting a repeat performance in 2000, but they were looking for a lot more than 6 percent. If Greenspan was serious about disappointing them, which he seemed to be, it could only mean one thing: higher interest rates were on the way.

## II

**The day after Greenspan's speech, the Dow hit an intra-day high of** 11,908.50 and closed at 11,723. Nobody knew it at the time, but the index had peaked, at least for this economic cycle. During the following two weeks, the Dow fell by almost 1,000 points, taking it back below the 11,000 level, as investors began to digest the possibility of an interest rate hike. Internet stocks slumped, particularly the stocks of online retailers, which were hit by disappointment over the holiday buying season. Amazon.com had shipped 20 million orders, 5 million more than it expected, but in early January 2000 it announced that its losses for the fourth quarter of 1999 would be considerably higher than the $150 million that Wall Street was already expecting. Its stock, which a month earlier had been trading above $100, fell back to $70. Stock in eToys, which had reached $70 before Christmas, dropped below $20. Value America, which once traded at $75, fell to

$5. The stocks of online communities, once a raging fad, were being ravaged. IVillage, a $130 stock in the wake of its IPO, was below $20, and so was TheStreet.com. As for TheGlobe.com, it was trading in single figures. At the end of January, Todd Krizelman and Stephan Paternot, the two former Cornell students who had founded the company, said they were stepping down as co–chief executives in favor of a more experienced manager. The announcement was laden with symbolism. Just fourteen months earlier, TheGlobe.com's IPO had marked the beginning of the Internet bubble's epic stage. The Internet stocks that continued to defy gravity were mainly Internet infrastructure companies, such as Akamai Technologies and Inktomi, and B2B plays, such as Ariba and Commerce One. But even some B2B stocks were falling. Healtheon, Jim Clark's ambitious attempt to move the health care industry online, was one of the strugglers. Despite acquiring its main rival, Web MD, the Silicon Valley company had persuaded only 80,000 doctors, about one in eight, to use its physician site. Healtheon's stock, which peaked at more than $125 in May 1999, had fallen back to $70, and it was still heading in the wrong direction.

On Sunday, January 30, 2000, Super Bowl XXXIV took place in Atlanta. The St. Louis Rams beat the Tennessee Titans 23–16, but the real business of the day took place during the commercials. In 1996, Autobytel, an online car retailer, started the trend of Internet companies advertising during the Super Bowl. When its ad generated a lot of traffic on its Web site, other companies noticed. Due to the demand from dotcom companies, the cost of a thirty-second Super Bowl spot had now risen to about $2 million. In 2000 there were seventeen Internet advertisers willing to pay that price. They included some familiar names—Charles Schwab, E★Trade, Pets.com—but also a number of unknown firms that were desperate to increase their name recognition in the hopes of scoring a successful IPO before time ran out: Computer.com, Epidemic.com, Onmoney.com, Lifeminders.com, kForce.com, and Ourbeginning.com. The sight of these companies spending millions of dollars to try to attract the attention of sozzled and semisozzled football fans was an apt metaphor for the Internet boom. A once good idea had degenerated into a nonsensical ritual.

Even sober television viewers seldom remember more than one or two of the ads they watch—a fact confirmed by Harris Interactive, a Rochester-based polling firm, which surveyed the Super Bowl viewers.[7] More than half of the respondents said they recalled seeing E★Trade's offbeat ad, which featured a dancing chimpanzee and the line "We just wasted two million bucks," and four out of ten remembered the Pets.com sock puppet. But just three in a hundred recalled Computer.com's ad, and even fewer remembered kForce.com.

On the morning of February 2, Greenspan and the rest of the FOMC gathered around a twenty-five-foot-long table in the Fed's grand boardroom. During World War II, Franklin D. Roosevelt and Winston Churchill commandeered this room to plan the allied campaign to liberate Europe. Greenspan and his colleagues didn't have Nazi Germany to worry about, but they were increasingly concerned about the economic expansion, which at 107 months old was now the longest ever. They had come close to raising interest rates in December, but had held back because of fears about Y2K computer problems. When the change of dates passed off uneventfully, there was no need for further restraint.

The Fed's senior economists started the meeting with a review of recent developments, which confirmed that the economy was still growing strongly. Consumer price inflation remained low, but there were signs that wage inflation and commodity prices, particularly the price of oil, might be picking up. The presidents of the twelve regional reserve banks reported that all parts of the country, agricultural areas excepted, were sharing in the boom. When the policy discussion began, the only issue of contention was how far to raise the federal funds rate. Some members of the committee wanted an immediate half-point increase in order to signal the Fed's determination to get a grip on the economy. The majority thought that a quarter-point hike would do the job, at least for now. Greenspan, who usually favored moving gradually, sided with the majority. The committee agreed to raise rates by a quarter point and couple the move with a public warning that more hikes might well lie ahead. The meeting ended just before noon. After lunch, the Fed announced it was raising the federal funds rate from 5.5 percent to 5.75 percent. In a statement, the FOMC said it "remains concerned that over time increases in demand will continue to exceed the growth in potential supply, even after taking account of the pronounced rise in productivity growth. Such trends could foster inflationary imbalances that would undermine the economy's record economic expansion."[8] It was a historic moment. In language that was almost the same as that Greenspan had used in New York a few weeks earlier, the Fed had formally abandoned its hands–off approach to the stock market. The speculative bubble had entered its terminal phase.

## III

**There was no immediate panic. The Dow closed the day down 37.85** points, but the Nasdaq posted a gain of twenty points. Many people on Wall Street were relieved that the Fed had only raised rates by a quarter of a percent. In the following days, a more elaborate form of denial took hold: investors and analysts convinced themselves that higher interest rates wouldn't affect technology companies. The day after the rise in interest rates, the Nasdaq shot up 137 points to 4,210.98, a record high. The Nasdaq rose again the next day, and the day after that, and the day after that. A week after the Fed's move, the index had risen by almost 10 percent. In the middle of February, the Nasdaq broke through 4,500, and for the first time the number of shares traded on the exchange topped 2 billion. The Dow, meanwhile, was stuck in a correction that had begun in January. On February 11, it closed below 10,500. "When Alan Greenspan speaks, the Old Economy trembles," Floyd Norris, a financial columnist for *The New York Times*, noted. "But the new one thinks it is impervious to higher interest rates, and shrugs off warnings from the Federal Reserve chairman."[9]

What was happening made no sense. Technology companies were leading the economy's growth, and a Fed-engineered slowdown was bound to hit their business hardest. But investors had developed a blind faith in anything to do with the Internet and computers. "The Italians want to be in this market, and they want to own technology," John Manley, an equity strategist at Salomon Smith Barney who had just returned from a trip across the Atlantic, assured a reporter. "That is true throughout Europe."[10] One commentator, to his credit, did face up to reality. Michael Mandel, *Business Week*'s economics editor, who had previously been a big supporter of the New Economy, pointed out that in a downturn many technology firms would be hit by a "double whammy" of fixed costs and slumping revenues. "Sooner rather than later, the New Economy boom is likely to be followed by a New Economy bust," Mandel wrote.[11]

On Wall Street, where Internet IPOs were still coming thick and fast, nobody wanted to listen to that sort of scaremongering. But despite the Nasdaq's upward march, the days had gone when any company with ".com" in its name was guaranteed a hero's welcome from investors. The market had entered what Hyman Minsky, an economist who specialized in financial manias, termed the stage of "revulsion." This takes place at the very peak of a bubble. Investors realize the game is almost up, and they become more discriminating. Some discreetly cash in their gains. The market has some good days, and it may even rise further, but it also becomes increasingly volatile amid the general recognition that the easy money has already been made.

On Friday, February 11, there were no fewer than ten IPOs, including the Wall Street debut of Pets.com. Despite its memorable Super Bowl commercial, the San Francisco–based company's financial report card looked disturbingly similar to those of other online retailers whose stocks had recently been battered. In 1999, Pets.com lost $62 million on revenues of less than $6 million. It was still selling its products below cost, and there was no sign of the ruinous competition in its market abating. Merrill Lynch managed the Pets.com IPO. Since hiring Henry Blodget a year earlier, the big retail brokerage had made a determined push into the Internet IPO business, and Pets.com was its best-known client. There were rumors on Wall Street that Morgan Stanley and Goldman Sachs had turned down the Pets.com offering, but Julie Wainwright, Pets.com's chief executive, insisted that she had chosen Merrill for its army of retail stockbrokers and because of Blodget, whom she described as "an A+ analyst." Finding buyers for Pets.com stock was not easy. Before the market opened, Merrill priced 7.5 million shares at $11 each. When trading started, the stock rose to $14, but by the close it had fallen back to $11. When the markets reopened after the weekend, the stock fell back below the offering price. On Tuesday, February 15, it closed at 7½.

This was sad news for Pets.com's investors, who had been hoping for a big IPO pop, for PetsMart.com and Petopia.com, whose IPO plans were now threatened, and for many other Internet companies. Pets.com had faithfully followed the Wall Street recipe for online success. It had raised a lot of money from investors and then spent heavily to build up its brand name, even though this meant incurring massive losses. The Pets.com sock puppet, which had featured in thirteen different ads, was now instantly recognizable; it had even appeared on *Good Morning America* and *Nightline*. But the sock puppet's popularity hadn't done much for Pets.com's business or its stock. Brand awareness, it turned out, didn't guarantee success.

Slowly but surely, Internet investors were beginning to concentrate on the one performance measurement they had previously avoided: profitability. Companies like America Online and eBay, which both made money, continued to do well. On February 8, eBay's stock, which had started the year at $125, reached $175. Strangely enough, the new focus on profits also gave Amazon.com's stock a temporary boost. At the start of February, the company announced that it lost $323 million in the fourth quarter of 1999, a 700 percent increase on the previous year. But Jeff Bezos insisted that these losses represented a "high-water mark" that would now recede as he led a "drive toward profitability."[12] Amazon.com was already making a profit on book sales, which still accounted for almost half its revenues, Bezos insisted. The Wall Street analysts applauded. Jamie Kiggen, of Donaldson, Lufkin & Jenrette, said the quarterly results demonstrated that Amazon.com was "a business that can become quite profitable."[13] Blodget, who had previously criticized Amazon.com for ignoring profitability, upgraded the stock from "accumulate" to "buy."

For a few days, the market accepted this upbeat analysis, and Amazon.com's stock rose from below $70 to above $80. When investors looked closely at the earnings report, they had second thoughts. For all Bezos's protestations to the contrary, the numbers showed that his company was still subject to what might be called Amazon's Law: the more money it took in, the more money it lost.

Comparing 1999 to 1998, Amazon.com's sales had more than doubled, from $609 million to $1.6 billion, but its marketing and sales costs had more than tripled, from $133 million to $413 million, and its net losses had increased almost sixfold, from $125 million to $720 million. Thanks to this dismal performance, the $1.75 billion that the company had raised from investors was fast running down. The cash and marketable securities in Amazon.com's treasury—$705 million—didn't even cover its annual losses. By the end of February, the stock had fallen back below $70.

## IV

**On February 23, 2000, Greenspan, appearing before the Senate** Banking Committee, defended his new policy toward the stock market. Senator Phil Gramm of Texas, the chairman of the Senate Banking Committee, introduced Greenspan by saying that he, for one, was not going to question the policies of "the most successful central banker in the history of the United States."[14] Senator Jim Bunning of Kentucky, another Republican, was less reticent. He called the Fed's decision to raise interest rates "misguided" and said it could become "more of a threat to our economy than inflation will ever be." Greenspan's prepared statement was a recitation of the arguments he had made in New York a month earlier. The economy, fueled by the stock market's remarkable ascent, was growing too strongly. Although there were few visible signs of inflation, the pool of available workers was shrinking, and this could not continue indefinitely without sparking rising prices. The only way to close the gap between supply and demand was to raise interest rates.

When the Fed chairman had finished reading, the senators didn't hide their displeasure. Paul Sarbanes of Maryland, the ranking Democrat, said Greenspan's fixation on the "wealth effect" threatened the job prospects of inner-city youths who had never owned a stock in their lives. Connie Mack, a Florida Republican, presented a graph that he claimed showed that there was no historical relationship between stock prices and inflation. Even Gramm sounded a critical note: "I think people hear what you are saying and conclude that you believe that equities are overvalued. I would guess that equities are not only not overvalued but may still be undervalued."[15] Bunning, his face stern, let the Fed chairman have it. "Why do we want to contain the growth and wealth effect in this country?" he demanded. Greenspan tried to explain, but Bunning cut him off: "If we get interest rates at double digits, we are going to stop the economy in its tracks. I don't want to see that happen on your watch, and I surely don't want to see it happen on my watch." "I appreciate that, Senator," Greenspan said quietly. "I have the same view."[16]

For once, the Fed chairman looked taken aback. His lined face, with its bulbous nose and long, narrow mouth turned down slightly at the corners, had an even more mournful cast than usual. As he stared through his thick spectacles and blinked his sad brown eyes, it was easy to see why his nickname in Ayn Rand's circle had been "the undertaker." For more than two hours, he patiently tried to explain why it was necessary to bring to an end to the great stock market boom that the country had enjoyed for the past five years. The people's representatives, faithfully reflecting the views of their electors, howled. The last thing they wanted in an election year was a stock market crash.

Greenspan was now facing the biggest challenge of his career. At the start of the 1990s, he had raised interest rates to head off rising prices and caused a recession, but then, at least, the threat of rising inflation had been visible. Now, most people outside the FOMC couldn't see any sign of inflation picking up. "We are suggesting, as an institution, that the stock market is too high, and that we are going to rein in inflation that's not there yet," a senior Fed official lamented. "What [Greenspan] did in 1987 was important, but it was what you would expect a central banker to do—try to calm the markets and assure financial stability. This is much less straightforward."[17]

For the moment, technology investors continued to ignore the Fed. The day of Greenspan's appearance on Capitol Hill, the Nasdaq enjoyed its biggest points gain ever—168.21—and closed at another all-time high. Internet stocks had a particularly strong session. EBay jumped twenty points; America Online jumped eight. Henry Blodget and a colleague of his contributed to the good cheer, issuing a report that said America Online "seems undervalued by almost any measure."[18] The rotation from stocks that would be vulnerable in a slowdown (Old

Economy companies) to those that would supposedly prosper indefinitely (New Economy companies) continued apace. On February 25, the Dow closed below 10,000 for the first time in almost twelve months.

Internet investors were not the only ones looking on the bright side. When Bob Simon, a veteran CBS News war reporter, interviewed a number of prominent young Internet executives for *60 Minutes II*, he found few signs of nervousness. Josh Harris, the founder of Pseudo.com, a fledgling online television network that produced about sixty youth-oriented shows from its studios in Soho, told Simon that his aim was "to take you guys out of business. I'm in a race to take CBS out of business." A couple of weeks after Simon's interview aired, *New York* magazine ran a cover story on Silicon Alley's "Early True Believers," a group of artsy Ivy League types who had become involved in the Internet when it was still an alternative medium. "We had amazing cultural timing," Rufus Griscom, the cofounder of Nerve.com, said. "It's incredibly powerful to feel that you are one of seventeen people who really understand the world."[19] Jason McCabe Calcanis, the editor of the *Silicon Alley Reporter*, a fawning glossy magazine, was equally portentous: "The metaphor for Silicon Alley is the people who reinvented film in the late sixties. It's the Dennis Hoppers and Scorceses and Coppolas—the people who didn't care about Hollywood and wanted to build something new."[20]

In the stock market, the rush to embrace technology continued. In the first three days of March, the Nasdaq gained another two hundred points. On March 2, 3Com, a Silicon Valley telecommunications equipment manufacturer, issued shares in its Palm Computing subsidiary. The underwriters originally estimated the issue price at $12 to $14, but demand was so strong that on the eve of the offering they raised the price to $38. When trading started, the stock surged almost $60, closing at 95$\frac{1}{16}$. At that price, Palm's $54.3 billion stock market valuation dwarfed the $28 billion valuation of its parent company, 3Com. To a connoisseur of Wall Street mathematics, there was a certain beauty in these numbers. Since 3Com still owned the 95 percent of Palm's stock that hadn't been issued, the market was placing an implicit value on the rest of the company of about *negative* $22 billion.

Investors had lost faith in second-tier online retailers, but they were still willing to pay almost any price for companies that appeared to embody the electronic future. Among companies in the Nasdaq 100 index, the average PE ratio was now well over 100. Cisco Systems, which supplied routers for the Internet, was vying with Microsoft and General Electric to be the company with the biggest stock market valuation. Seven of the fifteen most valuable companies in the world were technology firms: Microsoft, Cisco Systems, Intel, Oracle, Lucent Technologies, Nortel Networks, and Sun Microsystems. Every one of these firms made products that were used on the Internet. Speaking to an investment conference in Miami, James Cramer told the crowd to forget everything they thought they knew about the stock market: forget profits; forget value; and forget long-term investing. The only stocks worth holding, Cramer claimed, were technology companies. "Winners win!" he bellowed. (In his saner moments, even Cramer was having some doubts about the market. Writing on TheStreet.com, he advised investors to cash in some of their profits.)

## V

On March 6, 2000, Greenspan turned seventy-four. To celebrate his birthday, he appeared at a conference on the New Economy at Boston College, where Edward Markey, a Democratic congressman from Massachusetts, introduced him as the "Babe Ruth of our economic policy." A chocolate cake with six lighted candles was brought on stage, and as Greenspan blew them out Markey led the crowd in a rousing version of "Happy Birthday, Mr. Chairman." Greenspan walked over to the microphone and said, sheepishly: "If I'd known all this was about to happen, I would have been on my way to San Francisco." In the speech that followed, he traced the New Economy to the development of the transistor after World War II. "It brought us the microprocessor, the computer, satellites, and the joining of laser and fiber-optic technologies. By the 1990s, these and a number of lesser but critical innovations had, in turn, fostered an enormous new capacity to capture, analyze, and disseminate information. It is the growing use of information technology throughout the economy that makes the current period unique."[21] The changes in the economy were exemplified by the "multiplying uses of the Internet" and the proliferation of start-up firms trying to exploit them. Investors were "groping for the appropriate valuations of these companies," which indicated the "difficulty of divining the particular technologies and business models that will prevail in the decades ahead."

As he stood there and described the benefits of technology-driven capitalism, Greenspan sounded much like he must have done in the early 1960s, when he was writing for Rand's *Objectivist Newsletters*, describing capitalism as a "superlatively moral system"[22] and dismissing the welfare state as "nothing more than a mechanism by which governments confiscate the wealth of productive members of a society."[23] Back then, Greenspan's right-wing views were considered extreme; forty years later, faith in the free market was practically universal. Ironically, Greenspan, though still a true believer, was now the government official charged with bringing American capitalism to heel. After the rhapsody portion of his speech, he turned to the more prosaic issues of monetary policy. Continued prosperity, he said, depended upon a "macroeconomic environment of sustained growth and continued low inflation. That, in turn, means that the expansion of demand must moderate into alignment with the more rapid growth of aggregate supply."[24] The message was clear: interest rates would be going up further.

Still, most people on Wall Street weren't listening. The following day, March 7, the Nasdaq broke through 5,000 for the first time, but then dropped back. On Thursday, March 9, 2000, the index jumped 150 points, and this time it held on to the gain. When the market closed, the Nasdaq stood at 5,046.86. Moving from 3,000 to 5,000 had taken just four months. Internet stocks, despite the setbacks some of them had encountered, were also at an all-time high. On Thursday, March 9, the Dow Jones Internet Composite Index closed above 500 for the first time, at 509.84. In the past twelve months the index had risen by about 130 percent.

# chapter 20  crash

I

**Over the long run—years and decades—the stock market rises and** falls in line with economic growth and corporate profits. But in the short run—days and weeks—the market bounces up and down randomly, like a cork in a stream. Once the Fed embarked on a policy of raising interest rates, it was eminently predictable that technology and Internet stocks would fall, but it was impossible to know when, though there were hints that the moment of reckoning might not be far away. Outside of the technology sector, much of the market was already in a bear market: during the past year, more than 80 percent of the stocks in the S&P 500 index had fallen by 20 percent or more. The market was becoming much more volatile. Between 1988 and 1995, the Nasdaq moved up or down by more than 3 percent in a day just ten times. Since the start of 2000, there had already been twelve such days, six up and nine down. Even some longtime bulls were getting worried. On March 10, 2000, when the Nasdaq closed above 5,000, Jeremy Siegel, the Wharton economist who had previously argued that buying stocks was a good strategy regardless of their price, told CNN, "a big decline is very possible."

On Monday, March 13, the volatility resumed. In three days, the Nasdaq fell by almost 500 points before recovering somewhat later in the week. There were signs that the technology wave might be cresting. In two days, March 15 and March 16, the Dow, which had dipped back below 10,000, shot up 819 points as investors rediscovered Old Economy stocks like Ford Motor, Dow Chemical, and Home Depot.

At the end of the week, the Dow stood at 10,595.20, up almost 7 percent on the week. The Nasdaq finished the week at 4,798.13, down about 5 percent, and the Dow Jones Internet Composite Index closed the week at 466.5, down about 8 percent. In this confused environment, on Saturday, March 18, *Barron's* published a long article about Internet stocks under the headline "Burning Up." Written by reporter Jack Willoughby, the piece asked:

> When will the Internet Bubble burst? For scores of 'Net upstarts, that unpleasant popping sound is likely to be heard before the end of this year. Starved for cash, many of these companies will try to raise fresh funds by issuing more stock or bonds. But a lot of them won't succeed. As a result, they will be forced to sell out to stronger rivals or go out of business altogether. Already, many cash-strapped Internet firms are scrambling to find financing.[1]

With the help of a research firm, Pegasus Research International, Willoughby had examined the financial statements of more than two hundred Internet companies. For each firm, he calculated the rate at which it was spending money and compared this to the cash and marketable securities on its balance sheet. His conclusion: within twelve months at least fifty Internet firms would have no money left, and some of them would run out of cash a lot sooner than that. Among the companies facing immediate problems were CDNOW, whose takeover by Time Warner and Sony had recently fallen through; Peapod, the online grocery, and drkoop.com, the medical Web site set up by Dr. C. Everett Koop, a former U.S. surgeon general. The situation facing many other firms was only slightly less dire. MotherNature.com would run out of money in four and a half months. Drugstore.com and PlanetRx.com had enough cash to last nine months; eToys would be out of money in eleven months.

The *Barron's* piece was the most damaging piece of journalism that the Internet boom had produced, but most devastating of all was its timing. Investors had been tacitly assuming that Internet companies, whatever their losses, would always be able to raise more cash. For a long time, this had been a reasonable assumption, but given the setbacks already suffered by a number of Internet stocks it no longer was.

The *Barron's* article pointed out what would happen if the cash spigot got turned off permanently, and Internet companies were left to fend for themselves.

On Monday, March 20, many of the stocks on the *Barron's* list fell sharply; it was another bad day for technology stocks generally. The Nasdaq fell 188 points, nearly 4 percent, to 4,610. During the next few days, there was a predictable attempt to discredit the *Barron's* piece. "I didn't set my performance record, which is about the best in the business, with any help from *Barron's*," Alberto Vilar, head of the $700 million Amerindo Technology Fund, declared. Investors who avoided Internet stocks during the next five or ten years would miss "the biggest explosion of profits and growth ever seen," Vilar continued. Many of the firms mentioned by *Barron's* insisted that their burn rates had been overestimated. In some cases, this was true. The magazine's figures only went up to the end of 1999, since when some Internet firms had raised more money. Amazon.com and Digital Island, for example, had both issued hundreds of millions of dollars' worth of convertible bonds. But even if some of the figures quoted in the piece were out of date, the overall thrust of its argument was incontrovertible.

Some Internet companies were already facing a cash crunch. Firms like CDNOW and Peapod had seen their stocks collapse, and they didn't have the option to issue more shares. Theoretically, they could have tried to sell some bonds, but given the state of the market, that would have been a formidable challenge. Even market leaders like Amazon.com and E★Trade were being forced to pay higher yields on their loans because of the growing nervousness among investors. For struggling firms, the only real hope was to find another company either to invest in them or to buy them outright, but that was no easy matter. Potential buyers had an incentive to let the troubled business go bankrupt and then buy its assets on the cheap. Given this environment, the only option for the most cash-strapped Internet companies was to cut costs and hope for the best.

But even while the *Barron's* article made investors think about an issue they had been studiously avoiding, it didn't lead to an immediate slump. After falling for a day, most Internet stocks stabilized. On Tuesday, March 21, the FOMC met to discuss another interest rate hike. During the first three months of the year there had been no sign of an economic slowdown. Consumer spending had been particularly strong, and the overall level of demand was still outstripping the economy's capacity, which was the reason the Fed had started raising rates in the first place. The FOMC voted unanimously to increase the federal funds rate by another quarter point, to 6.0 percent. Repeating the formula used at its previous meeting, the committee said the economic risks "are weighted mainly toward conditions that may generate heightened inflation pressures in the future"[2]—an indication that yet more interest rate hikes might still be on the way.

If the Fed had been hoping for an immediate fall in the stock market, it was disappointed. Wall Street had already discounted the rate increase, and all the major markets rallied strongly. The Nasdaq rose by more than a hundred points, the Dow rose by more than two hundred points, and the S&P 500 closed at a new record. Internet stocks also had a good day. Yahoo!, which had split two-for-one a few weeks earlier, rose to 191¾, a gain of almost $20 a share. EBay rose by more than $18, to 214½. The buying continued for the rest of the week. On Wednesday, March 22, the Nasdaq jumped another 153.07 points, or almost 3 percent, to 4,864.75. The following day, the Dow rose by 253.20 points, to 11,119.90, its first close above 11,000 in a month and a half. At the end of the week, the Nasdaq was at 4,963.03—almost back to 5,000. Greenspan didn't comment on these developments, but people on Wall Street did. "The market is spitting in his eye," Harry Cohen, manager of the Smith Barney Appreciation Fund, told *The New York Times*.[3]

Taking advantage of the market's strength, investment bankers quickly offloaded more Internet companies on the public. Snowball.com, a San Francisco–based company that targeted "Generation i"— the 68 million individuals in the United States between the ages of thirteen and thirty—was one of the IPO candidates. Snowball.com was the twenty-ninth most popular destination on the Web. Its sites included ChickClick.com, for teenage girls, and TheForce.com, for *Star Wars* fans. Given the fate of iVillage and TheGlobe.com, it was perhaps surprising that investors could be found for an online community that had lost $34.8 million on revenues of $6.7 million in 1999, but they were. On March 21, Goldman Sachs issued 6.25 million shares in Snowball.com at $11, and they climbed to 15¼. A week later, Websense, a San Diego firm whose software allowed corporations to track their employees' Internet usage and prevent "cyber-slacking," the practice of visiting non-work-related Web sites on company time, also went public. Calvin Klein, Compaq Computer, and Morgan Stanley were among the firms that were already using Websense's Orwellian products. Hambrecht & Quist, which was now part of Chase Manhattan, issued 4 million shares in Websense at $18, and they rose 165 percent to 47¾. The successful IPOs showed that investors retained a basic faith in technology and the Internet. The day before the Websense IPO, Cisco Systems passed Microsoft to become the world's most valuable company, with a market capitalization of $555 billion.

## II

**Just when confidence seemed to be returning, the stock market came** under friendly fire on two fronts. First, *Business Week*, in an issue that came out on Friday, March 24, ran a cover story on the Wall Street "Hype Machine."[4] After some intrepid reporting, the magazine had discovered that Wall Street was peddling high-risk investment strategies to the public, such as momentum trading and buying Internet stocks. Worse, the media, "including *Business Week*, have fueled the explosion in do-it-yourself stock picking and short-term trading by amateurs."[5] The article singled out CNBC, noting that it had "become a mainstay of armchair momentum investors" and sometimes served as a "conduit for hype by its guests." On Tuesday, March 28, Abby Joseph Cohen, of Goldman Sachs, advised investors to lighten up on stocks, particularly technology stocks. Cohen, while claiming she remained optimistic for the long term, said technology was "no longer undervalued" and reduced the share of stocks in her model portfolio from 70 percent to 65 percent. The move stunned Wall Street. It was as if Madonna had advised girls to dress more conservatively. The Nasdaq dropped 124.67 points, to 4,833.89. The next day it fell another 189.22 points, to 4,644.67.

Mark Mobius, a well-known stock market strategist at the Templeton mutual funds group, added to the selling by suggesting that the worldwide mania for Internet stocks was coming to an end. "If you look closely, it's beginning," he said on March 29. "Look at the number of Internet stocks that have come off their highs, look at the number of Internet stocks that are below their offering price."[6] In response to these comments, Yahoo! fell $18, to $177; Inktomi fell $23, to $182; and eBay, which a few days earlier had hit an all-time high of $255, fell $25, to $199. The Dow Jones Internet Composite Index dropped by 8.6 percent, to 406. Shares in CDNOW dropped to a new low of $3.50 after the company's auditors, Arthur Andersen, voiced "substantial doubt" that the online retailer would be able to survive.

Many veteran investors were increasingly alarmed by the market's manic mood swings. Julian Robertson, the head of Tiger Management, a big hedge fund group, announced that he would start liquidating many of his funds at the end of the month because he no longer understood what was happening in the market. Barton Biggs told CNBC that in his forty years on Wall Street he had never seen anything like the current volatility. Asked about his investment strategy, Biggs said he was "hugging very close to the index" because "I'm scared to be a hero and really go very short tech or raise a lot of cash." There wasn't any particularly bad economic news to justify the widespread sense of dread—the Fed's intention to raise interest rates had been known for months—but that was one of the things that alarmed old-timers like Biggs and Robertson. Stock market crashes often happen in a news vacuum. There was no particularly bad news in October 1929 and October 1987 either, but both episodes were preceded by periods of increased volatility. Volatility is the stock market equivalent of a nervous rash. It indicates that investors are agitated and unsure what is going to happen next. In such circumstances, any hint of bad news tends to get exaggerated, and stocks can move sharply for no apparent reason. The best analogy is with the collapse of a sand castle. There is no way of knowing, in advance, which grain of sand will finally topple the structure, but at some point, if the grains keep getting piled on top of each another, one of them will prove decisive.

On Monday, April 3, the Nasdaq slumped again. This time it suffered its biggest-ever points fall and its fifth biggest percentage fall, tumbling 349.15 points, or 7.6 percent, to 4,223.68. Many analysts blamed the sell-off on the collapse of efforts to resolve the long-running Microsoft antitrust case. Judge Richard Posner, the conservative jurist who had been trying to mediate between the Justice Department and Microsoft, had announced at the previous week's end that his efforts to broker an out-of-court settlement had failed. Microsoft's stock fell 15⅜, to 90¹³⁄₁₆, dragging other technology stocks down with it. But the selling was too broad for the Microsoft case to be fully responsible. The Dow Jones Internet Composite Index fell 13.5 percent, to 332.3. Since peaking on March 10, it had dropped 35 percent. EBay fell 32¾, to $143.25; Yahoo! fell 11½, to 160⅛. In an ominous sign, even B2B stocks faced heavy selling. Ariba fell 16⅛, to 88⁵⁄₁₆; Commerce One fell 31¼, to $118. The small technology issues favored by momentum investors and day traders were hit hardest of all. Redback Networks, not a dotcom stock but a firm associated with the Internet all the same, fell 61¼, to 238¹¹⁄₁₆; WebMethods fell $51, to $189. These were the sorts of stocks that Alan Greenspan had in mind when he had compared day trading to casino gambling. During the past-twelve months, Redback Networks' stock had traded between $32.50 and $397. As investors sold technology stocks, many of them switched into Old Economy companies. The Dow rose by 300.01 points, to 11,221.93.

The next morning, April 4, things got worse. After the previous day's drop, many investors were facing margin calls they couldn't meet. When they failed to put up the money, the brokerage houses sold some of their stocks to raise cash. This was the traditional recipe for a stock market crash. At noon, the Dow was down by 504 points. An hour later, the Nasdaq was down by 575 points, and the atmosphere on Wall Street was one of near-panic. As luck would have it, Steve Case and many other leading figures from the media world were attending a conference in New York organized by *Variety* magazine. Between sessions, they ran to the phones to check on the market. Henry Blodget was on the road. Every time he looked at his handheld computer, the market seemed to be down another hundred points. The situation was serious enough for the White House to have its top economic official brief reporters. "We believe that the fundamentals of our economy still look very, very strong," Gene Sperling, the chairman of the National Economic Council, said.[7] It wasn't the most original statement, and by the time it appeared the stock market had started to bounce back of its own accord, as it is apt to do. When the markets closed, the Nasdaq was down by just 74.79 points, at 4,148.89, and the Dow was down by 57.09 points, at 11,164.84.

Of the buyers responsible for the recovery, some were mutual fund managers picking up old favorites, such as Microsoft, Intel, and Cisco Systems, on the cheap. Many were individual investors following the time-honored method of buying on the dips. EBay closed at $167, up 23¾; Yahoo! closed at 167⅜, up 7¼. It had been one of the busiest trading sessions in Wall Street history, a nerve-wracking day to rank with October 1929 and October 1987. On the floor of the New York Stock Exchange, 1.5 billion shares had changed hands. On the Nasdaq's computers, a stunning 2.88 billion shares were traded. To put these numbers into perspective, on October 19, 1987, when the Dow fell 22.6 percent, about 600 million shares were traded. And at that time a 600-million-share trading day was considered remarkable.

The rest of the week was calmer. On Wednesday, April 5, Alan Greenspan, Bill Gates, and Abby Joseph Cohen were among the attendees at a conference on the New Economy at the White House. With a presidential election just seven months away, the Clinton administration was keen to take some credit for nine years of economic expansion. Investors were more interested in what Greenspan and Cohen might have to say. Greenspan didn't make any comment on the stock market, but Cohen, perhaps alarmed by the reaction to her previous comments, was reassuring: "For the past decade, we have been enthusiastic about the outlook for stock prices in the United States, and we remain so."[8] The Nasdaq closed the day at 4,169.22, up 20.33 points.

On Thursday, April 6, and Friday, April 7, technology stocks staged a broad comeback. Friday was a particularly joyful day for technology investors, with the Nasdaq leaping 178.89 points, its biggest ever points rise, to 4,446.5. Intel rose by $7, to 136¹³⁄₁₆; Sun Microsystems jumped 6⅛, to 98¹³⁄₁₆. The news that Jim Clark was preparing to invest another $200 million in Healtheon/WebMD, which in two years had lost more than $140 million, helped to boost Internet stocks.

Despite all of Healtheon's problems, Clark still had faith in his magic diamond. "I am more confident than ever in Healtheon WebMD's vision on connecting physicians, payers, and consumers via the Internet," he said. The company's stock, which earlier in the week had fallen to an all-time low, rose 7½, to 29¾. Amazon.com rose 3⁵⁄₁₆, to 67⁷⁄₁₆; America Online rose 3⅞, to 68¾.

Investors headed into the weekend relieved, if a little dizzy. In the month since the Nasdaq topped 5,000, the stock market had shot up and down like a stunt plane. The past week had been particularly unsettling, but after all the gyrations the Nasdaq was just 13 percent below its peak, and for 2000 as a whole it was still up about 6 percent. The Dow Jones Internet Composite Index was 26.4 percent below its peak, but year-to-date it was down just 7 percent, which, compared to previous gains, was only a minor correction.

On the key question of whether the recent volatility had now ended, opinion was divided. Speaking on TheStreet.com's weekly television show, James Cramer claimed the worst was over: "We've got a great low yield on interest rates; we've got a Fed that I think is less worried because a lot of the dotcom madness has come out. I see more groups to like than I ever have. This was a very solid week for the bulls."[9] *Business Week* rejoined the stock market boosters with a cover that asked: "WALL STREET: IS THE PARTY OVER?" The answer, also emblazoned on the front page, was unequivocal: "High-tech stocks are undergoing a much-needed correction. But relax, the overall market probably won't tank. What we're seeing looks more like a healthy flight to quality."[10] *The Economist*, which had warned of a stock market bubble as far back as 1998, was more skeptical. It told its readers that technology stocks "could have further to fall, because their valuations have become so stretched. How stretched is difficult to determine, because traditional valuation methods are not good at coping with fast-growing companies—especially if they have neither dividends nor profits. For what it is worth, however, Nasdaq trades at a price/earnings ratio of 62 times trailing earnings. Between 1973 and 1995, its p/e never exceeded 21."[11]

*The Economist* piece highlighted an important point. In historical terms, technology stocks, particularly Internet stocks, were as overvalued as ever. They had risen to their current heights because investors had been willing to ignore old measures of valuation, preferring to focus on more general justifications of higher stock prices, such as the aging of the baby boomers and the revolutionary impact of the Internet. These arguments were so vague that they could be used to justify practically any level of stock prices. While the market was rising, this vagueness was a great advantage, because it meant there were no limit on the upside. But should stock prices start to fall and keep falling, rather than rebounding as in the week just gone, there would be no logical limit on the downside either—a fact investors were about to discover.

## III

**On Monday morning, April 10, the technology selling resumed, and** this time it continued through the day. At market close, the Nasdaq was down by 258.25 points, or 5.8 percent. Intel fell 5⅝, to 131⅛; Sun Microsystems lost 7¹³⁄₁₆, to $91. The Dow Jones Composite Internet Index fell by 37.65 points, or 10 percent, to 337.65. EBay slumped by 25³⁄₁₆, to 155¹¹⁄₁₆; Yahoo! dropped 9³⁄₁₆, to 141¹⁵⁄₁₆. Again, there was no apparent trigger for the selling, but its intensity forced some of Wall Street's bulls finally to acknowledge the obvious. "The technology sector has begun an important corrective trend," said Richard McCable, who had replaced Charles Clough as Merrill Lynch's senior stock strategist.[12] Old Economy stocks rallied: General Motors rose 1³⁄₁₆, to $86; International Paper rose $3, to 42⅝. The Dow finished the day at 11,186.56, up 75.08 points.

The technology sell-off continued on Tuesday, April 11, with the Nasdaq falling by 132.30 points, to 4,055.90, and the Dow Jones Internet Composite Index sliding another 7.1 percent, to 313.83. Again there was remorseless selling of previous favorites: Oracle fell 5⅛, to 77⅜; Yahoo! fell 8½, to 133½. At the close of trading, for the first time since the start of February, the Nasdaq was in negative territory for 2000. The only good news was that it hadn't fallen through the 4,000 mark. At one point during the day, it had come close, but it had bounced back, raising hopes for a more sustained rally.

When the market reopened the next morning, Wednesday, April 12, these hopes were disappointed. Rick Sherlund, a respected analyst at Goldman Sachs, had lowered his revenue expectations for Microsoft, citing lower than expected sales in March, thereby shattering the illusion that the Fed's effort to restrain the economy wouldn't have any impact on technology companies. Microsoft's stock slipped 4½, to 79⅜. IBM and Hewlett-Packard both fell sharply, too, and they helped to drag down the Dow, which closed at 11,125.13, off 161.95 points. Losers on the Nasdaq included Sun Microsystems, which dropped another 7⅞, to $80, and Cisco Systems, which fell $5, to $65. The Nasdaq index closed at 3,769.63, down 286.27 points, or 7 percent. The decline in Internet stocks was exacerbated by Forrester Research, which, defying its usual optimism, issued a report predicting the ultimate demise of many online retailers. Said an analyst at the firm: "It's time to face facts: online retail's honeymoon is over." Amazon.com slumped by $7, to 56⅜, but selling wasn't restricted to online retailers. America Online fell $3, to 62½; eBay fell 12⅞, to 142⅜; Inktomi slipped 12¹⁄₁₆, to $123. The Dow Jones Internet Composite Index fell by another 10 percent, to 283.33. The index was now 44 percent below its March 9 peak, and the Nasdaq was 25 percent below its March 10 peak, which meant that both were now in a bear market. (A fall of 20 percent or more is usually considered a bear market.)

The same self-reinforcing process that had propelled stock prices into the stratosphere was now operating in reverse, sending stocks hurtling back to earth. The herd mentality was as strong as ever, but investors were now copying each other selling. The technology that had made it so easy to buy stocks made it just as easy to sell them: all it took was a simple phone call or a few clicks of a mouse. As people shifted their savings out of technology funds and aggressive growth funds, mutual fund managers were forced to sell stocks that were already slumping, causing them to fall even further. The deep falls in many stocks prompted more margin calls, some of which couldn't be met, which, in turn, prompted further selling by the brokerage houses in order to raise cash. The falling market was feeding on itself, just as the rising market had fed on itself.

The morning of Thursday, April 13, brought some relief, with the

Nasdaq gaining almost 150 points early on but this proved temporary. A strong retail sales report raised fears of further interest rates by the Fed, and the markets turned around sharply. The Nasdaq ended the day down another 92.85 points, at 3,676.78. The Dow closed at 10,923.55, off 201.58 points. Internet stocks slipped yet again, with the Dow Jones Composite Internet Index falling 5.4 percent, to 267.96. Since the start of the week, Amazon.com had fallen by 29 percent, America Online had fallen by 14 percent, eBay had fallen by 23 percent, and Yahoo! had fallen by 10 percent. Where the bottom would come for these stocks, and many like them, nobody could tell, since even at their reduced levels they were prohibitively expensive according to traditional valuation measures. EBay's PE ratio was 1,262; Yahoo!'s PE ratio was 389; Amazon.com's PE ratio was negative, since it was still making a loss.

The Nasdaq's slide was now dominating the television news and knocking the saga of Elián Gonzalez, whose Miami relatives were refusing to let him be returned to Cuba, off the front pages. Tens of millions of Americans had their life savings invested in stocks. An entire generation had grown up knowing only a rising Dow and economic good times. If stock prices continued to plummet, the prosperity that the country had enjoyed for the past nine years would be threatened, with profound implications for the presidential race, the federal budget, and much else besides.

On the morning of Friday, April 14, 2000, investors tuned in to CNBC and CNNfn with trepidation, especially those with a historical bent. Eighty-eight years before, to the day, the *Titanic* had sunk. Now, new inflation figures showed prices rising faster than at any point in the last five years. This development, combined with another strong report on retail sales, meant that further interest rate hikes were virtually inevitable. Some analysts were predicting that the FOMC would raise rates by half a point at its next meeting. Shortly after 11 A.M. CNNfn's Terry Keenan reported: "We are seeing waves of selling hitting the Nasdaq right now. Yahoo! is down seven, Oracle down five, Amazon.com down five, Cisco is down two. And the carnage continues—an incredible sell-off. We are now down in percentage terms more than during the week of the October 1987 stock market crash." Unlike on Black Monday, when the stock ticker fell hopelessly behind and many brokers refused to answer their phones, there was no outright panic. The trading systems had been improved since 1987, which made it easier to track the market's fall. At 12:45 P.M., the Dow was down 320.56 points, almost 3 percent, and Nasdaq was down 245.21 points, or 6.7 percent. Losers were beating gainers by seven to one on the Nasdaq and by four to one on the New York Stock Exchange.

If investors were pinning their hopes on an afternoon recovery of the type that had taken place ten days earlier, they were disappointed. At 2 P.M., another wave of margin calls added to the selling pressure, which wasn't alleviated by Alan Greenspan, who had been making a lunchtime appearance at the American Enterprise Institute in Washington, the scene of his "irrational exuberance" speech in 1996. This time, Greenspan didn't mention the stock market or interest rates. At 2:45 P.M., the Dow was off more than 500 points, and the Nasdaq was off more than 300 points. The selling continued during the last hour of trading, reversing only slightly in the final few minutes, when a few bargain hunters stepped in. When the closing bell rang on the New York Stock Exchange, the Dow was at 10,305.77, down 617.58 points, its biggest ever points drop. The Nasdaq was at 3,321.29, down 355.49 points. This was not only the biggest points drop ever recorded by the index; it was also the second biggest percentage fall, bested only by October 19, 1987, Black Monday. Taking the week as a whole, the Nasdaq had suffered its worst week in history. After falling for five days in a row, it was down 1,125.15 points, or 25.3 percent, easily surpassing its 19.3 percent fall in the week of Black Monday. The Dow's slide had been less historic, but it was down 7.3 percent on the week.

The selling on Black Friday, as it came to be known, was across the board. Banks, airlines, and consumer companies got marked down alongside New Economy stocks: Citigroup fell $9\frac{9}{16}$; American Airlines fell \$5; Procter & Gamble fell $6\frac{5}{8}$. In the technology sector, the big names all got hit: Cisco Systems fell $4\frac{1}{8}$, to \$57; Microsoft fell $5\frac{1}{8}$, to $74\frac{1}{8}$; Intel fell $10\frac{5}{8}$, to $110\frac{1}{2}$. Internet stocks, already battered, were pummeled once more: Yahoo! dropped $20\frac{1}{8}$, to \$116; America Online dropped \$4.25, to \$55; and Amazon.com dropped $1\frac{1}{8}$, to $46\frac{7}{8}$. (Surprisingly, eBay managed to eke out a gain of $\frac{3}{4}$, to $139\frac{9}{16}$.)

Many smaller Internet stocks were crushed, a fact reflected in the Dow Jones Composite Internet Index, which dropped 31.24 points, or 12 percent, to 236.72. For the week, the index was off 37.1 percent.

After the market closed, the Treasury Secretary, Lawrence Summers, appeared on CNN and issued an appeal for calm: "We are watching the developments in the markets, as we always do, but our focus continues to be on what is most important—the fundamentals of the American economy and their contribution to our economic expansion. And I'm confident that the economy will continue to grow over the next while, with fluctuations from quarter to quarter as always, but our fundamentals are sound."[13] Summers's words had a familiar ring to them. On October 25, 1929, the day after Black Thursday, President Herbert Hoover said: "The fundamental business of the country—that is, the production and distribution of commodities—is on a very sound and prosperous basis."

## IV

**Try as they might, Wall Street's bulls were unable to write off what** had happened as a "healthy correction" or a "flight to quality." A five-week-long slump had climaxed in a panic. It had been an unusually long crash, but a crash all the same. Since peaking on March 10, the Nasdaq had dropped 1,727.33 points, or 34.2 percent. The Dow Jones Composite Internet Index was down 53.6 percent from its March 9 high. In just one week, $2 trillion of stock market wealth had been eviscerated. Microsoft alone had shed $240 billion in market capitalization since its peak. As for the Internet bubble, it had well and truly burst, as Table 1, which shows the performance of twenty leading Internet stocks during the five-week period from March 10 to April 14, demonstrates:

**TABLE 1:**

**Internet Stock Prices (March–April 2000)**

| | 3/10/00 | 4/14/00 | % Fall |
|---|---|---|---|
| Akamai Technologies | 296 | 64 7/8 | 78.1 |
| Amazon.com | 66 7/8 | 46 7/8 | 29.9 |
| America Online | 58 5/8 | 55 | 6.2 |
| Ariba | 305 3/8 | 62 1/4 | 79.6 |
| CMGI | 136 7/16 | 52 1/16 | 61.8 |
| Commerce One | 257 9/16 | 66 | 74.4 |
| DoubleClick | 117 5/8 | 60 9/16 | 48.5 |
| EBay | 193 1/4 | 139 5/16 | 27.9 |
| Excite/At Home | 28 9/16 | 21 3/4 | 23.9 |
| Healtheon/WebMD | 41 | 18 5/16 | 55.3 |
| Inktomi | 169 5/16 | 100 13/16 | 40.5 |
| Internet Capital Group | 143 9/16 | 40 | 72.1 |
| iVillage | 23 7/8 | 10 5/16 | 55.8 |
| Priceline.com | 94 1/2 | 58 9/16 | 38.0 |
| Razorfish | 36 | 15 5/8 | 56.6 |
| TheGlobe.com | 8 | 3 | 62.5 |
| TheStreet.com | 12 9/16 | 5 3/4 | 54.3 |
| VeriSign | 239 15/16 | 97 13/16 | 59.2 |
| Webvan | 11 13/16 | 7 1/2 | 36.5 |
| Yahoo! | 178 1/16 | 116 | 34.8 |

The bullish psychology, upon which everything depended, had been shattered. Even Henry Blodget, the ultimate optimist, conceded that there was little chance of putting it together again, at least for now. "We're going to see the weaker companies come under more pressure," Blodget told *The Washington Post*. "There's no reason everything should suddenly recover in the near term."[14] In a report issued by Morgan Stanley to its clients, Mary Meeker and her colleagues urged investors to concentrate their holdings in the market leaders like Amazon.com, eBay, and Yahoo! and hang on: "Perhaps we haven't seen a bottom yet, but for the leaders we certainly should be closer to the bottom than the top."[15] For investors who were still shareholders in Meeker's other stock picks—Ariba, VeriSign, Healtheon/WebMD, Priceline.com, Women.com, Tickets.com, and the rest—such words offered little consolation.

Even James Cramer, perhaps the loudest and most vociferous voice of the bull market, admitted to Matt Lauer on the *Today* show that the bubble had burst. "And I can tell you," he said, "that it's a sobering and humbling experience. I feel I went from being, you know, top of the game to being pretty humiliated."[16] Stock in Cramer's company, TheStreet.com, had slipped further during the crash and was presently trading at $5. Asked whether the era of entrepreneurs raising millions of dollars on the basis of an idea had come to an end, he replied, "Yeah, it's over. The Gold Rush is over."[17]

# chapter 21  dead dotcoms

I

**The collapse of the Nasdaq was a turning point in American history.**
For the past five years, the stock market, particularly the Nasdaq, had
been a symbol of American technological leadership and economic
power. Most of all, it had been a symbol of American self-confidence.
Ronald Reagan used to claim that the 1980s represented "morning in
America," but this claim rang somewhat hollow in an age when
gnarled operators like Ivan Boesky and Robert McFarlane were busy
going about their business. It was during the 1990s, following the collapse of the Soviet Union and victory in the Gulf War, that the
United States really rediscovered a feeling of youth and vigor. Old
restrictions seemed to slip away, and the country stepped into the
future like an animal shedding its winter coat. The rise of Silicon Valley and the Internet was something fresh—something untarnished by
financial scandal or memories of Vietnam. It gave new life to the most
potent American myth of all: that the future is boundless.

Now this myth had been exposed. Suddenly the country faced a
future with limits: economic limits, political limits, and cultural limits.
In Washington, the assumption of budget surpluses stretching out
indefinitely would have to be rethought. On campuses, students
would be forced to reconsider their careers. With the lure of instant
riches in an Internet start-up removed, law school or medical school
wouldn't look like such a bad bet after all. In boardrooms, corporate
executives would have to revise their strategies for creating shareholder value. Simply creating an online division or floating an Inter-

net tracking stock would no longer be enough. And everywhere, the belief that it was possible to make easy money by buying and selling pieces of paper would have to be let go.

The United States is a nation of many strengths, but facing up to reality is not one of them. For almost a year and a half after the April 2000 Nasdaq crash, there would be a marked reluctance to accept that the long boom had come to an end. From Alan Greenspan down, officials in the public and private sector would repeatedly insist that any economic downturn would be shallow and short-lived. On Wall Street, while the Nasdaq would show no signs of recovering, the Dow would remain stubbornly above 10,000, despite the fact that the financial outlook for many of its constituent companies was steadily deteriorating. Most remarkably of all, American consumers, the mainstay of the economy, would refuse to concede that they couldn't carry on spending every dollar they earned, and that, at some point, they would have to start rebuilding their savings. Even in the early summer of 2001, when economic growth had practically ceased, consumer spending would increase at a healthy clip. It wasn't until the terrorist attacks of September 11, 2001, that Americans would finally acknowledge that the 1990s were truly over, and that a darker, more uncertain future had dawned. Until then, the consequences of the bursting of the speculative bubble would play themselves out, but with few people ready to concede that things had changed irrevocably.

A collapse in asset prices can affect an economy in three main ways. It can reduce consumer spending by making people poorer; it can damage the banking system, especially if banks have lent a lot of money against assets whose value has collapsed; and it can hit investment spending because firms find it more difficult to raise money. The importance of each channel varies depending on the specific circumstances, but the overall impact is usually major. In Britain at the start of the 1990s, a collapse in house prices led to a steep drop in consumer spending, which plunged the economy into a recession that cost Margaret Thatcher the prime ministership. In Japan, at around the same time, a collapse in the stock market and the price of real estate led to big losses for the banks, which had lent recklessly during the 1980s boom, and the decrepit state of the banking system hobbled the Japanese economy throughout the 1990s. The most famous bust of all was the Great Depression, which followed the Great Crash of October 1929. Economists are still divided about exactly what caused the Great Depression, but a combination of all three factors—a reverse "wealth effect on consumption," a stricken banking system, and a slump in investment spending—was probably to blame, together with some policy mistakes by the Fed.

Following the Nasdaq crash, consumer spending and the banks both held up pretty well, at least initially. The collapse in stock prices impacted the economy mainly through reduced investment spending, but even this took a while to manifest itself. When it did, the effect was dramatic: Throughout the late 1990s, a virtuous circle had prolonged the economic expansion. As stock prices rose, firms could raise as much money as they wished for investment projects. (In effect, the Internet was one huge investment project.) The resultant surge in investment led to faster economic growth and faster productivity growth, which in turn boosted corporate profits. When investors saw profits rising, they poured more money into the stock market, which forced stock prices even higher, starting the process over. After the stock market bubble burst, the virtuous circle was replaced by a vicious circle. Many firms struggled to raise money, which led to a sharp decline in investment spending, especially on technology. The fall in investment caused a slowdown in economic growth and productivity growth, which, in turn, led to a drop in corporate earnings. With earnings falling, the stock market came under more selling pressure, thus restarting the process. At each turn of the circle, more of the economy was affected. To begin with, the damage was largely restricted to Internet firms. Then it spread to the rest of the technology sector, before finally encompassing the entire economy. As had been the case during the long boom, the logic of the downturn was self-reinforcing and inexorable. By the time of the terrorist attack in September 2001, the economy was already on the brink of a recession. And even before the attacks, there were signs that things were about to get a lot worse.

## II

**The first victim of the Nasdaq crash to be publicly identified was** Baruch Israel Hertz, the proprietor of Track Data Corporation, an online brokerage, whose advertising slogan, "You don't have to be a pro to trade like one," often ran on CNBC. Hertz, a heavy trader on his own account, owed $45 million to four brokerages that had lent him money on margin. To satisfy his debtors, he was forced to pledge more than half his stake in Track Data Corporation. In the grand scheme of things, Hertz was a small player. At the end of April, it emerged that one of the biggest, George Soros's Quantum Fund, had lost close to $2.5 billion, and the Quota Fund, another Soros operation, had lost several hundred million dollars. Soros had long been warning of a possible crash, and his skepticism with regard to technology issues was common knowledge. But it transpired that in the summer of 1999, Stanley Druckenmiller, the portfolio manager of the Quantum Fund, had persuaded Soros to go along with massive bets on stocks like Qualcomm and Cisco Systems. After the losses were announced, Druckenmiller resigned, as did Nicholas Roditi, the London-based manager of the Quota Fund. A chastened Soros said their successors would follow a more conservative trading strategy.

The majority of the crash's victims remained anonymous. In all walks of life, there were a few people who had placed their life savings in technology and Internet stocks. For the past few years, these intrepid souls had been the envy of their colleagues and friends, but now they didn't seem too clever. Most investors had maintained a diverse portfolio, and their losses in technology were cushioned by the resilience of the broader market. After its April slump, the Dow spent most of the next eighteen months trading between 10,000 and 11,000. Gone were the big gains of the late 1990s, but most people who had been in the market for several years were still ahead on their investments.

Partly for this reason, the Nasdaq's slump had little immediate impact on consumers' spending patterns. In April, retail spending appeared to strengthen, and the unemployment rate fell to 3.9 percent, a thirty-year low. When Greenspan and his colleagues on the FOMC met on May 16, 2000, their first meeting since March, the economy was still powering ahead. During the first quarter of the year, it had grown at an annual rate of 5.4 percent, down slightly from the 7.3 percent rate recorded in the fourth quarter of 1999, but still much too high for the Fed's taste. The demand for goods and services was still growing faster than the economy's capacity to supply them. In view of this, the FOMC voted unanimously to raise the federal funds rate by half a point, from 6.0 percent to 6.5 percent.

The sight of a central bank tightening monetary policy *after* a stock market crash was unusual. The orthodox reaction is to pump more money into the economy in order to prevent a recession from developing, which is what the Fed did in 1987. In raising interest rates, Greenspan and his colleagues seemed to be following the disastrous precedent of 1929, when their predecessors maintained a tight policy following the stock market's collapse. Greenspan was well aware of the Fed's errors following the Great Crash, but on this occasion he didn't think there was any danger of an economic slump. In a statement, the FOMC defended its decision to raise interest rates "in light of the extraordinary and persisting strength of overall demand."[1] There were few signs that the prosperity of the 1990s had been seriously dented. In May, the average cost of a two-bedroom apartment in Manhattan reached $958,202.

But if the economy as a whole was still growing strongly, the Internet sector was already contracting. The IPO window, which had been open since November 1998, had slammed shut. The investment bankers were forced to call up Internet companies they had been preparing for IPOs, such as Kozmo.com and Petopia.com, to tell them they would have to fend for themselves for the foreseeable future. Firms that had already gone public but needed more cash to survive, such as those on the *Barron's* list, were also left stricken.

Boo.com, a wildly ambitious attempt to create a global online retailer catering to fashion-conscious consumers, was the first big casualty. Ernst Malmsten, one of the three Swedes who founded Boo.com in 1998, referred to it as "a gateway to world cool."[2] In 1999, *Fortune* magazine picked it as one of its "Cool Companies" of the year. Boo.com was headquartered in London, but it also had offices in New York, Paris, Stockholm, and several other trendy locales. Its four hundred employees were highly paid, traveled in style, and had fresh fruit delivered daily. In eighteen months, they ran through about $185 million that had been raised from a variety of investors including Benetton, the Italian fashion house, LVMH, the French fashion conglomerate, J. P. Morgan, Goldman Sachs, and the Lebanese Hariri family. Boo.com's Web site, when it finally launched in November 1999, was slow, cumbersome, and inaccessible to Apple users. Customers were scarce. Between February and April 2001, total sales were $1.1 million. The Nasdaq crash, which removed any prospect of an IPO, was the final blow. On April 16, J. P. Morgan informed Malmsten that it couldn't raise any more money. On May 17, Boo.com shut down and filed for bankruptcy.

A few days later, Toysmart.com, whose backers included the Walt Disney Company, bowed out of the brutal battle in the online toys market. EToys, an ambitious California-based start-up that had gone public in May 1999, was the market leader, but ToysRUs.com, Wal-Mart.com, and Amazon.com were all fighting for the same customers. Two smaller companies, RedRocket.com and ToyTime.com, had already folded. Competition in the online pets market was equally intense. On June 13, Pets.com agreed to acquire the assets of Petstore.com, for $10 million in stock. Pets.com had been fortunate enough to go public before the Nasdaq crash, but its stock was now trading at about $2, which meant it would have great difficulty raising any more money. The two other main competitors in the industry—Petopia.com and PetsMart.com—had been forced to cancel their IPOs.

June also saw the collapse of Reel.com, an online video store. The vast majority of online retailers were now struggling to survive. Value America, the Virginia-based firm that styled itself as the "Wal-Mart of the Internet," had already fired half its staff and ousted its founder, Craig Winn, whom *CEO* magazine had once dubbed "the prince of e-commerce." Winn's vision of having manufacturers send products to customers direct, so Value America wouldn't have to maintain any costly inventories, had turned out to be as illusory as his plans to run for president. In 1999 alone, Value America lost more than $175 million. It somehow managed to raise another $90 million in March 2000, but this money didn't last long. On August 11, 2000, Value America closed its Web site and filed for bankruptcy.

The following month, Pseudo.com, the online television network, shut down. The closure came just seven months after founder Josh Harris had boasted that he was trying to put CBS out of business. In May, Harris had defied the post–Nasdaq crash gloom to raise $15 million. In July, Pseudo.com attracted a lot of media attention by providing live online coverage of the Republican National Convention in Philadelphia, but its viewing figures remained dismal. With fewer than 50,000 visitors a day, Pseudo.com didn't even show up on Media Matrix's ranking of news and content sites. (Since less than 5 percent of all Internet users had high-speed connections, which were essential for downloading streaming video, this was hardly surprising.) On September 18, Pseudo.com ran out of money. At least Harris could say that his firm had made some programs, lots of them, before going under. Pop.com, a West Coast online network backed by Steven Spielberg and Ron Howard, also went out of business in September, but without producing a single show.

By now, spotting the next dotcom to turn up its toes had turned into a popular spectator sport, with Web sites like Dotcomfailures.com and FuckedCompany.com leading the cheering. Philip Kaplan, a twenty-four-year-old New Yorker, launched FuckedCompany.com over the Memorial Day weekend of 2000 to poke fun at what he called the "ridiculousness" of many Internet business plans. The site quickly developed a cult following, attracting (Kaplan claimed) 300,000 visitors a day. Kaplan encouraged users to submit predictions for the next dotcom demise, and they scored points if they were proved right. Employees of troubled Internet companies used the site to vent their anger at their bosses (and their stock losses), while Kaplan, using the handle "Pud," kept up a sarcastic running commentary.

## III

**In August 2000, the National Association of Purchasing Manage-**ment's monthly index of manufacturing activity, an economic indicator that is closely watched on Wall Street, dipped significantly. In normal times, this wouldn't have been too disturbing. Manufacturing currently comprises about a fifth of the economy—the service sector is far bigger—and a fall in manufacturing output doesn't necessarily cause a recession. But since the middle of the 1990s, spending on high-end computers, software, and networking gear had been growing at an annual rate of 15 percent to 20 percent a year, and the technology sector had accounted for up to a third of overall economic growth. The Fed initially welcomed signs that its efforts to slow down the economy might finally be working. At the central bank's annual getaway in Jackson Hole in mid-August the atmosphere was almost giddy. Productivity was still rising strongly, which augured well for the economy's long-term prospects. "In public and in private, the worrywarts, killjoys, and practitioners of the dismal science who inhabit the Fed's marble halls are sounding like 49ers who have stumbled into a saloon with a sackful of nuggets," the Washington bureau chief of *The Financial Times* reported in early September. And he went on: "This autumn the U.S. central bank looks out on an economic landscape that, for the first time in four years, is not pockmarked with potential catastrophes."[3]

This was an optimistic prognosis, to say the least. On September 21, Intel, the world's largest chipmaker, warned that its revenue growth in the third quarter would be half what Wall Street had been expecting. Within two weeks, Intel's stock had fallen by 40 percent, eviscerating $215 billion in paper wealth. The Nasdaq, which had climbed back above 4,000 during the summer, entered a steep decline that would last through the end of the year and beyond. With public attention focused on the presidential election, the economy was no longer dominating the headlines, but the turndown in investment spending was getting serious. In the second quarter of the year, orders for information technology equipment had risen by 34 percent. Between July and September, they rose by just 1.2 percent. When the fourth quarter started, on October 1, many technology firms found their orders falling at an alarming rate. Some of their customers had gone out of business. Others had simply stopped buying. To many technology company executives, it seemed as if somebody had thrown a bucket of water over the economy. In November, the Nasdaq fell below 3,000.

Meanwhile, the carnage in the Internet sector continued. On

November 7, five days after the presidential election and less than nine months after its IPO, Pets.com announced that it was shutting up shop and firing most of its employees. Mortgage.com, a Florida-based dotcom, had already announced its intention to close, but Pets.com was the first publicly traded Internet company actually to go out of business. Merrill Lynch had contacted fifty potential investors on Pets.com's behalf, but only eight were even willing to meet the company. None was prepared to put up the $20 million or more that Pets.com needed. This was hardly surprising. In the previous quarter, the company had lost $21.7 million on sales of $9.4 million, and its cumulative losses since the start of 1999 amounted to $147 million. In a statement, Julie Wainwright, Pets.com's chairman and chief executive, said: "It is well known that this is a very, very difficult environment for business-to-consumer Internet companies. With no better offers and avenues effectively exhausted, we felt that the best option was an orderly wind-down with the objective to try to return something to the shareholders."[4]

The demise of Pets.com was an embarrassment to all concerned, especially Hummer Winblad, the Silicon Valley venture capital firm that had backed it in the beginning, Amazon.com, which had invested approximately $60 million in the company and ended up as its largest shareholder, and Merrill Lynch, which had touted its stock to the American public. Unsurprisingly, none of these firms had any comment, but Pets.com's sock puppet did have something to say when he appeared on *Good Morning America* a few weeks later. After admitting that recent events had left him "bummed a little bit," the sock puppet was asked by Jack Ford, the show's cohost, if he had any advice for investors. "Don't invest in dotcoms," the puppet replied.[5]

Many investors were wishing they had heeded that advice. On November 8, TheGlobe.com closed at 63 cents, Quepasa.com at 47 cents, E-Stamp at 59 cents, and eGreetings.com at 34 cents. The market was saying these companies would eventually go out of business. So many Web sites were closing that *The New York Post* created a "Dead Dotcom of the Day" column, which became a particular favorite of the paper's proprietor, Rupert Murdoch, who had been widely criticized for turning his back on the Internet boom.

On December 18, the FOMC held its last meeting of the year. Greenspan and his colleagues were divided about what to do. Earlier in the month, the Fed chairman had seemed to hint at a forthcoming interest rate cut when he said that "weakening asset values in financial markets could signal or precipitate an excessive softening in household and business spending."[6] Some members of the committee supported an immediate reduction in the federal funds rate, but the majority favored monitoring developments for a while longer. Despite the growing problems in the technology sector, the economy as a whole still appeared to be growing at an annual rate of somewhere between 2 percent and 3 percent. After a debate, the FOMC left interest rates as they were but warned that economic risks were now "weighted mainly toward conditions that may generate economic weakness in the future" and said it would "continue to monitor closely the evolving economic situation."[7]

There was more disturbing economic news over Christmas and the New Year, including a slide in December auto sales and disappointing holiday sales for many retailers. This heightened the gloom on Wall Street. On December 29, the last trading day of the year, the Nasdaq fell 87.24 points, closing at 2,470.52, and the Dow fell 81.91 points, to 10,786.75. For 2000 as a whole, the Nasdaq was off 39.3 percent, its biggest fall since its founding in 1971, and the Dow was off 6.2 percent, its worst performance since 1981. Many individual stocks had suffered stunning declines. Lucent Technologies was down 81 percent on the year, Dell Computer down 66 percent, and Microsoft down 63 percent. The Internet stocks had fared worst of all. Priceline.com had dropped 97 percent, Yahoo! 86 percent, and Amazon.com 77 percent.

## IV

**On Tuesday, January 2, 2001, the National Association of Purchasing** Management announced that its index of manufacturing activity had fallen to its lowest level since the last recession ended in 1991. Greenspan had seen enough. The very next day, shortly after 1 P.M., the Fed announced that it was cutting the federal funds rate from 6.5

percent to 6.0 percent. Interest rate changes between FOMC meetings are unusual. The previous one was in October 1998, when the financial markets were in a crisis following the near collapse of Long Term Capital Management. In a statement, the Fed said it had acted "in light of further weakening of sales and production, and the context of lower consumer confidence, tight conditions in some segments of financial markets and high energy prices sapping household and business purchasing power."[8] Investors reacted to the interest rate cut with shock, then delight. The Dow jumped 299.60 points, to 10,945.75. The Nasdaq, after falling for months, posted its biggest ever gain in points and percentages. At the close of trading, the index was at 2,616.69, up 324.83 points, or 14.2 percent.

The celebrations were short-lived. On reflection, investors realized that the Fed's intervention was evidence of its growing concern about the economy. "They saw the N.A.P.M., and it scared the pants off them," Ian Richardson, an economist at the consulting firm High Frequency Economics, told *The New York Times*.[9] George W. Bush, the incoming president, seized on the rate cut as evidence that the country needed the tax cuts he had promised during the election campaign, saying: "One of the messages Dr. Greenspan sent was that we need bold action, not only at the Fed, but in the halls of Congress to make sure this economy stays vibrant."[10] At the end of January, the Conference Board reported that consumers' confidence in the future had suffered its biggest fall since the Gulf War, the clearest evidence yet that the problems in the technology sector were spreading to the economy at large.

One of the factors undermining public confidence was the ongoing wave of job cuts, many of them in the Internet sector. Early in the New Year, Excite/At Home laid off 250 workers and wrote off $4.8 billion in losses related to the precipitous decline in value of its Excite portal. Of all the money-eating Internet companies, the Excite/At Home combine was probably the most ravenous. Since 1995, it had lost almost $10 billion. On January 30, Amazon.com announced plans to shutter two distribution centers and lay off 1,300 people, about 15 percent of its workforce. Although he didn't concede as much publicly, Jeff Bezos was finally admitting that his "Get Big Fast" strategy was no longer sustainable because investors were no longer willing to accept big losses indefinitely. In the last quarter of 1999, Amazon.com had garnered revenues of almost $1 billion, but it had lost $545 million. Since hitting an intra-day peak of $113 in December 1999, Amazon.com's stock had fallen to less than $20. Stripped of its Internet glamour, Bezos's firm looked like any other struggling company that was cutting costs in a desperate attempt to make ends meet. Adding insult to injury, Ravi Suria, a bond analyst at Lehman Brothers, said that the online retailer might run out of working capital later in the year, a claim the company firmly denied.

With the stock market punishing rather than rewarding Internet investments, several big media companies, including CNN, News Corporation, and Walt Disney, slashed their online divisions. CNN, now a part of AOL Time Warner, said it was firing up to 1,000 workers. Disney announced the closure of Go.com because there was no longer any point in trying to compete with America Online and Yahoo! Speaking for many of his fellow moguls, Michael Eisner, the chairman of Disney, said: "We were waiting for something at the end of the rainbow that was looking less and less worth waiting for."[11]

On January 31, 2001, the FOMC, citing the risk that "demand and production could remain soft," reduced the federal funds rate by another half point, from 6.0 percent to 5.5 percent. The economy was still growing, at least according to the official figures, but there was now no doubt that the Greenspan boom had come to an end. The vicious circle started by the Nasdaq crash had already completed one turn, with the slide in the stock market leading to a slowdown in the economy, leading to further falls in stock prices. Another turn was now beginning.

On March 7, eToys went out of business, having run up debts of $274 million. Once valued at $10 billion, the Santa Monica–based retailer was now worthless. When the liquidators tried to sell its Web site and its $80 million warehouse management system to pay off some of its creditors, there were no bids. Even the inventory of toys had to be sold at a 75 percent markdown. Three days after eToys filed for Chapter 11, Cisco Systems, the technology supplier that had benefited most from the growth of the Internet, announced it was firing 11 percent of its workforce because of a slump in demand. Many technology buyers had simply run out of money. NorthPoint Communications, which had built a nationwide network of high-speed Internet connections, was a typical example. When the market was at its peak, NorthPoint had been valued at $5.6 billion. In March, AT&T bought the company for $135 million.

On Friday, March 9, 2001, the anniversary of the Nasdaq first closing above 5,000, the index ended the day at 2,052.78. In twelve months, the total market value of companies listed on the Nasdaq had dropped from $6.7 trillion to $3.2 trillion: $3.5 trillion in stock market wealth had vanished. Cisco Systems, which a year earlier had been the world's most valuable company, worth $466.5 billion, was now valued at $164.2 billion. Yahoo!'s stock market value had fallen from $93.7 billion to $9.7 billion, Amazon.com's from $22.8 billion to $4.2 billion. The Dow Jones Composite Internet Index, which on March 10, 2000, closed at 509.84, now stood at 80.74, a fall of 84.2 percent.

On Monday, March 11, the Nasdaq fell another 129.40 points to 1,923.38, the first time it had dropped through 2,000 since November 1998, the month TheGlobe.com went public. Two days later, the Dow fell by 317 points and closed below 10,000. Deflationary forces were buffeting the economy, and the Fed's actions didn't seem to be having any effect. On March 20, the FOMC reduced the federal funds rate from 5.5 percent to 5.0 percent, the third half-point rate cut since the start of the year. In a statement explaining its move, the committee referred to the chain reaction that was sending the economy into a downward spiral: "Persistent pressures on profit margins are restraining investment spending, and, through declines in equity wealth, consumption."[12] Wall Street had been hoping for an even bigger move from the Fed. The Nasdaq closed the day at 1,857.44, off 93.74 points, and the Dow closed at 9,720.76, down 238.5 points. The willingness to cast aside old valuation methods was now coming back to haunt investors. Even after the dramatic drops of the last year, many stocks were still expensive on a historical basis. Since March 2000, the average PE ratio for stocks listed on the Nasdaq had fallen from 400 to 154, but that was still almost three times the average PE since 1985, which was 52.

On April 2, Inside.com became the latest Internet company to introduce drastic retrenchments when it merged with Brill Media Holdings, the publisher of *Brill's Content*, and announced heavy job

cuts. Michael Hirschorn and Kurt Andersen had produced an informative online magazine for media junkies, but from a business perspective Inside.com never made much sense, and once the bubble burst its
prospects of survival were minimal. (Later in the year, it would be shut
down.) On April 12, Kozmo.com closed shop, having spent more
than $250 million making life easier for couch potatoes. Since the can-
cellation of its IPO, the online delivery service had ousted its founders,
instituted a $5 minimum order, and started charging $2 for all orders
under $30, but none of these measures had stemmed its losses.

A day later, George Shaheen resigned as chief executive of
Webvan. Just six months earlier, Shaheen's decision to leave Andersen Consulting for the online grocer had been hailed as the ultimate
legitimization of e-commerce. But Shaheen had been unable to
alter the harsh economics of Webvan's business. Revenues remained
much lower than expected, and neither the acquisition of rival
HomeGrocer nor the imposition of a $4.95 delivery fee on orders
under $75 had stopped the flow of red ink. Webvan's stock was trad-
ing at 12 cents, and its auditors had recently warned it could go out
of business by the end of the year. Shaheen's signing-on package of
stock and options, which had once been worth $280 million, was
practically worthless. In a statement, he said he was resigning because
Webvan needed a "different kind of executive" as it concentrated on
survival.[13]

Online commerce was turning into a bad joke. In May, Inter-
net.com, a Connecticut-based publishing company, changed its name
to INTMedia Group. Since going public in June 1999, its stock had
gone from $14 to 72¼ to $4. "We have been the whipping boy
because of the name," Alan Meckler, the founder of Internet.com,
complained to *The Wall Street Journal*.[14] It now seemed conceivable
that the Internet bubble would vanish without a trace. To help save
some of it for posterity, Steve Baldwin, a freelance writer, set up a
Web site, www.disobey.com/ghostsites, where he preserved the
home pages of deceased dotcoms. Having once worked at Time
Warner's Pathfinder site, Baldwin knew a thing or two about troubled online ventures. Whenever an Internet company announced a
restructuring, he would take a digital copy of its home page and post
it on his site. "I've worked on so many Web projects and now they're

all gone," Baldwin told *The New York Times*. "I realized there's no proof I actually did anything."[15]

Throughout the summer of 2001, the carnage continued. On July 10, Webvan, arguably the most ambitious e-commerce venture of all, closed down, having spent about $1.2 billion building a nationwide distribution system. "It's easy to say we could have opened a few less markets," David Beirne, a partner at Benchmark Capital, who had championed Webvan from the early days, told *The New York Times*.[16] "But we had Catch 22. We had a unique opportunity to raise a lot of capital and build a business faster than Sam Walton rolled out Wal-Mart. But in order to raise the money, we had to promise investors rapid growth." On August 3, TheGlobe.com closed its online community site, vacated its Manhattan headquarters, and said it would now concentrate on its online games division. Less than three years had passed since the November 1998 IPO that turned Todd Krizelman and Stephen Paternot into instant multimillionaires, but it seemed like an eternity. Krizelman and Paternot had stepped down as co-CEOs during 2000, and Paternot had already written his memoir, *A Very Public Offering*, when the closure announcement came.

Having invested, intellectually as well as financially, in the Internet, many Americans were now looking around for somebody to blame. The media also fell into this behavior, targeting the VCs, stock analysts, and investment bankers who had promoted Internet stocks. In its issue of May 14, 2001, *Fortune* pictured Mary Meeker on its front page above the headline "Can We Ever Trust Wall Street Again?"[17] The magazine accused Meeker of compromising her position as a stock picker to win investment banking business for Morgan Stanley. Meeker admitted having put her name to some research reports that she hadn't authored, but she defended her decision to maintain buy ratings on stocks like Amazon.com, Priceline.com, and Yahoo! despite the catastrophic falls of the past year. Sometime during the next two or three years, the "nuclear winter" would give way to a "spring bloom," she insisted. "Our bet is that the winners that come out of this, the market value of the leaders, are going to make all the things that came before them look like chump change."[18]

The days when investors reacted to a favorable mention from Meeker by bidding a company's stock up ten or twenty points had long gone, and Internet issues continued to languish. In August, a group of investors in Amazon.com and eBay sued Meeker and Morgan Stanley, claiming that Meeker had issued favorable reports on these stocks in order to curry favor with the companies. Meeker "knew that the financial condition and future business prospects of Amazon did not support her positive comments and recommendations, but she nevertheless issued positive reports encouraging investors . . . to purchase shares of Amazon," one of the suits claimed.[19] Meeker wasn't the first Internet analyst to be sued by angry investors. In July, Merrill Lynch had paid about $400,000 to settle a similar suit brought against Henry Blodget. In the Meeker case, a judge dismissed the initial suits, but more seemed certain to follow. The Securities and Exchange Commission and the U.S. Attorney's office in Manhattan were investigating allegations that during the Internet boom certain brokerage firms received kickbacks for allowing certain clients to participate in sought-after IPOs. The probe was centered on Frank Quattrone and his colleagues at Credit Suisse First Boston, but it also involved other big Wall Street firms, including Morgan Stanley and Goldman Sachs.

On August 16, 2001, *The Industry Standard*, the weekly chronicle of the Internet economy, suspended publication after its parent company, Standard Media International, filed for bankruptcy. The demise of *The Industry Standard*, which during its three and a half years had earned a reputation for spirited and informative journalism, was yet another sign that the dotcom era was passing into history. During early 2000, when the magazine was thriving, its founders had raised $30 million from a group of outside investors, including Morgan Stanley and Chase Manhattan, and launched an aggressive expansion, with the intention of going public. At that juncture, Standard Media International was valuing itself at about $200 million. Like so many others, the company and its backers had mistaken an investing frenzy for permanent prosperity. In the first half of 2001, *The Industry Standard*'s advertising revenue fell by about 75 percent compared to the previous year. (Other Internet-related magazines, such as *Business 2.0* and *Red Herring*, suffered similar, if slightly less dramatic, falls.) By the summer of 2001, it was on track to lose about $50 million on the year. Attempts to raise more money failed, and *The Industry Standard* met the same fate that the *Railway Standard* and many other railway publications had met a century and a half previously: it failed to outlive the speculative bubble that had given it birth. Other publications would have to write the final chapter of the Internet story.

## VI

**The vicious circle of falling investment and profits was now affecting** firms of all kinds. In the second quarter of 2001, the economy grew by just 0.2 percent on an annualized basis: only the resilience of consumer spending, which increased at an annual rate of almost 2 percent, prevented it from contracting. The manufacturing sector was already in a deep slump, and corporate earnings had dropped by $150 billion in twelve months. Even on Wall Street, where analysts had repeatedly insisted that the slowdown would be short-lived, hopes of a rapid recovery were fading. The mighty Fed seemed powerless to arrest the decline. Between April and August, it reduced interest rates another four times, bringing the number of rate cuts in 2001 to seven. Since the start of the year, the federal funds rate had been reduced from 6.5 percent to 3.5 percent, but still the economy failed to respond. In August, the Ford Motor Company announced it was letting go of 5,000 workers because of falling demand.

On Tuesday, September 4, 2001, as Americans returned to their jobs after the Labor Day weekend, *The Wall Street Journal* published a report from Jackson Hole, Wyoming, where Alan Greenspan and his colleagues had been enjoying their annual policy retreat. The story said senior Fed officials had "expressed great uncertainty" over the course of the economy but also a determination to "continue cutting interest rates, a quarter point at a time, until signs of a recovery emerge." Such signs were hard to find. On Friday, September 7, the Labor Department announced that 100,000 jobs had been lost in August and that unemployment had risen from 4.5 percent to 4.9 percent, the biggest one-month jump in six years. Such a sharp rise in joblessness strongly suggested that the economy was now shrinking, although confirmation would not come until later in the year, when the third quarter gross domestic product figures were released. The historic economic expansion that had given rise to the greatest speculative bubble the country had ever seen was over. The stock market fell sharply, with the Dow shedding 234.00 points, or 2.4 percent, to close at 9,605.85. The Nasdaq, already in the doldrums for a year and a half, fell another 17.94 points, to 1,687.70. Shortly after the unemployment figures were released, President Bush summoned reporters to the Rose Garden and said he wanted the American people to know "we're deeply concerned about the unemployment rates and we intend to do something about it." Four days later, any lingering hopes of an economic recovery were extinguished when terrorists attacked the World Trade Center and the Pentagon.

# epilogue

**The events of Tuesday, September 11, 2001, drew a thick line under**
the dotcom era. During one radiant late-summer morning, nineteen
young men armed with box-cutters and knives destroyed many of the
intellectual assumptions that had underpinned the Internet bubble.
The myth of American invulnerability, which resulted from the end
of the Cold War and victory in the Gulf War, was only the most
obvious one. Allied to that belief was an overwhelming faith in technology. Perhaps the most disturbing aspect of the terrorist attack was
its determinedly low-tech nature and the ease with which it over-
came the overwhelming technical advantage of the perceived foe: the
U.S. financial and military establishment. The terrorists occasionally
exchanged e-mails, but for the most part they communicated via
voice and paper. Their principal weapons—jetliners loaded with fuel—
were invented in the 1940s. Against such a primitive but dedicated
enemy, the U.S. government's inventory of high-technology surveil-
lance equipment— spy satellites, reconnaissance aircraft, phone taps,
and so on—counted for nothing. A single informer with pencil and
paper would have been far more useful.

The promise of the Internet wasn't just technological: it was also
ideological. Once digital networks had liberated them from the con-
fines of tradition and physical location, human beings would come
together and transcend ancient divisions: tribal, religious, racial, and
economic. After September 11, it seems ludicrous to speculate about
an escape from history or geography. The gulf between radical Islam

and the West is deeply rooted in both. In retrospect, the period from 1989 to 2001 looks like an historic aberration, an extended time-out, during which the normal conditions of human conflict and international rivalry were temporarily suspended (for most people living in the West, at least). In this vacuum, technological utopianism and several other varieties of mushy thinking flourished.

One of the mushiest was the belief in eternal prosperity. The terrorist attacks hit the post-bubble economy where it was most vulnerable: in the minds of consumers. Stunned by the dreadful images from New York and Washington, many Americans deferred or canceled expenditures, and firms throughout the country (not just those in the travel industry) faced potentially catastrophic falls in demand. Until the terrorist attacks, the only thing preventing a deep recession had been the surprising willingness of consumers to keep spending at record levels despite the economic slowdown. Now this prop was removed. When the stock market reopened on Monday, September 17, it suffered one of its worst weeks ever, during which the Dow fell by more than 1,300 points, or 14.8 percent, to 8,235.81. This sell-off represented a perfectly rational reaction by investors to heightened uncertainty about the future, but it had negative economic consequences of its own. With more stock market wealth being eviscerated, both business and consumer spending were likely to be hit further. If they were, corporate profits would suffer more damage, which would put yet more pressure on stock prices.

In short, the events of September 11, 2001, attacks gave another sharp twist to the deflationary circle that had been buffeting the economy since the Nasdaq's collapse in March and April 2000. Had they occurred in a situation where consumers and firms were more upbeat about the future they would have been considerably less damaging. In financial terms, the direct impact of the terrorist attacks—the destruction of about 15 million square feet of office space and the temporary grounding of the airline industry—was relatively minor, but this was much less important than the indirect impact. By September 2001, the American economy was already on the brink of a psychological breakdown. The bear market was already more than a year and a half old. The Dow peaked in January 2000, the Nasdaq in March 2000. Repeated promises of an economic recovery had failed to materialize, and Alan Greenspan seemed unable to do anything about it. Confidence in the future seemed to be slipping away. In such circumstances, the sight of jetliners crashing into the World Trade Center and the Pentagon was a devastating blow.

Economists like to tally things in dollars and cents, but the significance of what happened cannot be expressed in purely monetary terms. It was too fundamental for that. For capitalism to operate successfully, at least two things have to be in place: a working system of laws, to ensure safety of person and property; and hope for the future, to encourage capital accumulation. If either doesn't exist—and the phenomenon of commercial jets being used as incendiary bombs to destroy office buildings is potentially fatal to both of them—the economic system will break down. That is what appeared to be happening in the days immediately following September 11, when large swaths of American business practically ground to a halt. It wasn't until the sheer savagery of the attacks started to recede into memory that any semblance of normality returned. By then, the financial outlook seemed utterly changed, although, in reality, the attacks had largely accentuated existing weaknesses in the economy.


**II**


**Now that the dotcom era is receding into history, it is easier to see** what is left of it. To begin with, the Internet remains a technological wonder. According to the latest estimates, more than 300 million people around the world use it to communicate in ways that would have been unthinkable a generation ago. As a research tool, mail service, and repository of human fascinations, the Internet is incomparable. Vannevar Bush, were he to rise from the grave and subscribe to America Online, would be astonished, not only at the volume of information at his fingertips but at its geographic and cultural diversity. None of this will be affected by the collapse of the stock market bubble. In decades to come, when companies like Webvan and TheGlobe.com are long forgotten, historians will look back on the 1990s as the decade during which the information society became a reality.

What the historians will have to say about e-commerce will be less complementary. Most of the early claims made about the online economy turned out to be grossly exaggerated. The Internet, it transpired, was not a "disruptive technology" that would destroy any company locked into old ways of doing things, such as selling books in stores, printing news on paper, or using people to sell stocks. The bookstores, newspaper companies, and brokerage houses are still in business, and most of them are doing fine. In each of these industries, old economy firms, far from being displaced by the Internet, have used it to get closer to their customers. Barnesandnoble.com allows people to return unwanted books to Barnes & Noble bookstores and continues to take market share from Amazon.com. The online edition of *The Wall Street Journal* boasts almost 500,000 subscribers, most of whom also buy the print edition. Merrill Lynch offers online trades for $29.95, but the majority of its clients also use the firm's brokers, who are much more expensive. These "clicks and mortar" strategies work because they treat the Internet as a unique distribution channel, but don't rely on it to the exclusion of all else. It is difficult to think of a single example in which an Internet company has supplanted a major old economy firm.

Most Internet start-ups failed because they were based on the mistaken premise that the Internet represented a revolutionary new business model, which it didn't. It is a tool that companies can use to build their business if they can combine it with distinctive products and avoid ruinous price wars, but nothing more than that. The Internet companies that will survive will be those providing services that wouldn't otherwise exist, such as eBay, and those providing services that complement existing products, such as Travelocity.com. It is no accident that both eBay and Travelocity.com deal in information goods. The Internet's great strength is its capacity to process information. Any good that can be standardized and converted into ones and zeroes has the potential to support online commerce. When the legal issues surrounding copyright are finally resolved, this category of goods will include music. When the money is finally found to make broadband connections the norm rather than the exception, it will also include film. Some things it won't include are groceries, pet food, and furniture. People still prefer to buy most goods in a store, where they can look at them, pick them up, and try them out. In 2000, online purchases came to less than 1 percent of total retail sales. In the publishing industry, where online stores were well established, only one book in fifteen was being bought online.

The main reason that Internet retailing has been such a financial disappointment is that it is more about retailing than the Internet. Any retailer is basically a distributor, purchasing goods from the manufacturers at wholesale and getting them into customers' hands at retail. Whether the goods are delivered to the nearest shopping mall (regular retailers) or to the doorstep (online retailers) is a secondary matter. Either way, building a distribution system is an arduous and costly operation. Whereas a state-of-the-art retail Web site might cost $25 million a year to develop and maintain, a nationwide system of warehouses and delivery trucks can cost $1 billion to construct and another $200 million to operate. The savings that Amazon.com enjoyed by not having any stores turned out to be largely eaten up by the extra costs of packing, shipping, and promotion. (Since online firms don't have a retail presence they have to spend more on advertising to remind consumers of their existence.)

Competitive pressures also make the Internet a tough place to do business. In the debate about whether online commerce would most closely resemble the economic model of "perfect competition" or "winner-takes-all," the supporters of Adam Smith have come out on top. Barriers to entry remain low, and being the first mover is no guarantee of success. Pets.com and eToys both had plenty of name recognition, but they still went bankrupt. As even more of the bubble companies go out of business, the intensity of competition on the Internet will diminish, but profits will still be hard to find. Online shoppers are extremely price-sensitive, and they tend to compare prices on a variety of sites. The Internet has even affected the cost of life insurance, hardly a product that most people associate with e-commerce. Jeffrey Brown, an economist at Harvard, and Austan Goolsbee, an economist at the University of Chicago, calculated that between 1995 and 1997 the presence of Web sites where people could compare prices reduced the price of term life insurance by somewhere between 8 percent and 15 percent.[1]

The impact of information technology on the economy as a whole is also coming into sharper relief. Even before the terrorist attacks, the three central tenets of the New Economy thesis—lengthy slumps are a thing of the past; Alan Greenspan is omnipotent; and the "productivity miracle" is real—had all been seriously undermined. In the first quarter of 2000 productivity growth was zero. It picked up again in the second quarter, but not to the previous rapid rate. If the economy's efficiency had really taken a quantum leap, as the optimists claimed, then productivity growth should have continued to accelerate despite the economic slowdown. The fact that it faltered suggests that a good deal of the previous surge was a temporary artifact of the boom, rather than a permanent change.

The "miracle" was further tarnished in August 2001, when the Bureau of Labor Statistics revised down its estimates of productivity growth for the previous few years: for 2000, from 4.3 percent to 3.0 percent; and for 1999, from 2.6 percent to 2.3 percent. For the period from 1995 to 2000 as a whole, the annual rate of productivity growth was revised down from 2.9 percent to 2.6 percent. Taken at face value, the latter figure indicates that productivity growth did pick up during the second half of the 1990s, if not as dramatically as once thought. (Between 1973 and 1995, productivity grew by just 1.4 percent a year.) But since some of the acceleration was undoubtedly cyclical, the underlying improvement was less dramatic than even the new numbers suggest. It now seems reasonable to assume that the underlying rate of productivity growth is about 2 percent, or perhaps 2.25 percent. If this is the case, the economy can sustain growth of about 3 percent, or perhaps 3.25 percent, a year.[2] To be sure, this is an improvement over the Old Economy speed limit of 2.5 percent a year, but it hardly adds up to a miracle.

There are several reasons why the New Economy argument turned out to be flawed. One of the most basic was that it exaggerated the role that information technology plays in the economy. Despite the rapid growth of the Internet, firms still spend more money on old-fashioned capital equipment, such as drills and welding machines, than they do on computers, telephones, and other information gadgets. In 2000, at the end of the Internet boom, information technology industries accounted for just 8 percent of gross domestic product. Many big industries that employ millions of people, such as construction, catering, and health care, were largely unaffected by the Internet. In the final analysis, manufacturing still has more to do with assembling bits of wood and metal than it does with exchanging information. Wings have to be attached to planes; roofs have to be put on houses; airbags have to be installed in SUVs. The Internet helps with the planning and organization of such tasks, but it doesn't turn screws or lay bricks. Nor does it operate on patients or serve businessmen lunch.

What of Alan Greenspan's theory that information technology made the economy more efficient by reducing the level of uncertainty facing companies? Alas, that too remains unproven. Technology giants like Dell Computer and Cisco Systems had installed sophisticated software to track their customers' needs, but they failed to predict the disastrous slump in demand at the end of 2000, and they were left with large stockpiles of unwanted inventories. That is not the only problem with Greenspan's theory. If it were correct, the firms and industries that invested most heavily in information technology would have enjoyed the biggest gains in productivity growth. But some of the biggest buyers of information technology, such as the banking and media industries, recorded hardly any productivity growth at all. The industries that enjoyed the most productivity growth during the 1990s were the producers of information technology (such as the personal computer industry), which benefited from Moore's Law, not the users of information technology.

For the Internet to alter living standards substantially over the long term, it would have to boost productivity growth throughout the economy, and of that there is little sign. One of the most optimistic, and widely quoted, estimates of the Internet's impact came from Robert Litan and Alice Rivlin, two economists at the Brookings Institution, a Washington think tank, who claimed it could boost overall productivity growth by 0.4 percent a year.[3] However, in arriving at this figure Litan and Rivlin assumed that the Internet would eventually generate big efficiency gains in health care, financial services, and government services—all sectors where productivity growth has lagged in recent years. The forecast may turn out to be accurate, but at the moment it is little more than wishful thinking.

The recent slowdown in productivity growth raises anew the question of where the Internet ranks in the history of great inventions. It is probably more important than the air-conditioner (pace Barton Biggs), but what about electricity? Clean drinking water? The internal combustion engine? Petroleum? Radio and television? Robert Gordon, an economist at Northwestern University, compared the Internet to all five of these inventions, most of which were developed in the last two-decades of the nineteenth century. His conclusion: "Internet surfing may be fun, but it represents a far smaller increment in the standard of living than achieved by the extension of day into night by electric light, the revolution in factory efficiency achieved by the electric motor, the flexibility and freedom achieved by the automobile, the saving of time and the shrinking of the globe achieved by the airplane, the new materials achieved by the chemical industry, the first sense of live two-way communication achieved by the telephone, the arrival of live news and entertainment into the family parlor achieved by radio and then television, and the enormous improvements in life expectancy, health, and comfort achieved by urban sanitation and indoor plumbing."[4] Some of Gordon's individual points may be questionable, but his overall argument is difficult to dispute. The Internet is a revolutionary means of communication, but it hasn't made people live longer, changed where they live, or made it any easier for them to get from Paris to New York.

## III

**When a speculative bubble bursts, there is usually an angry search** for the he culprits who pumped it up. After the South Sea bubble, several directors of the South Sea Company were arrested, and the chancellor of the Exchequer, the British equivalent of the secretary of the treasury, was imprisoned in the Tower of London. The United States doesn't have a Tower of London, but it does have an adversarial legal system, and there have already been lawsuits relating to the role that stock analysts like Mary Meeker and Henry Blodget played in the Internet boom. Most likely, the recriminations from the dot-com era will keep the courts busy for years to come.

Meeker, Blodget, and their opposite numbers at other Wall Street firms are obvious targets. For years, they promoted investments that were ridiculously overvalued, motivated, at least in part, by the desire to win investment-banking business for their employers. Even when the bubble burst, the analysts largely refused to acknowledge the obvious: that they had compromised their objectivity in order to ride the boom. But Meeker and Blodget were hardly the only ones to blame. They were just the most visible figures in an entire industry that created and ballyhooed Internet stocks. From John Doerr, who claimed that the Internet had been under-hyped, to Harvey Houtkin, who described day trading as "entertainment," countless individuals took part in the big sell. Whether they actually believed what they were saying is an intriguing question. Some did. The Internet appealed to the same human proclivity that spiritual sects and political fanatics have exploited down the ages: a desire to toss out received wisdom and embrace a new creed. Even in the humdrum world of business there was an almost religious aspect to the Internet fervor, and it was by no means restricted to Silicon Valley. Many of the Harvard and Wharton MBAs who flocked to online start-ups sincerely thought they were making business history, rather than playing out their allotted roles in a vast Shakespearean farce.

The attitude of investors and other participants in the bubble varied. Some of them swallowed the notion that the Internet changed everything. Others harbored serious doubts but suspended their disbelief in the interests of making money. (As history has often demonstrated, there is nothing like an investment portfolio that doubles in value every year or two to soothe the skeptical mind.) Still others got caught up in the crowd. If they tried to break away, they risked being punished. When Morgan Stanley and Goldman Sachs declined the opportunity to take TheGlobe.com public, Bear Stearns stepped in and organized the most successful IPO in history. When Mary Meeker downgraded At Home and the stock continued to rise, she looked like a fool.

The fundamental lesson of a speculative bubble is that behavior that seems rational at the individual level can lead to collective insanity. Trapped in the logic of herd behavior, Wall Street will inevitably keep inflating the bubble until it bursts. It is up to journalists and government officials to try to maintain sanity, but in this case neither proved up to the task. Despite some honorable exceptions, the overall standard of reporting on the Internet stock phenomenon was dismal. In many cases, CNBC being only the most obvious example, the media became an active participant in the bubble, turning entrepreneurs like Jeff Bezos into celebrities, and parroting the Wall Street line on stocks like Yahoo! and Amazon.com. Economics was largely responsible for this deterioration. The Internet boom created a vast new source of advertising, which newspapers, magazines, and television networks rushed to exploit. Some journalists genuinely believed in the Internet; others were reluctant converts. Either way, the result was the same: more hot air pumped into the bubble.

The Federal Reserve, which was created expressly to prevent speculative excesses, also failed in its duty. If anybody had the legal, moral, and intellectual authority to prick the bubble, it was Alan Greenspan, but he refused to exercise this power until too late. After his "irrational exuberance" speech in December 1996, Greenspan rarely mentioned the stock market, and when he did, it was usually to say that prices reflected the actions of well-informed investors. There were some valid reasons for Greenspan's hands-off policy. The long economic expansion that accompanied the stock market boom reduced welfare rolls, raised wages for the poor, and drew many previously excluded members of society into the mainstream. Greenspan was understandably reluctant to raise interest rates when there was no sign of inflation, but rising consumer prices are not the only indicator of an unbalanced economy. During the latter stages of the Internet boom, a soaring trade deficit, a plunging savings rate, and sharply rising indebtedness were all signs that the stock market was driving the economy into an increasingly precarious position. Still Greenspan stood aside—a fact that cannot be totally separated from his ideological beliefs.

As a fervent disciple of the free market, Greenspan believed that people's investment decisions were largely a matter for them, even if they didn't make sense. When Nobel Prize–winning economists warned publicly about a dangerous speculative bubble developing, Greenspan refused to act. As a faithful apostle of Ayn Rand, he believed that American capitalism was renewing itself before his eyes. In speech after speech, he stressed the historic changes that were sweeping the economy thanks to the application of information technology. The New Economy thesis would never have become so widely accepted if Greenspan hadn't seized upon it and made it his own. He liked to play the role of professor, hedging his public statements with qualifications, but Wall Street ignored these qualifications, especially when it was repackaging his lectures for distribution to investors. The message passed to the public was unequivocal: the Fed chairman believed that the New Economy was a reality, therefore higher stock prices were justified. Greenspan knew this was happening and did little to stop it.

Silicon Valley, Wall Street, the media, and the Fed all played roles in the Internet bubble, but when all is said and done it was primarily a story of greed and gullibility on the part of the American public. H. L. Mencken once wrote: "The notion that Americans are a sordid, money-grubbing people, with no thought above the dollar, is a favorite delusion of continentals, and even the English, on occasion, dally with it. It has, in fact, little solid basis. The truth is that Americans, as a race, set relatively little store by money; surely all their bitterest critics are at least as eager for it."[5] Had he lived through the 1990s, Mencken might have altered his views. At the height of the boom, the United States was consumed by the idea of getting rich on the Internet. College students, cabdrivers, construction workers, dentists, doctors, journalists, congressmen, Hollywood stars—they were all buying and selling Internet stocks. No glossy magazine or television newsmagazine was complete without its profile of the latest Internet billionaire. While it is true that Internet stocks eventually spread to Britain, Germany, and Japan, the Internet mania in those countries was nowhere near as intense as it was in the United States, and for good reason.

The Internet economy was an American creation, dominated by American firms, peopled with instantly recognizable American types. There was Marc Andreessen, the gawky farm boy; Jerry Yang, the hardworking Asian immigrant; Jeff Bezos, the high school valedictorian; Henry Blodget, the smooth-talking preppie; James Cramer, the fast-talking Jewish kid; and Jim Clark, the crusty engineer. With this cast of characters, the Internet boom and bust was like an epic miniseries that grabbed the imagination of the country and held it rapt until the final episode had ended. But unlike the case of a television program, the viewers were not passive couch potatoes. By quitting their jobs and joining an Internet start-up, or by simply buying a few hundred shares in Yahoo!, they could become actors in the ongoing drama. The desire not to feel left out fuels all mass movements. Coupled with greed, it is virtually irresistible.

## IV

**After the bursting of the bubble, the mood of the country changed** sharply. Dozens of day-trading firms closed down, while online trading firms such as E★Trade and Charles Schwab suffered big falls in turnover. George Gilder and Jim Cramer fell silent, or, if they didn't, most people stopped noticing what they were saying. Americans finally switched off CNBC and concentrated on other things in life apart from the stock market. When At Home filed for bankruptcy at the end of September 2001, *The New York Times* relegated the story to the bottom of its business section.[6] Especially in the wake of the terrorist attacks, many of the things that had seemed so important only two years previously now appeared mundane and minor. In 2000 and 2001, applications for the Peace Corps rose sharply, as college graduates and refugees from failed dotcoms looked for more worthwhile things to do. In the nation's boardrooms, corporate executives set aside their plans for Internet tracking stocks and concentrated on more basic matters, such as preventing the company from going broke. In Washington, the bickering over how to spend the budget surplus was replaced by weighty debates about how to prevent an economic downturn from turning into a chronic slump. After several years indulging itself in fanciful thoughts about the future, America had gotten serious, leaving behind the trivial pursuits of a speculative bubble. Until the next one comes along, that is.

Which probably won't be for quite a while. Memories of the Great Crash persisted for decades, and it wasn't until the 1950s that there was another major bout of stock market speculation. The Internet bust wasn't as traumatic as the Great Crash, but its ultimate consequences remain unclear. It wasn't the events of October 1929 that seared the events of October 1929 into the public memory, after all, but the Great Depression that followed the crash. Until September 11, 2001, the notion that the Internet bust might be succeeded by another economic cataclysm seemed fanciful. The most likely outcome was a lengthy but relatively shallow recession, during which businesses gradually eliminated the excess capacity they had created during the boom years and consumers gradually rebuilt their savings. Following the terrorist attacks, the economic calculus changed dramatically. For the first time in at least a generation, it was possible to construct a plausible scenario for the American economy involving a sharp contraction in gross domestic product, a wave of major bankruptcies, and mass unemployment. This grim version of the future involved all three major categories of private-sector expenditure—business investment, consumer spending, and exports—falling together, as the United States, Japan, and Europe entered a global recession simultaneously. In such a situation, the onus would fall on fiscal and monetary policy, but as the experiences of the United States in the 1930s and Japan in the 1990s demonstrated, it is extremely difficult for a government to revive a depressed economy if the private sector doesn't cooperate.

The depression scenario was only that, of course, and much depended on how quickly consumers would get over the initial wave of panic that the attacks produced. If Americans could be persuaded to return to the airports and the shopping malls pretty quickly, the economic outlook would improve appreciably, and there would be a fair chance of a reasonably rapid recovery once the excesses of the Internet boom had finally been wrung out of the system. Whichever outcome came to pass, however, one thing was certain: the halcyon days of the dotcom era would not return.

In November 2001, Henry Blodget resigned from Merrill Lynch after accepting a buyout offer that the firm had extended to thousands of its employees. Said Blodget to *The New York Times:* "It just seemed like a good time to pursue the next thing."[7]

# notes

## prologue

1 "Queen of the 'Net," *Barron's,* 21 December 1998.
2 "It doesn't matter what these companies do . . ." Saul Hansell, "Priceline.com Stock Zooms in Offering," *The New York Times,* 31 April 1998: C1.
3 Charles Mackay, *Extraordinary Popular Delusions and the Madness of Crowds* (London: Richard Bentley, 1841).
4 "Speculation . . . the act of knowingly assuming above-average risks," *The Concise McGraw-Hill Dictionary of Modern Economics,* 1983 ed.
5 "Speculation tends to detach itself . . ." Charles Kindleberger, *Manias, Panics, and Crashes: A History of Financial Crises* (New York: John Wiley, 1996), 14.
6 Priceline.com Prospectus, 18 March 1999: 1–21.

## chapter one: from memex to world wide web

1 "The investigator is staggered by the findings . . ." Vannevar Bush, "As We May Think," *Atlantic Monthly,* July 1945. <http://www.theatlantic.com/unbound/flashbks/computer/bushf.htm.>
2 Ibid.
3 Ibid.
4 Ibid.
5 "Most people are stupid . . ." John Naughton, *A Brief History of the Future* (London: Weidenfeld & Nicolson, 1999), 221.
6 "Lay down thy packet . . ." Janet Abbate, *Inventing the Internet* (Cambridge: MIT Press, 1999), 195.
7 "Suppose all the information stored . . ." Tim Berners-Lee, *Weaving the Web* (New York: HarperCollins, 1999), 4.
8 Ibid., 36.
9 Ibid., 73.
10 Karen D. Frazer, *The NSFNET Backbone Project, 1987–1995* <http://www.merit.edu/merit/archive/nsfnet/final.report/phenom.html>.

## chapter two: popular capitalism

1 Janos Kornai, "What the Change of System from Socialism to Capitalism Does and Does Not Mean," *Journal of Economic Perspectives* 14 (2000): 27–42.

2 "the final form of human government," Francis Fukuyama, "The End of History," *National Interest*, Summer 1989: 3–18.

3 "Computing is not about computers anymore. . . ." Nicholas Negroponte, *Being Digital* (New York: Vintage, 1996), 7.

4 "My approach was that if the code doesn't say, 'Thou shalt not' . . ." Pamela Yip, *Dallas Morning News*, 9 January 2001.

5 "It is not a case of choosing those . . ." John Maynard Keynes, *The General Theory of Employment, Interest and Money* (New York: Harcourt Brace Jovanovich, 1964), 156.

6 "Investors learned firsthand in the 1980s . . ." Jane Bryant Quinn, "Time to Time the Market?" *Newsweek*, 6 September 1993: 56.

7 "Stocks have been chronically undervalued . . ." Jeremy Siegel, *Stocks for the Long Run* (New York: McGraw Hill, 1994), xvii.

8 Ibid., 30.

9 "Plot the two, and it looks like the same chart . . ." Jeffrey M. Laderman, "Call It a Boomer Boom," *Business Week*, 27 March 2000: 209.

## chapter three: information superhighway

1 "During my service in the United States Congress . . ." Jules Siegel <http://www.redrat.net/gorebush/gore net.htm>.

2 "Just as the Interstate highway system . . ." Al Gore, "We Need a National 'Superhighway' for Computer Information," *The Washington Post*, 15 July 1990: B3.

3 "The information superhighway is a convenient metaphor . . ." Tosca Moon Lee, "The Information Interstate: Superhighway or Superhype?" *Smart Computing* 5.9 (1994) <http://www.smartcomputing.com/editorial/article.asp?article=articles%2F1994%2Fpcn0925%2Fpcn0925%2Easp>.

4 "We are seeing a revitalization of society . . ." Michael Hauben, <http://www.eff.org/pub/Net_culture/netizen.paper>.

5 Ibid.

6 William Gibson, *Neuromancer* (New York: Ace Books, 1994).

7 Donna Haraway, *Cyborgs, Simians and Women: The Reinvention of Nature* (New York: Routledge, 1991).

8 "It just seemed to me to be the most important thing . . ." Tom Bethell, "The Prophet of Profits: George Glider Extends His Seamless Web," *The American Spectator*, August 1999.

9 "The microchip will reshape not only the television and computer industries . . ." George Gilder, *Life After Television: The Coming Transformation of Media and American Life* (New York: Norton, 1992), 15–16.

10 Ibid., 53.

11 Ibid., 40.

12 "creating social changes so profound that their only parallel . . ." Louis Rossetto, *Wired*, January 1993.

13 "within ten or twenty years the world will be completely transformed . . ." Paul Keegan, "The Digerati," *The New York Times Magazine*, 21 May 1997: 38.

14 "It's very hard to think outside the boxes . . ." Peter Schwartz, "Shock Wave (Anti) Warrior," *Wired*, November 1993.

15 Mitchell Kapor, "Where Is the Digital Highway Really Heading?" *Wired*, July/August 1993.

16 "When I met with the Japanese Prime Minister . . ." *The Boston Globe*, 1 March 1995.

17 "The idea that twenty years from now . . ." Nicholas Negroponte, *Being Digital* (New York: Vintage, 1996), 148.

18 Ibid., 179.

19 Ibid., 212.

20 "A Conversation with Vice President Gore about the 'Information Superhighway,'" *The National Journal* 25 (1993): 676.

21 "Our new electronic superhighway will change the way people use television. . . ." Michael Wolff, *Burn Rate* (New York: Touchstone, 1999), 117.

22 John Cassidy, "Bell Rings Multi-Media Revolution," *Sunday Times of London*, 17 October 1993.

## chapter four: netscape

1 "By the power vested in me by nobody in particular . . ." John Naughton, *A Brief History of the Future* (London: Weidenfeld & Nicolson, 1999), 245.

2 "Say we were talking about God or something . . ." Rick Tetzeli, "What It's Really Like to be Marc Andreessen," *Fortune*, 9 December 1996: 50.

3 "There was a definite element of not wanting to make it easier . . ." Naughton, 243.

4 "It had a very large established budget . . ." Ibid., 242.

5 "Face it, they made pages look cool," Ibid., 247.

6 "I was right. People abused it horribly . . ." Ibid., 246.

7 " 'Tim bawled me out' . . . Andreessen later recalled . . ." Robert H. Reid, *Architects of the Web: 1,000 Days that Built the Future of Business* (New York: John Wiley, 1997), 12.

8 "There's no infrastructure at all in Illinois . . ." Ibid., 21.

9 "so different and so obviously useful . . ." Ibid., 17.

10 "Marc. You may not know me . . ." Jim Clark, *Netscape Time: The Making of the Billion-Dollar Start-Up That Took on Microsoft* (New York: St. Martin's, 2000), 34.

11 "Along with its brother, impatience . . ." Michael Lewis, *The New New Thing: A Silicon Valley Story* (New York: Norton, 1999), 36.

12 "This *is* an information superhighway . . ." Reid, 19.

13 "I'm finished with all that Mosaic shit," Clark, 42.

14 "Well, we could always build a Mosaic killer." Ibid., 49.

15 "How could anyone make money on the Internet? . . ." Ibid., 45.

16 "If you can hire the entire Mosaic team to do this . . ." Ibid., 49.

17 "We had this twenty-two-year-old kid who was pretty damn interesting . . ." Reid, 24.

18 "When you ask people for millions of dollars . . ." Clark, 74.

19 "When I started Convergent, I got commitments for $2.5 million in twenty minutes . . ." Annalee Saxenian, *Regional Advantage: Culture and Competition in Silicon Valley and Route 128* (Cambridge: Harvard UP, 1996), 65.

20 Saxenian, 39.

21 "a highly caffeinated Clark Kent," John Heilemann, "The Networker," *The New Yorker*, 11 August 1997: 29.

22 "This is so big, the only thing to do is dive right in," Ibid.

23 "the nearest thing to a working prototype of the information superhighway . . ." Philip Elmer-Dewitt, "Battle for the Soul of the Internet," *Time*, 25 July 1994: 50.

24 "info-suck" and "info-nipple," Reid, 29.

25 "It's basically a Microsoft lesson, right? . . ." Ibid., 31.

26 "It blew us all away," Clark, 160.

27 "I'm astonished. I've never seen anything like this in my life," Peter H. Lewis, "Netscape Knows Fame and Aspires to Fortune," *The New York Times*, 1 March 1995: D1.

## chapter five: the stock market

1 Edward Chancellor, *Devil Take the Hindmost: A History of Financial Speculation* (New York: Farrar Strauss & Giroux, 1999), 3–6.

2 "full of instability, insanity, pride and foolishness . . ." Ibid., 13.

3 "for carrying out an undertaking of great advantage . . ." Charles Mackay, *Extraordinary Popular Delusions and the Madness of Crowds* (London: Richard Bentley, 1841), 55.

4 "The universal deluge of the S. Sea . . ." Chancellor, 84–85.

5 "Dread seemed to take possession of the multitude . . ." Robert Sobel, *Panic on Wall Street: A History of American Financial Disasters* (New York: Macmillan, 1968), 179.

6 "October. This is one of the peculiarly dangerous months . . ." Burton G. Malkiel, *A Random Walk Down Wall Street* (New York: W. W. Norton, 1985), 28.

7 "a new era without depressions," Chancellor, 193.

8 Gene Epstein, "Can Anything Stop This Economy?" *Barron's*, 4 September 2000.

9 Malkiel, 50.

10 "dividend discount model," John Burr Williams, *The Theory of Investment Value* (Cambridge: Harvard UP, 1938).

11 Benjamin Graham and David L. Dodd, *Security Analysis* (New York: McGraw Hill, 1988).

## chapter six: ipo

1 "We had a belief that goods will be sold electronically . . ." Kara Swisher, *aol.com: How Steve Case Beat Bill Gates, Nailed the Netheads, and Made Millions in the War for the Web* (New York: Three Rivers, 1999), 89.

2 "It's like the land rush in Oklahoma . . ." Amy Cortese, "Cyberspace," *Business Week*, 27 February 1995: 78.

3 "This is a rocket that has been launched . . ." John W. Verity, "Planet Internet," *Business Week*, 3 April 1995: 118.

4 "Anything that even sounds like it's an Internet play . . ." Karen Southwick, "Smitten with the Internet," *Upside,* June 1995: 16.

5 "I continued to preach the gospel, assuring the unsaved . . ." Jim Clark, *Netscape Time: The Making of the Billion-Dollar Start-Up That Took on Microsoft* (New York: St. Martin's, 2000), 205.

6 "With this company, and in this market . . ." Joshua Quittner and Michelle Slatalla, *Speeding the Net: The Inside Story of Netscape and How It Challenged Microsoft* (New York: Atlantic Monthly Press, 1998), 239.

7 "If Spyglass could score a successful IPO . . ." Clark, 212.

8 "It's just like church . . ." Ibid., 218.

9 "The weather at seven A.M . . ." Ibid., 3.

10 "Press one if you're calling about Netscape," Quittner and Slatalla, 248.

11 Clark, 13.

12 "It was the best opening day for a stock in Wall Street history . . ." Ibid., 221.

13 "People started drinking my Kool-Aid," Michael Lewis, *The New New Thing: A Silicon Valley Story* (New York: Norton, 1999), 88.

14 "Today another frontier yawns before us . . ." John Perry Barlow, "Jack In, Young Pioneer!" *Computerworld College Edition*, 1994.

15 Ibid.

16 "like other Microsoft programs, may smother all competitors," Joshua Quittner, "Browser Madness," *Time,* 21 August 1995: 56.

17 "displace both the telephone and the television over the next five years . . ." George Gilder, "The Coming Software Shift," *Forbes,* 28 August 1995.

18 "George, George, George—what took you so long?" Howard Anderson, "George Gilder and His Critics," *Forbes ASAP,* 9 October 1995.

## chapter seven: yahoo!

1 "pure marketing hype," Randall E. Stross, "How Yahoo! Won the Search Wars," *Fortune,* 2 March 1998: 148.

2 "every mother's idea of the bedroom that she wished her sons never had," Andrew Gumbel, "Analysis: The Cyberpunks," *The Independent* (London), 24 March 1999.

3 "If you've got thirteen Madonna sites . . ." Stross, *Fortune.*

4 "The office was in the right-hand corner of a little industrial building . . ." Tim Koogle, interview with the author, 7 February 2000.

5 "charging too much money and getting too little done," Ibid.

6 "We really wanted to keep the service free—that was a fundamental goal," Jerry Yang, interview with the author, 7 February 2000.

7 "In spite of no real marketing spending and no infrastructure . . ." Koogle, interview.

8 "If you looked at Microsoft and believed Bill Gates . . ." John Cassidy, "The Woman in the Bubble," *The New Yorker,* 26 April 1999: 54.

9 "a new way of financing companies," Cassidy, Ibid., 56.

10 "a big market opportunity for lots of companies," Mary Meeker and Chris DePuy, *The Internet Report* (New York: HarperBusiness, 1996), 1–2.

11 Ibid., 1.

12 Ibid., back cover.

13 "the number of pure-play investment vehicles related to the Internet . . ." Ibid., 1–3.

14 "Investors should hold off in the near term . . ." Ibid., 1–1.

15 "For now, it's important for companies to nab customers . . ." Ibid., 1–20.

16 "I remember that in 1995 I would speak with Marc Andreesen . . ." Cassidy, *New Yorker,* 56.

17 "Morgan Stanley's great insight . . ." Roger McNamee, interview with the author, March 1999.

18 "The lack of any sales was a major negative in our rating," Joseph Radigan, "CyberCash's Investors Get a Wild Ride," *U.S. Banker,* April 1996.

19 "I really wanted a few more quarters," Joseph Nocera, "Do You Believe? How Yahoo! Became a Blue-Chip Stock," *Fortune,* 7 June 1999: 79.

20 "We couldn't afford to be boxed in," Ibid., 80.

21 "I was, like, Yahoo!, you know, just a search engine . . ." Mary Meeker, interview with the author, March 1999.

22 "The valuations are into the sphere of surrealism," Jon Auerbach, "Yahoo, Indeed," *Boston Globe*, 13 April 1996, City Edition.

23 "a new kind of global, diversified media company . . ." Jerry Useem, "All Dressed Up and No IPO," *Inc.,* February 1998: 98.

24 "a piece of junque du jour," Ibid.

25 "Mistake. Big mistake. I knew it . . ." Michael Wolff, *Burn Rate* (New York: Touchstone, 1999), 101.

26 "The honeymoon is over," Kora McNaughton, "Fixing the Pipes," *Upside,* October 1996.

27 Ibid.

## chapter eight: battle for the 'net

1 "something far less expensive than a PC which is powerful enough for Web browsing," Charles H. Ferguson, *High Stakes, No Prisoners* (New York: Three Rivers Press, 1999), 144–45.

2 "poorly debugged set of device drivers," Ibid., 150.

3 "hard core about the Internet," Ibid., 244.

4 James Collins, "High Stakes Winners," *Time,* 19 February 1996: cover.

5 "I could never have imagined myself standing there with Gates . . ." Kara Swisher, *aol.com: How Steve Case Beat Bill Gates, Nailed the Netheads, and Made Millions in the War for the Web* (New York: Three Rivers, 1999), 140.

6 "we must leverage Windows more . . ." Joshua Quittner and Michelle Slatalla,

*Speeding the Net: The Inside Story of Netscape and How It Challenged Microsoft* (New York: Atlantic Monthly Press, 1998), 283.

7 "It is Case's America Online that has shown . . ." Amy Cortese and Amy Barrett, "The Online World of Steve Case," *Business Week,* 15 April 1996.

8 "I never knew anybody who took AOL seriously as an Internet company," Michael Wolff, *Burn Rate* (New York: Touchstone, 1999), 203.

9 "the closest thing to marketing," Cortese and Barrett, *Business Week.*

10 "make it easy and make it fun," Swisher, 98.

11 Ibid., 226.

12 Ibid.

13 "nobody does a better job of making general information available for a mass market than America Online," Mary Meeker and Chris DePuy, *The Internet Report* (New York: HarperBusiness, 1996), 1–18.

14 "The Emperor hath no Pants, AOL hath no Profits," Swisher, 201.

15 Rupert Murdoch, interview with the author, 16 February 2001.

16 "black hole," Wolff, 135.

17 "A wealth of information creates a poverty of attention," Carl Shapiro and Hal R. Varian, *Information Rules: A Strategic Guide to the Network Economy* (Cambridge: Harvard Business School Press, 1998), 6.

18 "We'll be doing our best to get advertising income . . ." NBC, transcript of press conference, 14 December 1995.

19 "This is a big deal for GE . . ." Ibid.

## chapter nine: irrational exuberance

1 Robert McGough, "Stock Funds' Intake: $99 Billion in 4 Months," *The Wall Street Journal,* 29 May 1996.

2 "You've got stocks selling at absolutely unbelievable multiples of earnings and revenues . . ." Barton Biggs, interview with the author, June 1996.

3 "The sociological signs are very bad, too . . ." Ibid.

4 "Believe me, the investment bankers would love me to be wildly bullish . . ." Byron Wien, interview with the author, June 1996.

5 "The powerful 1995 rally in stock prices is not a bubble but rather a signal that the valuation paradigm has changed," David Shulman, "1996: Stock Market Bubble or Paradigm Shift?" Salomon Brothers circular, December 1995.

6 "The tape has a way of telling you . . ." David Shulman, interview with the author, June 1996.

7 "the wonderful things going on in the U.S. economy," Abby Joseph Cohen, interview with the author, June 1996.

8 "I believe that the government's productivity figures are wrong . . ." Ibid.

9 "so dramatic that one cannot expect them to be quickly incorporated by investors," Ibid.

10 "The people who say the stock market is up x percent and therefore is overpriced are not looking at the right thing . . ." Ibid.

11  Neither Mr. Buffett nor Munger "would currently buy shares . . ." Bloomberg, "Buffett says offering is overpriced," *Financial Post*, 3 April 1996: 6.

12  "euphoria," Edward Wyatt, "Manager of Biggest Mutual Fund Quits After Recent Subpar Gains," *The New York Times*, 24 May 1996: A1.

13  "It sent a message that you had better be right or else your job is on the line . . ." Barton Biggs, interview with the author, June 1996.

14  "When the rest of the world is mad, we must imitate them in some measure," John Carswell, *The South Sea Bubble* (London: Cresset Press, 1960), 161.

15  "A fad is a bubble if the contagion of the fad occurs through price . . ." Robert J. Schiller, *Market Volatility* (Cambridge: MIT Press, 1993), 56.

16  "We're all looking at the performance of Internet companies that have come out since Netscape . . ." Peter H. Lewis, "Yet Again, Wall Street is charmed by the Internet," *The New York Times*, 3 April 1996.

17  "Is there a reason for concern here that some of us don't know about?" Lisa Bransten, "Lost in Cyberspace with a Motley Fool," *Financial Times*, 22 June 1996.

18  "disquieting similarities between our present prosperity and the fabulous twenties," Justin Martin, *Greenspan: The Man Behind Money* (Cambridge: Perseus, 2000), 216.

19  "I think investors can accommodate themselves to a 7 percent gain rather than a 30 percent gain . . ." Arthur Levitt, interview with the author, June 1996.

20  "I think we partially broke the back of an emerging speculation in equities," Bob Woodward, *Maestro: Greenspan's Fed and the American Boom* (New York: Simon & Schuster, 2000), 122.

21  Ibid., 173.

22  Ibid., 174.

23  "Clearly, sustained low inflation implies . . ." Bloomberg, "Excerpt From the Speech by Greenspan," *The New York Times*, 7 December 1996: A37.

24  "I wonder if I had anything to do with that," Bob Shiller, interview with the author, 21 February 2000.

25  "The Fed has no intention of tightening monetary policy simply to push the equity market down," Floyd Norris, "Greenspan Asks a Question and Global Markets Wobble," *The New York Times*, 7 December 1996: A1.

26  "Instead of raising rates, he is going to make speeches," Ibid.

**chapter ten: amazon.com**

1  "In the three years since the Internet has taken off, the slow growth of electronic commerce has been one of its big disappointments . . ." *Economist* survey, "In Search of the Perfect Market," *The Economist*, 10 May 1997.

2  Chip Bayers, "The Inner Bezos," *Wired*, March 1999.

3  "You have to keep in mind that human beings aren't good at understanding exponential growth . . ." Robert Spector, *Amazon.com: Get Big Fast* (New York: John Wiley & Sons, 2000), 25.

4  "no eight-hundred-pound gorillas in book publishing and distribution," Michael H. Martin, "The Next Big Thing: A Bookstore?" *Fortune*, 9 December 1996.

5  "I knew that when I was eighty . . ." Spector, 30.

6 "Though it hasn't yet posted a profit, the company is on its way to ringing up more than \$5 million . . ." G. Bruce Knecht, "How Wall Street Whiz Found a Niche Selling Books on the Internet," *The Wall Street Journal*, 16 May 1996: A1.

7 "If we'd thought all this was purely about money . . ." John Heilemann, "The Networker," *The New Yorker*, 11 August 1997: 34.

8 "Amazon.com is truly virtual," Martin, *Fortune*, 9 December 1996.

9 "three floors above an art gallery on a slightly seedy street in Seattle . . ." Economist survey, "A River Runs Through It," *The Economist*, 10 May 1997.

10 Jonathan Chait and Stephen Glass, "Amazon.con," *Slate*, 4 January 1997.

11 "enormous benefit to the [publishing] business because it's not about selling big, best-selling authors . . ." Spector, 174.

12 "We have to be a player. Online bookselling is going to be a very big thing," Ibid., 124.

13 "virtually unlimited online shelf space . . ." Amazon.com Prospectus, March 1997: 3.

14 "believes that it will incur substantial operating losses for the foreseeable future . . ." Ibid.

15 Ibid.

16 "If we're profitable within the next two years, it will be an accident," *Fortune*, 9 December 1996.

17 "stocks only a few hundred titles," Spector, 168.

18 "caused every investment banker and every venture capitalist in Silicon Valley to just go absolutely nuts," Roger McNamee, "Discussion about Hi Tech IPOs," *CNNfn*, Cable News Network, 19 May 1997.

## chapter eleven: the new economy

1 "The Net provides a powerful, efficient new channel of retailing . . ." Mary Meeker and Sharon Pearson, *Internet Retailing Report* (New York: Morgan Stanley, 1997), i.

2 "I saw a lot of research that kept saying people dislike grocery shopping . . ." "Consumer-Direct: Will Stores Survive?" *Progressive Grocer*, 1 April 1997.

3 Lucien Rhodes, "The Race for more Bandwidth," *Wired*, January 1996.

4 "Because of the foregoing factors, among others, the Company is unable to forecast its revenues . . ." At Home prospectus, 16 May 1997:5.

5 "Now, as Doerr and a handful of At Home's bosses and boosters hovered anxiously over a blue computer screen . . ." John Heilemann, "The Networker," *The New Yorker*, 11 August 1997: 28.

6 "My-oh-my, you talk about a joyous Fourth of July!" *Wall Street Week*, ann. Louis Rukeyser, PBS, 4 July 1997.

7 "So, let's make it three cheers for the red, white and green," Ibid.

8 "I remember when we held a press conference around this time in 1972 . . ." David E. Sanger, "The Mantra for 1999: It's the Best of Times," *New York Times*, 3 May 1997.

9 "The unique nature of an expansion led by high-technology . . ." Michael J. Mandel, "The New Business Cycle," *Business Week*, 31 March 1997: 58.

10 Michael J. Mandel, "The New Growth Formula," *Business Week,* 19 May 1997: 31.

11 Ibid., 32–33.

12 "new era without depressions . . ." Edward Chancellor, *Devil Take the Hindmost: A History of Financial Speculation* (New York: Farrar Strauss & Giroux, 1999), 193.

13 "Civilization is taking on new aspects . . ." John Moody, "The New Era in Wall Street," *Atlantic Monthly,* August 1928: 260.

14 Rik Kirkland, "America in the world: still on top, with no challenger," *Fortune,* 9 June 1997: 86.

15 "non-regulatory, market-oriented approach," John M. Broder, "Let It Be: Ira Magaziner Argues for Minimal Internet Regulations," *The New York Times,* 30 June 1997: D1.

16 "exceptional . . . once or twice in a century phenomenon . . ." Alan Greenspan, *Monetary Policy Testimony and Report to the Congress,* 22 July 1997.

17 "What we may be observing in the current environment . . ." Ibid.

18 "sharp, incisive action . . ." John Cassidy, "Pricking the Bubble," *The New Yorker,* 17 August 1998: 37.

19 Ibid., 40.

20 "There's no guarantee that even if you get a 1929, you'll end up with a 1932," Lawrence B. Lindsey, *Economic Puppetmasters: Lessons from the Halls of Power* (Washington: AEI Press, 1999), 53.

21 "At the time of the weekly Board of Governors meeting, the U.S. economy was literally linked together by a single bridge . . ." Ibid., 30.

22 "What she did—through long discussions and lots of arguments into the night . . ." John Cassidy, "The Fountainhead," *The New Yorker,* 24 April & 1 May 2000: 167.

23 "Ayn, this is *incredible*. . . ." Ibid.

24 "She did things in her personal life which I would not approve of . . ." Ibid., 168.

25 "Everybody is tired of being bearish and being wrong . . ." Barton Biggs, interview with the author, July 1997.

26 "I was at a dinner the other night. There were a lot of older people there who are very bearish," Ibid.

27 "international stock market crash," Anna-Patricia Kahn, "Nennen Sie mich ruhig einen Phantasten," *Focus,* July 1997.

28 "rational exuberance about profits and near-zero inflation," "Wall St. Contrarians Have It Tough," *Associated Press,* 13 July 1997.

29 "an outstanding platform that I think will in three to five years lead to some fairly significant profits," Brenda Dalglish, "Investors Bet Big on Pure Cable-Modem Play," *Financial Post,* 9 October 1997.

30 "This has gotten more ink than my last six books," Bob Minzesheimer, "Updike in the Teeth of Technology," *USA Today,* 11 September 1997: 1D.

31 "We are making a long-term bet on this company . . ." Mary Meeker, "U.S. and the Americas Investment Research," Morgan Stanley Dean Witter, 26 September 1997: 1.

32 Ibid.

## chapter twelve: a media bubble

1 "I don't think anybody should do anything right now. . . ." Author's notes.
2 "Asia's down; Latin America's down . . ." John Cassidy, "Department of Jitters," *The New Yorker,* 10 November 1997: 41.
3 "We caught on to a Gulf War that's going to last forever . . ." Ibid.
4 "We had a chance to define our brand, and we took it . . ." Ibid.
5 "A lot of financial journalists seem to hate capitalism . . ." Charles Fishman, "Colour Commentary of the New Economy," *Financial Post,* 17 June 2000: D1.
6 "America is experiencing a serious asset-price bubble," "America's Bubble Economy," *The Economist,* 18 April 1998: 15.
7 "This is unquestionably a bubble," "Addressing the U.S. Bubble," *Financial Times,* 22 April 1998: 1.
8 "America today is nothing like Japan eight years ago . . ." "The Economic Bubble Theory," editorial, *The New York Times,* 29 April 1998.
9 Michael Hirsh, "Bubble Trouble?" *Newsweek,* 11 May 1998: 46.
10 "confidence-shattering crash" Susan E. Kuhn, "How Crazy Is This Market?" *Fortune,* 15 April 1996: 83.
11 Nelson D. Schwartz, "Time to Cash In Your Blue Chips," *Fortune,* 21 July 1997.
12 "Seeing such price gains, you may have two questions . . ." Duff McDonald, "It's Not Too Late to Grab Some Net," *Money,* July 1998.
13 "In our 20th century consumer culture, it may seem almost too good to be true . . ." Michael Krantz, "Click Till You Drop," *Time,* 20 July 1998: 39.
14 "more than the 30 million who tune in weekly to NBC's top-rated TV show, *ER,*" Linda Himelstein, "Yahoo! The Company, the Strategy, the Stock," *Business Week,* 7 September 1998: 67.
15 "We happened to launch on the same day that the Communications Decency Act was dealt a fatal blow . . ." Casey Kait and Stephen Weiss, *Digital Hustlers: Living Large and Falling Hard in Silicon Valley* (New York: ReganBooks, 2001), 163.
16 "It was unbelievable how traditional media . . ." Ibid., 165.
17 "a new generation of businesspeople . . ." The Founding Editors, "Annual Report," *Fast Company,* February 1997.
18 Ibid.
19 "the senior level person who wakes up at night and wonders how the Net affects my business. . . ." Lisa Granastein, "Journals of E-Commerce," *Mediaweek,* 22 June 1998.
20 "Imagine Media Launches Business 2.0: The Magazine for Business in the Internet Age," *PR Newswire,* 2 April 1998.
21 "The New Economy—decentralized and antihierarchical—is the most promising opportunity in years. . . ." Ibid.
22 "The personal computer is the communications tool that has made all the difference. . . ." James J. Cramer, "Special: Cramer on the Power of the Individual Investor," TheStreet.com, 4 April 1997.

23 "We'll have stuff that will blow your mind. . . ." Melanie Warner, "The Trader Who Won't Shut Up," *Fortune,* 12 May 1997: 19.

24 "I am a big believer in the Internet. . . ." ABCNews.com, 27 March 1998.

25 "We simply don't have enough pieces of paper . . ." TheStreet.com, 24 June 1998.

26 "There are companies whose businesses wouldn't exist . . ." Kathleen Doler, "A Conversation with Co-Founder of TheStreet.com: James Cramer, Columnist, Trader and Wild Man," *Upside,* November 1998.

27 "He's on track to enter Wall Street's hall of fame for ubiquity . . ." Kimberly S. McDonald, "High-Profile Hedger," *New York Post,* 14 December 1997: 66.

## chapter thirteen: greenspan's green light

1 "I think there is a good deal of comparison between the market in 1929 and the market today," Cassidy, "Pricking the Bubble," 38.

2 "I define a bubble as a situation in which the level of stock prices is high . . ." Ibid.

3 "Some members expressed concern that the widespread perception of reduced risk . . ." Minutes of the Federal Open Market Committee, 19 May 1998.

4 "a number of members indicated that the decision was a close call for them," Ibid.

5 "Failing that, firming actions on the part of the Federal Reserve may be necessary to ensure a track of expansion . . ." Monetary Policy Testimony and Report to the Congress; Testimony of Alan Greenspan, 21 July 1998.

6 "History tells us that there will be a correction of some significant dimension . . ." Jacob M. Schlesinger, "Greenspan Tempers Economic Optimism," *The Wall Street Journal,* 23 July 1998.

7 S. C. Gwynne, "Is the Boom Over?" *Time,* 14 September 1998.

8 "just not credible that the United States can remain an oasis of prosperity . . ." Ibid., 28.

9 "I think we know where we have to go," Richard W. Stevenson, "Fed Chairman Renews Hopes for a Rate Cut," *The New York Times,* 24 September 1998: C1.

10 "to cushion the effects on prospective economic growth . . ." Federal Reserve Press Release, 29 September 1998.

11 David Wessel, "How the Fed Fumbled, and Then Recovered, in Making Policy Shift," *The Wall Street Journal,* 17 November 1998.

12 "Without actually saying it, Greenspan is saying: 'We're going to supply liquidity to the system . . . '" Tom Petruno, "Fed Cut Sends Many Signals," *The Los Angeles Times,* 16 October 1998: C1.

13 "This is a way of telling everyone, the lifeguard is back on duty; you can go back in the pool," John M. Berry, "Greenspan Orders Interest Rate Cut," *The Washington Post,* 16 October 1998: A1.

14 "We feel the cyclical bear market is over," Christopher Byron, "Byron's Index Shows Investors Still Buying Everything," TheStreet.com, 6 November 1998.

15 "I agree, things are bound to get even crazier . . ." TSC Staff, "Net Stocks: Is Now the Time to Buy?" 10 November 1998.

### chapter fourteen: euphoria

1 "I have enquired of some that have come from London, what is the religion there? . . ." Edward Chancellor, *Devil Take the Hindmost: A History of Financial Speculation* (New York: Farrar Strauss & Giroux, 1999), 77.
2 "miserable mercenary Period," Ibid., 76.
3 "The demon stock jobbing is the genius of this place . . ." Ibid., 77.
4 "Few Men, who follow Reason's Rules, Grow Fat with South-Sea Diet . . ." Ibid., 70.
5 "There is nothing so disturbing to one's well-being and judgment as to see a friend get rich," Charles P. Kindleberger, *Manias, Panics, and Crashes: A History of Financial Crises* (New York: John Wiley, 1996), 13.
6 Randall E. Stross, *eBoys* (New York: Crown Business, 2000).
7 "EBay's market opportunity is huge," Mary Meeker, "U.S. and the Americas Investment Research," 24 September 1998: 1.
8 "I sold my TGLO at 88—who wouldn't?" Cory Johnson, "Are Net IPOs out to Lunch?" TheStreet.com, 22 November 1998.
9 "I've had days similar to this, but this definitely feels good," Walter Hamilton, "TheGlobe.com Sets Record for 1st-Day Trading," *Los Angeles Times,* 14 November 1998: C1.
10 Beth Piskora and Andy Geller, "Net Geeks Strike Gold in $97M Stock Bonanza," *New York Post,* 14 November 1998: 5.
11 "Although conditions in financial markets have settled down materially . . ." Federal Reserve Press Release, 11 November 1998.
12 "This ought to be the preeminent Internet company over the next decade," Steve Lohr and John Markoff, "Deal Is Concluded on Netscape Sale to America Online," *The New York Times,* 25 November 1998: A1.
13 "In an emerging and dynamic industry like the Internet . . ." News Release, *PR Newswire,* 9 November, 1998.
14 *"incredibly expensive,"* Suzanne Galante, "The 400 Blow," TheStreet.com, 16 December 1998.
15 "Amazon's valuation is clearly more art than science . . ." Ibid.
16 "If there must be madness, something may be said for having it on a heroic scale," John Kenneth Galbraith, *The Great Crash: 1929* (New York: Houghton Mifflin, 1997), 64.
17 "First of all, you wouldn't get 'hype' working if there weren't something fundamentally, potentially sound . . ." Steven Mufson and John M. Berry, "Frenzy for Internet Stocks Gains Backer—Greenspan," *The Washington Post,* 29 January 1999: A1.
18 "the Fed's gentle genius," Rich Miller, "Fed's Gentle Genius Brings a Unique Grace to the Job," *USA Today,* 23 February 1999: A1.
19 Lewis, 104.
20 Ibid., 187.

## chapter fifteen: queen of the 'net

1 "Based on my experience at, and my knowledge of, iVillage . . ." Sandra Rubin, "Controversy Hits iVillage as Stock Debut Looms," *National Post,* 9 March 1999.

2 "With every IPO the envelope is being pushed a little further . . ." John Cassidy, "The Woman in the Bubble," *The New Yorker,* 26 April 1999: 65.

3 "We are seeing the second generation of Internet entrepreneurs, and they have market cap envy of the Jerry Yangs and Marc Andreessens. . . ." Mary Meeker, interview with the author, 25 March 1999.

4 "There are 1.9 million items for sale . . ." Ibid.

5 "The overall Internet stock phenomenon may well be a 'bubble' . . ." Henry Blodget, Internet/Electronic Commerce Report, 9 March 1999.

6 "I don't want to be the Internet stock poster child," Mary Meeker, interview with the author, 25 March 1999.

7 "If Amazon.com executes to its plan, it's a very powerful business . . ." Mary Meeker, interview with the author, 15 March 1999.

8 "(Meeker) has been a terrific adviser in many ways . . ." Meg Whitman, interview with the author, March 1999.

9 "The people buying Internet stocks don't think they are buying Morgan Stanley, American Express, or Berkshire Hathaway . . ." Joseph Perella, interview with the author, March 1999.

10 "Mary is one of a kind," Ibid.

11 "This is a time to be rationally reckless . . ." Mary Meeker, interview with the author, 25 March 1999.

12 "We just think Mary is the best . . ." Cassidy, "The Woman in the Bubble," 56.

13 "What we are looking at is confirmation in the stock market that the U.S. economy is in excellent condition . . ." Ianthe Jean Dugan and Robert O'Harrow, "Dow Tops 10,000, Fueling Debate on Its Future," *The Washington Post,* 30 March 1999: A1.

14 "It's no longer a ceiling; it's a floor," Ibid.

15 "The difference is that the real values are being created . . ." Mary Meeker, interview with the author, 1 April 1999.

16 "THIS WEEK'S BILLIONAIRES," *The Industry Standard,* 12 April 1999.

17 "wagering billions of dollars on complex business stories . . ." Michael Parsons, "I Want to Believe," *The Industry Standard,* 12 April 1999: 2.

18 "Jewish guy with a lot of guilt, slightly misunderstood, trying to change an industry . . ." Vanessa Grigoriadis, "Silicon Valley 10003," *New York,* 6 March 2000.

19 "I'm thrilled. TheStreet.com is like the people's choice . . ." Gary Strauss, "Sunny Side of TheStreet.com," *USA Today,* 12 May 1999: 1B.

## chapter sixteen: trading nation

1 "As soon as I wake up in the morning, I turn on CNBC. . . ." Author's notes.

2 Matthew Schifrin, "Free Enterprise Comes to Wall Street," *Forbes,* 6 April 1998.

3 "investment should be for the long run—not for minutes or hours," Steven Mufson, "Levitt Warns of Online Trading," *The Washington Post,* 28 January 1999.

4 "Anyone who has ever played Space Invaders knows the drill . . ." Steve Bodow, "Short Term Prophets," *Wired,* January 1999: 165.

5 "If they follow the rules, they'll succeed . . ." Mike Snow, "Day-Trade Believers Teach High-Risk Investing," *The Washington Post,* 6 July 1998: 15.

6 "I don't plan to live very much longer . . ." Evan Thomas and T. Trent Gegax, "It's a Bad Trading Day . . . And It's About to Get Worse," *Newsweek,* 9 August 1999: 22.

7 Ibid.

8 Ibid.

9 "the best entertainment since television. . . ." Geoffrey Smith, Mike McNamee, and Leah Nathans Spiro, "Day of Reckoning for Day-Trading Firms?" *Business Week,* 18 January 1999: 88.

10 "a serious threat to Americans' financial lives," James Kim and David Rynecki, "Merrill Lynch Hears Net's Call," *USA Today,* 2 June 1999: 1B.

11 "It's clear that there is a segment of the marketplace that wants access to Merrill Lynch . . ." David Komansky, transcript of CNBC broadcast, 1 June 1999.

12 Fidelity Investments, press release, 9 March 2000.

13 Robert Putnam, *Bowling Alone: The Collapse and Revival of American Community* (New York: Touchstone, 2000).

14 Deborah Adamson, "Stock Together: Investor Clubs Seek to Make Fake Fortunes in Stock Contest," *The Daily News of L.A.,* 15 February 1999.

15 Brad M. Barber and Terrance Odean, "Trading Is Hazardous to Your Health: The Common Stock Investment Performance of Individual Investors," *Journal of Finance* 55.2 (April 2000): 773–806.

16 "Recent Changes in U.S. Family Finances: Results from the 1998 Survey of Consumer Finances," Federal Reserve Bulletin, February 2000.

17 Sushil Bikhchandani, David Hirshleifer, and Ivo Welch, "Learning from the Behavior of Others: Conformity, Fads, and Informational Cascades," *The Journal of Economic Perspectives,* Summer 1998: 151–170.

18 "However, this can be costly and time-consuming . . ." Ibid., 152–153.

19 "allowing individuals to take advantage of the hard-won information . . ." Ibid., 152.

20 "Public information stops accumulating . . ." Ibid., 155.

21 "is a grain of sand amid other grains of sand, which the wind stirs up at will," http://paradigm.soci.brocku.ca/lward/LeBon/lebon-01-01.html

22 "The fact that (individuals) have been transformed into a crowd puts them in possession of a sort of collective mind. . . ." Ibid.

23 Charles Gasparino, "Leading Merrill Stock Strategist to Leave Firm by Year End," *The Wall Street Journal,* 27 August 1999.

**chapter seventeen: web dreams**

1 "I'm going to start an Internet company," Author's notes.

2 "I didn't want to miss the next Industrial Revolution," Betsy Morris, "Take Your Blue-Chip Job and Shove It!" *Fortune,* 2 August 1999: 60.

3 "There's never been a time in contemporary history . . ." Steven Wilmsen, "MBAs Are the Latest Net Gain," *The Boston Globe,* 9 May 1999: A1.

4 "Annual Report," *Fast Company,* February 1997.

5 "It was absurdly easy . . ." Interview with the author, March 2001.

6 "Naw. It's going to be ten billion. Or zero," Randall E. Stross, *eBoys* (New York: Crown, 2000), 43.

7 "may be the most innovative E-commerce venture to date," Linda Himelstein, "Can You Sell Groceries Like Books?" *Business Week,* 26 July 1999.

8 "This is the first back-end re-engineering of an entire industry," Ibid.

9 "set the rules for the largest consumer sector in the economy," Mary Dejevsky, "Totally Bananas," *Independent* (London), 10 November 1999: 1.

10 "We invest only in companies that share our passion for customers . . ." *PR Newswire,* "Amazon.com Announces Investment in Pets.com," 29 March 1999.

11 "There is a huge potential for growth in the pet category as an e-commerce play . . ." *PR Newswire,* "Petopia.com Announces $9 Million Equity Investment from Technology Crossover Ventures," 10 May 1999.

12 "half the potheads in New York," Adam L. Penenberg, "The Internet May Be Global, but Kozmo is Going Local," *Forbes,* 18 October 1999: 164.

13 " 'We're going to put the fun back into funerals,' . . ." Randy Komisar, *The Monk and the Riddle* (Boston: HBS Press, 2000), 7.

14 "It wasn't just about the money . . ." Michael Hirschorn, interview with the author, March 2001.

15 " 'I think we can end up nicely north . . .' " Kurt Andersen, *Turn of the Century* (New York: Random House, 1999), 432.

16 "No one feels guilty about being rich anymore . . ." Joanna Coles, "The New American Gold Rush," *Times* (London), 10 August 1999.

### chapter eighteen: warning signs

1 George Soros, *The Alchemy of Finance* (New York: John Wiley & Sons, 1987).

2 "Additionally, drugstore.com maintained a level of 48 percent engaged shoppers (a unique user . . . )," Gretchen Morgenson, "How Did They Value Stocks? Count the Absurd Ways," *The New York Times,* 10 March 2001.

3 "How Much Is the Stock Market Overvalued?" http://fairmodel.econ.yale.edu

4 "looks more plausible all the time . . ." Kevin Kelly, "The Good News Is, You'll Be a Millionaire Soon," *Wired,* September 1999: 151.

5 "I don't think Internet valuations are crazy . . ." Kevin Kelly, "Prophets of Boom," *Wired,* September 1999: 156.

6 "For the past ten years I have been one of the most bullish forecasters about the future . . ." Kevin Kelly, "Happy Days," *Wired,* September 1999: 159.

7 "Face it: Out there in some garage an entrepreneur is forging a bullet with your company's name on it," Gary Hamel, "Bringing Silicon Valley Inside," *Harvard Business Review,* September/October 1999.

8 Helen Jung, "Amazon's Bezos: Internet's Ultimate Cult Figure," *Seattle Times,* 19 September 1999: A1.

9 "When we try to comprehend something as vast, amorphous, and downright

scary as the Internet . . ." Robert D. Hof, "A New Era of Bright Hopes and Terrible Fears," *Business Week,* 4 October 1999: 84.

10 "It's not only the dominant online bookseller . . ." Steven Levy, "Special Report," *Newsweek,* 11 October 1999: 50.

11 "Sixteen months ago, we were a place where people came to buy books . . ." Leslie Kaufman, "Amazon.com Plans a Transformation to Internet Bazaar," *The New York Times,* 30 September 1999: A1.

12 "It's a completely new model," Josh McHugh, "The $29 Billion Flea Market," *Forbes,* 1 November 1999: 66.

13 "as tired as we are of endless postponement of gratification," Gretchen Morgenson, "Market Watch: Over the Rainbow With Amazon.com," *The New York Times,* 31 October 1999: C1.

14 "The thing that always amazed me was how powerful his vision was . . ." Joshua Quittner, "An Eye on the Future," *Time,* 27 December 1999: 56.

15 "The new media stock market valuations are real . . ." Steve Lohr, "Medium for Main Street," *The New York Times,* 11 January 2000: C10.

16 "The Internet boom looks less ephemeral today," Editorial, "The Biggest Media Merger Yet," *The New York Times,* 11 January 2000.

17 "marks the beginning of the end of the old mass media," Peter Huber, "The Death of Old Media," *The Wall Street Journal,* 11 January 2000.

18 "It was a brilliant piece of financial engineering . . ." Rupert Murdoch, interview with the author, 16 February 2001.

19 "We really believe in saying, 'Hey, these are the opportunities that are ahead of us . . .'" Jerry Yang, interview with the author, 7 February 2000.

## chapter nineteen: the fed strikes

1 "the power and impact of the new technologies on the New Economy . . ." William Jefferson Clinton, White House Transcript, 4 January 2000.

2 "judgments of millions . . ." Jacob M. Schlesinger, "How Greenspan Finally Came to Terms with the Stock Market," *The Wall Street Journal,* 8 May 2000: A1.

3 "awesome changes . . ." Alan Greenspan, "Technology and the Economy," Remarks before the Economic Club of New York, 13 January 2000.

4 "In short, information technology raises output per hour . . ." Ibid.

5 "imbalance between growth of supply and growth of demand . . ." Ibid.

6 "does not mean that prices of assets cannot keep rising . . ." Ibid.

7 Greg Johnson, "Super Bowl's 'Dot-Com' Ads Mostly Unmemorable," *Los Angeles Times,* 2 February 2000: C3.

8 "remains concerned that over time increases in demand will continue to exceed the growth in potential supply . . ." Federal Reserve, press release, 2 February 2000.

9 "When Alan Greenspan speaks, the Old Economy trembles . . ." Floyd Norris, "Technology Investors Tune Out Greenspan," *The New York Times,* 18 February 2000.

10 "The Italians want to be in this market, and they want to own technology . . ."

Kenneth L. Gilpin, "The Market Stocks: Demand for Technology Shares Drives Nasdaq to Record," *The New York Times,* 8 February 2000: C15.

11 "Sooner rather than later, the New Economy boom is likely to be followed by a New Economy bust," Michael J. Mandel, "The Risk that Boom Will Turn to Bust," *Business Week,* 14 February 2000: 120.

12 "drive toward profitability," Roger Yu, "Amazon Sales Soar as Red Ink Spreads," *Seattle Times,* 3 February 2000: E1.

13 "a business that can become quite profitable," Saul Hansell, "Amazon Loss Soared 543% in 4th Quarter" *The New York Times,* 3 February 2000: C1.

14 "the most successful central banker in the history of the United States," Phil Gramm, "Humphrey-Hawkins Report on U.S. Monetary Policy," transcript, 23 February 2000.

15 "I think people hear what you are saying and conclude that you believe that equities are overvalued. . . ." Ibid.

16 "If we get interest rates at double digits, we are going to stop the economy in its tracks . . ." Ibid.

17 "We are suggesting, as an institution, that the stock market is too high . . ." John Cassidy, "The Fountainhead," *The New Yorker,* 24 April 2000: 162.

18 "seems undervalued by almost any measure," Robert D. Hershey Jr., "Nasdaq in Record Gain to New High, but Blue Chips Fall," *The New York Times,* 24 February 2000: C14.

19 "We had amazing cultural timing . . ." Vanessa Grigoriadis, "Silicon Alley 10003," *New York,* 6 March 2000.

20 Ibid.

21 "It brought us the microprocessor, the computer, satellites . . ." Alan Greenspan, remarks before the Boston College conference on the New Economy, 6 March 2000.

22 "superlatively moral system," Cassidy, "The Fountainhead," 168.

23 Ibid.

24 Greenspan, Boston College conference.

## chapter twenty: crash

1 "When will the Internet Bubble burst? . . ." Jack Willoughby, "Burning Up," *Barron's,* 20 March 2000: 29.

2 "are weighted mainly toward conditions that may generate heightened inflation pressures . . ." Federal Reserve, press release, 21 March 2000.

3 "The market is spitting in his eye," Robert D. Hershey, "Technology Lifts Nasdaq and Pushes S. & P. Over 1,500," *The New York Times,* 23 March 2000: C12.

4 Marcia Vickers and Gary Weiss, "Wall Street's Hype Machine," *Business Week,* 3 April 2000.

5 "including *Business Week,* has fueled the explosion . . ." Ibid., 117.

6 "If you look closely, it's beginning . . ." Walter Hamilton, "Nasdaq Falls 189 As Tech Sell-Off Widens; Dow Up," *Los Angeles Times,* 30 March 2000: C1.

7 "We believe that the very fundamentals of our economy still look very, very strong," Thomas S. Mulligan, "Wall Street Nose-Dives, Then Rallies By Day's End," *Los Angeles Times,* 5 April 2000: A1.

8 "For the past decade, we have been enthusiastic about the outlook for stock prices . . ." Times Staff, "Calm Follows Storm, Market Indexes Mixed," *Los Angeles Times,* 6 April 2000: C1.

9 "We've got a great low yield on interest rates . . ." TSC Staff, TV transcripts, TheStreet.com, 10 April 2000.

10 Marcia Vickers and Jeffrey M. Laderman, "Wall Street: Is the Party Over?" *Business Week,* 17 April 2000.

11 "could have further to fall . . ." Economist staff, "Monopoly Money," *The Economist,* 8 April 2000.

12 "The technology sector has begun an important corrective trend," Times staff and wire reports, "Nasdaq gets hammered again as techs slump," *Los Angeles Times,* 11 April 2000: C1.

13 "We are watching the developments in the markets, as we always do . . ." Larry Summers, interview on *CNN Street Sweep,* 14 April 2000.

14 "We're going to see the weaker companies come under more pressure," Sandra Sugawara, "Wall St. Collapse Tests Faith in 'New Economy,'" *The Washington Post,* 15 April 2000: A1.

15 "Perhaps we haven't seen a bottom yet . . ." Times Staff, Bloomberg News, "Market Savvy," *Los Angeles Times,* 20 April 2000: C4.

16 "And I can tell you that it's a sobering and humiliating experience . . ." NBC News transcripts, "Jim Cramer, TheStreet.com, Discusses Rebound in Stock Market," *Today,* 18 April 2000.

17 "Yeah, it's over. The Gold Rush is over," Ibid.

## chapter twenty-one: dead dotcoms

1 "in light of the extraordinary and persisting strength of overall demand," Federal Reserve, press release, 16 May 2000.

2 "a gateway to world cool," Susan Orenstein, "Boo.com: A Cautionary Tale," *Industry Standard,* 5 June 2000.

3 "In public and in private, the worrywarts, killjoys, and practitioners of the dismal science . . ." Gerard Baker, "Fed Passes Round the Punchbowl in Celebration," *The Financial Times,* 7 September 2000: 15.

4 "It is well known that this is a very, very difficult environment for business-to-consumer Internet companies . . ." Reed Abelson, "Pets.com: Sock Puppet's Home, Will Close," *The New York Times,* 8 November 2000: C4.

5 "Don't invest in dotcoms," ABC News transcripts, "Sock Puppet Talks About Surviving a Plummeting Stock Market," *Good Morning America,* 1 December 2000.

6 "weakening asset values in financial markets . . ." Michael Mandel, "Tech Leads—Both Up and Down," *Business Week,* 8 December 2000: 62.

7 "weighted mainly toward conditions that may generate economic weakness . . ." Federal Reserve Press Release, 18 December 2000.

8  "in light of further weakening of sales and production . . ." Richard W. Stevenson and Louis Uchitelle, "Markets Surge, but Full Effects on Consumers Will Take Longer," *The New York Times,* 4 January 2001: C9.
9  "They saw the N.A.P.M., and it scared the pants off them," Ibid.
10 "One of the messages Dr. Greenspan sent was that we need bold action . . ." Ibid.
11 "We were waiting for something at the end of the rainbow . . ." Saul Hansell, "Disney, in Retreat from Internet, to Abandon Go.com Portal Site," *The New York Times,* 30 January 2001.
12 "Persistent pressures on profit margins are restraining investment spending . . ." Federal Reserve Press Release, 21 March 2001.
13 "different kind of executive," David Leonhardt, "Early Defector to a Dot-Com Is Leaving an Online Grocer," *The New York Times,* 16 April 2001: C1.
14 "We have been the whipping boy because of the name . . ." Cassell Bryan-Low, "By Any Other Name, A Dot-Com Would Be Sweeter to Investors," *The Wall Street Journal,* 15 April 2000.
15 "I've worked on so many Web projects, and today they're all gone . . ." Paul Andrews, "The Virtual Dead Live on in Museum of Web Failures," *International Herald Tribune,* 25 May 2001: 13.
16 "It's easy to say we could have opened a few less markets . . ." Saul Hansell, "An Ambitious Internet Grocer Is Out of Both Cash and Ideas," *The New York Times,* 10 July 2001.
17 Peter Elkind, "Can We Ever Trust Wall Street Again," *Fortune,* 14 May 2001.
18 "nuclear winter . . ." Ibid.
19 "knew that the financial condition and future business prospects of Amazon.com did not support her positive comments . . ." Colleen DeBaise and Nick Wingfield, "Morgan Stanley Star Tech Analyst Faces Lawsuit Over Bullish Calls," *The Wall Street Journal,* 2 August 2001.

## epilogue

1  Jeffrey R. Brown and Austan Goolsbee, "Does the Internet Make Markets More Competitive? Evidence form the Life Insurance Industry." October 2000.
2  Bureau of Labor Statistics, "Productivity and Costs: Second Quarter 2001," 7 August 2001.
3  Robert E. Litan and Alice M. Rivlin, "The Economy and the Internet: What Lies Ahead?" Conference report, Brookings Institution, December 2000.
4  "Internet surfing may be fun. . . ." Robert J. Gordon, "Does the 'New Economy' Measure Up to the Great Inventions of the Past?" National Bureau of Economic Research, Working Paper 7833, August 2000.
5  "The notion that Americans are a sordid, money-grubbing people . . ." Marion Elizabeth Rogers, ed. *The Impossible H. L. Mencken* (New York: Anchor Books, 1991), 21.
6  "At Home Files for Bankruptcy; Will Sell a Unit,'" Matt Richtel, *The New York Times,* 29 September 2001: C1.
7. "Wall Street's Internet-Stock Star Calls It Quits," Patrick McGeehan, *The New York Times,* 15 November 2001: A1.

# appendix  dot.con data bank

| Company | IPO Date | # Shares Issued (m) | T4Q rev. offer[1] ($m) | Offer Price | Adjusted Offer[2] | P/S offer | 1st day close |
|---|---|---|---|---|---|---|---|
| America-Online | 19-Mar-92 | | | $11.50 | $0.09 | | $14.75 |
| Network Associates | 6-Oct-92 | | | $4.00 | $0.79 | | $4.00 |
| CMGI | 25-Jan-94 | 1.24 | $17.20 | $8.00 | $0.17 | 1.4 | $8.00 |
| RSA Security | 14-Dec-94 | 2.20 | | $16.00 | $4.00 | | $16.38 |
| PSINet* | 2-May-95 | 4.00 | $18.03 | $12.00 | $6.00 | 20.1 | $15.25 |
| Spyglass* | 28-Jun-95 | 2.00 | | $8.50 | $4.25 | | $27.25 |
| Newsedge | 11-Aug-95 | 1.98 | $9.05 | $13.50 | | | $24.75 |
| Netscape* | 14-Aug-95 | 5.00 | $22.51 | $28.00 | | 47.5 | $58.25 |
| CheckFree | 28-Sep-95 | 6.00 | | $18.00 | | | $21.50 |
| Verity | 6-Oct-95 | 3.00 | | $12.00 | $6.00 | | $18.50 |
| Secure Computing | 17-Nov-95 | 2.00 | $23.31 | $16.00 | | 4.2 | $48.25 |
| Globix Corp | 25-Jan-96 | 1.15 | $11.16 | $7.00 | $1.75 | 0.7 | $8.00 |
| VocalTec | 7-Feb-96 | 2.50 | | $19.00 | | | $17.25 |
| CyberCash* | 15-Feb-96 | 2.00 | $0.02 | $17.00 | | 11,413.0 | $28.25 |
| Cylink | 16-Feb-96 | 4.00 | $34.90 | $15.00 | | 15.1 | $22.50 |
| Sterling Commerce* | 8-Mar-96 | 12.00 | $286.39 | $24.00 | | 7.6 | $29.00 |
| Mindspring* | 14-Mar-96 | 1.95 | $2.23 | $8.00 | $1.33 | 18.0 | $8.88 |
| Terra Lycos | 1-Apr-96 | 3.00 | $1.05 | $16.00 | $4.00 | 286.4 | $21.94 |
| Excite, Inc.* | 3-Apr-96 | 2.00 | $20.90 | $17.00 | | 9.6 | $20.00 |
| Sapient Corp | 4-Apr-96 | 1.00 | $21.93 | $21.00 | $2.63 | 36.1 | $32.00 |
| Yahoo | 12-Apr-96 | 2.60 | $3.10 | $13.00 | $1.08 | 304.8 | $33.00 |
| WorldTalk Corp* | 12-Apr-96 | 2.00 | $7.93 | $8.00 | | 12.1 | $10.00 |
| Axent* | 23-Apr-96 | 3.00 | $16.07 | $14.00 | | 11.6 | $18.75 |
| Infonautics* | 30-Apr-96 | 2.00 | $0.61 | $14.00 | | 202.9 | $13.25 |
| Edify Corp* | 6-May-96 | 2.00 | $19.09 | $15.00 | | 25.5 | $31.25 |
| S1 Corporation | 23-May-96 | 2.44 | | $20.00 | $10.00 | | $41.00 |
| OpenMarket | 23-May-96 | 4.00 | $4.39 | $18.00 | | 244.5 | $39.88 |
| Disney Internet Group | 11-Jun-96 | 3.46 | $2.76 | $12.00 | | 126.6 | $14.00 |
| BroadVision | 21-Jun-96 | 4.00 | $1.94 | $7.00 | $0.78 | 75.7 | $7.13 |
| CheckPoint | 28-Jun-96 | 4.00 | | $14.00 | $3.50 | | $24.00 |
| Primix Solutions | 3-Jul-96 | 3.75 | $8.03 | $16.00 | | 29.3 | $18.00 |
| CNET | 9-Jul-96 | 2.00 | $6.93 | $16.00 | $4.00 | 30.6 | $16.50 |
| Connectinc.com* | 15-Aug-96 | 2.40 | $7.00 | $6.00 | $30.00 | 17.6 | $6.00 |
| E*Trade | 16-Aug-96 | 5.67 | $42.67 | $10.50 | $2.63 | 7.5 | $11.25 |
| Internet C&C (RMI.net) | 5-Sep-96 | 1.37 | $2.51 | $3.50 | | 6.0 | $3.06 |
| V-ONE | 25-Oct-96 | 3.00 | $8.44 | $5.00 | | 7.2 | $4.81 |
| VoxWare | 30-Oct-96 | 2.70 | $6.03 | $7.50 | | 16.4 | $8.25 |
| MessageMedia | 13-Dec-96 | 3.00 | $0.61 | $9.00 | | 163.6 | $9.00 |
| Earthlink | 22-Jan-97 | 2.00 | $32.50 | $13.00 | $6.50 | 4.5 | $13.00 |
| Ameritrade | 4-Mar-97 | 2.00 | $69.61 | $15.00 | $1.25 | 4.1 | $19.50 |
| Egghead.com* | 17-Apr-97 | 2.50 | $14.27 | $6.00 | | 6.9 | $5.88 |
| Onsale* | 17-Apr-97 | 2.50 | $21.01 | $6.00 | | 4.7 | $5.88 |
| Go2Net* | 23-Apr-97 | 1.60 | | $8.00 | $2.00 | | $9.88 |
| Amazon.com | 15-May-97 | 3.00 | $30.88 | $18.00 | $1.50 | 18.2 | $23.50 |
| Bluefly | 16-May-97 | 1.50 | $8.60 | $5.00 | | 1.7 | $5.38 |
| NetSpeak* | 29-May-97 | 2.40 | $1.72 | $8.75 | | 56.2 | $9.13 |
| Peapod* | 10-Jun-97 | 4.00 | $35.54 | $16.00 | | 7.3 | $16.00 |
| Excite@Home | 11-Jul-97 | 9.00 | $1.48 | $10.50 | $5.25 | 1,351.3 | $17.00 |
| Net.B@nk | 28-Jul-97 | 4.30 | | $12.00 | $4.00 | | $14.38 |
| Concentric Ntwk* | 1-Aug-97 | 3.30 | $31.59 | $18.00 | $9.00 | 10.3 | $23.31 |
| Fine.com Int'l* | 12-Aug-97 | 1.00 | $2.07 | $8.00 | | 10.0 | $9.75 |
| Network Solutions* | 26-Sep-97 | 2.50 | $30.76 | $11.00 | $2.75 | 5.3 | $11.00 |
| N2K Inc* | 17-Oct-97 | 3.00 | $4.06 | $19.00 | | | $24.25 |
| SportsLine | 13-Nov-97 | 3.00 | $7.13 | $12.50 | | 34.2 | $17.88 |
| Preview Travel* | 20-Nov-97 | 3.00 | $13.10 | $7.50 | | 9.8 | $11.00 |
| RealNetworks | 21-Nov-97 | 3.00 | $28.16 | $12.50 | $3.13 | 17.5 | $17.88 |
| MarchFirst* | 5-Dec-97 | 1.10 | $31.65 | $6.50 | | 4.4 | $7.00 |

| Adjusted D1 close[3] | D1% change | All-time high | Price 3/10/00 | Price 8/31/01 | % ch from hi[4] | MktCap Offer ($m) | MktCap 3/10/00 ($m) | MktCap 8/31/01 ($m) |
|---|---|---|---|---|---|---|---|---|
| $0.12 | 28.3% | $93.75 | $58.63 | $37.35 | (60%) | $62 | $131,056 | $165,945 |
| $0.79 | 0.0% | $36.69 | $31.19 | $15.85 | (57%) | | $4,342 | $2,177 |
| $0.17 | 0.0% | $153.25 | $136.44 | $1.78 | (99%) | $23 | $33,555 | $616 |
| $4.09 | 2.3% | $90.25 | $87.19 | $19.24 | (79%) | $91 | $3,362 | $1,078 |
| $7.63 | 27.1% | $68.13 | $55.88 | — | — | $362 | $7,264 | — |
| $13.63 | 220.6% | $85.13 | $81.38 | — | — | $85 | $1,383 | |
| | 83.3% | $12.25 | $4.63 | $2.28 | (81%) | $27 | $80 | $42 |
| | 108.0% | $0.00 | $0.00 | — | — | $1,069 | | |
| | 19.4% | $104.69 | $88.63 | $21.91 | (79%) | $575 | $4,627 | $1,901 |
| $9.25 | 54.2% | $60.00 | $55.44 | $10.60 | (82%) | $114 | $1,659 | $377 |
| | 201.6% | $27.88 | $26.50 | $14.95 | (46%) | $97 | $556 | $422 |
| $2.00 | 14.3% | $62.75 | $62.00 | $0.85 | (99%) | $8 | $1,029 | $36 |
| | (9.2%) | $52.31 | $41.63 | $1.03 | (98%) | $139 | $477 | $12 |
| | 66.2% | $14.88 | $13.63 | — | — | $251 | $313 | — |
| | 50.0% | $22.50 | $21.63 | $0.47 | (98%) | $526 | $643 | $15 |
| | 20.8% | $44.19 | $43.63 | — | — | $2,175 | $0 | — |
| $1.48 | 10.9% | $39.06 | $30.50 | — | — | $40 | $1,940 | — |
| $5.48 | 37.1% | $135.21 | $111.76 | $7.03 | (95%) | $300 | $11,354 | $3,663 |
| | 17.6% | $0.00 | $0.00 | — | — | $200 | — | — |
| $4.00 | 52.4% | $140.94 | $57.03 | $5.41 | (96%) | $792 | $3,262 | $671 |
| $2.75 | 153.8% | $432.69 | $178.06 | $11.86 | (97%) | $944 | $93,746 | $6,794 |
| | 25.0% | $20.31 | $13.19 | — | — | $96 | $191 | — |
| | 33.9% | $31.81 | $30.50 | — | — | $187 | $854 | — |
| | (5.4%) | $15.94 | $12.50 | — | — | $124 | $147 | — |
| | 108.3% | $17.25 | $0.00 | — | — | $486 | — | — |
| $20.50 | 105.0% | $129.25 | $105.00 | $11.57 | (91%) | $49 | $3,943 | $684 |
| | 121.5% | $65.38 | $60.44 | $0.73 | (99%) | $1074 | $2651 | $34 |
| | 16.7% | $37.88 | $24.13 | — | — | $349 | $3,596 | — |
| $0.79 | 1.8% | $175.94 | $86.08 | $1.29 | (99%) | $147 | $20,045 | $359 |
| $6.00 | 71.4% | $170.00 | $139.94 | $31.99 | (81%) | $458 | $10,154 | $7,366 |
| | 12.5% | $14.13 | $12.88 | $0.21 | (98%) | $235 | $188 | $4 |
| $4.13 | 3.1% | $79.00 | $67.75 | $9.18 | (88%) | $212 | $4,978 | $1,264 |
| $30.00 | 0.0% | $5.25 | $2.81 | — | — | $123 | $42 | — |
| $2.81 | 7.1% | $39.19 | $26.50 | $6.40 | (84%) | $319 | $6,477 | $2,170 |
| | (12.5%) | $12.50 | $10.44 | $3.87 | (69%) | $15 | $189 | $118 |
| | (3.8%) | $13.50 | $6.38 | $1.06 | (92%) | $61 | $109 | $24 |
| | 10.0% | $12.50 | $8.44 | $0.19 | (98%) | $99 | $113 | $3 |
| | 0.0% | $20.75 | $14.00 | $0.32 | (98%) | $100 | $699 | $22 |
| $6.50 | 0.0% | $39.06 | $23.75 | $13.51 | (65%) | $147 | $774 | $1,775 |
| $1.63 | 30.0% | $30.75 | $21.50 | $5.96 | (81%) | $283 | $3,750 | $1,128 |
| | | $26.63 | $9.69 | — | — | $98 | $359 | — |
| | (2.0%) | $26.63 | $0.00 | — | — | $98 | — | — |
| $2.47 | 23.5% | $100.06 | $85.06 | — | — | $42 | $2,366 | |
| $1.96 | 30.6% | $106.69 | $66.88 | $8.94 | (92%) | $561 | $22,790 | $3,243 |
| | 7.6% | $15.44 | $11.50 | $0.90 | (94%) | $15 | $57 | $8 |
| | 4.3% | $27.19 | $24.00 | — | — | $96 | $311 | — |
| | 0.0% | $15.00 | $8.38 | — | — | $260 | $152 | — |
| $8.50 | 61.9% | $57.00 | $28.56 | $0.42 | (99%) | $2,003 | $10,861 | $172 |
| $4.79 | 19.8% | $31.25 | $12.13 | $8.20 | (74%) | $88 | $356 | $248 |
| $11.66 | 29.5% | $60.00 | $57.44 | — | — | $327 | $2,419 | — |
| | 21.9% | $0.00 | $0.00 | — | — | $21 | — | — |
| $2.75 | 0.0% | $272.25 | $244.53 | — | — | $163 | $16,344 | — |
| | 27.6% | $0.00 | $0.00 | — | — | $272 | — | — |
| | 43.0% | $63.25 | $57.75 | $0.91 | (99%) | $244 | $1,362 | $25 |
| | 46.7% | $59.75 | $46.00 | — | — | $128 | $641 | — |
| $4.47 | 43.0% | $177.75 | $81.63 | $7.22 | (96%) | $494 | $12,146 | $1,166 |
| | 7.7% | $51.75 | $38.88 | — | — | $140 | $3,335 | — |

| Company | IPO Date | # Shares Issued (m) | T4Q rev. offer[1] ($m) | Offer Price | Adjusted Offer[2] | P/S offer | 1st day close |
|---|---|---|---|---|---|---|---|
| Verisign | 30-Jan-98 | 3.00 | $9.38 | $14.00 | $3.50 | 54.8 | $25.50 |
| CDNow* | 10-Feb-98 | 4.10 | $17.37 | $16.00 | | 19.6 | $22.00 |
| DoubleClick | 20-Feb-98 | 3.50 | $30.60 | $17.00 | $4.25 | 13.0 | $26.75 |
| Exodus Comm. | 19-Mar-98 | 4.50 | $12.41 | $15.00 | $0.94 | 38.8 | $27.63 |
| GSV (Cybershop) | 23-Mar-98 | 3.20 | $1.50 | $6.50 | | 36.9 | $8.75 |
| Verio* | 12-May-98 | 5.50 | $35.69 | $23.00 | $11.50 | 20.5 | $23.00 |
| Frontline Comm. | 14-May-98 | 1.60 | $0.32 | $4.00 | | 42.1 | $4.88 |
| Inktomi | 10-Jun-98 | 2.25 | $9.38 | $18.00 | $4.50 | 78.8 | $36.00 |
| NetGravity* | 12-Jun-98 | 3.00 | $7.01 | $9.00 | | 18.4 | $9.75 |
| Beyond.com | 17-Jun-98 | 5.00 | $19.84 | $9.00 | | 17.7 | $13.25 |
| Broadcast.com* | 17-Jul-98 | 2.50 | $8.95 | $18.00 | | 118.4 | $62.75 |
| Telebank Financial* | 22-Jul-98 | 4.50 | $13.87 | $14.50 | $7.25 | 7.7 | $18.63 |
| Cyberian Outpost | 31-Jul-98 | 4.00 | $30.35 | $18.00 | | 14.9 | $20.50 |
| Pilot Network* | 11-Aug-98 | 3.25 | $12.58 | $14.00 | | 14.9 | $13.63 |
| Digital River | 11-Aug-98 | 3.00 | $7.76 | $8.50 | | 21.3 | $9.88 |
| GeoCities* | 11-Aug-98 | 4.75 | $8.49 | $17.00 | | 134.7 | $37.31 |
| 24/7 Media | 14-Aug-98 | 3.25 | $3.02 | $14.00 | | 101.3 | $20.25 |
| Entrust Tech. | 18-Aug-98 | 7.77 | $36.05 | $16.00 | | 26.4 | $20.00 |
| eBay | 24-Sep-98 | 3.50 | $19.01 | $18.00 | $3.00 | 99.1 | $47.38 |
| EarthWeb* | 11-Nov-98 | 2.10 | $1.52 | $14.00 | | 253.6 | $48.69 |
| Theglobe.com | 13-Nov-98 | 3.10 | $1.74 | $9.00 | $4.50 | 358.3 | $63.50 |
| FatBrain.com* | 20-Nov-98 | 3.00 | $17.27 | $10.00 | | 12.3 | $19.94 |
| uBid* | 4-Dec-98 | 1.58 | $24.13 | $15.00 | | 17.7 | $48.00 |
| TicketMaster-CitySearcl | 4-Dec-98 | 7.00 | $13.84 | $14.00 | | 216.2 | $43.06 |
| NBCi* | 9-Dec-98 | 4.00 | $5.29 | $14.00 | | 85.3 | $34.44 |
| Internet America | 10-Dec-98 | 2.30 | $11.37 | $13.00 | | 8.2 | $14.88 |
| AboveNet Comm.* | 10-Dec-98 | 5.00 | $4.80 | $13.00 | | 44.7 | $16.75 |
| Infospace.com | 15-Dec-98 | 5.00 | $6.13 | $15.00 | $1.88 | 65.7 | $20.00 |
| Audiohighway.com* | 18-Dec-98 | 2.00 | $0.06 | $6.50 | | 945.3 | $15.38 |
| MarketWatch.com | 15-Jan-99 | 2.75 | $5.26 | $17.00 | | 217.8 | $97.50 |
| Allaire* | 22-Jan-99 | 2.50 | $16.96 | $20.00 | $10.00 | 26.2 | $43.75 |
| Tut Systems | 29-Jan-99 | 2.50 | $10.56 | $18.00 | | 59.7 | $57.50 |
| Modern Media, Inc | 5-Feb-99 | 2.60 | $37.87 | $16.00 | $8.00 | 12.7 | $45.00 |
| Pacific Internet | 10-Feb-99 | 2.50 | $43.54 | $17.00 | | 13.6 | $48.00 |
| VerticalNet | 11-Feb-99 | 3.50 | $2.10 | $16.00 | $4.00 | 350.8 | $45.38 |
| WebMD | 11-Feb-99 | 5.00 | $39.62 | $8.00 | | 54.6 | $31.38 |
| Prodigy | 11-Feb-99 | 8.00 | $133.80 | $15.00 | | 12.4 | $28.13 |
| Vignette Corp. | 19-Feb-99 | 4.00 | $16.21 | $19.00 | $3.17 | 69.3 | $42.69 |
| Web Trends* | 19-Feb-99 | 3.50 | $8.01 | $13.00 | $6.50 | 37.9 | $27.06 |
| Intraware | 26-Feb-99 | 4.00 | $10.39 | $16.00 | | 42.8 | $18.88 |
| pcOrder* | 26-Feb-99 | 2.20 | $21.71 | $21.00 | | 32.9 | $47.13 |
| RoweCom | 9-Mar-99 | 3.10 | $19.05 | $16.00 | | 12.4 | $24.50 |
| FlashNet Comm* | 16-Mar-99 | 3.00 | $26.89 | $17.00 | | 21.8 | $43.63 |
| Multex.com | 17-Mar-99 | 3.00 | $13.18 | $14.00 | | 53.9 | $33.63 |
| iVillage | 19-Mar-99 | 3.65 | $15.01 | $24.00 | | 123.4 | $80.13 |
| AutoWeb.com* | 23-Mar-99 | 5.00 | $13.00 | $14.00 | | 76.9 | $40.00 |
| About.com* | 24-Mar-99 | 3.00 | $3.72 | $25.00 | | 147.9 | $47.50 |
| Onemain.com* | 25-Mar-99 | 8.50 | $56.69 | $22.00 | | 13.2 | $39.56 |
| autobytel.com | 26-Mar-99 | 4.50 | $23.80 | $23.00 | | 30.3 | $40.25 |
| Critical Path | 29-Mar-99 | 4.50 | $0.90 | $24.00 | | 2,504.9 | $65.88 |
| Priceline.com | 30-Mar-99 | 10.00 | $35.24 | $16.00 | | 278.7 | $69.00 |
| ZDNet Group* | 31-Mar-99 | 10.00 | $56.10 | $19.00 | | 45.9 | $36.00 |
| Claimsnet.com | 6-Apr-99 | 2.50 | $0.18 | $8.00 | | 585.9 | $16.50 |
| Rhythms Net Connect.* | 7-Apr-99 | 9.38 | $0.53 | $21.00 | | 8,862.6 | $69.19 |
| Value America* | 8-Apr-99 | 5.50 | $41.54 | $23.00 | | 57.0 | $55.19 |
| USinternetworking | 9-Apr-99 | 6.00 | $4.12 | $21.00 | $9.33 | 543.5 | $57.50 |
| D*liad (iTurf) | 9-Apr-99 | 4.20 | $4.01 | $22.00 | | 239.0 | $57.44 |

| Adjusted D1 close[3] | D1% change | All-time high | Price 3/10/00 | Price 8/31/01 | % ch from hi[4] | MktCap Offer ($m) | MktCap 3/10/00 ($m) | MktCap 8/31/01 ($m) |
|---|---|---|---|---|---|---|---|---|
| $6.38 | 82.1% | $251.25 | $239.94 | $41.05 | (84%) | $514 | $24,596 | $8,328 |
| | 37.5% | $17.00 | $9.44 | – | – | $340 | $286 | |
| $6.69 | 57.4% | $126.75 | $117.63 | $8.03 | (94%) | $397 | $10,589 | $1,086 |
| $1.73 | 84.2% | $92.03 | $82.28 | $0.88 | (99%) | $482 | $14,025 | $489 |
| | 34.6% | $12.88 | $2.75 | $0.22 | (98%) | $55 | $26 | $0 |
| $11.50 | 0.0% | $80.00 | $56.00 | – | – | $732 | $4,319 | – |
| | 22.0% | $7.81 | $5.56 | $0.18 | (98%) | $14 | $22 | $1 |
| $9.00 | 100.0% | $231.63 | $169.31 | $3.96 | (98%) | $739 | $16,543 | $511 |
| | 8.3% | $35.94 | $0.00 | – | – | $129 | – | |
| | 47.2% | $12.75 | $6.00 | $1.11 | (91%) | $352 | $218 | $4 |
| | 248.6% | $0.00 | $0.00 | – | – | $1,059 | – | – |
| $9.31 | 28.4% | $37.94 | $27.19 | – | – | $107 | $915 | – |
| | 13.9% | $14.75 | $10.25 | $0.36 | (98%) | $451 | $241 | $11 |
| | (2.6%) | $50.38 | $49.50 | – | – | $187 | $681 | – |
| | 16.2% | $41.13 | $31.38 | $4.70 | (89%) | $165 | $651 | $115 |
| | 119.5% | $0.00 | $0.00 | – | – | $1,144 | | |
| | 44.6% | $64.63 | $58.25 | $0.17 | (100%) | $306 | $1,300 | $8 |
| | 25.0% | $138.44 | $128.19 | $4.35 | (97%) | $953 | $6,390 | $276 |
| $7.90 | 163.2% | $179.50 | $96.63 | $56.23 | (69%) | $1,883 | $12,497 | $15,366 |
| | 247.8% | $51.88 | $28.44 | – | – | $385 | $278 | – |
| $31.75 | 605.6% | $12.38 | $8.00 | $0.08 | (99%) | $622 | $213 | $2 |
| | 99.4% | $39.75 | $15.88 | – | – | $212 | $181 | – |
| | 220.0% | $44.50 | $34.81 | – | – | $428 | $401 | – |
| | 207.6% | $44.13 | $33.00 | $16.35 | (63%) | $2,992 | $2,748 | $2,314 |
| | 146.0% | $100.17 | $56.00 | – | – | $451 | $2,908 | |
| | 14.5% | $21.00 | $12.13 | $0.50 | (98%) | $94 | $86 | $5 |
| | 28.8% | $0.00 | $0.00 | – | – | $215 | – | |
| $2.50 | 33.3% | $130.53 | $122.47 | $1.20 | (99%) | $402 | $23,612 | $364 |
| | 136.6% | $13.50 | $6.63 | – | – | $53 | $38 | – |
| | 473.5% | $62.19 | $44.00 | $2.25 | (96%) | $1,146 | $609 | $37 |
| $21.88 | 118.8% | $174.94 | $88.38 | – | – | $444 | $2,314 | – |
| | 219.4% | $115.50 | $63.13 | $1.02 | (99%) | $631 | $739 | $17 |
| $22.50 | 181.3% | $71.31 | $52.88 | $5.00 | (93%) | $480 | $1,202 | $129 |
| | 182.4% | $74.88 | $52.00 | $2.28 | (97%) | $590 | $638 | $29 |
| $11.34 | 183.6% | $172.00 | $136.59 | $0.90 | (99%) | $738 | $9,619 | $88 |
| | 292.2% | $71.06 | $41.00 | $4.90 | (93%) | $2,163 | $6,017 | $1,763 |
| | 87.5% | $32.13 | $19.06 | $5.66 | (82%) | $1,660 | $1,222 | $399 |
| $7.12 | 124.7% | $163.75 | $99.00 | $6.83 | (96%) | $1,123 | $5,819 | $1,687 |
| $13.53 | 108.2% | $98.56 | $68.25 | – | – | $304 | $1,740 | |
| | 18.0% | $81.25 | $74.25 | $1.16 | (99%) | $444 | $1,789 | $33 |
| | 124.4% | $70.50 | $30.00 | – | – | $714 | $487 | – |
| | 53.1% | $50.38 | $20.56 | $0.68 | (99%) | $236 | $209 | $9 |
| | 156.6% | $10.88 | $6.44 | – | – | $585 | $92 | – |
| | 140.2% | $38.38 | $29.25 | $3.17 | (92%) | $710 | $784 | $103 |
| | 233.9% | $30.50 | $23.88 | $1.01 | (97%) | $1,853 | $705 | $53 |
| | 185.7% | $13.25 | $7.50 | – | – | $1,000 | $188 | – |
| | 90.0% | $101.75 | $92.88 | – | – | $550 | $1,426 | – |
| | 79.8% | $22.00 | $11.63 | – | – | $748 | $273 | – |
| | 75.0% | $18.88 | $10.17 | $1.00 | (95%) | $720 | $185 | $31 |
| | 174.5% | $116.75 | $113.91 | $0.32 | (100%) | $2,247 | $4,903 | $24 |
| | 331.3% | $95.94 | $94.50 | $5.52 | (94%) | $9,820 | $13,838 | $1,216 |
| | 89.5% | $33.25 | $29.75 | – | – | $2,574 | $2,193 | – |
| | 106.3% | $12.19 | $7.19 | $2.00 | (84%) | $103 | $48 | $21 |
| | 229.5% | $48.88 | $40.38 | – | – | 4,679 | $3,115 | – |
| | 140.0% | $15.13 | $6.09 | – | – | $2,370 | $273 | – |
| $25.56 | $173.8% | $79.00 | $62.25 | $0.47 | (99%) | $2,241 | $5,691 | $68 |
| | 161.1% | $23.94 | $11.38 | $6.24 | (74%) | $959 | $215 | $288 |

| Company | IPO Date | # Shares Issued (m) | T4Q rev. offer[1] ($m) | Offer Price | Adjusted Offer[2] | P/S offer | 1st day close |
|---|---|---|---|---|---|---|---|
| Worldgate Comm. | 15-Apr-99 | 5.00 | $1.02 | $21.00 | | 687.3 | $34.00 |
| Proxicom* | 20-Apr-99 | 4.50 | $42.41 | $13.00 | $6.50 | 11.0 | $19.50 |
| Internet Financial Svs* | 20-Apr-99 | 2.00 | $10.84 | $7.00 | | 7.7 | $11.00 |
| Log On America | 22-Apr-99 | 2.20 | $0.76 | $10.00 | | 313.7 | $35.00 |
| NetPerceptions | 23-Apr-99 | 3.65 | $4.48 | $14.00 | | 142.0 | $29.81 |
| Launch Media | 23-Apr-99 | 3.40 | $5.01 | $22.00 | | 68.1 | $28.38 |
| Razorfish | 27-Apr-99 | 3.00 | $30.97 | $16.00 | $8.00 | 26.1 | $33.50 |
| HearMe.co | 29-Apr-99 | 3.90 | $8.03 | $18.00 | | 134.1 | $50.63 |
| Marimba | 30-Apr-99 | 4.00 | $17.09 | $20.00 | | 79.5 | $60.75 |
| Applied Theory | 30-Apr-99 | 4.50 | $15.08 | $16.00 | | 27.8 | $20.50 |
| Town Pages Net.com | 30-Apr-99 | 2.20 | $1.86 | $10.00 | | 45.0 | $11.63 |
| Flycast Comm.* | 4-May-99 | 3.00 | $8.03 | $25.00 | | 52.3 | $29.75 |
| MapQuest.com* | 4-May-99 | 4.60 | $24.72 | $15.00 | | 29.1 | $22.38 |
| Silknet Software* | 5-May-99 | 3.00 | $10.71 | $15.00 | | 49.2 | $35.13 |
| NorthPoint Comm.* | 5-May-99 | 15.00 | $0.93 | $24.00 | | 5,225.2 | $40.19 |
| Comps.com* | 5-May-99 | 4.50 | $13.12 | $15.00 | | 13.2 | $14.25 |
| Portal Software | 6-May-99 | 4.00 | $26.67 | $14.00 | $7.00 | 104.7 | $37.38 |
| AdForce* | 7-May-99 | 4.50 | $7.09 | $15.00 | | 80.9 | $29.94 |
| Jupiter Media Metrix | 7-May-99 | 3.00 | $8.35 | $17.00 | | 91.3 | $45.56 |
| NetObjects | 7-May-99 | 6.00 | $20.52 | $12.00 | | 16.5 | $13.00 |
| TheStreet.com | 11-May-99 | 5.50 | $5.70 | $19.00 | | 248.7 | $60.00 |
| BiznessOnline.com | 12-May-99 | 2.90 | $6.20 | $10.00 | | 13.2 | $11.88 |
| CareerBuilder* | 12-May-99 | 4.50 | $8.76 | $13.00 | | 41.5 | $16.00 |
| Copper Mountain | 13-May-99 | 4.00 | $34.72 | $21.00 | $10.50 | 44.1 | $68.44 |
| Bankrate | 13-May-99 | 3.50 | $2.58 | $13.00 | | 67.6 | $13.00 |
| Scient Corp. | 14-May-99 | 3.00 | $20.68 | $20.00 | $10.00 | 54.1 | $32.63 |
| NextCard | 14-May-99 | 6.00 | $1.13 | $20.00 | | 1,295.7 | $33.50 |
| Alloy Online | 14-May-99 | 3.70 | $10.21 | $15.00 | | 27.9 | $20.00 |
| Redback Networks | 18-May-99 | 2.50 | $15.25 | $23.00 | $5.75 | 116.1 | $84.13 |
| OneSource Info. | 19-May-99 | 3.64 | $30.62 | $12.00 | | 4.6 | $14.25 |
| eToys* | 20-May-99 | 8.32 | $34.73 | $20.00 | | 224.4 | $76.56 |
| @plan.inc* | 21-May-99 | 2.50 | $4.40 | $14.00 | | 39.6 | $16.00 |
| fashionmall.com | 21-May-99 | 3.00 | $2.41 | $13.00 | | 40.5 | $13.00 |
| BarnesandNoble.com | 25-May-99 | 25.00 | $85.14 | $18.00 | | 6.7 | $22.94 |
| StarMedia | 26-May-99 | 7.00 | $6.61 | $15.00 | | 209.4 | $26.06 |
| Juno Online Svs | 26-May-99 | 6.50 | $27.14 | $13.00 | | 14.8 | $11.63 |
| ZipLink* | 26-May-99 | 3.50 | $8.16 | $14.00 | | 19.3 | $12.38 |
| EDGAR Online | 26-May-99 | 3.60 | $2.26 | $9.50 | | 48.8 | $9.56 |
| DLJdirect* | 26-May-99 | 16.00 | $141.07 | $20.00 | | 21.5 | $30.00 |
| iXL Enterprises | 3-Jun-99 | 6.00 | $104.73 | $12.00 | | 10.9 | $17.88 |
| F5 Networks | 4-Jun-99 | 3.00 | $9.51 | $10.00 | | 28.0 | $14.88 |
| Online Resources | 4-Jun-99 | 3.10 | $3.25 | $14.00 | | 46.8 | $14.06 |
| High Speed Access | 4-Jun-99 | 13.00 | $90.92 | $13.00 | | 11.6 | $20.38 |
| Wit Soundview | 4-Jun-99 | 7.60 | $5.87 | $9.00 | | 179.1 | $14.88 |
| Medium4.com | 7-Jun-99 | 1.70 | $0.00 | $6.00 | | | $6.25 |
| BackWeb Tech. | 8-Jun-99 | 5.50 | $12.06 | $12.00 | | 57.2 | $19.69 |
| drkoop.com | 8-Jun-99 | 9.38 | $0.45 | $9.00 | | 1,011.4 | $16.44 |
| Openwave (phone.com) | 11-Jun-99 | 4.00 | $1.76 | $16.00 | $8.00 | 694.3 | $40.13 |
| onlinetradinginc.com* | 11-Jun-99 | 2.25 | $6.84 | $7.00 | | 16.0 | $9.88 |
| GenesisIntermedia.com | 14-Jun-99 | 2.00 | $18.12 | $8.50 | | 2.5 | $8.38 |
| CareInsite* | 16-Jun-99 | 5.65 | $0.21 | $18.00 | | 10,110.0 | $30.94 |
| GoTo.com | 18-Jun-99 | 6.00 | $2.24 | $15.00 | | 446.6 | $22.38 |
| AppNet Systems* | 18-Jun-99 | 6.00 | $37.12 | $12.00 | | 10.0 | $12.00 |
| Viant Corp | 18-Jun-99 | 3.00 | $23.83 | $16.00 | $8.00 | 21.0 | $24.38 |
| Student Advantage | 18-Jun-99 | 6.00 | $18.27 | $8.00 | | 13.4 | $8.00 |
| Easylink (Mail.com) | 18-Jun-99 | 6.85 | $2.60 | $7.00 | | 141.6 | $8.75 |
| Streamline.com* | 18-Jun-99 | 4.50 | $8.73 | $10.00 | | 15.6 | $7.63 |

| Adjusted D1 close[3] | D1% change | All-time high | Price 3/10/00 | Price 8/31/01 | % ch from hi[4] | MktCap Offer ($m) | MktCap 3/10/00 ($m) | MktCap 8/31/01 ($m) |
|---|---|---|---|---|---|---|---|---|
| | 61.9% | $48.63 | $34.81 | $2.75 | (94%) | $702 | $746 | $65 |
| $9.75 | 50.0% | $124.31 | $49.25 | — | — | $466 | $2,573 | — |
| | 57.1% | $0.00 | $0.00 | — | — | $84 | — | — |
| | 250.0% | $27.50 | $14.25 | $0.27 | (99%) | $238 | $109 | $2 |
| | 112.9% | $60.38 | $57.50 | $1.20 | (98%) | $636 | $1,264 | $32 |
| | 29.0% | $26.25 | $21.00 | $0.91 | (97%) | $342 | $268 | $13 |
| $16.75 | 109.4% | $55.00 | $36.00 | $0.20 | (100%) | $807 | $3,124 | $20 |
| | 181.3% | $37.50 | $21.94 | $0.07 | (100%) | $1,007 | $525 | $2 |
| | 203.8% | $65.25 | $56.13 | $2.75 | (96%) | $1,358 | $1,295 | $66 |
| | 28.1% | $35.88 | $34.75 | $0.31 | (99%) | $420 | $742 | $9 |
| | 16.3% | $9.38 | $8.25 | $0.15 | (98%) | $84 | $71 | $2 |
| | 19.0% | $145.00 | $122.50 | — | — | $420 | $1,857 | — |
| | 49.2% | $32.50 | $18.25 | — | — | $720 | $613 | — |
| | 134.2% | $275.88 | $273.00 | — | — | $527 | $4,483 | — |
| | 67.5% | $37.63 | $29.50 | — | — | $4,865 | $3,702 | — |
| | (5.0%) | $9.63 | $7.56 | — | — | $173 | $0 | — |
| $18.69 | 167.0% | $83.94 | $77.69 | $1.86 | (98%) | $2,792 | $12,286 | $323 |
| | 99.6% | $80.00 | $72.00 | — | — | $574 | $1,439 | — |
| | 168.0% | $51.50 | $43.94 | $0.76 | (99%) | $762 | $864 | $27 |
| | 8.3% | $43.50 | $40.00 | $0.28 | (99%) | $339 | $986 | $9 |
| | 215.8% | $20.50 | $12.56 | $1.21 | (94%) | $1,416 | $308 | $35 |
| | 18.8% | $9.44 | $8.50 | $0.07 | (99%) | $82 | $62 | $1 |
| | 23.1% | $9.25 | $5.75 | — | — | $364 | $136 | — |
| $34.22 | 225.9% | $123.69 | $108.00 | $1.51 | (99%) | $1,532 | $5,078 | $80 |
| | 0.0% | $7.31 | $5.28 | $0.69 | (91%) | $175 | $72 | $10 |
| $16.32 | 63.2% | $130.00 | $121.00 | $0.45 | (100%) | $1,119 | $8,501 | $33 |
| | 67.5% | $41.00 | $18.69 | $8.93 | (78%) | $1,463 | $947 | $477 |
| | 33.3% | $21.88 | $15.31 | $16.00 | (27%) | $285 | $222 | $401 |
| $21.03 | 265.8% | $191.03 | $191.03 | $4.08 | (98%) | $1,770 | $16,644 | $628 |
| | 18.8% | $14.00 | $9.13 | $8.73 | (38%) | $141 | $93 | $110 |
| | 282.8% | $77.81 | $13.06 | — | — | $7,793 | $1,564 | — |
| | 14.3% | $16.06 | $10.00 | — | — | $174 | $109 | — |
| | 0.0% | $7.50 | $4.19 | $2.35 | (69%) | $98 | $31 | $17 |
| | 27.4% | $20.31 | $9.00 | $1.23 | (94%) | $574 | $1,298 | $200 |
| | 73.7% | $58.25 | $50.00 | $0.32 | (99%) | $1,385 | $3,218 | $23 |
| | (10.5%) | $66.75 | $19.88 | $0.90 | (99%) | $402 | $688 | $37 |
| | (11.6%) | $21.13 | $17.75 | — | — | $158 | $226 | — |
| | 0.6% | $15.13 | $14.88 | $2.20 | (85%) | $110 | $185 | $33 |
| | 50.0% | $19.50 | $13.06 | — | — | $3,030 | $1,341 | — |
| | 49.0% | $56.75 | $36.50 | $0.32 | (99%) | $1,137 | $2,557 | $31 |
| | 48.8% | $155.88 | $115.75 | $15.82 | (90%) | $266 | $2,431 | $392 |
| | 0.4% | $22.63 | $22.00 | $1.40 | (94%) | $152 | $240 | $16 |
| | 56.8% | $27.56 | $18.63 | $0.32 | (99%) | $1,056 | $1,009 | $19 |
| | 65.3% | $23.56 | $17.50 | $1.84 | (92%) | $1,051 | $1,266 | $224 |
| | 4.2% | $7.19 | $5.00 | $0.15 | (98%) | $62 | $50 | $3 |
| | 64.1% | $58.00 | $58.00 | $0.69 | (99%) | $689 | $2,032 | $26 |
| | 82.7% | $19.00 | $9.38 | $0.14 | (99%) | $452 | $284 | $6 |
| $20.07 | 150.8% | $200.75 | $170.19 | $16.04 | (92%) | $1,224 | $11,025 | $2,711 |
| | 41.1% | $12.63 | $8.31 | — | — | $110 | $370 | — |
| | (1.4%) | $28.00 | $21.94 | $17.17 | (39%) | $44 | $116 | $400 |
| | 71.9% | $83.00 | $50.38 | — | — | $2,153 | $3,547 | — |
| | 49.2% | $113.25 | $57.13 | $19.75 | (83%) | $994 | $2,601 | $1,047 |
| | 0.0% | $70.00 | $49.88 | — | — | $372 | $1,621 | — |
| $12.19 | 52.4% | $118.88 | $38.13 | $1.20 | (99%) | $500 | $1,713 | $61 |
| | 0.0% | $28.00 | $16.88 | $1.93 | (93%) | $244 | $594 | $91 |
| | 25.0% | $27.13 | $16.44 | $0.30 | (99%) | $368 | $737 | $27 |
| | (23.7%) | $12.81 | $6.50 | — | — | $136 | $120 | — |

| Company | IPO Date | # Shares Issued (m) | T4Q rev. offer[1] ($m) | Offer Price | Adjusted Offer[2] | P/S offer | 1st day close |
|---|---|---|---|---|---|---|---|
| Ramp Networks* | 22-Jun-99 | 4.00 | $11.10 | $11.00 | | 30.3 | $16.75 |
| Salon.com | 22-Jun-99 | 2.50 | $2.92 | $10.50 | | 36.6 | $10.00 |
| Ariba | 23-Jun-99 | 5.00 | $23.49 | $23.00 | $5.75 | 163.6 | $90.00 |
| TD Waterhouse | 23-Jun-99 | 42.00 | $0.80 | $24.00 | | 1,206.7 | $25.63 |
| Medinex Systems | 23-Jun-99 | 2.50 | $0.89 | $10.00 | | 93.1 | $9.56 |
| Software.com* | 24-Jun-99 | 6.00 | $28.79 | $15.00 | | 28.3 | $20.00 |
| CyberSource | 24-Jun-99 | 4.00 | $4.45 | $11.00 | | 68.9 | $14.25 |
| quepasa.com | 24-Jun-99 | 4.00 | $0.00 | $12.00 | | | $17.13 |
| Jupiter Networks | 25-Jun-99 | 4.80 | $13.85 | $34.00 | $11.33 | 349.8 | $98.88 |
| Internet.com | 25-Jun-99 | 3.40 | $5.11 | $14.00 | | 64.2 | $14.00 |
| Stamps.com | 25-Jun-99 | 5.00 | $0.00 | $11.00 | | | $13.06 |
| Persistence Software | 25-Jun-99 | 3.00 | $8.59 | $11.00 | | 29.6 | $13.81 |
| US SEARCH Corp.com | 25-Jun-99 | 6.00 | $10.74 | $9.00 | | 11.2 | $6.94 |
| Digital Island | 29-Jun-99 | 6.00 | $5.45 | $10.00 | | 77.4 | $11.88 |
| nFront* | 29-Jun-99 | 3.90 | $1.87 | $10.00 | | 102.5 | $13.50 |
| E Loan | 29-Jun-99 | 3.50 | $11.11 | $14.00 | | 127.6 | $37.00 |
| Primus Knowledge | 1-Jul-99 | 4.15 | $11.16 | $11.00 | | 21.3 | $17.56 |
| Commerce One | 1-Jul-99 | 3.30 | $4.54 | $21.00 | $3.50 | 301.2 | $61.00 |
| Ask Jeeves | 1-Jul-99 | 3.00 | $1.71 | $14.00 | | 924.7 | $64.94 |
| Musicmaker.com | 7-Jul-99 | 8.40 | $0.72 | $14.00 | | 10,106.8 | $23.94 |
| Interliant | 8-Jul-99 | 7.00 | $10.33 | $10.00 | | 68.7 | $16.81 |
| Liquid Audio | 9-Jul-99 | 4.20 | $3.11 | $15.00 | | 211.6 | $36.56 |
| CommTouch Software | 13-Jul-99 | 3.00 | $0.70 | $16.00 | | 484.5 | $24.00 |
| China.com | 13-Jul-99 | 4.20 | $3.50 | $20.00 | $5.00 | 401.9 | $67.11 |
| National Info Consortiur | 15-Jul-99 | 13.00 | $39.83 | $12.00 | | 22.8 | $17.31 |
| Audible | 16-Jul-99 | 4.00 | $0.57 | $9.00 | | 919.4 | $21.00 |
| Engage Tech. | 20-Jul-99 | 6.00 | $10.60 | $15.00 | $7.50 | 177.8 | $41.00 |
| Convergent Comm.* | 20-Jul-99 | 8.40 | $85.56 | $15.00 | | 6.0 | $21.50 |
| Talk City* | 20-Jul-99 | 5.00 | $2.31 | $12.00 | | 140.4 | $13.69 |
| Art Tech Group | 21-Jul-99 | 5.00 | $14.66 | $12.00 | $6.00 | 37.7 | $18.06 |
| MP3.com* | 21-Jul-99 | 12.30 | $1.83 | $28.00 | | 2,308.3 | $63.31 |
| Voyager.net* | 21-Jul-99 | 9.00 | $34.27 | $15.00 | | 13.3 | $15.06 |
| Hoover's | 21-Jul-99 | 3.25 | $9.23 | $14.00 | | 27.2 | $22.00 |
| Versa Tel Telecom | 23-Jul-99 | 21.25 | $23.23 | $10.50 | | 23.0 | $13.75 |
| Tanning Tech | 23-Jul-99 | 4.00 | $39.41 | $15.00 | | 9.3 | $18.44 |
| InsWeb | 23-Jul-99 | 5.00 | $11.66 | $17.00 | | 88.1 | $31.56 |
| JFax.com | 23-Jul-99 | 8.50 | $4.44 | $9.50 | | 70.2 | $9.50 |
| Ventro | 27-Jul-99 | 7.50 | $0.19 | $15.00 | | 4,176.7 | $25.50 |
| Liberate Tech. | 28-Jul-99 | 6.30 | $17.31 | $16.00 | $8.00 | 48.4 | $20.38 |
| drugstore.com | 28-Jul-99 | 5.00 | $4.20 | $18.00 | | 507.2 | $50.25 |
| Quokka Sports* | 28-Jul-99 | 5.00 | $4.67 | $12.00 | | 106.5 | $11.38 |
| Net2Phone | 29-Jul-99 | 5.40 | $34.21 | $15.00 | | 36.9 | $26.56 |
| Perficient | 29-Jul-99 | 1.00 | $1.10 | $8.00 | | 29.9 | $9.38 |
| Digex | 30-Jul-99 | 10.00 | $28.16 | $17.00 | | 47.5 | $22.31 |
| WatchGuard Tech. | 30-Jul-99 | 3.50 | $14.94 | $13.00 | | 15.0 | $12.13 |
| Accrue Software | 30-Jul-99 | 3.90 | $2.95 | $10.00 | | 81.0 | $12.19 |
| N2H2 | 30-Jul-99 | 4.50 | $4.39 | $13.00 | | 58.7 | $12.81 |
| Pacific Softworks | 30-Jul-99 | 0.95 | $2.86 | $5.25 | | 9.6 | $6.50 |
| Continuus Software* | 30-Jul-99 | 3.10 | $28.87 | $8.00 | | 2.6 | $7.88 |
| Splitrock Services* | 3-Aug-99 | 9.00 | $63.47 | $10.00 | | 8.1 | $9.00 |
| Quotesmith.com | 3-Aug-99 | 5.00 | $5.87 | $11.00 | | 30.5 | $9.69 |
| BigStar Entertainment | 3-Aug-99 | 2.50 | $2.24 | $10.00 | | 33.3 | $8.16 |
| Internet Capital Group | 5-Aug-99 | 14.90 | $5.87 | $12.00 | $6.00 | 496.5 | $24.44 |
| Pivotal | 5-Aug-99 | 3.50 | $25.33 | $12.00 | | 9.5 | $12.31 |
| HomeStore.com | 5-Aug-99 | 7.00 | $16.59 | $20.00 | | 92.0 | $22.75 |
| Cobalt Group | 5-Aug-99 | 4.45 | $7.62 | $11.00 | | 18.2 | $8.31 |
| Tumbleweed Comms | 6-Aug-99 | 4.00 | $2.72 | $12.00 | | 94.7 | $12.06 |

| Adjusted D1 close[3] | D1% change | All-time high | Price 3/10/00 | Price 8/31/01 | % ch from hi[4] | MktCap Offer ($m) | MktCap 3/10/00 ($m) | MktCap 8/31/01 ($m) |
|---|---|---|---|---|---|---|---|---|
| | 52.3% | $25.75 | $25.75 | – | – | $337 | $542 | – |
| | (1.8%) | $9.44 | $6.56 | $0.40 | (96%) | $107 | $75 | $6 |
| $22.50 | 291.3% | $183.00 | $152.69 | $2.28 | (99%) | $3,843 | $28,067 | $590 |
| | 6.8% | $25.69 | $19.88 | $8.13 | (68%) | $961 | $7,481 | $3,076 |
| | (4.4%) | $9.50 | $8.75 | $0.18 | (98%) | $83 | $81 | $2 |
| | 33.3% | $193.00 | $142.25 | – | – | $814 | $5,865 | – |
| | 29.5% | $66.50 | $45.00 | $1.19 | (98%) | $306 | $1,161 | $41 |
| | 42.8% | $15.00 | $7.94 | $0.19 | (99%) | $236 | $116 | $3 |
| $32.96 | 190.8% | $243.00 | $141.22 | $14.00 | (94%) | $4,845 | $21,941 | $4,503 |
| | 0.0% | $66.56 | $57.06 | $2.80 | (96%) | $328 | $1,331 | $71 |
| | 18.7% | $88.25 | $33.13 | $2.42 | (97%) | $454 | $1,161 | $122 |
| | 25.5% | $24.13 | $21.00 | $0.35 | (99%) | $254 | $402 | $7 |
| | (22.9%) | $10.88 | $4.53 | $1.63 | (85%) | $121 | $79 | $29 |
| | 18.8% | $144.63 | $108.50 | $3.38 | (98%) | $422 | $3,783 | $465 |
| | 35.0% | $44.00 | $41.94 | – | – | $192 | $0 | – |
| | 164.3% | $28.31 | $11.00 | $0.73 | (97%) | $1,417 | $459 | $39 |
| | 59.6% | $135.50 | $129.63 | $2.40 | (98%) | $237 | $1,856 | $45 |
| $10.17 | 190.5% | $256.44 | $128.78 | $3.26 | (99%) | $1,368 | $9,297 | $642 |
| | 363.9% | $186.00 | $84.69 | $0.97 | (99%) | $1,581 | $2,270 | $36 |
| | 71.0% | $67.50 | $44.38 | $2.00 | (97%) | $725 | $1,464 | $7 |
| | 68.1% | $54.44 | $48.00 | $0.38 | (99%) | $710 | $2,097 | $19 |
| | 143.7% | $43.75 | $23.06 | $2.39 | (95%) | $658 | $493 | $54 |
| | 50.0% | $66.50 | $66.50 | $0.43 | (99%) | $341 | $846 | $8 |
| $16.78 | 235.6% | $98.13 | $64.05 | $2.29 | (98%) | $1,407 | $2,704 | $235 |
| | 44.3% | $67.88 | $65.88 | $3.06 | (95%) | $909 | $3,499 | $172 |
| | 133.3% | $16.50 | $14.00 | $0.46 | (97%) | $525 | $359 | $13 |
| $20.50 | 173.3% | $92.50 | $74.50 | $0.22 | (100%) | $1,885 | $7,262 | $43 |
| | 43.3% | $16.88 | $12.81 | – | – | $511 | $358 | – |
| | 14.1% | $26.13 | $11.63 | – | – | $324 | $283 | – |
| $9.03 | 50.5% | $128.13 | $95.81 | $1.49 | 99% | $552 | $6,235 | $102 |
| | 126.1% | $61.25 | $23.19 | – | – | $4,219 | $1,589 | – |
| | 0.4% | $14.63 | $13.00 | – | – | $457 | $411 | – |
| | 57.1% | $13.00 | $11.19 | $3.22 | (75%) | $251 | $136 | $50 |
| | 31.0% | $77.25 | $76.75 | $0.70 | (99%) | $534 | $4,533 | $64 |
| | 22.9% | $70.38 | $39.50 | $4.14 | (94%) | $366 | $798 | $89 |
| | 85.6% | $30.63 | $14.00 | $0.45 | (99%) | $1,026 | $485 | $19 |
| | 0.0% | $7.69 | $5.88 | $3.50 | (54%) | $312 | $193 | $39 |
| | 70.0% | $239.81 | $181.31 | $0.38 | (100%) | $810 | $5,945 | $18 |
| $10.19 | 27.4% | $128.53 | $98.00 | $14.32 | (89%) | $838 | $8,189 | $1,507 |
| | 179.2% | $49.25 | $21.13 | $0.95 | (98%) | $2,131 | $916 | $63 |
| | (5.2%) | $17.00 | $13.63 | – | – | $497 | $600 | – |
| | 77.1% | $70.25 | $55.50 | $4.11 | (94%) | $1,262 | $2,864 | $244 |
| | 17.3% | $26.50 | $22.00 | $2.18 | (92%) | $33 | $77 | $14 |
| | 31.2% | $171.50 | $171.50 | $5.96 | (97%) | $1,339 | $10,547 | $382 |
| | (6.7%) | $103.00 | $94.50 | $9.93 | (90%) | $224 | $1,834 | $268 |
| | 21.9% | $70.00 | $50.63 | $0.25 | (100%) | $239 | $1,269 | $8 |
| | (1.5%) | $31.25 | $19.13 | $0.46 | (99%) | $257 | $403 | $10 |
| | 23.8% | $12.94 | $11.13 | $0.12 | (99%) | $28 | $49 | $1 |
| | (1.5%) | $16.69 | $9.81 | – | – | $74 | $88 | – |
| | | $55.50 | $55.50 | – | – | $516 | $3,154 | – |
| | (11.9%) | $12.13 | $7.50 | $2.04 | (83%) | $179 | $144 | $11 |
| | (18.4%) | $63.00 | $5.13 | $0.10 | (100%) | $75 | $44 | $1 |
| $12.22 | 103.7% | $192.50 | $143.56 | $0.76 | (100%) | $2,914 | $37,534 | $217 |
| | 2.6% | $70.23 | $63.88 | $6.68 | (90%) | $240 | $1,279 | $160 |
| | 13.8% | $122.25 | $57.72 | $16.57 | (86%) | $1,525 | $4,044 | $1,804 |
| | (24.5%) | $24.13 | $12.63 | $3.43 | (86%) | $139 | $213 | $71 |
| | 0.5% | $129.25 | $108.00 | $3.33 | (97%) | $257 | $2,332 | $101 |

| Company | IPO Date | # Shares Issued (m) | T4Q rev. offer[1] ($m) | Offer Price | Adjusted Offer[2] | P/S offer | 1st day close |
|---|---|---|---|---|---|---|---|
| Interactive Pictures* | 6-Aug-99 | 4.20 | $3.85 | $18.00 | | 78.8 | $18.00 |
| InterWorld Corp | 10-Aug-99 | 3.00 | $19.18 | $15.00 | $750.00 | 24.4 | $17.75 |
| Braun Consulting | 10-Aug-99 | 4.60 | $36.18 | $7.00 | | 3.3 | $7.06 |
| U.S. Interactive* | 10-Aug-99 | 4.60 | $18.39 | $10.00 | | 10.9 | $10.63 |
| HotJobs.com | 10-Aug-99 | 3.00 | $4.65 | $8.00 | | 43.6 | $7.63 |
| Mortgage.com* | 11-Aug-99 | 7.06 | $42.09 | $8.00 | | 7.1 | $7.16 |
| Active Software* | 13-Aug-99 | 3.50 | $13.86 | $11.00 | | 24.0 | $14.00 |
| Quest Software | 13-Aug-99 | 4.40 | $49.04 | $14.00 | $7.00 | 36.5 | $47.00 |
| SilverStream Software | 17-Aug-99 | 3.00 | $9.97 | $16.00 | | 53.6 | $31.50 |
| Headhunter.net | 19-Aug-99 | 3.00 | $3.24 | $10.00 | | 33.8 | $10.19 |
| Agile Software | 20-Aug-99 | 3.00 | $16.81 | $21.00 | $10.50 | 47.1 | $39.88 |
| LookSmart | 20-Aug-99 | 9.00 | $24.01 | $12.00 | | 61.5 | $17.31 |
| MyPoints.com* | 20-Aug-99 | 5.00 | $4.92 | $8.00 | | 53.0 | $11.00 |
| Lionbridge Tech. | 20-Aug-99 | 3.50 | $44.06 | $10.00 | | 4.4 | $12.63 |
| Internet Pictures Corp. | 26-Aug-99 | 4.00 | $0.57 | $7.00 | $70.00 | 623.5 | $17.56 |
| ImageX.com | 26-Aug-99 | 3.00 | $3.99 | $7.00 | | 59.7 | $13.94 |
| PurchasePro.com | 14-Sep-99 | 4.00 | $2.82 | $12.00 | $4.00 | 166.9 | $26.13 |
| Luminant Worldwide | 16-Sep-99 | 4.06 | $71.54 | $18.00 | | 8.7 | $26.38 |
| garden.com* | 16-Sep-99 | 4.10 | $5.39 | $12.00 | | 59.7 | $19.06 |
| Vitria Technology | 17-Sep-99 | 3.00 | $17.42 | $16.00 | $4.00 | 83.8 | $48.25 |
| E.piphany | 22-Sep-99 | 4.15 | $7.64 | $16.00 | $24.00 | 152.8 | $45.19 |
| Kana Comms | 22-Sep-99 | 3.30 | $4.97 | $15.00 | $7.50 | 285.4 | $51.50 |
| Broadbase Software* | 22-Sep-99 | 4.00 | $4.34 | $14.00 | | 108.0 | $27.25 |
| Bluestone Software* | 23-Sep-99 | 4.00 | $10.88 | $15.00 | | 29.8 | $18.75 |
| eGain Comms | 23-Sep-99 | 5.00 | $1.02 | $12.00 | | 627.8 | $23.00 |
| yesmail.com* | 23-Sep-99 | 3.40 | $6.18 | $11.00 | | 43.0 | $13.06 |
| NetZero | 23-Sep-99 | 10.00 | $4.63 | $16.00 | | 646.9 | $29.13 |
| Cybergold* | 23-Sep-99 | 5.00 | $2.01 | $9.00 | | 115.5 | $12.00 |
| Ashford.com | 23-Sep-99 | 6.25 | $1.45 | $13.00 | | 329.6 | $13.00 |
| Keynote Systems | 24-Sep-99 | 4.00 | $4.70 | $14.00 | | 132.1 | $27.25 |
| Promotions.com | 24-Sep-99 | 3.58 | $5.59 | $14.00 | | 29.3 | $11.50 |
| Foundry Ntwks | 28-Sep-99 | 5.00 | $52.32 | $25.00 | $12.50 | 166.1 | $156.25 |
| ITXC | 28-Sep-99 | 6.25 | $9.12 | $12.00 | | 107.8 | $28.25 |
| FreeShop.com* | 28-Sep-99 | 3.20 | $2.97 | $12.00 | | 68.5 | $13.56 |
| Medscape* | 28-Sep-99 | 6.60 | $9.51 | $8.00 | | 63.2 | $13.81 |
| InterNAP Ntwk Svs | 29-Sep-99 | 9.50 | $4.64 | $20.00 | $10.00 | 710.2 | $52.98 |
| Envision Development* | 29-Sep-99 | 3.50 | $0.39 | $7.00 | | 129.8 | $6.75 |
| Network Commerce | 29-Sep-99 | 7.25 | $21.22 | $12.00 | | 19.9 | $12.69 |
| Telemate.Net Software | 29-Sep-99 | 3.50 | $10.78 | $14.00 | | 9.3 | $14.19 |
| FTD.com | 29-Sep-99 | 4.50 | $49.62 | $8.00 | | 8.1 | $8.63 |
| RADWARE | 30-Sep-99 | 3.50 | $4.90 | $18.00 | | 86.1 | $28.88 |
| LoisLaw.com* | 30-Sep-99 | 3.98 | $5.68 | $14.00 | | 53.4 | $14.50 |
| Digital Insight | 1-Oct-99 | 3.50 | $11.83 | $15.00 | | 38.4 | $32.13 |
| AltiGen Comm. | 5-Oct-99 | 3.25 | $5.60 | $10.00 | | 36.6 | $16.00 |
| Breakaway Solutions | 6-Oct-99 | 3.00 | $6.49 | $14.00 | $7.00 | 110.0 | $42.25 |
| DSL.net | 6-Oct-99 | 7.20 | $0.21 | $7.50 | | 2,425.0 | $8.53 |
| Calico Commerce | 7-Oct-99 | 4.00 | $24.19 | $14.00 | | 75.7 | $56.00 |
| PlanetRx.com* | 7-Oct-99 | 6.00 | $0.82 | $16.00 | | 1,610.7 | $26.00 |
| Interwoven | 8-Oct-99 | 3.15 | $8.12 | $17.00 | $8.50 | 109.1 | $41.00 |
| TriZetto Group | 8-Oct-99 | 4.20 | $19.09 | $9.00 | | 9.3 | $9.00 |
| Jupiter Comm.* | 8-Oct-99 | 3.13 | $23.29 | $21.00 | | 21.6 | $35.50 |
| E-Stamp* | 8-Oct-99 | 7.00 | $0.00 | $17.00 | | | $22.38 |
| VitaminShoppe.com* | 8-Oct-99 | 4.55 | $6.68 | $11.00 | | 29.8 | $9.75 |
| Netcentives | 14-Oct-99 | 6.00 | $3.54 | $12.00 | | 112.8 | $12.56 |
| iGo | 14-Oct-99 | 5.00 | $14.26 | $12.00 | | 19.0 | $14.06 |
| NetRadio | 14-Oct-99 | 3.20 | $0.55 | $11.00 | $49.50 | 190.9 | $10.00 |
| Cysive | 15-Oct-99 | 3.35 | $15.37 | $17.00 | $8.50 | 27.3 | $37.75 |

| Adjusted D1 close[3] | D1% change | All-time high | Price 3/10/00 | Price 8/31/01 | % ch from hi[4] | MktCap Offer ($m) | MktCap 3/10/00 ($m) | MktCap 8/31/01 ($m) |
|---|---|---|---|---|---|---|---|---|
| | 0.0% | $25.25 | $0.00 | — | — | $304 | — | — |
| $887.50 | 18.3% | $4,293.75 | $84.13 | $0.85 | (100%) | $468 | $2,276 | $0 |
| | 0.9% | $83.50 | $55.00 | $7.25 | (91%) | $120 | $905 | $148 |
| | 6.3% | $70.25 | $43.88 | — | — | $200 | $850 | — |
| | (4.6%) | $45.00 | $31.94 | $9.58 | (79%) | $203 | $985 | $367 |
| | (10.5%) | $10.63 | $4.06 | — | — | $297 | $175 | — |
| | 27.3% | $139.94 | $124.63 | — | — | $333 | $2,998 | — |
| $23.50 | 235.7% | $116.50 | $97.50 | $20.80 | (82%) | $1,792 | $7,568 | $1,827 |
| | 96.9% | $124.63 | $93.63 | $5.64 | (95%) | $535 | $1,644 | $123 |
| | 1.9% | $24.38 | $15.63 | $9.20 | (62%) | $109 | $168 | $188 |
| $19.94 | 89.9% | $217.23 | $72.81 | $10.00 | (95%) | $79 | $3,329 | $478 |
| | 44.3% | $69.63 | $69.63 | $0.65 | (99%) | $1,478 | $5,956 | $60 |
| | 37.5% | $88.50 | $66.13 | — | — | $261 | $1,668 | — |
| | 26.3% | $26.25 | $19.88 | $0.85 | (97%) | $192 | $324 | $26 |
| $175.60 | 150.9% | $450.00 | $39.50 | $1.92 | (100%) | $358 | $846 | $13 |
| | 99.1% | $41.88 | $24.25 | $1.01 | (98%) | $238 | $405 | $31 |
| $8.71 | 117.8% | $158.38 | $61.01 | $0.80 | (99%) | $471 | $1,733 | $58 |
| | 46.6% | $50.63 | $23.56 | $0.58 | (99%) | $621 | $570 | $18 |
| | 58.8% | $14.38 | $7.50 | — | — | $322 | $131 | — |
| $12.06 | 201.6% | $136.50 | $93.41 | $2.76 | (98%) | $1,460 | $11,567 | $358 |
| $67.79 | 182.4% | $253.38 | $211.66 | $6.44 | (97%) | $1,167 | $5,710 | $454 |
| $25.75 | 243.3% | $234.00 | $169.81 | $0.85 | (100%) | $1,419 | $9,805 | $80 |
| | 94.6% | $164.13 | $124.25 | — | — | $469 | $2,238 | — |
| | 25.0% | $135.13 | $74.50 | — | — | $324 | $1,342 | — |
| | 91.7% | $68.50 | $57.50 | $1.66 | (98%) | $640 | $1,668 | $60 |
| | 18.7% | $38.00 | $33.88 | — | — | $265 | $0 | — |
| | 82.1% | $35.56 | $23.25 | $0.51 | (99%) | $2,998 | $2,431 | $64 |
| | 33.3% | $24.00 | $16.88 | — | — | $232 | $326 | — |
| | 0.0% | $24.88 | $8.75 | $0.14 | (99%) | $479 | $323 | $7 |
| | 94.6% | $162.00 | $151.13 | $8.25 | (95%) | $621 | $3,568 | $232 |
| | (17.9%) | $29.25 | $16.00 | $0.21 | (99%) | $164 | $228 | $3 |
| $78.13 | 525.0% | $207.56 | $201.19 | $10.95 | (95%) | $8,693 | $23,048 | $1,317 |
| | 135.4% | $119.75 | $85.06 | $3.00 | (97%) | $983 | $3,043 | $135 |
| | 13.0% | $59.94 | $33.75 | — | — | $203 | $522 | — |
| | 72.6% | $13.38 | $9.25 | — | — | $601 | $415 | — |
| $26.49 | 164.9% | $105.91 | $91.06 | $1.00 | (99%) | $3,295 | $11,982 | $151 |
| | (3.6%) | $72.75 | $42.63 | — | — | $51 | $320 | — |
| | 5.7% | $23.44 | $19.63 | $0.33 | (99%) | $423 | $689 | $2 |
| | 1.4% | $20.94 | $15.13 | $1.85 | (91%) | $101 | $111 | $17 |
| | 7.9% | $8.25 | $3.88 | $6.55 | (21%) | $404 | $183 | $318 |
| | 60.4% | $80.00 | $58.63 | $12.94 | (84%) | $422 | $856 | $212 |
| | 3.6% | $44.00 | $24.00 | — | — | $303 | $503 | — |
| | 114.2% | $83.88 | $55.88 | $17.07 | (80%) | $454 | $825 | $502 |
| | 60.0% | $23.00 | $18.69 | $0.91 | (96%) | $205 | $240 | $13 |
| $21.13 | 201.8% | $79.00 | $76.94 | $0.04 | (100%) | $714 | $2,681 | $2 |
| | 13.7% | $31.88 | $29.31 | $0.30 | (99%) | $509 | $1,711 | $19 |
| | 300.0% | $71.88 | $36.06 | $0.07 | (100%) | $1,831 | $1,215 | $2 |
| | 62.5% | $23.50 | $9.50 | — | — | $1,321 | $495 | — |
| $20.50 | 141.2% | $169.38 | $99.47 | $8.15 | (95%) | $886 | $2,280 | $844 |
| | 0.0% | $88.50 | $74.81 | $11.33 | (87%) | $177 | $1,481 | $503 |
| | 69.0% | $42.00 | $30.13 | — | — | $504 | $436 | — |
| | 31.6% | $39.25 | $10.06 | — | — | $837 | $393 | — |
| | (11.4%) | $17.19 | $4.50 | — | — | $199 | $92 | — |
| | 4.7% | $80.63 | $58.44 | $0.09 | (100%) | $399 | $1,890 | $4 |
| | 17.2% | $22.25 | $8.75 | $0.40 | (98%) | $271 | $169 | $9 |
| $45.00 | −9.1% | $46.69 | $5.69 | $0.71 | (98%) | $105 | $57 | $2 |
| $18.88 | 122.1% | $74.00 | $52.25 | $2.48 | (97%) | $419 | $595 | $74 |

| Company | IPO Date | # Shares Issued (m) | T4Q rev. offer[1] ($m) | Offer Price | Adjusted Offer[2] | P/S offer | 1st day close |
|---|---|---|---|---|---|---|---|
| Women.com* | 15-Oct-99 | 3.75 | $13.93 | $10.00 | | 60.0 | $18.50 |
| ZapMe!* | 20-Oct-99 | 9.00 | $0.15 | $11.00 | | 2,740.1 | $9.50 |
| NaviSite | 22-Oct-99 | 5.50 | $10.52 | $14.00 | $7.00 | 86.6 | $34.63 |
| Viador | 26-Oct-99 | 4.00 | $5.36 | $9.00 | | 33.0 | $11.13 |
| InterTrust Tech. | 27-Oct-99 | 6.50 | $0.59 | $18.00 | $9.00 | 3,484.0 | $54.38 |
| Data Return | 28-Oct-99 | 6.30 | $2.84 | $13.00 | | 199.0 | $16.38 |
| Akamai Tech. | 29-Oct-99 | 9.00 | $66.98 | $26.00 | | 198.1 | $145.19 |
| Cavion Tech.* | 29-Oct-99 | 1.20 | $0.46 | $6.50 | | 60.3 | $6.00 |
| Be Free | 3-Nov-99 | 5.60 | $2.10 | $12.00 | $6.00 | 361.8 | $29.00 |
| Tickets.com | 4-Nov-99 | 6.70 | $34.95 | $12.50 | | 33.5 | $19.25 |
| Webvan Group* | 5-Nov-99 | 25.00 | $0.40 | $15.00 | | 19,748.5 | $24.88 |
| Collectors Universe | 5-Nov-99 | 4.00 | $22.56 | $6.00 | | 6.5 | $6.00 |
| Netzee | 9-Nov-99 | 4.40 | $4.94 | $14.00 | | 58.2 | $14.81 |
| iBasis | 10-Nov-99 | 6.80 | $13.22 | $16.00 | | 92.9 | $40.25 |
| Expedia | 10-Nov-99 | 5.20 | 47.91 | $14.00 | | 42.6 | $53.44 |
| SonicWALL | 11-Nov-99 | 4.00 | $14.29 | $14.00 | $7.00 | 43.0 | $26.06 |
| NetCreations* | 12-Nov-99 | 3.30 | $11.59 | $13.00 | | 25.9 | $20.00 |
| Quintus* | 16-Nov-99 | 4.50 | $36.54 | $18.00 | | 46.8 | $55.00 |
| iManage | 17-Nov-99 | 3.60 | $15.64 | $11.00 | | 33.7 | $24.63 |
| Web Street* | 17-Nov-99 | 3.50 | $20.69 | $11.00 | | 14.9 | $12.38 |
| Retek | 18-Nov-99 | 5.50 | $72.96 | $15.00 | | 20.1 | $32.56 |
| LifeMinders.com | 19-Nov-99 | 4.20 | $6.01 | $14.00 | | 73.1 | $22.38 |
| Mediaplex | 19-Nov-99 | 6.00 | $14.58 | $12.00 | | 61.1 | $29.00 |
| SciQuest | 19-Nov-99 | 7.20 | $1.41 | $16.00 | | 518.4 | $30.00 |
| Exactis.com* | 19-Nov-99 | 3.53 | $8.06 | $14.00 | | 36.0 | $24.00 |
| Digital Impact | 23-Nov-99 | 4.50 | $4.44 | $15.00 | | 293.8 | $55.50 |
| GetThere.com* | 23-Nov-99 | 5.00 | $9.34 | $16.00 | | 82.1 | $24.50 |
| SmarterKids.com* | 23-Nov-99 | 4.50 | $1.13 | $14.00 | | 240.4 | $14.00 |
| Mcafee | 2-Dec-99 | 6.25 | $18.12 | $12.00 | | 102.6 | $44.00 |
| Knot | 2-Dec-99 | 3.50 | $2.85 | $10.00 | | 74.2 | $15.00 |
| E-Cruiter.com | 7-Dec-99 | 2.45 | $0.95 | $6.00 | | 68.5 | $8.56 |
| HealthCentral.com | 7-Dec-99 | 7.50 | $0.50 | $11.00 | | 386.5 | $9.88 |
| Preview Systems | 8-Dec-99 | 3.80 | $2.82 | $21.00 | | 468.3 | $83.75 |
| Andover.Net* | 8-Dec-99 | 4.00 | $2.63 | $18.00 | | 363.7 | $63.75 |
| NetRatings | 8-Dec-99 | 4.00 | $1.59 | $17.00 | | 261.7 | $28.00 |
| Agency.com | 8-Dec-99 | 5.90 | $94.98 | $26.00 | | 27.0 | $76.00 |
| Fogdog* | 9-Dec-99 | 6.00 | $2.83 | $11.00 | | 165.6 | $13.13 |
| Freemarkets | 10-Dec-99 | 3.60 | $16.04 | $48.00 | | 593.5 | $280.00 |
| eBenX | 10-Dec-99 | 5.00 | $15.20 | $20.00 | | 44.6 | $44.88 |
| MedicalLogic | 10-Dec-99 | 5.30 | $20.64 | $17.00 | | 32.5 | $22.00 |
| El Sitio* | 10-Dec-99 | 8.20 | $28.22 | $16.00 | | 45.5 | $33.31 |
| MotherNature.com* | 10-Dec-99 | 4.10 | $2.70 | $13.00 | | 57.7 | $10.31 |
| HealthExtras | 14-Dec-99 | 5.50 | $2.59 | $11.00 | | 95.9 | $9.00 |
| Gric Communications | 15-Dec-99 | 4.60 | $6.27 | $14.00 | | 59.3 | $21.00 |
| Optio Software | 15-Dec-99 | 5.00 | $29.66 | $10.00 | | 9.3 | $16.31 |
| eCollege.com | 15-Dec-99 | 4.50 | $3.54 | $11.00 | | 55.8 | $14.25 |
| Xpedior* | 16-Dec-99 | 8.50 | $137.40 | $19.00 | | 9.5 | $26.00 |
| OnDisplay* | 17-Dec-99 | 3.50 | $7.69 | $28.00 | | 189.2 | $77.00 |
| C-Bridge Internet | 17-Dec-99 | 4.00 | $15.68 | $16.00 | | 44.2 | $40.06 |
| Egreetings.com* | 17-Dec-99 | 6.00 | $1.66 | $10.00 | | 218.9 | $10.56 |
| Neoforma.com | 24-Jan-00 | 7.00 | $0.46 | $13.00 | $130.00 | 6,417.6 | $52.38 |
| HealthGate Data | 26-Jan-00 | 3.75 | $2.33 | $11.00 | | 87.2 | $11.75 |
| Extensity | 27-Jan-00 | 4.00 | $6.81 | $20.00 | | 238.5 | $71.25 |
| 724 Solutions | 28-Jan-00 | 6.00 | $2.73 | $26.00 | | 931.2 | $71.81 |
| L90, Inc. | 28-Jan-00 | 6.50 | $4.70 | $15.00 | | 99.3 | $23.56 |
| SkillSoft | 1-Feb-00 | 3.10 | $2.37 | $14.00 | | 95.5 | $18.00 |
| Centra Software | 3-Feb-00 | 5.00 | $4.23 | $14.00 | | 182.0 | $33.25 |

| Adjusted D1 close[3] | D1% change | All-time high | Price 3/10/00 | Price 8/31/01 | % ch from hi[4] | MktCap Offer ($m) | MktCap 3/10/00 ($m) | MktCap 8/31/01 ($m) |
|---|---|---|---|---|---|---|---|---|
| | 85.0% | $20.98 | $10.38 | — | — | $836 | $474 | — |
| | −13.6% | $12.94 | $7.94 | — | — | $403 | $347 | — |
| $17.32 | 147.4% | $159.16 | $153.75 | $0.40 | (100%) | $911 | $8,625 | $24 |
| | 23.7% | $61.50 | $40.75 | $0.22 | (100%) | $177 | $671 | $7 |
| $27.19 | 202.1% | $181.38 | $87.25 | $1.32 | (99%) | $2,056 | $3,435 | $124 |
| | 26.0% | $89.50 | $85.75 | $0.66 | (99%) | $565 | $3,036 | $24 |
| | 458.4% | $327.63 | $296.00 | $4.21 | (99%) | $13,270 | $27,066 | $485 |
| | −7.7% | $36.38 | $28.88 | — | — | $28 | $136 | — |
| $14.50 | 141.7% | $84.00 | $47.88 | $1.80 | (98%) | $760 | $2,511 | $118 |
| | 54.0% | $21.88 | $12.81 | $2.24 | (90%) | $1,172 | $731 | $17 |
| | 65.9% | $25.44 | $11.81 | — | — | $7,899 | $3,802 | — |
| | 0.0% | $10.13 | $7.63 | $1.50 | (85%) | $146 | $186 | $37 |
| | 5.8% | $30.38 | $21.88 | $1.39 | (95%) | $287 | $424 | $5 |
| | 151.6% | $90.50 | $74.50 | $1.10 | (99%) | $1,228 | $2,275 | $50 |
| | 281.7% | $56.00 | $34.81 | $37.36 | (33%) | $2,041 | $1,330 | $1,891 |
| $13.03 | 86.1% | $66.25 | $66.25 | $18.71 | (72%) | $615 | $1,568 | $1,215 |
| | 53.8% | 62.00 | $60.88 | — | — | $300 | $913 | — |
| | 205.6% | $56.50 | $40.50 | — | — | $1,711 | $1,302 | — |
| | 123.9% | $37.94 | $24.88 | $5.00 | (87%) | $527 | $534 | $117 |
| | 12.5% | $17.38 | $6.56 | — | — | $308 | $163 | — |
| | 117.1% | $93.94 | $65.50 | $27.98 | (70%) | $1,465 | $2,980 | $1,419 |
| | 59.9% | $91.00 | $85.50 | $1.65 | (98%) | $439 | $1,678 | $44 |
| | 141.7% | $102.00 | $75.13 | $0.80 | (99%) | $890 | $2,375 | $29 |
| | 87.5% | $84.13 | $72.13 | $0.90 | (99%) | $731 | $1,797 | $26 |
| | 71.4% | $35.00 | $32.69 | — | — | $290 | $395 | — |
| | 270.0% | $61.75 | $40.00 | $1.26 | (98%) | $1,304 | $942 | $36 |
| | 53.1% | $50.00 | $21.63 | — | — | $767 | $678 | — |
| | 0.0% | $15.31 | $4.63 | — | — | $272 | $90 | — |
| | 266.7% | $55.50 | $49.00 | $14.50 | (74%) | $1,859 | $2,070 | $660 |
| | 50.0% | $15.69 | $6.38 | $0.55 | (96%) | $211 | $89 | $8 |
| | 42.7% | $8.75 | $7.75 | $3.12 | (64%) | $63 | $57 | $24 |
| | −10.2% | $13.69 | $7.00 | $3.55 | (74%) | $195 | $138 | $4 |
| | 298.8% | $83.75 | $64.63 | $0.09 | (100%) | $1,321 | $1,019 | $2 |
| | 254.2% | $77.50 | $39.00 | — | — | $956 | $585 | — |
| | 64.7% | $53.00 | $33.94 | $12.77 | (76%) | $416 | $505 | $422 |
| | 192.3% | $76.00 | $32.63 | $3.30 | (96%) | $2,565 | $1,101 | $128 |
| | 19.3% | $14.63 | $8.19 | — | — | $468 | $292 | — |
| | 483.3% | $341.31 | $202.63 | $14.46 | (96%) | $9,520 | $6,881 | $576 |
| | 124.4% | $76.50 | $61.00 | $4.19 | (95%) | $678 | $926 | $83 |
| | 29.4% | $51.00 | $29.38 | $0.37 | (99%) | $671 | $895 | $21 |
| | 108.2% | $41.00 | $22.69 | — | — | $1,285 | $875 | — |
| | −20.7% | $10.31 | $4.50 | — | — | $156 | $68 | — |
| | −18.2% | $12.00 | $6.13 | $6.10 | (49%) | $248 | $169 | $178 |
| | 50.0% | $69.00 | $56.00 | $0.92 | (99%) | $372 | $992 | $18 |
| | 63.1% | $27.50 | $20.75 | $0.56 | (98%) | $276 | $351 | $10 |
| | 29.5% | $14.25 | $9.06 | $4.20 | (71%) | $198 | $133 | $68 |
| | 36.8% | $32.63 | $16.94 | — | — | $1,300 | $847 | — |
| | 175.0% | $125.94 | $113.63 | — | — | $1,455 | $2,182 | — |
| | 150.4% | $60.38 | $48.31 | $0.66 | (99%) | $693 | $836 | $14 |
| | 5.6% | $11.25 | $6.75 | — | — | $363 | $232 | — |
| $523.75 | 302.9% | $735.31 | $44.31 | $7.26 | (99%) | $2,952 | $2,498 | $133 |
| | 6.8% | $13.00 | $8.88 | $0.83 | (94%) | $203 | $153 | $5 |
| | 256.3% | $78.25 | $68.50 | $5.04 | (94%) | $1,625 | $1,562 | $124 |
| | 176.2% | 231.88 | $207.00 | $4.10 | (98%) | $2,542 | $7,328 | $239 |
| | 57.1% | $30.06 | $20.25 | $1.29 | (96%) | $467 | $401 | $32 |
| | 28.6% | $30.00 | $25.75 | $28.00 | (7%) | $227 | $324 | $456 |
| | 137.5% | $36.50 | $33.50 | $9.85 | (73%) | $773 | $779 | $248 |

| Company | IPO Date | # Shares Issued (m) | T4Q rev. offer[1] ($m) | Offer Price | Adjusted Offer[2] | P/S offer | 1st day close |
|---|---|---|---|---|---|---|---|
| FirePond | 4-Feb-00 | 5.00 | $34.29 | $22.00 | | 95.8 | $100.25 |
| Streamedia Comm.* | 21-Dec-99 | 1.00 | $0.00 | $8.50 | | | $9.00 |
| eMerge Interactive | 4-Feb-00 | 6.50 | $19.03 | $15.00 | | 80.0 | $47.25 |
| WorldQuest | 4-Feb-00 | 2.75 | $5.07 | $13.00 | | 32.2 | $27.44 |
| FastNet | 8-Feb-00 | 4.00 | $7.29 | $12.00 | | 32.8 | $16.62 |
| Buy.com | 8-Feb-00 | 14.00 | $596.85 | $13.00 | | 5.4 | $25.12 |
| Vicinity | 9-Feb-00 | 7.00 | $7.46 | $17.00 | | 176.1 | $48.75 |
| Delano Tech | 9-Feb-00 | 5.00 | $5.36 | $16.00 | | 275.0 | $50.50 |
| Landacorp | 9-Feb-00 | 3.50 | $8.64 | $10.00 | | 24.4 | $15.94 |
| Organic | 10-Feb-00 | 5.50 | $58.77 | $20.00 | | 53.6 | $39.94 |
| The LightSpan Partners | 10-Feb-00 | 7.50 | $10.87 | $12.00 | | 53.5 | $13.50 |
| Xcare.net | 10-Feb-00 | 5.00 | $3.36 | $18.00 | | 142.9 | $31.25 |
| webMethods | 11-Feb-00 | 4.10 | $14.88 | $35.00 | | 430.4 | $212.62 |
| Lante | 11-Feb-00 | 4.00 | $32.96 | $20.00 | | 65.3 | $54.94 |
| VIA NET.WORKS | 11-Feb-00 | 14.30 | $25.71 | $21.00 | | 110.6 | $49.81 |
| Pets.com* | 11-Feb-00 | 6.00 | $5.79 | $11.00 | | 56.2 | $11.00 |
| Chordiant Software | 15-Feb-00 | 4.50 | $17.59 | $18.00 | | 78.1 | $39.44 |
| Stardrive (Sunhawk.com) | 15-Feb-00 | 1.40 | $100.58 | $12.00 | | 0.5 | $18.50 |
| Savvis Comm. | 15-Feb-00 | 17.00 | $17.63 | $24.00 | | 126.4 | $24.00 |
| b2bstores.com* | 15-Feb-00 | 4.00 | $0.00 | $8.00 | | 29,728.8 | $8.12 |
| VarsityBooks.com | 15-Feb-00 | 4.08 | $8.90 | $10.00 | | 17.3 | $9.88 |
| VantageMed | 15-Feb-00 | 3.00 | $15.79 | $12.00 | | 5.5 | $10.06 |
| Lending Tree | 16-Feb-00 | 3.65 | $6.96 | $12.00 | | 44.5 | $18.00 |
| Choice One | 17-Feb-00 | 7.15 | $4.52 | $20.00 | | 195.9 | $29.56 |
| Inforte | 18-Feb-00 | 2.00 | $30.09 | $32.00 | | 28.4 | $72.94 |
| GigaMedia | 18-Feb-00 | 8.83 | $0.58 | $27.00 | | 7,408.7 | $88.00 |
| eSafetyworld | 18-Feb-00 | 1.00 | $0.00 | $7.00 | | | $7.44 |
| DigitalThink | 25-Feb-00 | 4.40 | $7.18 | $14.00 | | 132.7 | $29.00 |
| hotel reservations network | 25-Feb-00 | 5.40 | $161.81 | $16.00 | | 8.7 | $26.00 |
| Niku | 29-Feb-00 | 8.00 | $2.98 | $24.00 | | 1,603.6 | $69.12 |
| Avenue A | 29-Feb-00 | 5.25 | $69.70 | $24.00 | | 59.0 | $73.88 |
| Net.Genesis | 29-Feb-00 | 4.25 | $6.54 | $18.00 | | 176.5 | $56.38 |
| MatrixOne | 1-Mar-00 | 5.00 | $53.66 | $25.00 | | 52.5 | $73.81 |
| ONVIA.com | 1-Mar-00 | 8.00 | $27.18 | $21.00 | | 178.4 | $61.50 |
| Switchboard | 2-Mar-00 | 5.50 | $8.30 | $15.00 | | 76.6 | $26.81 |
| Register.com | 3-Mar-00 | 5.00 | $9.64 | $24.00 | | 182.6 | $57.25 |
| Asiainfo | 3-Mar-00 | 5.00 | $60.28 | $24.00 | | 61.9 | $99.56 |
| Versata | 3-Mar-00 | 3.85 | $12.58 | $24.00 | | 279.9 | $92.75 |
| Prime Response* | 3-Mar-00 | 3.50 | $20.52 | $18.00 | | 23.1 | $23.88 |
| FirstWorld Comm.* | 8-Mar-00 | 8.50 | $54.50 | $17.00 | | 7.2 | $25.00 |
| iPrint.com | 8-Mar-00 | 4.50 | $3.26 | $10.00 | | 139.8 | $15.75 |
| Selectica | 10-Mar-00 | 4.00 | $10.60 | $30.00 | | 460.3 | $141.23 |
| OTG Software | 10-Mar-00 | 5.00 | $25.44 | $19.00 | | 56.3 | $56.19 |
| HomeGrocer.com* | 10-Mar-00 | 22.00 | $21.65 | $12.00 | | 81.4 | $14.13 |
| RADVision | 14-Mar-00 | 3.80 | $17.55 | $20.00 | | 57.5 | $55.94 |
| Digitas | 14-Mar-00 | 6.20 | $187.01 | $24.00 | | 9.0 | $29.50 |
| FairMarket | 14-Mar-00 | 5.00 | $2.12 | $17.00 | | 607.3 | $48.50 |
| Loudeye Tech. | 15-Mar-00 | 4.50 | $2.65 | $16.00 | | 527.1 | $40.00 |
| ImproveNet | 16-Mar-00 | 2.76 | $2.07 | $16.00 | | 112.7 | $14.13 |
| TippingPoint (Netpliance) | 17-Mar-00 | 8.00 | $0.03 | $18.00 | $270.00 | 51,283.4 | $22.06 |
| Integrated Information | 17-Mar-00 | 4.60 | $21.21 | $15.00 | | 19.8 | $20.94 |
| Snowball.com | 21-Mar-00 | 6.25 | $6.67 | $11.00 | | 85.5 | $15.31 |
| PartsBase.com | 22-Mar-00 | 3.50 | $0.36 | $13.00 | | 442.6 | $11.38 |
| Blaze Software* | 23-Mar-00 | 4.00 | $14.76 | $16.00 | | 40.1 | $27.75 |
| Digital Lighthouse* | 24-Mar-00 | 4.50 | $24.70 | $12.00 | | 9.1 | $12.38 |
| Eprise | 24-Mar-00 | 4.00 | $3.66 | $15.00 | | 158.3 | $25.25 |
| Websense | 28-Mar-00 | 4.00 | $8.70 | $18.00 | | 106.4 | $47.75 |

| Adjusted D1 close[3] | D1% change | All-time high | Price 3/10/00 | Price 8/31/01 | % ch from hi[4] | MktCap Offer ($m) | MktCap 3/10/00 ($m) | MktCap 8/31/01 ($m) |
|---|---|---|---|---|---|---|---|---|
| | 355.7% | $100.25 | $81.00 | $0.71 | (99%) | $3,283 | $2,653 | $28 |
| | 5.9% | $9.00 | $4.50 | — | — | $39 | $19 | — |
| | 215.0% | $66.88 | $66.88 | $1.83 | (97%) | $1,523 | $2,156 | $65 |
| | 111.1% | $36.00 | $34.50 | $2.05 | (94%) | $163 | $205 | $13 |
| | 38.5% | $18.88 | $18.38 | $1.16 | (94%) | $239 | $264 | $21 |
| | 93.2% | $27.50 | $15.00 | $0.11 | (100%) | $3,244 | $1,937 | $15 |
| | 186.8% | $74.88 | $64.00 | $1.48 | (98%) | $1,314 | $1,725 | $42 |
| | 215.6% | $51.50 | $47.00 | $0.25 | (100%) | $1,473 | $1,371 | $9 |
| | 59.4% | $16.25 | $14.13 | $1.04 | (94%) | $211 | $187 | $16 |
| | 99.7% | $39.94 | $29.63 | $0.32 | (99%) | $3,150 | $2,336 | $28 |
| | 12.5% | $24.38 | $24.38 | $1.45 | (94%) | $582 | $1,051 | $67 |
| | 73.6% | $31.25 | $22.63 | $16.41 | (47%) | $480 | $348 | $454 |
| | 507.5% | $308.00 | $232.50 | $12.03 | (96%) | $6,404 | $7,003 | $595 |
| | 174.7% | $86.13 | $69.00 | $0.96 | (99%) | $2,153 | $2,704 | $39 |
| | 137.2% | $71.75 | $63.63 | $0.88 | (99%) | $2,843 | $3,631 | $54 |
| | 0.0% | $11.00 | $7.63 | — | — | $325 | $225 | — |
| | 119.1% | $39.44 | $39.38 | $2.84 | (93%) | $1,373 | $1,371 | $150 |
| | 54.2% | $27.25 | $27.25 | $0.91 | (97%) | $52 | $76 | $6 |
| | 0.0% | $28.06 | $23.00 | $0.96 | (97%) | $2,229 | $2,136 | $90 |
| | 1.5% | $18.38 | $16.25 | — | — | $65 | $130 | — |
| | −1.2% | $10.06 | $9.81 | $0.58 | (94%) | $154 | $153 | $10 |
| | −16.2% | $12.00 | $5.56 | $0.99 | (92%) | $87 | $48 | $9 |
| | 50.0% | $18.00 | $14.06 | $4.13 | (77%) | $310 | $242 | $78 |
| | 47.8% | $61.88 | $42.13 | $4.56 | (93%) | $885 | $1,261 | $172 |
| | 127.9% | $80.06 | $71.81 | $11.00 | (86%) | $855 | $842 | $141 |
| | 225.9% | $90.75 | $68.00 | $1.03 | (99%) | $4,297 | $3,320 | $50 |
| | 6.3% | $8.00 | $7.13 | $0.65 | (92%) | $22 | $21 | $2 |
| | 107.1% | $59.44 | $53.88 | $12.20 | (79%) | $953 | $1,770 | $431 |
| | 62.5% | $42.61 | $22.38 | $41.60 | (2%) | $1,414 | $1,217 | $2,359 |
| | 188.0% | $105.00 | $70.50 | $0.57 | (99%) | $4,772 | $4,868 | $43 |
| | 207.8% | $75.00 | $60.13 | $1.35 | (98%) | $4,113 | $3,347 | $78 |
| | 213.2% | $56.38 | $50.50 | $0.52 | (99%) | $1,154 | $1,033 | $12 |
| | 195.3% | $74.00 | $70.00 | $10.71 | (86%) | $2,817 | $2,671 | $488 |
| | 192.9% | $61.50 | $48.06 | $0.41 | (99%) | $4,849 | $3,790 | $34 |
| | 78.8% | $44.25 | $35.00 | $4.04 | (91%) | $636 | $830 | $104 |
| | 138.5% | $99.75 | $99.25 | $8.43 | (92%) | $1,761 | $3,053 | $316 |
| | 314.8% | $99.56 | $85.00 | $14.25 | (86%) | $3,732 | $3,186 | $595 |
| | 286.5% | $92.75 | $71.00 | $0.39 | (100%) | $3,522 | $2,696 | $17 |
| | 32.6% | $30.13 | $27.50 | — | — | $473 | $545 | — |
| | 47.1% | $37.13 | $37.13 | — | — | $395 | $586 | — |
| | 57.5% | $24.00 | $24.00 | $0.24 | (99%) | $455 | $694 | $7 |
| | 370.8% | $141.23 | $141.23 | $3.92 | (97%) | $4,880 | $4,880 | $142 |
| | 195.7% | $56.19 | $56.19 | $6.21 | (89%) | $1,431 | $1,431 | $205 |
| | 17.7% | $14.75 | $14.13 | — | — | $1,763 | $1,763 | — |
| | 179.7% | $57.88 | — | $5.36 | (91%) | $1,009 | — | $105 |
| | 22.9% | $30.00 | — | $4.24 | (86%) | $1,679 | — | $253 |
| | 185.3% | $48.50 | — | $0.98 | (98%) | $1,288 | — | $28 |
| | 150.0% | $44.56 | — | $0.79 | (98%) | $1,394 | — | $35 |
| | −11.7% | $16.00 | — | $0.17 | (99%) | $233 | — | $3 |
| $330.94 | 22.6% | $4,963.50 | — | $8.30 | (100%) | $1,333 | — | $34 |
| | 39.6% | $25.88 | — | $0.80 | (97%) | $420 | — | $13 |
| | 39.2% | $15.31 | — | $0.29 | (98%) | $570 | — | $3 |
| | −12.5% | $14.00 | — | $0.55 | (96%) | $160 | — | $8 |
| | 73.4% | $31.13 | — | — | — | $592 | — | — |
| | 3.2% | $12.75 | — | — | — | $225 | — | — |
| | 68.3% | $25.38 | — | $0.69 | (97%) | $579 | — | $16 |
| | 165.3% | $48.06 | — | $17.89 | (63%) | $926 | — | $358 |

| Company | IPO Date | # Shares Issued (m) | T4Q rev. offer[1] ($m) | Offer Price | Adjusted Offer[2] | P/S offer | 1st day close |
|---|---|---|---|---|---|---|---|
| ARTIST direct | 28-Mar-00 | 5.00 | $10.27 | $12.00 | | 33.3 | $9.41 |
| Telocity* | 29-Mar-00 | 11.00 | $0.19 | $12.00 | | 5,937.7 | $13.25 |
| ArrowPoint Comm.* | 31-Mar-00 | 5.00 | $12.38 | $34.00 | | 327.6 | $118.48 |
| ValueClick | 31-Mar-00 | 4.00 | $21.10 | $19.00 | | 27.7 | $20.94 |
| Vyyo | 5-Apr-00 | 6.75 | $4.23 | $13.50 | | 161.3 | $20.25 |
| i3 Mobile | 6-Apr-00 | 5.10 | $1.73 | $16.00 | | 319.9 | $25.00 |
| Saba Software | 7-Apr-00 | 4.00 | $6.70 | $15.00 | | 211.1 | $33.00 |
| GoAmerica | 7-Apr-00 | 10.00 | $2.70 | $16.00 | | 279.3 | $16.00 |
| LivePerson | 7-Apr-00 | 4.00 | $0.60 | $8.00 | | 464.6 | $9.50 |
| Opus360 | 7-Apr-00 | 5.95 | $2.00 | $10.00 | | 312.3 | $12.50 |
| HealthStream | 11-Apr-00 | 5.00 | $7.23 | $9.00 | | 22.9 | $8.50 |
| Corillian | 12-Apr-00 | 4.00 | $7.74 | $8.00 | | 33.2 | $8.50 |
| PEC Solutions | 20-Apr-00 | 3.00 | $53.20 | $9.50 | | 3.7 | $9.00 |
| Embarcadero Tech | 20-Apr-00 | 4.20 | $18.85 | $10.00 | | 21.8 | $16.00 |
| Software Technologies | 28-Apr-00 | 4.00 | $55.17 | $12.00 | | 21.8 | $17.88 |
| Sequoia Software* | 12-May-00 | 4.20 | $8.40 | $8.00 | | 32.6 | $10.06 |
| iBeam | 18-May-00 | 11.00 | $2.20 | $10.00 | | 675.5 | $14.00 |
| CrossWorlds | 1-Jun-00 | 4.00 | $23.20 | $10.00 | | 10.9 | $10.13 |
| Exult | 2-Jun-00 | 6.00 | $10.43 | $10.00 | | 81.0 | $10.00 |
| taketoAUCTION | 13-Jun-00 | 1.30 | $0.49 | $8.00 | | 126.2 | $8.50 |
| Rediff.com | 14-Jun-00 | 4.60 | $1.91 | $12.00 | | 252.3 | $19.31 |
| eChapman.com | 15-Jun-00 | 1.26 | $10.55 | $13.00 | | 10.1 | $7.38 |
| eFunds | 26-Jun-00 | 5.50 | $334.74 | $13.00 | | 1.8 | $13.00 |
| Click Commerce | 26-Jun-00 | 5.00 | $13.54 | $10.00 | | 48.5 | $17.63 |
| Busybox* | 27-Jun-00 | 2.50 | $351.16 | $5.00 | | 0.1 | $5.56 |
| Genuity | 28-Jun-00 | 173.90 | $797.04 | $11.00 | | 2.3 | $9.41 |
| Precise Software | 29-Jun-00 | 4.25 | $13.93 | $16.00 | | 36.5 | $24.00 |
| Virage | 29-Jun-00 | 3.50 | $5.56 | $11.00 | | 58.7 | $16.88 |
| CareScience | 29-Jun-00 | 4.00 | $5.26 | $12.00 | | 24.3 | $10.02 |
| I-Many | 13-Jul-00 | 7.50 | $21.88 | $9.00 | | 17.6 | $12.48 |
| Support.com | 19-Jul-00 | 4.25 | $4.75 | $14.00 | | 229.4 | $32.62 |
| Interland* | 25-Jul-00 | 5.00 | $14.38 | $12.00 | | 28.9 | $8.94 |
| Raindance Comm. (Evo | 25-Jul-00 | 7.00 | $7.25 | $8.00 | | 52.4 | $8.13 |
| Blue Martini | 25-Jul-00 | 7.50 | $21.67 | $20.00 | | 171.1 | $54.78 |
| Mainspring Comm.* | 27-Jul-00 | 4.00 | $7.03 | $12.00 | | 36.8 | $14.31 |
| WebEx | 28-Jul-00 | 3.50 | $8.30 | $14.00 | | 143.8 | $33.06 |
| ValiCert | 28-Jul-00 | 4.00 | $3.34 | $10.00 | | 77.6 | $11.88 |
| Convergent Group* | 1-Aug-00 | 5.00 | $70.43 | $7.00 | | 4.3 | $7.00 |
| Resonate | 3-Aug-00 | 4.00 | $14.70 | $21.00 | | 64.6 | $36.13 |
| ScreamingMedia | 3-Aug-00 | 5.00 | $5.40 | $12.00 | | 72.7 | $10.50 |
| iAsiaWorks | 3-Aug-00 | 9.00 | $19.80 | $13.00 | | 18.9 | $9.50 |
| EXE Technologies | 4-Aug-00 | 8.00 | $96.70 | $8.00 | | 3.5 | $8.13 |
| AOL Latin America | 8-Aug-00 | 25.00 | $6.02 | $8.00 | | 365.1 | $8.44 |
| Mind C.T.I. | 8-Aug-00 | 3.00 | $9.78 | $10.00 | | 20.6 | $10.00 |
| Radview Software | 9-Aug-00 | 4.00 | $6.75 | $10.00 | | 21.9 | $9.03 |
| PeoplePC | 16-Aug-00 | 8.50 | $22.38 | $10.00 | | 44.9 | $8.88 |
| Avistar Comm. | 17-Aug-00 | 3.00 | $14.48 | $12.00 | | 23.2 | $13.38 |
| ServiceWare Tech. | 25-Aug-00 | 4.50 | $25.18 | $7.00 | | 8.2 | $8.75 |
| Zengine | 21-Sep-00 | 4.29 | $4.09 | $13.00 | | 56.9 | $14.13 |
| OmniSky | 21-Sep-00 | 9.10 | $2.10 | $12.00 | | 546.9 | $17.64 |
| AvantGo | 27-Sep-00 | 5.50 | $9.62 | $12.00 | | 69.4 | $20.00 |
| Docent | 29-Sep-00 | 8.00 | $3.08 | $11.00 | | 236.4 | $18.31 |
| Elastic Networks | 29-Sep-00 | 7.80 | $20.31 | $13.00 | | 21.5 | $13.94 |
| Asia Global Crossing | 6-Oct-00 | 53.00 | $108.00 | $7.00 | | 36.9 | $7.38 |

1. T4Q Revenue at Offer is the trailing four quarters of sales at the time of the IPO
2. Adjusted offer is the original offering price adjusted for stock splits

| Adjusted D1 close[3] | D1% change | All-time high | Price 3/10/00 | Price 8/31/01 | % ch from hi[4] | MktCap Offer ($m) | MktCap 3/10/00 ($m) | MktCap 8/31/01 ($m) |
|---|---|---|---|---|---|---|---|---|
|  | −21.6% | $12.00 | — | $6.32 | (47%) | $342 | — | $23 |
|  | 10.4% | $15.88 | — | — | — | $1,110 | — | — |
|  | 248.5% | $146.63 | — | — | — | $4,054 | — | — |
|  | 10.2% | $20.94 | — | −$2.18 | (90%) | $584 | — | $80 |
|  | 50.0% | $44.13 | — | $1.00 | (98%) | $682 | — | $37 |
|  | 56.3% | $25.00 | — | $2.84 | (89%) | $555 | — | $65 |
|  | 120.0% | $38.81 | — | −$8.25 | (79%) | $1,414 | — | $382 |
|  | 0.0% | $16.06 | — | $1.38 | (91%) | $754 | — | $74 |
|  | 18.8% | $9.50 | — | $0.12 | (99%) | $279 | — | $4 |
|  | 25.0% | $12.50 | — | $0.08 | (99%) | $625 | — | $9 |
|  | −5.6% | $10.13 | — | $1.50 | (85%) | $166 | — | $31 |
|  | 6.3% | $28.00 | — | $2.52 | (91%) | $257 | — | $87 |
|  | −5.3% | $11.94 | — | $18.00 | 51% | $198 | — | $466 |
|  | 60.0% | $64.63 | — | $13.24 | (80%) | $412 | — | $359 |
|  | 49.0% | $34.75 | — | — | — | $1,204 | — | — |
|  | 25.8% | $19.50 | — | — | — | $274 | — | — |
|  | 40.0% | $27.88 | — | $0.10 | (100%) | $1,486 | — | $13 |
|  | 1.3% | $26.38 | — | $2.57 | (90%) | $253 | — | $69 |
|  | 0.0% | $19.00 | — | $14.00 | (26%) | $845 | — | $1,432 |
|  | 6.3% | $8.81 | — | $1.01 | (89%) | $62 | — | $8 |
|  | 60.9% | $16.81 | — | $1.15 | (93%) | $481 | — | $29 |
|  | −43.2% | $13.00 | — | $2.05 | (84%) | $107 | — | $26 |
|  | 0.0% | $13.00 | — | $17.28 | 33% | $592 | — | $799 |
|  | 76.3% | $43.00 | — | $6.05 | (86%) | $657 | — | $238 |
|  | 11.2% | $5.00 | — | — | — | $48 | — | — |
|  | −14.5% | $11.00 | — | $1.78 | (84%) | $1,808 | — | $1,734 |
|  | 50.0% | $43.13 | — | $19.16 | (56%) | $508 | — | $512 |
|  | 53.5% | $21.63 | — | $2.58 | (88%) | $326 | — | $53 |
|  | −16.5% | $12.00 | — | $1.40 | (88%) | $128 | — | $19 |
|  | 38.7% | $27.25 | — | $5.45 | (80%) | $384 | — | $190 |
|  | 133.0% | $34.13 | — | $3.65 | (89%) | $1,090 | — | $122 |
|  | −25.5% | $12.00 | — | — | — | $416 | — | — |
|  | 1.6% | $11.00 | — | $1.21 | (89%) | $380 | — | $57 |
|  | 173.9% | $69.75 | — | $1.00 | (99%) | $3,709 | — | $68 |
|  | 19.3% | $16.63 | — | — | — | $259 | — | — |
|  | 136.1% | $55.38 | — | $17.27 | (69%) | $1,193 | — | $679 |
|  | 18.8% | $25.25 | — | $2.45 | (90%) | $260 | — | $56 |
|  | 0.0% | $8.00 | — | — | — | $304 | — | — |
|  | 72.0% | $47.50 | — | $4.99 | (89%) | $949 | — | $137 |
|  | −12.5% | $14.25 | — | $2.50 | (82%) | $393 | — | $96 |
|  | −26.9% | $13.00 | — | $0.11 | (99%) | $373 | — | $4 |
|  | 1.6% | $20.38 | — | $3.80 | (81%) | $341 | — | $173 |
|  | 5.5% | $9.44 | — | $3.59 | (62%) | $2,198 | — | $241 |
|  | 0.0% | $13.81 | — | $2.17 | (84%) | $201 | — | $43 |
|  | −9.7% | $10.00 | — | $0.50 | (95%) | $148 | — | $8 |
|  | −11.2% | $10.00 | — | $0.17 | (98%) | $1,005 | — | $19 |
|  | 11.5% | $12.00 | — | $1.65 | (86%) | $335 | — | $41 |
|  | 25.0% | $10.25 | — | $0.30 | (97%) | $206 | — | $7 |
|  | 8.7% | $15.19 | — | $3.55 | (77%) | $233 | — | $52 |
|  | 47.0% | $19.94 | — | $0.71 | (96%) | $1,149 | — | $52 |
|  | 66.7% | $18.00 | — | $1.74 | (90%) | $667 | — | $61 |
|  | 66.5% | $25.75 | — | $4.95 | (81%) | $729 | — | $209 |
|  | 7.2% | $13.00 | — | $0.93 | (93%) | $436 | — | $29 |
|  | 5.4% | $7.25 | — | $3.87 | (47%) | $3,982 | — | $2,252 |

3. Adjusted 1st day close is the original 1st day closing price adjusted for stock splits
4. % change from high rounded to nearest percent
*Indicates companies that no longer exist as an independent company

# index